A BILINGUAL GUIDE

JAPAN AS IT IS

日本タテヨコ

D0514705

Gakken

JAPAN AS IT IS

©GAKKEN 1985
Published by GAKKEN CO., LTD.
4-40-5, Kami-ikedai, Ohta-ku, Tokyo 145, Japan

Printed in Japan.
All rights reserved.
No part of this book may be reproduced in any form
without the written permission of the publisher.

First published 1985
Fourteenth impression 1989

Printed in Japan by Kosaido Co., Ltd. Tokyo

まえがき

この本はビジネスマンや留学生を主な対象とします。特に外国の人に日本を紹介したいと思っている日本人、日本に関心を持ち、日本をよく知りたいと考えている外国人、日本語や英語を習っている人たちに使っていただきたいと考えています。

内容はたいへん幅広くなっています。取り上げた項目は、日本の政治・経済とか、能・歌舞伎・相撲といった伝統文化だけでなく、日本人のものの考え方、行動のパターン、動物や植物に対するイメージのような分野にまで及んでいます。いわば、この本は小型の日本百科事典になっていて、日本に関することならなんでも、これ1冊でほぼ間に合うようになっています。

各項目の解説は次のような視点から行っています。

1. 日常生活面の解説に力を入れる

私たち日本人にはわかりきった日常的なことが、外国人にわからないことが多いので、その解説をていねいに行う。

2. 日本的なものの見方、考え方の背景を解説する

日本独特のものの見方、考え方を、単なる現象の説明に終わらせないで、できるかぎり根源にさかのぼって解説する。

3. 比較文化的な視点から解説する

解説をわかりやすく、また客観的にするために、可能な範囲で他国文化との比較を行う。

4. 客観的な解説を心がける

あまり変動しない大まかな統計的数字を踏まえ、内外の研究者の諸説を参考にして、客観的な解説を目ざす。

5. 読みやすさ、使いやすさを考慮する

どこからでも気軽に読めるよう、1項目1ページを原則とする。

執筆と翻訳にあたられた方々にはご苦労をおかけしました。学問的に未開拓の分野が多い上に、1項目1ページという制約をしたために、当初の予想よりはるかにむずかしい仕事をお願いすることになりました。ご尽力に対して心からお礼申し上げます。

1985年10月

学研・語学ソフトウエア開発部部長　田中好夫

Preface

This book was compiled for both the businessman and the scholar. It is for the Japanese who wants to explain Japan to his foreign friends, the friend who wants to know more about Japan, and students of Japanese and English alike.

It is very broad in scope. Among the hundreds of topics discussed are such current concerns as politics and economics, traditional arts such as kabuki, noh, and sumo, Japanese thinking and behavioral patterns, the associations that the various flora and fauna have, and many other underlying aspects of Japan as it is. It is, if you will, a miniature encyclopedia giving the reader ready access to understanding Japan.

In compiling the text, the primary emphasis was on explaining everyday life. There are many things which are second nature to Japanese and inscrutable to the uninitiated. These have been explained as best we could.

The next priority was to explain things that are distinctively Japanese — going beyond the surface phenomena to explore underlying reasons.

For the sake of both clarity and specificity, the explanations have been set in an international comparative context.

Every effort has been made to stay objective. Statistics have been marshaled, authorities consulted, and balances struck.

Finally, all of this has been packaged for readability and understandability. Each explanation is in Japanese and English on facing pages, each a self-contained unit allowing the reader to start anywhere, to find things easily, and to browse with enjoyment.

Because of these demands, it has been a trial for the writers and translators involved. Not only do many of the questions posed defy answering, the one-page format imposed restrictions and complications far beyond anything we had first imagined. They are to be commended for their skill in putting it all together.

October 1985

Yoshio Tanaka
Senior Editor

Contents

まえがき	Preface	1
協力者一覧	Editorial Staff	8
Part-1　日本と日本人	**JAPAN AND THE JAPANESE**	**9**
1　日本の自然環境	The Japanese Land and People	10
2　日本の歴史(1)	Japanese History (1)	12
3　日本の歴史(2)	Japanese History (2)	14
4　日本の歴史(3)	Japanese History (3)	16
5　日本の歴史(4)	Japanese History (4)	18
6　日本人の起源	Origins of the Japanese People	20
7　日本文化の起源	Sources of Japanese Culture	22
8　日本文化の特性	Characteristics of Japanese Culture	24
9　日本人の自然観	Japanese Concepts of Nature	26
10　日本人の宗教心	Japanese Religion	28
11　日本人の勤労意識	The Japanese Work Ethic	30
12　日本人の娯楽観	Relaxing Japanese-style	32
13　日本人の美意識	Japanese Aesthetics	34
14　日本人の死生観	Views of Life and Death	36
15　集団主義	Groupism	38
16　義理人情	*Giri* and *Ninjō*	40
17　日本人の脳	The Japanese Brain	42
18　高齢化社会	Longevity	44
19　日本人の１年	The Japanese Year	46
20　日本人の一生	The Japanese Life Cycle	48
21　日本人の言語行動	Japanese Verbal Signals	50
22　日本人のジェスチャー(1)	Japanese Gestures (1)	52
23　日本人のジェスチャー(2)	Japanese Gestures (2)	54
24　日本語	The Japanese Language	56
25　日本人の好きな英雄	Popular Heroes	58
26　日本人論の好きな日本人	The Japanese Identity Crisis	60
27　日本人と付き合う法	Getting along with the Japanese	62
NOTES		64

Part-2 日本人の生活	LIVING IN JAPAN	73
1 暮らし	Standard of Living	74
2 生活時間	The Japanese Day	76
3 家庭	The Family	78
4 家計	The Household Budget	80
5 住宅	Housing	82
6 耐久消費財と日本的家具	Consumer Durables	84
7 洋服と着物	Clothing and Kimono	86
8 食生活	The Japanese Diet	88
9 日本食と材料	Japanese Food	90
10 伝統的な日本食	Traditional Japanese Dishes	92
11 結婚・離婚	Marriage and Divorce	94
12 死の儀式	Funerals	96
13 正月・盆	*Shōgatsu* and *Bon*	98
14 子供の年中行事	Children's Festivals	100
15 七夕・クリスマス	Tanabata and Christmas	102
16 日本の祭り	Japanese Festivals	104
17 消費生活	The Japanese Consumer	106
18 贈答	Gift-giving	108
19 新聞	Newspapers	110
20 テレビ・ラジオ	Radio and Television	112
21 出版	Publishing	114
22 道路網	Roads	116
23 鉄道網	Rail Transport	118
24 日本の治安	Public Order in Japan	120
25 公害問題	Pollution	122
26 社会保障	Social Welfare	124
27 教育制度	The Japanese Education System	126
28 学校生活	Student Life	128
29 塾	Cram Schools	130
30 観光	Tourism	132
31 温泉巡り	Japan's Hot Springs	134
32 花見・紅葉狩り	Cherry-blossom and Maple-leaf Viewing	136
33 野球	Baseball	138
34 ゴルフ・テニス・釣り	Golf, Tennis, and Fishing	140
35 相撲	Sumo	142
36 柔道	Judo	144

37	剣道・弓道・空手道・合気道	*Kendō*, *Kyūdō*, Karate, and *Aikidō*	146
38	映画	Films	148
39	碁・将棋・マージャン	*Go*, *Shōgi*, and Mahjong	150
40	公営ギャンブル	Legalized Gambling	152
41	子供の遊び	Children's Games	154
NOTES			156
Part-3	**日本の社会**	**JAPANESE SOCIETY**	**163**
1	統治のしくみ	Government	164
2	戦後政治の流れ	Postwar Politics	166
3	天皇と皇室	The Imperial Institution	168
4	内閣	The Cabinet	170
5	政党	Political Parties	172
6	選挙	Elections	174
7	派閥	Political Factions	176
8	官僚	The Bureaucracy	178
9	裁判	The Japanese Judicial System	180
10	税制	Taxes	182
11	外交	Foreign Policy	184
12	防衛	Japanese Defense Policy	186
13	経済協力	International Economic Cooperation	188
14	戦後日本経済の復興	Japan's Postwar Economic Recovery	190
15	高度成長から安定成長へ	From Rapid Growth to Stable Growth	192
16	産業構造の変遷	Changes in the Industrial Structure	194
17	産業組織	Japan's Industrial Structure	196
18	産業政策	Industrial Policy	198
19	貿易構造と貿易摩擦	Trade Structure and Trade Friction	200
20	農林水産業	Farming, Forestry, and Fisheries	202
21	主要製造業	Japan's Principal Manufacturing Industries	204
22	先端技術製品	High-technology Products	206
23	物価と流通産業	Prices and Distribution	208
24	日本の原子力利用	Japan's Nuclear Power Industry	210
25	意思決定のしくみ	The Japanese Decision-making Process	212
26	雇用関係の特徴	Japanese Employment	214
27	年功序列	Seniority-based Rewards	216
28	労使関係	Industrial Relations	218
29	勤務時間・賃金	The Japanese Workweek and Wages	220

30 定年	Retirement	222
31 ビジネスマンの付き合い	Socializing	224
32 ビジネスマンの1日	A Day in the Life of a Japanese Businessman	226
33 ビジネスマンの一生	The Life of a Businessman	228
34 日本的商談	Japanese Business Practices	230
NOTES		232
Part-4 日本の文化	**CULTURAL HERITAGE**	**235**
1 建築	Architecture	236
2 庭園	Gardens	238
3 音楽	Music	240
4 邦楽	Traditional Japanese Music	242
5 能	Noh	244
6 歌舞伎	Kabuki	246
7 文楽・日本舞踊	*Bunraku* and *Buyō*	248
8 大衆芸能	Popular Entertainment	250
9 生け花(華道)	Flower Arrangement	252
10 茶の湯(茶道)	The Tea Ceremony	254
11 書道	Calligraphy	256
12 絵画	Painting	258
13 浮世絵	Ukiyo-e	260
14 陶磁器	Ceramics	262
15 漆器	Lacquer ware	264
16 日本刀	The Japanese Sword	266
17 日本人形	Japanese Dolls	268
18 日本の文学(1)—古代	Japanese Literature(1)(Formative Years)	270
19 日本の文学(2)—王朝	Japanese Literature(2)(Court Literature)	272
20 日本の文学(3)—武家もの	Japanese Literature(3)(Medieval)	274
21 日本の文学(4)—町人もの	Japanese Literature(4)(Town Pleasures)	276
22 日本の文学(5)—近代	Japanese Literature(5)(Post-restoration)	278
23 日本の文学(6)—現代	Japanese Literature(6)(Early Twentieth Century)	280
24 日本の文学(7)—戦後	Japanese Literature(7)(Postwar)	282
25 和歌	*Waka*	284
26 俳句	Haiku	286
27 日本のコミック	*Manga*	288
28 仏教	Buddhism	290
29 禅	Zen	292

30 神道	Shinto	294
31 キリスト教	Christianity	296
32 神話	Mythology	298
33 昔話	Folk Tales	300
34 伝説	Legends	302
NOTES		304
Part-5 超自然・動植物のイメージ	**AFFINITIES WITH NATURE**	**313**
1 犬・猫	Dogs and Cats	314
2 馬・牛	Horses and Cows	316
3 タヌキ・キツネ	*Tanuki* and *Kitsune*	318
4 タイ・コイ	Sea Bream and Carp	320
5 ツル・カラス	Cranes and Crows	322
6 松	Pine Trees	324
7 竹	Bamboo	326
8 桜	*Sakura*	328
9 梅・桃	Plum and Peach	330
10 幽霊	Ghosts	332
11 妖怪(1)—鬼・天狗	Monsters and Apparitions(1)	334
12 妖怪(2)—河童・1つ目小僧	Monsters and Apparitions(2)	336
NOTES		338
付録	**Appendix**	**341**
日本史年表	Chronology of Japanese History	342
索引	**Indices**	**348**
日本語索引	Japanese Index	348
英語索引	English Index	359

N.B.

日本文中の＊印(英文中の＊印)の項目は、Notesのページに、解説あるいは写真・イラストがあることを示しています。NotesはPartごとに、各Partの最後にあります。

Asterisks in the text indicate words that are further explained in the Notes section after each Part.

Editorial Staff

●企画・制作
学研・語学ソフトウエア開発部

●執筆協力（五十音順）

相川二元	AIKAWA Tsugumoto	サンケイ新聞編集委員
井尻千男	IJIRI Kazuo	日本経済新聞編集委員
奥西峻介	OKUNISHI Shunsuke	大阪外国語大学助教授
木村利行	KIMURA Toshiyuki	文芸評論家
佐藤　豊	SATO Yutaka	日本経済新聞速報部次長
杉戸清樹	SUGITO Seiju	国立国語研究所室長
清野真智子	SEINO Machiko	フリーライター
高橋美幸	TAKAHASHI Miyuki	サンケイ新聞記者
千野境子	CHINO Keiko	サンケイ新聞記者
堀内克明	HORIUCHI Katsuaki	明治大学教授
八木　甫	YAGI Hajime	松阪大学教授

●翻訳
㈱ジャパン・リサーチ　Japan Research Inc.

●デザイン
㈲フェイデアス・デザイン　Pheidias Design Ltd.

●イラスト
杵淵亮一　KINEBUCHI Ryoichi

●校正・編集協力
遠藤由紀子／沖田真知子／学研・調査資料室

●写真・取材協力
学研・写真部／学研・企画資料室
國田茂（表紙カバー）／共同通信社（p. 73大鳴門橋、p. 161花見）／慶応義塾大学考古学研究室（p. 64縄文式尖底深鉢）／東京大学総合研究資料館（p. 64弥生式壺形土器）／宮内庁（p. 65聖徳太子及二王子像）／法隆寺（p. 65釈迦三尊像、p. 65金堂壁画、p. 304金堂）／正倉院宝物（p. 65鳥毛立女屏風）／平等院（p. 66鳳凰堂）／神護寺（p. 66源頼朝像）／東大寺（p. 67金剛力士像）／鹿苑寺金閣（p. 67）／長興寺（p. 68織田信長像）／畠山記念館（p. 68豊臣秀吉像）／読売新聞社（p. 162碁、将棋）／毎日新聞社（p. 162マージャン、p. 306落語、p. 313鶴）／PPS通信社（p. 163集積回路）／妙法院門跡（p. 235千手観音座像）／龍安寺（p. 304方丈庭園）／伊勢神宮（p. 304）／池坊家元池坊専永（p. 306立華）／古流松藤会会長池田昌弘（p. 306生花）／小原流家元小原豊雲（p. 306盛花）／勅使河原和風会会頭勅使河原和風（p. 306投入）／東京国立博物館（p. 308埴輪）／吉徳コレクション（p. 308嵯峨人形）／吉徳（p. 308木目込人形）／斎藤良輔（p. 308鳴子こけし）／全生庵（p. 339円山応挙作「幽霊」）

Part-1
日本と日本人
JAPAN AND THE JAPANESE

1 日本の自然環境

自然環境と国民性や文化のあり方とは，深いかかわりがある。日本の場合も，置かれた自然の条件から影響を大きく受けている。

●位置

日本はアジア大陸の東端に位置する島国である。3000以上の島のうち，主なものは北海道，本州，四国，九州の4つ。海を隔てて北はサハリン・シベリア，西は朝鮮半島・中国と隣接している。この位置は，大陸の政治的変動に巻き込まれることなく，大陸の文化を取り入れられる有利さを持っているため，日本は建国以来，固有の文化を残しながら，外来文化を摂取し，独自の融合文化を築いてくることができた。

●国土と人口

全国土の4分の3が森林に覆われた山地である。山は高くなく，本州中央部に標高3000m級の，日本アルプスと呼ばれる山脈がそびえているほかは，2000mを超すのはわずかである。火山は著しく多く，主要なものだけで150を数える。大きな平野がないので，河川は短く急流を成している。日本列島は地殻変動帯に属しているため地震が多い。

面積は約38万km²。イギリスの1倍半，アメリカのカリフォルニア州とほぼ同じである。人口はアメリカの約半分，1億2000万人。うち70%が関東南部から北九州に至る地域に住む。ベルギーやオランダのほうが人口密度は高いが，居住可能面積で見れば日本が上である。

●気候

中緯度に位置して気候は温暖。中央部の東京の年平均気温は15.3℃である。列島の北端から南端まで3000kmあるので温度差があり，年平均気温は6～22℃。雨は多く，年間降水量は1600～1700mmに達する。早春から夏の植物生育期，特に6月から7月の梅雨期にはよく雨が降る。夏と秋に年数回は襲来する台風も多量の雨をもたらす。

日本列島は規則正しく季節風の支配を受け，冬は寒帯気団が南下し，夏は熱帯気団が北上する。両気団に覆われる冬と夏は各数か月と長く，季節風交替の谷間にあたる春と秋は各2か月程度である。

冬は，北西季節風が吹いて雪が降り続く日本海側と，晴天が多く乾燥した太平洋側と対照的な天候分布になる。本州南部の夏は暑く，東南アジア並みかそれ以上で，典型的な照葉樹林帯の気候である。夏の3～4か月間，東南アジアなどと同じ気候ということは，日本の農耕文化の基層となったイモ・イネをはじめ，南方系の生物が熱帯気団とともに北上した可能性があるということであり，この点が日本文化の基本的性格を南方型とする有力な根拠になっている。

The Japanese Land and People

In Japan as in any country, the nation's culture and national character have been largely molded by geography and climate.

● Location*

Japan is an island nation off the east coast of Asia. Among its 3,000-plus islands, the four major ones are Hokkaido, Honshu, Shikoku, and Kyushu. Bordered on the north by Sakhalin and Siberia and on the west by the Korean peninsula and China, Japan is far enough from Asia to have escaped involvement in continental upheavals and yet close enough to have benefited from continental culture. With unbroken cultural continuity, Japan has been able to adapt foreign influences into its own cultural development.

● Land and People

Japan is a mountainous land 75% covered by forests. Except for a range of mountains (called the Japan Alps) in central Honshu 3,000 meters or more above sea level, few of Japan's mountains exceed 2,000 meters. Many of the mountains are volcanic, and there are 150 important volcanoes. With few large plains, Japan's swiftly flowing rivers* tend to be short. Large-scale plate movements cause frequent earthquakes.

With about 380,000 square kilometers of land area, Japan is 50% larger than Great Britain or roughly the size of California, yet its population is over 120 million—half that of the United States. About 70% of the people live in the area from Tokyo to Kitakyushu. Belgium and the Netherlands have higher overall population densities, but Japan has the highest population per arable land area.

● Climate

Located in the temperate zone, Japan has a warm climate. The average temperature in Tokyo, roughly in the middle of the Japanese archipelago, is 15.3°C. Average temperatures throughout the 3,000-kilometer north-south islands vary widely between 6°C and 22°C. There is considerable rainfall, 1,600 to 1,700 millimeters per year, with especially heavy rains between early spring and the summer growing season. Summer and autumn typhoons also bring considerable rainfall.

There are four distinct seasons, with the cold moving south in the winter and the warmth north in the summer. Summer and winter are long compared to the two-month average for spring and autumn.

Winter weather conditions differ greatly between the Sea of Japan side and the Pacific side of the archipelago. Seasonal northwest winds bring heavy snow to western Japan while leeward eastern Japan tends to have dry, clear winter days. Except in the northern half of Japan, the summer heat is comparable to that in Southeast Asia. Southwestern Japan has a junglelike humidity in the summer, and there are many agricultural and lifestyle similarities with the South Pacific in addition to the tropical climate of the three to four summer months.

2 日本の歴史(1)

日本の歴史の大きな特徴として，次の点を挙げることができる。

①原始の時代から現代まで，１万年の間，在来文化を一変するような他民族との大規模な融合がなく，独自の文化を守り続けていること

②その一方で，古くから外国の文化を熱心に取り入れて日本化し，文明の一流の水準に達していること

●原始・古代（およそ１万年前～紀元後11世紀）

小国の乱立，国土の統一を経て，中国の制度に範をとった律令国家が成立する。しかし，しだいにその矛盾が広がって地方政治が乱れ，武士団が成長していく。

• 縄文時代　日本列島には洪積世の時代から人間が生活していたが，日本人種および日本語の原型が成立したと見られているのは，およそ１万年前から紀元前３世紀ごろまでの縄文期である。当時の人々は，数人から10人が１戸の竪穴住居に住み，生活を狩猟，漁労，採集に頼り，貧富・階級差のない社会を構成していた。

• 弥生時代　紀元前３世紀ごろ，朝鮮から九州北部に稲作と金属器使用の技術が渡来した。稲作技術は，生産を増大し，貧富・身分の差を生み，農村共同体を政治集団化するなど，画期的な社会変化をもたらした。農耕に伴う信仰，儀礼，習俗なども広がり，日本文化の原型が形造られた。弥生時代は紀元後３世紀ごろまで続き，後期には東北地方にまで及んだ。

• 古墳時代　紀元後４世紀半ばごろ，乱立していた小国が大和政権によって統一された。統一の進展とともに，前方後円墳によって代表される古墳が地方に広まった。この時代は中国から多くの知識，技術が流入した時代で，４世紀に大和政権は朝鮮半島へ進出して，大陸の高度の物質文化を輸入し，５世紀には朝鮮半島から渡来人(帰化人)が鉄器生産・製陶・機織り・金属工芸・土木などの諸技術を伝え，中国の文字である漢字の使用も始まった。６世紀に儒教の摂取が本格的になり，仏教も伝来した。

７世紀に聖徳太子が政治の刷新を図り，大化の改新を契機に，天皇を中心とした中央集権国家の建設を目ざした。この場合も，隋，唐を手本にしたが，このころから大陸文化の摂取にさらに積極的になり，９世紀末までに遣隋使，遣唐使を10数回も派遣することになる。

Japanese History (1)

The two main points which characterize Japanese history are (i) over 10,000 years of cultural continuity and (ii) the ability to adapt imported culture and technology to improve Japanese living standards.

● **Prehistory and Ancient History** (c. 8,000 BC to 11th century AD)

This period covers the early formation of tribes, their consolidation into scattered political entities, the establishment of a centralized government administered through the *ritsuryō** system adapted from China, and the gradual emergence of a powerful military caste.

• **Jomon Period*** (c. 8,000 to c. 300 BC) Humans first occupied the Japanese archipelago in the diluvial epoch, but the biological and linguistic roots of the modern Japanese are believed to have developed in the long period referred to as the Jomon period. The Jomon people lived in vertical caves housing anywhere from a few to a dozen people. They were hunters, gatherers, and fishers, and there seems to have been no stratification of their society into ruler and ruled, rich and poor.

• **Yayoi Period***(c. 300 BC to c. 300 AD) Some time in the 3rd century BC, wet-paddy rice agriculture and metal-working technology were introduced into northern Kyushu from the Korean peninsula. The agrarian life which resulted marked a significant social change in the creation of classes and stratification by wealth and poverty within the political community. Agrarian values, ceremonies, and customs were developed and spread to form the rudiments of modern Japanese culture. By the 3rd century AD, the Yayoi culture extended to northeastern Japan.

• **Kofun Period***(c. 300-710) In the middle of the 4th century, the independent tribes scattered throughout Japan were consolidated under the Yamato clan. This shift toward a unified state is marked by the construction of large keyhole-shaped tomb mounds,* *kofun*, for the ruling elite. Knowledge and technology from China spread in this period. While the several forays which the Yamato mounted against the Korean peninsula were unsuccessful, they enhanced Japanese access to mainland amenities as 5th-century Korean immigrants introduced new techniques in iron making, potting, weaving, smithing, and civil engineering. Chinese writing was adopted in the 5th century and Confucian* and Buddhist teachings in the 6th century.

In the 7th century, Prince Shotoku,* regent under Empress Suiko, further centralized the state and strengthend the imperial authority. His efforts were crystallized in the Taika Reforms* instituted by his successors in emulation of the Sui and Tang dynasty organizations. Envoys were dispatched repeatedly to China well into the 9th century.

3 日本の歴史(2)

• 奈良時代　710年に都を平城京(今の奈良市および近郊)に定めて律令国家の隆盛期を迎えるが，農民の窮乏，浮浪民の増加，荘園の拡大による公地公民制の事実上の崩壊など，矛盾が出始める。

この時代は国が仏教を厚く保護したため，仏教文化，とりわけ仏教美術が栄えた。日本最初の仏教文化である7世紀初めの飛鳥文化，人間的な若々しさに特色がある7世紀後半の白鳳文化，唐の最盛期の文化の影響を受け，写実的で豊かな人間感情を示す8世紀中期の天平文化などがそれである。

仏教美術と並ぶ，この時代の文化上の金字塔は『万葉集』である。『万葉集』は8世紀半ばまでの約400年間の，庶民から天皇に至る約4500首の歌を集めた歌集で，上代日本人の素朴な生活感情が率直に表現され，今でも多くの日本人に愛されている。このほか，現存する最古の歴史書『古事記』(712年)，最古の勅撰歴史書『日本書紀』(720年)，最古の漢詩集『懐風藻』(751年)などもこの時代の遺産である。

• 平安時代　8世紀末に平安京(今の京都市)へ都を移し，律令体制の再建を図ったが，公地公民制が崩れて国家は財政難に陥った。894年を最後に遣唐使を中止したので，大陸文化の大量輸入も途絶えた。

10～11世紀に藤原氏が政権を独占し，荘園を経済的基盤として全盛を誇るが，地方政治の混乱によって治安が乱れ，武士団が成長していった。11世紀末に藤原氏に対抗して院政が始まると，武士が中央政界に進出してくる。

平安時代は国風文化を特色とする。9世紀にはまだ唐の影響を受けて，密教と漢文学の弘仁・貞観文化が栄えたが，大陸との直接交流がなくなった10世紀以降になると，日本独特の貴族文化が生まれる。その代表が最初の勅撰和歌集『古今和歌集』(10世紀初め)，世界最古の長編小説『源氏物語』(11世紀初めごろ)，随筆『枕草子』(1000年ごろ)などの文芸作品群である。これらの作品は，漢字から日本人が独自に作りだした「仮名」で書かれており，感性的な和語を書き表す「仮名」の発明があって初めて生まれたものである。

仏教は現世利益を図る密教とともに，10世紀後半から来世での幸福を説く浄土教が流行した。建築・絵画・書・彫刻など，美術・工芸面でも国風化の傾向が著しかった。

Japanese History (2)

•**Nara Period** (710-794) Peaking with the 710 move to Heijokyo, the *ritsuryō* system collapsed as the peasantry's impoverishment, the growing numbers of the homeless, and the development of tax-immune *shōen** signaled the collapse of the *kōchi-kōmin** concept.

Under official patronage, Buddhist culture and art flourished. The artistic and cultural legacy of the period goes from the early 7th century Asuka culture* through the vibrant Hakuho culture* of the latter 7th century, and culminates in the Tang-influenced humanistic Tenpyo culture* of the mid-8th century.

The *Man'yōshū* collection of about 4,500 verses by Japanese of all classes composed over a nearly 400-year span dates from this period. This eloquent record is still widely read and admired. Other important works are *Kojiki* (Record of Ancient Matters), written around 712 and the oldest Japanese history extant, 720's *Nihon Shoki* (Chronical of Japan), the oldest known official history of Japan, and *Kaifūsō* (Fond Recollections of Poetry), the first (751) anthology of Chinese poetry by Japanese poets.

•**Heian Period** (794-1185) The capital was moved to Heiankyo at the end of the 8th century and an attempt made to revive the *ritsuryō* system, but the impotence of the *kōchi-kōmin* philosophy plunged the imperial government into financial difficulties. Missions to Tang China ceased after 894, stemming the flow of mainland culture into Japan.

The Fujiwara* family consolidated their grip on power in the 10th and 11th centuries, and the *shōen* became accepted as basic to the economy. The court's inability to control outlying regions led to widespread unrest and the emergence of a powerful warrior class. By the end of the 11th century, the Fujiwara regency had been thwarted by the *insei** system and the warrior class was increasingly influential in politics.

The Heian period is notable for its natively inspired art and culture.* In the 9th century, Tang influence was still strong, esoteric Buddhist sects* flourished, and *kanbun* writing in the Chinese style remained the leading form of literary expression. In the 10th century, however, a uniquely Japanese culture developed as shown by the first official anthology of *waka* poetry, the *Kokin Wakashū* (Collection from Ancient and Modern Times), the *Tale of Genji*, recognized as the world's first novel, and the *Makura no Sōshi* (Pillow Book), a collection of essays, all of which were written in the Japanese *kana* phonetic syllabary developed from Chinese. The invention of *kana* made the written expression of Japanese sensibilities possible for the first time.

Esoteric Buddhist sects introduced from China were joined in the latter half of the Heian period by the natively inspired Jodo sect,* and the trend toward native expression continued in the arts and literature.

日本の歴史(3)

●**中世**（12～16世紀）

今までの支配者，王朝貴族に代わって新興の武士が政権を握り，封建制度を築き上げていく。

• **鎌倉時代**　12世紀末，源頼朝(よりとも)が鎌倉に幕府を開いて武家政権が誕生した。それから1世紀半の間，東の鎌倉の武士は，西の京都の公家(くげ)と対立しながら，封建社会を形成していった。13世紀後半，モンゴル軍が2度にわたって九州北部に来襲したが，武士団の奮戦と大暴風雨のおかげでこれを退けた。しかし，これを契機に幕府の武士統制が困難となり，幕府は滅亡の道を歩むことになる。

文化面では，従来の公家文化を基盤に，宋伝来の禅宗文化を取り入れ，動的，写実的で素朴な独特の武家文化が育っていった。宗教面では，法然(ほうねん)・親鸞(しんらん)・日蓮(にちれん)などの名僧によって鎌倉仏教が生まれ，広い階層の信仰を集めた。関東の武士には12世紀に伝えられた禅宗が重んじられた。芸術にも新傾向が起こり，鎌倉時代初期の彫刻は力強い写実性，豊かな人間味の表出で新風を巻き起こした。文学では武士の好みを反映して『平家物語』(原作は13世紀初め)のような軍記物語の傑作が出た。その他，流麗な技巧美の『新古今和歌集』(1205年)，随筆集『方丈記』(13世紀)，『徒然草(つれづれぐさ)』(14世紀)などが著された。

• **室町時代**　14世紀前半，足利義満が京都の室町幕府を安定させてから2世紀余りの間に，政治・文化面とも，武家が公家を圧倒して優位に立った。室町幕府は諸国の有力な守護大名の力を集めて成立していたため，統制力が弱く，15世紀後半に入ると，全国各地の戦国大名が群立する戦乱の世，いわゆる戦国時代となった。戦国大名はその地域の土地・人民を支配する強力な独立政権となり，武士が農民を支配する封建社会が成立する。経済面では明貿易など商業の進展が見られた。

文化面では，公家と武家の文化に禅宗の影響が加わった，14世紀末の金閣に代表される北山文化，15世紀末の銀閣に代表される東山文化が栄えた。能・狂言・連歌(れんが)など庶民も楽しめる文化が発達し，地方へも広まった。日本の伝統文化を代表する茶道・華道も，この時代に基礎が固まった。16世紀半ばに，南蛮人(ポルトガル人・イスパニア人)が渡来して，鉄砲やキリスト教を伝え，文化面で活気がみなぎった時代である。

Japanese History (3)

●**Feudal Era** (12th to 16th centuries)

This era saw the transfer of power from the imperial court to the newly ascendant military class and the building of a feudal system.

•**Kamakura Period** (1185-1333) Near the end of the 12th century, Minamoto no Yoritomo* established a military government in Kamakura. Over the nearly 150 years of this period, the tug-of-war between the military in Kamakura and the court in Kyoto fashioned feudal society. In the latter half of the 13th century, Mongol invasions twice threatened northern Kyushu, but were thwarted by sudden storms and stalwart defenses. Ironically, military rule became increasingly difficult in the ensuing years.

Culturally, Zen Buddhism had a wide following among the warrior class, and a new aesthetic of naturalism and simplicity developed within the conventional court culture. In religion, popular Buddhist sects emerged led by such outspoken monks as Honen,* Shinran,* and Nichiren.* Early Kamakura sculpture* is notable for its powerful realism and humanistic touches. Although military epics such as the *Heike Monogatari* (Tale of the Heike; early 13th century) dominated the period's literature, the court produced such dazzling works as the 1205 *Shin Kokin Wakashū* (New Collection of Ancient and Modern Times), the *Hōjōki* (The Ten Foot Square Hut; 13th century), and the *Tsurezuregusa* (Essays in Idleness; 14th century).

•**Muromachi Period** (1333-1576) Named after the district in Kyoto where Ashikaga Yoshimitsu consolidated his government in the early 14th century, this period is distinguished by the military's political and cultural preeminence. Yet the Ashikaga clan was too dependent upon the independent warlords' support to form a strong central government, and battles between competing warlords each with absolute authority over his own landholdings and subjects, were frequent by the latter half of the 15th century as this period developed into the *Sengoku jidai* (age of civil wars). Despite this, trade with Ming China flourished.

Zen Buddhism remained influential in both military and court circles. The two main artistic trends were the Kitayama culture* of the late 14th century, symbolized by the Kinkakuji Gold Pavilion, and the Higashiyama culture* of the late 15th century symbolized by the Ginkakuji Silver Pavilion. Noh, kyogen, *renga* linked verse, and other popular arts evolved and spread, and the tea ceremony and flower arranging were founded. Portuguese and Spanish traders also contributed to Japanese culture in the mid-16th century with the introduction of firearms and Christianity.

5 日本の歴史(4)

●**近世**(16世紀～19世紀半ば)

将軍と大名が土地・人民を統治し，経済的には農業生産に支えられる，いわゆる幕藩体制が確立する。

• **安土・桃山時代**　戦国の戦乱が治まって全国の統一が完成し，織田信長と豊臣秀吉が政権を握った時代。国内の統一とともに海外との交渉も活発に展開して，豪華で壮大な桃山文化を生んだ。

• **江戸時代**　徳川家康は，1603年に幕府を江戸(今の東京)に開き，以後260余年間，徳川氏が全国を支配する。幕府は天皇・公家・寺社を厳しく統制し，幕藩体制を支える農民の支配に心を砕いた。17世紀後半，3代将軍家光のとき，鎖国によって幕藩体制の安定期を迎えるが，産業の発達，商品経済の発展に伴い，農民の自給自足の経営が崩れ，18世紀ごろから幕藩体制が揺らぎ始める。

庶民の文化がこの時代の特色。17世紀末から18世紀初めの元禄文化は，京都，大坂などの上方地方を中心とする武士と町人の文化で，人形浄瑠璃・歌舞伎・浮世絵・工芸などが盛んになった。特に町人文芸に優れ，小説の井原西鶴，俳諧の松尾芭蕉，人形浄瑠璃・歌舞伎の脚本作者近松門左衛門などが出た。19世紀初めの化政文化は舞台が江戸に移り，小説・歌舞伎・浮世絵・文人画など多彩な町人文化が栄えた。

教育，学問も普及した。武士は幕藩体制維持の理論的根拠となる儒学，特に朱子学を学んだ。18世紀以降，日本の古典を研究する国学や蘭学が発達した。多くの藩(大名の領地)で子弟教育用の藩校が設立され，民間では庶民の初等教育機関である寺子屋が多くできた。

●**近代・現代**(19世紀半ば～現代)

19世紀後半の開国を機に，日本は半世紀で近代国家に急成長する。

• **明治**　欧米の先進諸国に追いつくために，政府は富国強兵，殖産興業，文明開化をモットーに，憲法の制定，国会の開設，不平等条約の改正など，近代化政策を次々に実行した。日清戦争・日露戦争の勝利を契機に，産業革命が進行し，資本主義が発達して，国際的地位もしだいに上がった。明治の文化は，伝統文化と欧米文化が対立し，統合されていく方向で発展していった。

• **大正・昭和**　第一次世界大戦以降の日本は，大正デモクラシーのような民衆勢力の台頭はあったものの，帝国主義的傾向を強め，昭和前期の1930年代から十五年戦争に突入する。太平洋戦争の敗北を機に，日本は自由で平和な文化国家の建設を目ざすようになった。

Japanese History (4)

●**Early Modern Era** (16th to mid-19th centuries)

In this era the feudal lords* consolidated their control and a *bakuhan** administrative system was established with an agricultural economy.

•**Azuchi-Momoyama Period*** (1576-1600) Following decades of civil war, Oda Nobunaga* and Toyotomi Hideyoshi* bid for national reconciliation. Relative peace and revived overseas trade.

•**Edo Period** (1600-1867) Consolidating his position, Tokugawa Ieyasu* made himself shogun and established his government in Edo in 1603. The shogunate kept the emperor, the nobility, and the religious institutions on a tight rein and strictly regulated the lives of the common people, mostly farmers, on whom the government ultimately rested. In the latter 17th century, the third shogun Iemitsu closed the country to foreign commerce. While domestic commerce and industry flourished, agriculture fell upon hard times. By the 18th century, the *bakuhan* system was falling apart.

The Edo period had a vigorous popular culture. In the Genroku era the Kyoto-Osaka* area was a center of *jōruri* puppet theater, kabuki, *ukiyo-e* prints, and other arts. Literature soared to new heights with Ihara Saikaku's fiction, Basho's poetry, and Chikamatsu's drama. As the cultural focus shifted to Edo in the early 19th century, novels, kabuki, *ukiyo-e*, and *bunjin-ga** painting continued to prosper.

Advances were made in education and scholarship. The philosophical underpinning for the *bakuhan*, Confucianism and neo-Confucian *Shushigaku* were major subjects of study for early-Edo samurai. *Kokugaku*, a nationalistic school of learning, and Dutch learning* grew in popularity after the 18th century. Many clans set up schools for samurai children while townspeople sent their children to *terakoya** schools.

●**Modern Era** (late-19th century to the present)

•**Meiji*** (1868-1912) With the fall of the shogunate and the imperial restoration, the Meiji government ended its seclusion and rushed to catch up with the industrialized West. Seeking to "enrich the country and strengthen the military," industry was promoted, Western culture was encouraged, a constitution was drawn up, a parliament was established, and the unequal treaties of the late Edo period were revised. Victory in the Sino-Japanese* and Russo-Japanese wars* moved Japanese capitalism onto the international stage. Culturally, this was a time of Japanizing Western cultures.

•**Taisho* and Showa*** (1912 to the present) Despite a brief interlude of "Taisho democracy,"* Japan's imperialistic leanings intensified following the end of World War I, and in the early Showa period —the early 1930s—the nation embarked upon 15 years of war.* The loss of World War II both marked a new nadir for Japan and provided the impetus for building a new nation of peace and freedom.

6 日本人の起源

日本人のルーツ探しは，明治以後，考古学・人類学・言語学など多方面から行われ，住居や神話の類似性からポリネシア系の南方説，さまざまな文化の関連から中国南方説，古墳や埋蔵品の馬具などから北方系の騎馬民族説，シベリアからの南下説などが言われてきた。第二次世界大戦後，特に近年になって，考古学的な発掘が進み，多数の人骨や石器，遺物が見つかり，より客観的な研究とデータが整い，他民族，他人種との比較も容易になっている。

●日本人の原型

日本では10万年以上前の人骨も発見されているが，現在の日本人の原型とされる人類は約１万8000年くらい前，日本にやってきたと見られている。この時代は，氷河期の最も寒かった時期に当たっており，海面が現在よりも140mほど下がっていたため，当時の食料であったマンモスを追って全地球的規模で民族移動が行われ，モンゴロイドが北米，南米にも渡った時期である。

日本周辺では間宮，宗谷，津軽，対馬の各海峡や黄海，琉球列島などが陸続きになり，このため北方からは，寒い気候に適応した，顔の凹凸が少ない，身長も低い新モンゴロイドが，南方からは，アジア大陸南部に広く住んでいた丸顔の古モンゴロイドが渡ってきた。この２つはやがて混交して，やや新モンゴロイドの特徴が濃く古モンゴロイドの特徴も合わせ持つ「原日本人」が生み出された。身体的な特徴は，丸顔で，背の低い，多毛性の人種である。

●「原日本人」から現代日本人へ

「原日本人」は日本各地に住んでいたが，弥生時代から古墳時代にかけて，朝鮮半島や中国大陸から，細面で背の高いより進んだ技術と文明を持った民族が西日本に移住してきて，原日本人に文化的な影響を与えるとともに，しだいに広く移り住み，原日本人とも混交していき，現代日本人が生み出されていった。ただ，その波及が，北日本と南西諸島に至るのが遅れたために，それらの地域には，日本人のプロトタイプのさまざまな特徴が残ることになったと見られている。

なお，現代の日本人を調べると，北には丸顔で背の低い人，南には細面で背の高い人が多いことがわかっている。

Origins of the Japanese People

Since Meiji times, archaeologists, anthropologists, and linguists have attempted to trace the origins of the Japanese people. Housing types and myths suggest a Polynesian origin; varied cultural characteristics point to southern China; tomb artifacts suggest a relationship to the mounted nomads of Korea and northern China; and other clues hint that the first Japanese made their way from Siberia across ancient land bridges. Human skeletons, stone ware, and other finds since the Second World War have supplied a wealth of data and facilitated scientific comparison with other peoples and races.

● The Japanese Prototype

Human skeletons over 100,000 years old have been discovered, but the prototype of the modern Japanese is believed to have come to Japan about 18,000 years ago. This was the time of the last glacial period, when the world's oceans were 140 meters lower than they are now. Great migrations were being made all over the globe in pursuit of the mammoth and other sources of food. This was also when Mongoloid peoples migrated to north and south America.

Linked to the Asian continent by expanses of land bridging the Tatar, Soya, Tsugaru, and Tsushima straits and the Yellow Sea, and connected to the southern Ryukyu Islands, Japan was easily accessible to the migratory peoples. From the north came a new Mongoloid race, short and with relatively flat features adapted to hard northern climes, and from the south came the older Mongoloid race of round-faced people who populated much of the southern Asian continent. The intermixing of these two races resulted in the prototype Japanese distinguished primarily by new Mongoloid features but having old Mongoloid characteristics as well—hairy, short of stature, and with a round face.

● Modern Japanese

The commonly accepted hypothesis today is that prototype Japanese were fairly evenly distributed throughout Japan. From the Yayoi through the Kofun periods, tall, narrow-faced peoples representing more advanced Chinese and Korean civilizations immigrated to western Japan bringing their culture and technology with them. These immigrants were gradually assimilated into the indigenous stock, and the result was the modern Japanese. The intermingling of the tall immigrant peoples with the short indigenous Japanese took so long to spread, however, that examples of early prototype Japanese are still to be found in the northernmost and southwestern areas of Japan.

Interestingly, studies of modern Japanese racial characteristics have shown that people in the north tend to be short and round-faced while people in the south tend to be tall and narrow-faced.

7 日本文化の起源

●照葉樹林文化地帯

日本の文化の根底となっている縄文(じょうもん)文化には，シベリアなどの北方文化の要素と，東南アジアなどの南方文化の要素とが見られるが，植物学者中尾佐助を中心とした植物生態学者，考古学者，文化人類学者らのグループは，東南アジアでの広範囲なフィールドワークに基づき，縄文文化の南方系の要素が，東南アジア文化とさまざまな共通性を持つことを実証した。この東南アジアに特有の文化を「照葉樹林文化」と言う。照葉樹というのは，カシ，クスノキ，ツバキ，サザンカといった常緑で，葉が厚く，表面が光り，深緑色をしている樹木で，東南アジアの熱帯雨林のすぐ北側，つまり，中国の雲南省を中心に，西はヒマラヤからシッキム，南はビルマ，ベトナム北部，東は中国南岸部から日本まで，この樹林が生い繁っている地帯を照葉樹林帯と呼んでいる。

●共通の文化要素

この地帯は人種的にはモンゴロイドが住み，気候的にも似通っており，このため，共通した文化要素を持つに至ったものと思われる。特に，熱帯雨林ほど果物や芋類などに恵まれなかったため，早くから焼畑農耕が始まり，ヒエ，アワ，ソバ，大豆など，そして後には稲が栽培された。これらの雑穀類は，そのままでは食べられないために，水にさらしたり，あく抜きをした上で粉にして煮て，*もちとして食べた。このため，焼畑農耕，穀類を粉にするためのうすやきねなどの道具，煮たきするためのこしきなどの土器類の発達などが共通の文化となっている。

この地帯の特産品である*茶や*こんにゃく，*シソの飲食も特徴的であるし，大豆を原料とした納豆作りもこの地帯だけで行われている。食品以外では*漆や蚕の飼育による絹の使用，*鵜(う)飼いによる漁業も，雲南からベトナム，中国南岸から日本まで，この地帯で広く見られるものである。

神話では，日本の『古事記』『日本書紀』に出てくる「天岩屋(あめのいわや)型」の日食神話，神の死体から何種類かの作物が生まれるという「死体化生型」の作物起源神話なども，共通するものである。信仰では，死者が山や丘の頂に帰り，死者の霊は山に眠るという「山上他界」の考え方も焼畑農耕民に広く分布している。男女が自分の思いを歌い合う「歌垣(うたがき)」の習俗，男が女の所に通う「妻問い婚」なども行われていた。

Sources of Japanese Culture

●Shiny-leaf Culture

Japan's earliest civilization, the Jomon culture, shows signs of northern cultural influences from Siberia and southern influences from Southeast Asia. There is a group of botanists, archeologists, and cultural anthropologists led by the botanist Nakao Sasuke who claim a close relationship between the Jomon culture and the basic culture of Southeast Asia. This group has named this common culture the shiny-leaf culture because it is characterized by its emergence in forests of evergreen trees with thick, dark green, and shiny leaves such as *kashi* (oak), *kusunoki* (*Cinnamomum camphora*), *tsubaki* (*camellia japonica*), and *sazanka* (*camellia sasanqua*). Located just north of Southeast Asia's tropical rainforests, this shiny-leaf forest belt spreads from China's Yunnan Province to the Himalayas and Sikkim in the west, Burma and northern Vietnam in the south, and the southern Chinese coast in the east.

●Cultural Characteristics

The fact that the shiny-leaf forest belt's residents share a common climate and a Mongoloid racial heritage is believed to have given them a common culture as well. Agriculture started early in this region because its people lacked the fruits and tubers so abundantly available in the southern tropical rainforest zones. Food cultivation began with various types of millet, buckwheat, and soybeans, eventually extending to rice. These plants had to be processed before they could be eaten, and the soaking, grinding, and boiling needed to create a glutinous paste* eaten as a staple are common processes throughout the region. These common experiences have also given rise to such common tools as mortars and pestles for grinding and earthenware pots for cooking.

Other characteristics common to this zone include the drinking of tea* and the cultivation and eating of *konnyaku** (Devil's tongue) and perilla.* *Nattō*, a fermented bean product made of soybeans, is found in various forms wherever the shiny-leaf culture's writ runs. Besides these common foods, the region is noted for its lacquer ware,* silk, and cormorant fishing.*

The myths of the region all include an eclipse myth, and stories of food plants sprouting from corpses abound. The region's scorched-earth farming societies share a belief that the dead return to hilltops, and that their souls sleep within mountains. Although no longer practiced in some areas, similar customs of the past include the *utagaki* song festivals in which young boys and girls vied with each other in their songs, and the marriage custom of having the husband visit his wife regularly at her home instead of their living together.

8 日本文化の特性

内外の学者，研究者が挙げる日本文化の特性は多い。その中から代表的な4つを取り上げてみよう。

●重層性

日本の文化は，系統の異なる文化が併存ないしは混在する重層文化である。例は周囲にいくらでもある。政治には新旧の制度が混在し，衣食住は和洋折衷であり，宗教は神仏をともに受け入れ，日常使う日本語の中には漢語が半分以上も含まれている，といったぐあいである。

重層文化が生まれた理由として，日本人は異質文化への好奇心が強いこと，在来文化を根こそぎ否定するような侵略を受けず，必要に応じて外来文化を取り入れる環境にあったこと，などが挙げられる。

●均一性

日本の文化は，地域によって，宗教によって，あるいは人によって異なるということはなく，ほぼ均一，均質であると言うことができる。どこを切っても同じ断面が現れる「金太郎あめ」*というのがあるが，正に日本の文化は金太郎あめと同じである。狭い国土に多数の人が住んでいることのほかに，日本人は長い間，生活の末端まで国家の統制を受けてきた経験から，個人よりも集団や国家を考える習性を持っていることが，文化の均一性を生んだ原因と見られる。

●日本化

日本人は外来文化を日本化して，独自のものとしてしまう能力を持っている。平安時代に，漢字を日本化して仮名を作り出し，『源氏物語』などの傑作を生んだことは，日本の歴史(p. 14)で見たとおりである。

鎌倉仏教は仏教が日本化された例である。6世紀に伝来した仏教は，鎌倉時代に法然(ほうねん)とその弟子親鸞(しんらん)が出て，外来宗教の域を脱し，日本の仏教となった。法然は専修(せんじゅ)念仏の教え，親鸞は悪人正機(しょうき)説といった，日本人に即した独特の教義を説いて宗教活動を展開したため，広く民衆の信仰を集めることができたのである。

●現実的

日本人は現実的である。普遍的概念よりも個別的な事物を重んじる。仏教を現世利益的なものに変えたこともそうだし，江戸時代の幕藩体制の理論的根拠となった儒学も，理論面より応用面，実際面で優れていた。現代の科学でも，原理の追求より原理の応用・製品化の面で能力を発揮していることは周知のとおりである。

Characteristics of Japanese Culture

Japanese culture has many unique features, the following four being among the most characteristic.

●Multi-layered

As shown in innumerable ways, Japanese culture is made up of many layers—old and new, foreign and native. Politics is a mixture of old and new customs. The three essentials of food, clothing, and shelter are blends of Japanese and Western elements. Japanese practice both Buddhist and Shinto rites, and more than half of the Japanese language is comprised of Chinese-derivative words.

Among the reasons for this multi-layered quality of Japanese culture are the curiosity Japanese people have for other cultures and the historic process of assimilation as Japanese welcomed foreign cultural elements without discarding indigenous customs and traditions.

●Homogeneity

Varying little by region, religion, or person, Japanese culture is basically uniform throughout the country—like the *kintarō-ame** candy, which shows the same pattern no matter where it is cut. Not only does Japan have a large population on limited land, but the people have lived for centuries under centralized governments which regulated people's lives in minute detail. Primary importance has traditionally been placed on the group rather than on the individual, and this heritage accounts for much of Japanese society's uniformity.

●Japanization

Japanese have been very adept at making foreign elements their own to create something that is uniquely Japanese. This trait goes back beyond the Heian period when Japanese *kana* characters were created out of the more complex Chinese characters and this *kana* script then used to produce such great works as the *Tale of Genji*.

Kamakura Buddhism is another example of Japanization. Introduced to Japan in the 6th century, Buddhism did not spread until the appearance of Honen and Shinran, respectively founders of the Jodo and Jodo Shin sects. Honen taught that all that was needed to attain salvation was to recite the name of Amida Buddha, and Shinran, his disciple, elaborated on this by stressing that Amida Buddha had prepared the Pure Land precisely for the salvation of the wicked. These teachings, which stressed pure and simple faith over complicated rites and doctrines, appealed strongly to the common Japanese populace.

●Pragmatism

The Japanese are highly pragmatic, emphasizing specific circumstances more than universal truths. Indeed, it is this trait which made it possible to create Japan's this-worldly Buddhism and why the Confucian ethic of the Edo-period shogunate was far better in its practical applications than in its theory. Even in modern science, Japanese show more aptitude for scientific applications than for basic research.

9 日本人の自然観

●自然との一体化

日本人にとって古来，自然はあくまで恵みを与えるもの，親しむべきものであり，決して人間と対立する厳しく，むごいものではなかった。これは日本が温帯の湿潤な地域にあって，自然環境が温和なものであったのに加え，縄文時代以来の採集・漁労社会，それに次ぐ稲作を中心とした農耕社会にとって，自然は生育をもたらし，実りをもたらすものであったことによる。また，定着的な農耕社会である日本では，父祖代々がその自然とともに生き，やがて自然に帰っていき，自分自身もまたその道をたどる。それゆえ自然と自分を一体化し，自然の心をわが心として生きる感情が，日本人の哲学・思想・宗教などすべての精神活動の根本に流れている。

このような自然への親しみ，自然と我との一体化は，さらに，自然を楽しみ，現世を謳歌する現実肯定の考え方を生み出してゆく。それはまた，「長いものには巻かれろ」の精神であり，太平洋戦争を「鬼畜米英」と言って戦い，敗けると何の抵抗もなくアメリカ文化に染まったのも，和の精神の底に流れるものもこれである。日本の宗教が現世利益をうたわなければ信者を集められないのも，また，日本人の現実肯定の表れであると言われている。

●自然の観察と再現

他方，春夏秋冬の四季の微妙な変化が，農耕社会においては種まき，生育，収穫の兆候ともなるところから，自然の移ろいへの細かい観察が行われ，それは「松風の音を聞き，虫の音をめでる」といった自然への鋭敏な感覚をはぐくみ，それを基に，さまざまな芸術や生活習慣が生まれている。西洋絵画では17世紀に初めて独立した主題となった風景画も，日本では山水画と呼ばれて鎌倉時代以来，常に主要なテーマであった。文学においても，自然はいつも重要なテーマであり，特に和歌や俳句が，花鳥風月をうたい，俳句に季語を詠み込むのも，その小世界に自然を取り入れようとする姿勢の表れである。

日本人の自然観は仏教の無常感によって増幅されたものだが，特に禅宗の思想と結び付いてからは，幽玄・わび・さびの世界を生み出し，茶道や庭園，華道などにおいて，人工の極致として，ありのままの飾らない自然を再現するようになった。このような考え方は，芸術ばかりでなく武道でも行われ，後にスポーツ化した剣道・柔道・空手道などでも，その技量の奥儀は自然体，つまり，自然と一体となって，あるがままの力を発揮することであるとしている。

Japanese Concepts of Nature

●Oneness with Nature

Nature has always been a familiar and friendly blessing to the Japanese, not a cruel foe, and this concept of nature is readily understandable in view of the Japanese islands' temperate climate and abundant rainfall. To the gathering and fishing peoples of the Jomon period and the rice cultivating farmers who followed, this environment was not only mild and non-threatening but the source of all growth and fertility. The life cycles of the agricultural people of old Japan so closely followed the natural rhythm of the land that they were as one with nature, their very souls a part of the spirit of nature. This sense of oneness with nature underlies the Japanese ethos, its philosophy, thought, and religion, and it is part of the Japanese sensitivity to and enjoyment of nature.

The identification with nature has spawned a preference to flow with the tide. The Japanese situational ethic—its ready resignation to the way things are and its emphasis on harmony at all cost—is well-illustrated by the Japanese receptiveness to American culture after World War II even though they had vilified America and fought bravely against the United States during the war. Another aspect of this concern with their immediate situation is the lack of interest in religious promises of other-worldy rewards. They are more likely to be attracted by promises of immediate and this-worldly advantages.

●Observation and Re-creation

The need of an agricultural society to know when to plant, cultivate, and harvest its crops has sharpened the Japanese sensitivity to seasonal changes, heightening their awareness of the minutiae of nature—the wind in the pines and the singing of insects—and giving rise to a wide variety of arts and customs embodying this sensitivity. Landscapes did not become an accepted subject for Western painting until the 17th century, but in Japan they were already a major theme of the *sansui-ga** painting introduced from China in the Kamakura period. Nature has played a major part in Japanese literature as well, figuring prominently in seasonal references* in *waka* and haiku poetry and in the custom of using seasonal introductions in correspondence and other writing.

The Buddhist concept of transience has been incorporated into the indigenous concept of nature as an extension of oneself. Zen teachings have given rise to the mysticism and rustic simplicity of *yūgen*,* *wabi*,* and *sabi** inherent in the tea ceremony, the Japanese garden, and flower arrangements. In all of these arts, the ultimate goal is to represent nature as it is. This extends even into the traditional martial arts such as *kendō*, judo, and karate, which teach that strength comes only when one is completely relaxed and as much at one with nature as possible.

10 日本人の宗教心

●複雑な多神教国

日本人の宗教心は，世界の宗教の中でも最も複雑なものの１つであることは間違いない。よく言われるのが，「正月には神社に初もうでに行き，春秋の彼岸には寺に墓参りし，クリスマスには家中でケーキを食べ，子供にプレゼントする」という年中行事や，「七五三で神社にお参りし，結婚式は教会で挙げ，葬式はお寺で」という通過儀礼における宗教の多様性である。

ふつう，多神教と言った場合は，１つの宗教が多数の神を持っていることを指すが，日本の場合は，それぞれ体系化された多神教である仏教や神道があり，日本人の大部分はその両方の信徒で家には神棚も仏壇もある上，時にはさらに，他の新宗教の信徒であることもありうる。加えて，お稲荷さん，道祖神といったアニミズムやシャーマニズムに近い神にも抵抗なく手を合わせる。自動車を買えばおはらいをしてもらい，超近代的な工場のロボットに人名をつけて擬人化した扱いをするのなども，アニミズム的信仰の表れと言ってよさそうだ。

これを裏付けるのは，文化庁が編さんしている『宗教年鑑』である。1984年版によれば，日本の宗教人口は２億2000万人。このときの総人口が約１億2000万人なので，日本人すべてがほぼ２つずつの宗教の信徒となっていることになる。ところが，1982年のＮＨＫの調査によると，「あなたご自身は，何か宗教を信仰していますか」との問いに，「信仰を持っている」と答えたのは33％だけで，「信仰を持っていない」が65％であった。

●根底にある利益求心

このように，ある宗教に対する明確な信仰心は持たないが，心情として，あるいは基本的感覚として存在するのが日本人の宗教心と言えそうだ。その根本にあるのが，やはり，日本人の自然観に基づく現実肯定の宗教的表現である，現世利益を求める心である。日本固有の民族信仰である神道はもともと豊作や部族社会の安全を祈る祈願神であり，インドで発生したときには自らの救いを得る宗教であった仏教も，日本伝来とともに祈禱（きとう）する宗教となった。

こうして日本では，宗教は商売繁盛，家内安全，受験合格，安産に至るまで，多種多様な現世利益を祈る場となり，宗教法人の経済的基盤もそこにある。「苦しいときの神頼み」「いわしの頭も信心から」のことわざが，日本人の宗教心の現世利益という特色を物語っている。

Japanese Religion

●Overlapping Religions

Japanese beliefs are probably among the most complicated in the world because of the openness to all religions, as exemplified by the visits to Shinto shrines at New Year's,* trips to Buddhist temples in the spring and fall* to visit the family grave, and the modern custom of a cake and presents at Christmas. The *Shichi-go-san* celebration entails a trip to the local Shinto shrine, weddings are often held in Christian churches, and funerals are most often Buddhist.

Polytheism usually refers to a religion with many gods, but Japan doubles this by having many religions each of which may have many gods. It is not uncommon for a Japanese family to have both Shinto and Buddhist alters even though its members believe in yet a third faith. Many Japanese also feel a close affinity to Inari,* once an agrarian deity but now popular throughout Japan as an all-purpose god, and the *dōsojin** on the edges of villages to protect villagers. The same person who has a Shinto priest perform purification rites for his new car may also work in an ultra-modern factory where he animistically gives the robots both nicknames and a measure of affection and respect.

Statistics substantiate the evidence of Japanese culture's polytheistic quality. According to the Agency for Cultural Affairs' *Religion Yearbook*, Japan had a religious population of 220 million in 1984—nearly double the actual population of 120 million. In response to a survey done by the Japan Broadcasting Company in 1982, however, only 33% of those queried said that they had a religious affiliation, and 65% said that they had no religion.

●Here-and-now Orientation

While the Japanese tend to avoid identifying with any single religious doctrine, they do have an inherent reverence for all things, a reverence that stems from their strongly-rooted, nearly mystical affinity with nature and quest for this-worldly rewards. Shinto, Japan's indigenous religion, was originally a means of supplicating the gods for aid in agricultural endeavors and for protection at the tribal level. Buddhism, which started out preaching good works to attain salvation, was transformed in Japan to a religion of supplication.

In Japan religion is a tool for petitioning for business profits, the safety of the household, success on school entrance exams, painless childbirth, and numerous other concrete rewards now. It is this faith in the power and influence of the gods in this world which is the source of the secular affluence of many of Japan's institutionalized religious organizations. Common expressions such as *kurushii toki no kami danomi* (turning to religion in times of distress) and *iwashi no atama mo shinjin kara* (even the basest thing is sacred) further reveal the Japanese view of religion as a source of this-worldly benefits.

11 日本人の勤労意識

●よく働く日本人

日本人は非常によく働くという評価は，日本の経済発展とともに今では国際的にも定着している。ただ，そうした評価の裏に日本に対する羨望（せんぼう）と嫉妬（しっと）が潜んでいることは，例えば日本の経済活動に対して「エコノミック・アニマル」と称していることでもわかる。しかし，日本人からすると，欧米の評価にはどこか認識の誤りがあるようだ。

日本人にとって働くということは，必ずしも利益を求めることが第一義的な目的ではなく，働くという行為そのものに価値を見いだしているという説がある。評論家の山本七平氏（*）によれば，日本人の勤労というのは，すなわち仏教で言う成仏するための修業であり，経済的利益は宗教的に動機づけられた，つまり，私欲のない労働の結果とされる。このような，結果としての利潤は是認されると考えていると言うのである。現在の企業活動においても、この勤労に対する精神は生き続けており，それが，日本人が非常によく働くことの解答でもある。したがって，経済報酬は労働（時間）に対する対価であるという欧米的な勤労意識とは，その精神においてだいぶ異なることになる。この違いが，一方では契約社会に基づく企業経営を創出し，一方では独特のいわゆる日本的経営を生み出したと言う。

●変わりつつある労働観

しかし，最近は仕事に対する考え方もだいぶ変化している。基本的に労働に対する価値を依然認めてはいるものの，意欲の点になるとかなり減少してきている。その背景としては，1つに労働の目的の喪失がある。低成長時代になり，いくら働いたからといって収入は増えない。高齢化により，ポスト不足で出世も期待できない状況で，具体的な目標が立てにくい。

また一方，経済的に一応豊かになるとともに，価値観の多様化が進み，特に若い世代に働くこと以外の価値を認める傾向が強くなりつつある。そして，OA化やロボット化などが進むにつれ，熟練技術が単純労働に取って代わられたり，労働時間の短縮，余暇の増大などにより，従来の勤労そのものの条件も変わってくる。このことは，しだいに労働観の変化をもたらすだろうし，それにつれて当然勤労意欲というのも変わると思われる。少なくとも，今までのような企業中心的な勤労意欲というのは確実に減退していくであろう。

The Japanese Work Ethic

● Hard-working Japanese

As the Japanese economy has grown stronger, the Japanese people have come to be known the world over as hard workers. However, this perception of Japan often includes negative elements, including the view that Japanese are simply "economic animals" pursuing profit above all else. Yet for their part, the Japanese feel that Western perceptions are distorted by misunderstanding about a number of aspects of life in Japan.

To begin with, the zeal with which Japanese pursue their work is based not so much on the profit motive as it is on the value of working. The distinguished social commentator Yamamoto Shichihei,* for example, traces the Japanese work ethic to Japan's strong Buddhist tradition. As Yamamoto explains it, the act of working is subconsciously accepted as a spiritual discipline, and Buddhahood, not economic gain, is the prize to be gained through selfless devotion to one's work. Even today, this orientation lives on in Japanese companies, and this is a major reason why Japanese work so hard. As such, the Japanese work ethic differs radically from the modern European attitude that work is basically an exchange of labor (time) for money and that neither the work nor the act of working has any inherent value. This difference is also seen as a major cause of the differences between business management in the contractual West and what might be called the distinctively Japanese-style management.

● Changing Attitudes

However, the Japanese work ethic has been undergoing significant change in recent years. While work is still held in high esteem, there has been considerable erosion on the motivation side. This is partly because the goals have become more elusive. In today's slow-growth climate, extra work is not always rewarded by a higher income, and the graying of the Japanese population is creating a shortage of upper-management posts.

In addition, as the Japanese have attained a relatively high level of material affluence, their values have become more individualized, and many people—particularly young people—are placing a greater emphasis on personal-interest activities outside of their work. As tomorrow's increasingly sophisticated office and factory automation technologies change work conditions and make routine jobs out of tasks which formerly required skilled expertise, there will likely be a significant shortening of the work week and the creation of more leisure time, gradually changing the way work is perceived. This will naturally have an impact on people's motivation. At the very least, there will be less of the company-oriented work ethic that has been so pervasive until now.

12 日本人の娯楽観

●働き蜂(ばち)の暇つぶし

「ウサギ小屋に住む働き蜂」と西欧人に評されたように，日本人は元来，仕事第一で，遊ぶという観念に乏しい国民だった。いい仕事をすることこそが人生の生きがいであり，したがって仕事以外の自由な時間も，もっぱら仕事の疲れをいやし，ストレスを解消するために使われた。例を挙げれば，テレビを見てゴロ寝をするとか，盛り場で一杯飲むとか，同僚とマージャンをするなどである。なかでも日本独得の大衆娯楽*パチンコは，いつでも１人で遊べて，運がよければ景品稼ぎもできる点が受けて，最も人気のある暇つぶし法だった。スポーツではゴルフがあるが，これもあくまで仕事絡みであった。

●娯楽観の変化

しかし，こうした娯楽観が支配的だったのは高度経済成長時代の昭和40年代までで，最近の日本人のレジャーに対する考え方はだいぶ変わってきている。余暇を仕事の余り時間とするのではなく，もっと積極的な意味で考えるようになった。

その１つが，低成長時代に入った昭和50年代前半に典型的だった生活向上型あるいは自己投資型とでも呼ぶべき余暇利用法である。余暇をただ漠然と過ごすのではなく，生活の資源として有効に使おうというもので，日曜大工のようなＤＩＹ（do-it-yourself）活動や自分の教養を高めるための読書や学習，スポーツでも健康作りのためのジョギング，水泳などが盛んに行われるようになった。そして，安定成長時代に入った昭和50年代後半からは，若い世代を中心に，余暇そのものにより高度な楽しみを求める傾向が強くなってきている。高級レストランで豪華な食事を楽しんだり，国内旅行を節約しても海外旅行に出かける，テニス・ゴルフも道具に凝って，時には仲間と海外へ繰り出す――という具合に，これといった楽しみには投資を惜しまないというのが，最も新しい日本人のレジャーに対する考え方であり，レジャーは今や，所得や自由時間のゆとりの現れとなっている。

なお，こうした娯楽観の変化とは関係がないが，ここ数年，老若問わず圧倒的人気があるのが，音楽だけ入ったカセットテープに合わせて歌う*カラオケである。もともとは盛り場のバー，スナックだけにあったカラオケセットが今では家庭にまで普及し，歌う順番を巡って殺人が起きたり，騒音公害が問題になるほどはやっている。

Relaxing Japanese-style

● Work before Pleasure

Characterized by one Western observer as "workaholics who live in rabbit hutches," the Japanese have always put work before pleasure and have traditionally scorned play for play's sake. For most Japanese, work has been what gives life meaning, and people have tended to spend their leisure time at simple pursuits to relieve work-related exhaustion and stress. For instance, many Japanese prefer to loaf around the house watching television, go for a drink at a local pub, or get together with friends to play mahjong. One of the most popular pastimes is pachinko,* that peculiarly Japanese form of pinball that can be played any time of the day, needs only one player, and offers abundant prizes for high-scorers. There are also sports such as golf, but golf is played mainly for business reasons.

● Broadening Interests

However, while this tradition of free time as rest time was dominant throughout Japanese history, there have been some major changes in the way the Japanese view recreation since the mid-1970s end of the economy's rapid growth. No longer the odd hour or two left over after work, leisure has come into its own.

With the slower economic growth of the late-1970s, people began using their leisure time for what might be called lifestyle-enhancement or self-improvement purposes. Rather than just fritter away their free time, people began to take advantage of this time and to make it an important part of their lives by, for example, becoming weekend carpenters and do-it-yourselfers, reading and studying to augment their educations, or taking up sports and other fitness-oriented pursuits such as jogging and swimming. With the stable economic growth of the 1980s, many people (particularly younger people) are growing ever more adamant in their quest to derive maximun enjoyment from their leisure time. More and more people are dining out at luxury restaurants, traveling overseas even if this means cutting back on domestic travel, and occasionally even organizing overseas tennis, golf, or other affinity-group tours with friends. This tendency to spare no expense for the sake of quality leisure is Japan's newest trend, and one that bespeaks of the greater income and free time today's Japanese have at their disposal.

Another recent phenomenon in recreation, although one that does not involve any great change in how leisure time is perceived, is the popularity of *karaoke** sing-along tapes that provide instrumental accompaniment for people of all ages who like to sing. These tapes first appeared in bars, but now they are showing up in private homes, and the *karaoke* craze has even led to violence over who is going to sing first, complaints about the noise, and other problems.

13 日本人の美意識

日本人の美意識の底には常に自然との一体感と，仏教の諸行無常の考え方が流れている。しかし，時代の雰囲気によって，表現される美意識は異なる。

●「もののあわれ」

日本人が中国文化の影響を消化し，独自の文化・精神を作り上げたのは平安時代とされているが，この時代に支配的だった美意識が「もののあわれ」である。あらゆる物事の中に，はかなさを見て，心に感動を生じるようすを言い，『源氏物語』をはじめとする文学の世界にもそれは色濃く反映されていた。

●「わび」と「さび」

戦国の世が終わり，心の落ち着きを取り戻した時代に，力を得た町人が持った美意識である。「わび」は，茶道の中で生まれた美意識で，おごらず質素な中に，豊かさと静かな心を秘めたものである。千利休をはじめとする茶道の宗匠たちは，一輪の野の花や日常雑器の中に美を見いだした。「さび」は松尾芭蕉を中心とした俳句の世界で言われた美意識で，静かな孤高の心境を言う。「わび」も「さび」も禅の悟りの境地をバックボーンに持っている。

●「いき」

江戸時代に町人が作り上げた美意識で，気がきいてセンスのよいことを言う。「いき」には「張り・あだ・あか抜け」の３条件があるとされ，張りとは自分の考えを貫く心，あだは下品にならないコケトリー，あか抜けは人生の表裏に通じた軽妙さと言える。

●幕の内弁当の美意識

こうした伝統的な美意識を近代文明と調和させ，現代に花咲かせたものを「幕の内弁当の美意識」と言ったのが，栄久庵憲司である。幕の内弁当には，ご飯と煮物・焼き物・漬物などさまざまなおかずが少しずつ彩りよく入っている。１つ１つの素材はごくありふれたものであるが，それらが全体としては調和のとれた美として，狭い弁当箱の中にきっちり納まっている。「わび」「さび」そして「いき」の精神に立ち，見た目の美しさ，味という機能でも優れている。この幕の内弁当の美意識は，世界の市場で人気のあるコンパクトにパッケージされ，デザインも優れた家庭電器製品・オートバイ・自動車などの製品に生かされ，さらには日本が世界をリードしている大規模集積回路の極微小の世界の根底にも存在していると言ってよい。

Japanese Aesthetics

While oneness with nature and the Buddhist feeling* that worldly display counts for nothing underlie the Japanese aesthetic, this has been expressed differently in different ages.

● Pathos

It was in the Heian period that Chinese culture was adapted and Japanized into truly Japanese modes. The dominant aesthetic of that age was one of pathos and insignificance. Every event was seen as inspiring for its transience, touching for its insignificance, and this ethic is perhaps most starkly depicted in *Genji Monogatari* and the other literature of the times.

● *Wabi* and *Sabi*

When the raging civil wars ended and peace returned to people's hearts, it was the aesthetic of the newly powerful merchant class which prevailed. Born of the tea ceremony, *wabi* is an aesthetic of finding richness and serenity in simplicity. This was epitomized by the single wild flower and everyday plainness which decorated the tea houses of Sen no Rikyu* and other masters.* *Sabi* was a term for the beauty of such haiku as those by Basho, and it bespeaks of a quiet grandeur enjoyed in solitude. Both *wabi* and *sabi* are closely linked to the Zen striving for enlightenment through nothingness.

● Chic

Iki was the buzzword in the Edo period for the trendy fashionableness favored by the merchants. Generally, the three requirements for this chic *iki* were a persistence in being one's own person, a touch of class that refused to be vulgar, and a light lifestyle.

● *Maku-no-uchi* Beauty

Harmonized with modern civilization, this traditional sense of beauty finds expression today, says industrial designer Ekuan Kenji,* in the beauty of the *maku-no-uchi* boxed lunch. Here there are small portions of rice, pickled vegetables, grilled fish, and other foods—each quite ordinary in its own right—placed in harmonious arrangement to create a work of art in a small lacquered box. Embodying the principles of *wabi*, *sabi*, and *iki*, the lunch pleases both the eye and the palate. The same spirit which creates this elegantly compact *maku-no-uchi* boxed lunch also produces the home electronic appliances, automobiles, and other Japanese products that have proven so popular in the international marketplace—as well as the supercompact super-ICs where Japan commands a leading position. This is Japan's all-pervasive aesthetic of unostentatious functional beauty raised to its highest.

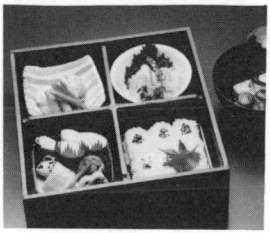

△幕の内弁当 (*maku-no-uchi* boxed lunch)

14 日本人の死生観

●武士道

日本人の死生観に最も大きな影響を与えたのは仏教である。浄土宗は「厭離穢土・欣求浄土」と言って，汚いこの世を早く去り，極楽浄土を求むべきだと唱えた。また禅宗の一派曹洞宗の日本における開祖道元は，その著『正法眼蔵』の中で，「生死を生死にまかす」として，生死の問題にとらわれることなく，死のときには生への執着を捨てて死に徹し，生のときには生に徹して一瞬一瞬に全力を尽くして生きることを教え，鎌倉時代以後，明日にも戦場に散るかもしれない武士たちの心の支えとなってきた。

江戸時代に入り，官僚化した武士に対する復古の動きとして，盛んに「武士道」が唱えられるようになる。江戸時代中期に九州佐賀藩の武士道の書『葉隠』では，「武士道といふは，死ぬ事と見つけたり」と言ってのけている。ここでは禅宗の言葉を一歩強めて，死に徹することが，完全なる生にもつながる，との考え方が示されている。

それを徹底したのが武士道における「切腹」で，腹という致死性の少ない部分を裂き，壮絶に死ぬことを演出して，自らの名と家名を活かし遺族への保障を得る。それが切腹という儀礼であり，また，制度でもあった。

●心中

心中も，江戸時代初めごろは，男女の愛情確認のための行為，例えば誓紙，断髪，入れ墨をすることを「心中立てる」「心中する」と言っていた。それが江戸時代半ばから2つとない生命をかけるようになったことから，「心中死」，または「心中情死」と呼ばれるようになり，歌舞伎や浄瑠璃でもてはやされたこともあって，心中，すなわち情死心中となったものである。ここでも，死によって，愛情を全うしたのであり，「死によって活かす」という，日本固有の死生観が貫かれているのである。

●自殺

日本は自殺が多いと言われるが，人口10万人当たりの自殺者は20.4人(1984年)，死亡者中の自殺者の割合は3.3%で，ルーマニア，ハンガリーなどとともに世界の上位である。

その原因は，日本では「死によって活かす」自殺は，それ自体が潔い行為と見られ，罪悪視されることはないからで，これには仏教の厭世思想が果たした役割が大きく，自殺をタブーとするキリスト教文化圏の思想とはたいへん異なっている。

Views of Life and Death

● *Bushi-dō*

Buddhist concepts have had a major effect upon Japanese perceptions of life and death. The Jodo sect, one of the most popular Buddhist sects, for example, teaches that the world as we know it is tainted and that we must strive for rebirth in the Jodo Pure Land paradise.* In Zen, also, Dogen, founder of Soto Zen, admonishes in his *Shōbō Genzō* (Treasury of the True Dharma Eye) that we should not question either life or death. Confronted with death, we should die readily, and while alive we should live every minute to the fullest. This concept of life and death was readily accepted in the Kamakura period and later by samurai who continually confronted death on the battlefield.

By the Edo period, the samurai were little more than bureaucrats, and *bushi-dō*, the way of the warrior with its ethics and guides for proper conduct, was stressed as part of the attempt to preserve the dignity of the warrior class. "*Bushi-dō* is a way of dying" is a famous saying from *Hagakure** (In the Shadow of Leaves), a book on *bushi-dō* written in the middle of the Edo period. *Hagakure* takes Zen teachings one step further by saying that being able to accept death is equivalent to living a full and complete life.

Seppuku, ritualistic suicide by disembowlment, was a means of protecting one's name and the honor of one's house through a dramatic and glorious death. In *bushi-dō*, *seppuku* was both a ritual and the epitome of ethical conduct.

● *Shinjū**

In the early Edo period, expressions of love between a man and a woman, such as exchanging pledges, cutting one's hair, and tattooing,* were referred to as *shinjū*. Sometime in the latter half of the Edo period *shinjū*, double love suicides, became prevalent and supplied ample story material for kabuki and *jōruri*.* To the Japanese, death marked the culmination of the love between two people, and by this reasoning, *shinjū* was a fulfillment of love.

● Suicide

Japan has a high suicide rate, with 20.4 suicides per 100,000 population in 1984. Suicide accounts for 3.3% of all deaths, ranking Japan alongside Rumania, Hungary, and other countries with high suicide rates.

One of the reasons that so many Japanese opt for suicide is that they see it as a means of fulfillment rather than a sinful act. This reflects Buddhist fatalism and is quite alien to Judeo-Christian admonishments against taking one's own life.

15 集団主義

●集団の重視

E.O.ライシャワーは『ザ・ジャパニーズ』の中で，日本人と欧米人とのいちばん顕著な違いを，日本人の集団重視に見ている。日本人といえどもこの見方に異論はないだろう。

確かに日本人の集団重視は過去，第2次世界大戦における玉砕や集団自決の悲劇，一億一心のスローガン，また今日，企業経営，サラリーマン社会などにおける集団の和の重視，果ては学校の生徒の制服に至るまで，広く深く根を張っている。「出る釘は打たれる」ということわざは日本人の処生術を端的に表しているし，集団に異を唱えたり，背を向けた者には「村八分」という処罰があった。例外はむろんあるが，日本の社会は個我の主張より，集団あっての個，個は集団にあって生かされると了解してきたと言える。

●集団主義の形成

集団主義の成立は，日本の歴史的背景と無縁ではない。第1に，はるか弥生時代に始まる稲作文化の影響がある。農村では今日もなお，田植えや稲刈り期には近隣どうしが助け合い，共同作業を行う習慣が一部に残っている。狩猟文化と異なり，そこでは集団作業と共同秩序とが必要であり，生活共同体なのである。儒教思想の影響も無視できない。忠孝を重んずるその道徳は江戸時代以降特に広まり，「家」制度にもつながった。家長は絶対の権限を持ち，家族は「家」に従わねばならず，武士階級にあっては一朝事あれば御家断絶と，連帯責任を取らされた。

狭い国土に多くの人口ということも有力な一因だろう。朝晩の通勤電車の殺人的ラッシュは外国人のしばしば瞠目するところだが，当の日本人は甘受せざるを得ないし，そこから集団の調和という社会生活の知恵を身に付けるのである。住宅事情しかり。学校教育しかり。

●集団主義の功罪

集団主義には当然ながらプラス，マイナスの両面がある。戦前の無批判な軍国主義化は後者であろうし，戦後の高度経済成長の原動力となったニッポン式経営は，たとえ一部にエコノミック・アニマルと批判を浴びても，全般的にはプラスの集団主義であり，外国から「日本に学べ」の声も出るわけである。しかし，当の日本ではこれとは逆に個性化，多様化への志向が年々強まっており，集団主義を日本人の永久不変の特性とする見方が見直される時代も来るかもしれない。

Groupism

● Perceptions of the Group

Edwin O. Reischauer writes in his book *The Japanese* that Japanese groupism and Western individualism mark one of the most conspicuous differences between Japanese and Westerners. Very few Japanese would disagree.

In the past, Japanese group spirit was alarmingly evident in the gung-ho zeal of World War II, the mass suicides, and slogans such as *ichioku isshin* (a nation united); and today it is still broadly and deeply entrenched not only in the blue-suit world of the office worker but also in the school-uniform world of children. The pressure to conform is described by a Japanese saying that "The nail that sticks out gets pounded down," and the ultimate punishment of *murahachibu** ostracism that awaits non-conformists. It can generally be said that the group defines the individual in Japanese society, and the individual is only significant in so far as he or she represents the group.

● Historical Roots

Japanese groupism's earliest traces can be found in the rice-farming civilization of the Yayoi period when rice cultivation required group effort. Even today, neighbors in many villages work together in planting and harvesting their crops. Unlike nomadic societies, agrarian cultures demand communal cooperation, discipline, and a sense of shared fate. Japanese groupism was also shaped by the nation's Confucian heritage. Confucian morality stressing filial piety became widespread in the Edo period as an integral part of the household system that made the home the basic unit of society. Under this system, the head of the house's authority was absolute, a person's status was based upon his household's, and all household members were collectively responsible for each other's actions, meaning that all could be punished for a serious offense by any.

Another fact that has helped shape Japanese groupism is that so many people live together on so little land. Foreign visitors stare in disbelief at the crowds who jam the commuter trains morning and evening, yet the Japanese put up with these conditions (at home and at school as well) because they know that harmony is the only choice.

● Pros and Cons

Naturally, Japanese groupism has its positive and negative sides. On the negative side, it is reminiscent of the earlier blind obedience to the military, but on the positive side group unity has contributed to the nation's phenomenal postwar economic growth, which, despite its "economic animal" aspects, is drawing positive comment from people interested in learning from Japan. In recent years, however, Japanese have turned increasingly to individualism, and the idea of Japan as a monolithic group is coming up for reexamination.

16 義理人情

「義理人情」という観念は，封建時代に確立し，重視された。しかし，現代においても芝居，映画，演歌，浪曲などによく取り上げられ，日本人の共感を呼ぶテーマとなっている。

●相克する義理と人情

義理人情は「義理」と「人情」という2つの言葉を合わせたものである。義理とは，社会生活を営むうえでの他人に対する道徳的なルールである。つまり，親子・主従・師弟などの上下関係，友人・隣近所などの対等の関係において守らなければならない道義である。例えば，「人に恩をかけてもらったら，必ずそれに報いる」などで，それを踏みはずせば「義理を欠く」ことになる。これに対して，人情は，人間がだれでも持っている自分や家族などへの愛情である。

したがって，義理と人情はしばしば対立するものであり，日本では，人情よりも義理を重んじるべきだと考えられてきた。君主への義理から自分の子供を殺す，などは人情を抑えて義理を通した典型的な例である。義理人情は，この相克する2つの言葉を並び用いることで，生きていくうえでのつらい感覚を，つまり「義理と人情の板挟み」に苦しむ様を表現している。

●近松の作品に見る義理人情

江戸時代の文芸は義理人情を題材にしたものが多い。中でも近松門左衛門は心中物で，義理と人情の板挟みに苦しむ人間たちを描いて人気があった。近松の物語は，妻子がありながら遊女に夢中になった商人が，商売も顧みずに破綻（はたん）し，その清算に遊女と心中する話である。登場人物がそれぞれの立場で義理と人情の板挟みになり，あれこれと悩み抜き，あれこれと行動し，あげくのはてに主人公とヒロインは心中するという悲劇に追い込まれていくようすが，人々の心を揺り動かしたのであろう。

●現代の義理人情

近代的な契約精神に基づくビジネス社会に，封建時代のような義理人情は，もはや不必要なことは言うまでもないことであるが，日常の心配りとしての「義理を欠かないこと」は，なお求められることが多い。社会的な付き合いを重んじる人のことを「義理堅い人」と言って評価するし，中元・歳暮や冠婚葬祭に際しての贈答なども，義理が日本人の生活習慣に深く入り込んでいる例と言える。

Giri and *Ninjō*

The concepts of *giri* and *ninjō* were well established by the feudal period and remain important themes in stage dramas, film, *enka** songs, and *Naniwa-bushi* narrative ballads even today.

●Conflict between *Giri* and *Ninjō*

Giri refers to the many social obligations which are needed for smooth relations in Japan's vertical society—between parent and child, master and servant, and teacher and disciple—and between equals such as friends and neighbors. As such, *giri* is the moral duty to fulfill obligations and repay favors received, and to fail to meet the requirements of *giri* is seen as a major moral shortcoming. In contrast, *ninjō* encompasses those all-too-human feelings and inclinations that we all share. *Giri* is what your mind tells you to do, and *ninjō* what your heart tells you to do.

It is only natural that *giri* and *ninjō* should come into conflict at times, and in Japan *giri* has most often taken precedence over *ninjō*. The classic case is that of the ancient warrior who had, in extreme cases, to kill his own child rather than betray his duty to his lord. Together, the combination of *giri* and *ninjō* (popularly represented by the run-on word *giri-ninjō*) symbolizes the anguish of being forced to choose between what your emotions want you to do and what your sense of duty tells you you have to do.

●Chikamatsu's *Giri-ninjō* Plays

Many Edo period literary works focused on the eternal conflict between *giri* and *ninjō*, none more poignantly than the double-suicide plays of Chikamatsu Monzaemon. Thus the typical Chikamatsu play might be about a merchant who falls madly and passionately in love with a courtesan,* to the dismay of his family and the detriment of his business, until eventually, because they cannot bear to be apart and society will not let them be together, they commit suicide together. Edo audiences were greatly moved by these plays in which every actor battled with the dilemma of the *giri-ninjō* conflict and which invariably culminated in tragic suicide as the only way out of the situation.

● *Giri* and *Ninjō* Today

Although the contractual foundations of modern business practices have alleviated the intensity of some *giri-ninjō* conflicts, the concept of *giri* remains an important element in social relationships. A person who is careful to meet all *giri* obligations is much-sought and greatly admired as *giri-gatai*; and such formal manifestations of one's social or business *giri* as the *chūgen* and *seibo* gift exchanges in summer and winter remain, along with all of the many social obligations that go with marriages, births, funerals, and the other rites of passage of life, an integral part of the contemporary Japanese lifestyle.

17 日本人の脳

日本の音楽会は，どこへ行ってもたいへん静かだ。聴衆は皆文字どおり息を殺して演奏を聴いている。外国の指揮者などは，日本人はマナーがよいと褒めるが，実はこれは日本人の脳のしくみに原因があることが，東京医科歯科大学の角田忠信教授の研究でわかっている。

●欧米型と日本型

人間の脳は左脳（言語脳）と右脳（音楽脳）に分かれ，その機能が異なる。左脳は言語や計算，論理的思考を扱い，右脳は音楽，直観的・非言語的世界をつかさどる。この脳の働きの一部が日本人と欧米人で異なるというのが，いわゆる「角田理論」である。

欧米人の脳は左で理性的認知，右で感性的認知とはっきり分かれているのに対し，日本人の左脳には理性的・感性的認知が混在している。母音，笑い声・泣き声などの感情音，風の音・虫の鳴き声のような自然音，邦楽器の音などを，日本人は欧米人とは逆に左脳で処理する。したがって，ため息・せき・嘆声などが音楽の途中に入ってくると，スイッチが左脳に切り替わり，音楽鑑賞が妨げられる。そのために日本の音楽会は静かなのである。

脳の機能の違いは，文化の差をもたらす。欧米文化の論理性，知的に自然と対決する姿勢に対し，日本文化は非論理性，情緒性，自然との融和を特色とするが，この違いは聴覚を通しての自然界の認知の仕方からくるものだと言う。

角田理論は，今はやりの日本人論や日本文化の科学的根拠になるものとして，たいへんなブームになった。湯川秀樹博士は，「近来こんなおもしろい話を聞いたことがない」と言ったくらいである。

●日本語が原因

日本人の脳がこういうしくみになった原因は，母音優位の日本語にあると言う。欧米語（例えば英語）では，「子音＋母音」（go），「子音＋母音＋子音」（cat）の音節が言葉の単位になるので，母音はそれ自体意味を持たず，楽音として右の音楽脳で扱われる。これに対して，日本語の母音は，「い」（胃），「え」（絵）のように単独でも意味を持つので，言葉として左の言語脳で処理される。母音と構造のよく似た多くの自然音も，同じように左脳で扱われることになる。

人間の脳は生まれたときは世界共通，生後6歳ぐらいから9歳までの使用言語によって型が決まる。今のところ，日本人と同じ脳の型は，母音の多いポリネシア語を話す人たちだけということである。同じ日本人でも欧米語を母語とする日系二世は欧米型の脳になる。

The Japanese Brain

Japanese concert audiences are very quiet, seemingly holding their breaths during the performance, yet according to Dr Tsunoda Tadanobu of the Tokyo Medical and Dental University, these highly praised good manners are caused by the way the Japanese brain is structured.

●Western vs Japanese Brain Functions

The left and right sides of the human brain are believed to have different functions, the left cerebral hemisphere responding to verbal, mathematical, and logical stimuli and the right side to musical, sensory, and non-verbal stimuli. It is this functional differentiation which lies at the heart of Tsunoda's theory distinguishing between Westerners and Japanese.

According to Tsunoda, while the Western brain is divided between the rational left and the emotional right side, the Japanese brain mixes rational and emotional responses in the left hemisphere. It is the left side of the Japanese brain—not the right as it would be for Westerners—which reacts to the sounds of vowels; laughter and crying; natural sounds such as the wind and chirping insects; and native Japanese musical instruments. Thus the Japanese audience is more likely to be sensitive to sighing and coughing during a concert because both the music and the coughing are heard by the left hemisphere.

Many cultural differences can be explained by this difference in the way the brain functions. Westerners tend to be logical and intellectual in confrontation with nature while Japanese culture is more emotional and seeks harmony with nature. These different perceptions then affect how the two cultures interact with nature.

Tsunoda's theory has thus become extremely popular as a scientific explanation for Japan's distinctive patterns of culture and logic. Nobel physicist Yukawa Hideki* has called it "one of the most incredible theories I've heard in years."

●The Role of Language

The Japanese brain's functioning is directly related to the many-voweled Japanese language. The basic English sound units are syllables of consonants and vowels, such as the word "go," and consonant-vowel-consonant combinations such as "cat." Since vowels in themselves are meaningless, they are received as non-verbal sounds by the music-oriented right side of the Western brain. In Japanese, however, vowels can stand alone as words—e.g., "*i*"(stomach) and "*e*"(picture)—and are therefore heard by the left side as language. Like vowels, natural sounds are also heard on the left side of the brain.

The brain's functional structure starts out the same for all people but changes depending upon what language the person learns as a child. Only Polynesian speakers, with their numerous vowels, evince Japanese-like brain functions. Even Japanese raised speaking a Western language, such as American nisei, display Western brain traits.

18 高齢化社会

●急速な高齢化

日本は今，急速な高齢化社会への道を歩んでいる。わずか35年ほど前までは「人生50年」と言われ，男女とも平均寿命は50歳を少し上回る程度だった。それが，その後生活条件，医療技術の向上によって出生率，死亡率が著しく低下した結果，1984年には，平均寿命が男子74.5歳，女子80.2歳と世界ではトップ。1983年段階で65歳以上の老人のいる世帯は900万世帯を越え，男65歳以上，女60歳以上の者のみか，それに18歳未満の者がいるだけの高齢者世帯も，280万と全世帯の7.7%を占める長寿大国になっている。

厚生省の「日本の将来人口新推計」によると，現在9.9%(1984年)の老年人口(65歳以上)比率は，今世紀末には15%，21世紀に入ると20%になり，欧米諸国の2～4倍のスピードで高齢化が進むと予測されている。

●高齢化社会への対応

こうした人口の高齢化は，長寿を喜ぶ一方で，さまざまな社会問題をも引き起こしている。独り暮らしの老人の孤独な死などはその象徴的な例である。核家族化が進む中で，家族がありながら独りで暮らしていた老人がだれにもみとられずひっそりと亡くなり，死後何十日もたって発見されたという記事がしばしば新聞をにぎわす。ボケや寝たきり老人の看護に家族が疲れ，ノイローゼが高じてその老人を殺してしまったり，心中したりするケースもしだいに増えている。これほどではないにしても，家庭に老人を抱えたらどうするか，自分の老後をどう過ごすかは，今や国民的な関心事と言える。

以上のような現状を踏まえ，厚生大臣の諮問機関である人口問題審議会は，1984年，10年ぶりにまとめた「人口白書」の中で，「人生80年」に変わったこれからの社会への対応について，いくつかの提言をしている。それによると，人口高齢化は，個人レベルだけでなく，生産年齢(15歳～64歳)人口による高齢者扶養の負担増や労働人口の中高年化など，社会経済にもきわめて大きな影響を及ぼすようになるだろうと指摘。こうした変化に対処するには，生涯教育の実施などによって自立する高齢者を育てていくとともに，次代を担う児童の健全な育成，医療の充実など生活の質にかかわる政策を推進させて，社会のしくみそのものを切り替えていく必要があるとしている。老人問題は日本の最重要課題となるだろう。

Longevity

● Rapid Graying

Japan is rapidly becoming a nation of old people. Only 35 years ago, people spoke of the two score and ten years of life. Yet by 1984 improvements in the standard of living and advances in medical science had brought about striking reductions in both the birth rate and the mortality rate to lengthen the average life span to 74.5 for males and 80.2 for females, making Japan the longevity leader. Over nine million households included at least one member 65 years old or older in 1983. Fully 2.8 million households—7.7% of all Japanese households—consist solely of old people (males 65 or older and females 60 or older) and minors under 18 years of age.

According to the Ministry of Health and Welfare's *Population Projections for Japan*, the percentage of the population aged 65 or older will grow from 9.9% today (1984) to 15% by 1999 and 20% later in the 21st century. Japanese society is expected to continue to age twice to four times as fast as Western societies.

● Social Responses

While people are glad to be living longer, this same trend poses a number of problems for society. Typical is the lonely death suffered by solitary old people. As the trend toward nuclear families intensifies, more and more old people live and die isolated from their kin, sometimes not being discovered until weeks after they have died. Likewise, there are increasing numbers of people who, mentally and physically exhausted from the trials of caring for senile or bedridden relatives, kill the old people and then themselves in despair. Even when things do not reach this extreme, there is widespread anxiety both about how to care for aging relatives and about how to plan for one's own declining years.

Given this situation, the Ministry of Health and Welfare's Population Issues Council made a number of recommendations in the 1984 *Population White Paper*—the first population white paper in ten years—for dealing with the social changes arising from the shift to this longer fourscore-years life span. According to the Council, population aging will have major ramifications not only for the individual but also for the society at large as the productive-age population (people aged 15-64) assumes a proportionately greater burden of support for elderly dependents and as the labor population itself shifts toward the older strata. This situation will require enhanced educational opportunities to encourage old people to be more independent, welfare and medical policies to improve the quality of life for all ages, and a total reworking of social institutions. In many ways, this is the most important problem facing Japanese society today.

19 日本人の1年

まとまった休暇がめったにとれない多くの日本人にとって，大半の職場が休みになる正月は，一年中でいちばんのんびりする期間である。日ごろ世話になっている知人，仕事の得意先への年始回りなど，まるきり仕事抜きというわけにもいかないが，それでも，こたつを囲んでおとそ*を飲みながらテレビの正月番組を見たり，いつもは接触時間の少ない子供たちとも親子の対話をして過ごせる。

1月5日か7日ぐらいから仕事が始まるが，2月初めぐらいまでは付き合いを大事にする日本社会の慣例として，職場の同僚や知人との新年会に忙殺されて，正月気分がなかなか抜けない。その期間を過ぎると，今度は4月まで落ちつかない季節が続く。というのも，職場や学校などの新年度が始まるのが4月だからで，自分自身の職場での人事異動がどうなるか，転勤はないか，子供がいる場合は子供たちの進・入学，就職は大丈夫かと，何かと心配事が多くなる。

どうにか新しい生活のペースに慣れるのが5月ごろ。一息ついたところで，6月半ば過ぎから7月にかけて，夏のボーナスが支給される。住宅ローンを払ったり貯蓄に回した残りで，自分の欲しかったゴルフクラブなどを買い，妻や子供たちにも何か買ってやるのが，日ごろ，宮仕えの身のサラリーマンにとってはささやかな楽しみである。

7月下旬から約1か月間，子供たちは学校が夏休みに入る。父親もその間に1週間ぐらいの夏休みをとるのが普通。日ごろ働きづめの父親としては家でゆっくりくつろぎたいところだが，旅行やドライブなどの家庭サービスでふだんの日より疲れてしまうか，逆に妻や子供たちだけ里帰り*や旅行に出し，父親は「にわかやもめ」で留守番というケースが多い。夏休みとは言えゆっくり憩えないのがつらいところだ。

気候が穏やかな秋は行楽シーズン。職場の運動会などに家族そろって参加して体を動かしたり，紅葉を求めてドライブやハイキングに行く家庭が多い。

12月に入ると，夫は年末の休みに入る27，8日まで仕事納め*に追われ，妻は大掃除や正月準備であわただしく過ごす。12月31日の大みそかには，家族そろって年越し*そばを食べながら，NHKの年末恒例番組「紅白歌合戦」などを見て，新年を迎える。

The Japanese Year

Largely unable to take any long vacations at other times of the year, most Japanese look forward to the New Year's holidays when most of the population is on vacation. Although not completely business-free, since it is a time for courtesy calls on the boss, good customers, and other people who have helped him during the year, this is a rare opportunity for the businessman to relax with his family, sitting around the *kotatsu*, sipping sweet sake,* watching the television specials, and talking leisurely with his children in a welcome change from the hectic pace of the rest of the year.

Work resumes about half a dozen days into January, yet the emphasis on congeniality means that the month is filled with new year's parties with friends and co-workers, and it is hard to get over the holiday spirit. Once these parties are over, a period of anxiety sets in from February to April. Because the business and school years start in April, people worry about personnel shifts and possible transfers at work and, if they have children, about whether or not the children will get into the school of their choice or find a good job after graduation.

It is not until May or so that people are able to settle down in the new year's routine. Soon afterward, in late June or early July, it is time for the summer bonus. This is a real treat for the beleagured employee, enabling him to make another large payment on the mortgage, to put a little money aside for a rainy day, and perhaps even to buy that new set of golf clubs that he wanted or to get something for the wife and kids.

Summer vacation for the children starts near the end of July and lasts about one month, and it is common for the man of the house to take a week off during this period. Although father would like to putter around the house and just do nothing for a change, the rest of the family wants to travel, and father often ends up more tired from vacation than from his normal work routine—that is, if he does not stay at home and bachelor while his wife takes the children to visit their grandparents.* It is a sad state of affairs when people cannot relax on their summer vacations.

The temperate fall is a season for enjoying outings. There are company field days with the whole family taking part in sports events, hikes or drives in the country to see the autumn foliage, and more.

Come December, and father wraps up the year's work* on the 27th or 28th, when his year-end vacation starts. Mother, of course, is busy with the year-end cleaning and many preparations for the New Year's holidays. On New Year's eve, the whole family joins together in eating *toshikoshi-soba*,* watching NHK's *Kōhaku Uta-gassen* and other special programs, and welcoming in the new year.

20 日本人の一生

人生80年。男は27，8歳，女は24，5歳で結婚し，結婚して2，3年の間に子供を1人か2人つくり，子供が成長して結婚するのが男女とも50代後半。60歳か65歳ぐらいで夫は仕事をやめ，その後は夫婦だけの老後を送る——というのが，現代の日本人のおおまかなライフサイクルである。

1950年代後半以降の高度経済成長時代には，諸外国から「エコノミック・アニマル」と評されたように，仕事に打ち込むためにはある程度，家庭を犠牲にしてもかまわないと考える「モーレツ型」がサラリーマンの主流だったが，現在では豊かで楽しい家庭を築くために働きたいとする「マイホーム型」が70%を占めている(日本リクルートセンターが1984年に実施した「新入社員は何を考えているか」の調査結果)。

●子供中心の一生

その家庭での中心は，やはり子供である。3歳と5歳の男の子，3歳と7歳の女の子の祝いである11月15日の七五三のほかにも，毎年，3月3日の桃の節句には女の子の，5月5日の端午(たんご)の節句には男の子の，無事な成長を祈って祝う。6，7歳で子供が小学校に入学すると，今度は教育が親の最大の関心事になる。日本の教育は6・3・3・4制で，小学校6年間，中学校3年間が義務教育である。その上の高校への進学率は94%，大学へも3人に1人の割合で進学している。こういう高学歴社会を反映して，多くの親は子供を少しでもいい学校へ入れようと，子供が小・中学生のころから塾通いをさせる。高校・大学の受験に失敗すると1，2年は予備校にも通わせる。したがって，教育費捻出(ねんしゅつ)は親にとっては頭の痛い問題になっている。

子供が20歳になって成人式を終えると，一応，親の責任を果たしたことになるが，アメリカなどと違って，日本の大学生は授業料も生活費も親がかり。結婚式の費用まで親に頼っている若者が少なくない現状だから，親が子供から解放されるのは，就職・結婚を経て，子供も自分の家庭を持ったときということになろう。気がついてみると，夫はもう定年が目の前。子供たちは自分の生活をエンジョイするばかりで，あまり親のことを顧みない。そのうち定年がやってくる。どこかで寂しさを感じながらも，ようやく夫婦2人して，趣味に生きがいを見いだしたり，旅行を楽しんだりして静かに余生を生きるというのが，日本人の一生である。

The Japanese Life Cycle

The average lifespan of the Japanese is nearly 80 years. Men usually marry around 27-8 and women 24-5 years of age. After two or three years of marriage, the typical Japanese couple has one or two children. By the time their children are out of the nest, Japanese parents are in their late 50s. With the husband generally retiring at 60-65, the elderly couple spend their remaining years enjoying life together and visiting their children from time to time.

During the rapid economic growth from the late 1950s through the early 1970s, when Japanese were referred to as economic animals, the typical employee devoted himself enthusiastically to his work, often at the expense of family life. Today, however, (according to a 1984 survey by Nippon Recruit) 70% of Japanese employees put their primary emphasis on home and family.

● Focus on Children

The Japanese family revolves around its children. Ancient festivals to pray for the children's sound development are still celebrated today: *Shichi-go-san* (7-5-3) on November 15 for boys 3 and 5 and girls 3 and 7 years old, the Doll Festival on March 3 for girls, and Children's Day on May 5, traditionally a celebration for boys and now a national holiday for all children. Children start school at age 6-7, at which point education becomes a major concern for Japanese parents. The Japanese school system is divided into six years of elementary education, three of junior high school, three of high school, and four of university. Only the first nine years are compulsory, but 94% of Japanese junior high students go on to high school and one out of three goes to college. In the highly educated Japanese society, parents work to get their children into as good a school as possible. Even as early as elementary school, children are sent to *juku* to prepare for their next-level entrance examinations, and those who do poorly the first time around often spend a year or two boning up at special cram schools. All of this costs money, of course, and education is a major expense for Japanese parents.

While parents are not responsible for their children after they come of age at twenty, most parents continue to pay their children's living expenses and tuition through university, and many Japanese still expect their parents to defray wedding costs. Japanese parents find it difficult to get free of financial responsibility for their children until well after the children have finished their education, found jobs, gotten married, and settled down with their own children. Before they know it, father is near retirement and the children too involved in their own lives to pay much attention to their parents. While post-retirement is a lonely time for some people, they are finally free to concentrate on travel and other hobby interests.

21 日本人の言語行動

●あいづちとうなずき

日本人は会話中にあいづちやうなずきを頻繁にする習慣があると言われる。「ハイ」とか「エーソウデスネ」とかの言葉によるものも，頭や上体を前に倒す身ぶりだけのものも含めて，ある調査によれば日常会話の場合には数秒に1回の割合で観察されるほどである。しかし，すべてが「そのとおりだ」「了解した」という肯定の意味で行われているわけではなく，単に「ああ，そうですか」「そういうこともあるのですか」と相手の話を聞いているサインとして発しているだけの場合が多いことに注意すべきである。

こうした日本人と接して欧米人が「彼は確かにあのとき肯定した」と受け取ったとすれば，当の日本人にとっては予想外のことである。逆に，こうしたあいづちやうなずきに慣れた日本人は，会話中に相手の話に何の反応も示してこない欧米人に不安感――この人は私の話を聞いていてくれるのか？――を感じることになる。

●婉曲（えんきょく）表現

日本人は自分の意見を確固として持っていても，「私はこう考える」「私の意見はこうだ」という直接的な表現は避け，「こうなのではないでしょうか」「こう考えたいのですがいかがでしょう」などといった婉曲な言い回しをするほうが適当で丁寧だと考える傾向が強い。相手に考慮や判断の余地を残してあることを言語表現の上でもはっきりと言い，相手から返ってくる反応を取り込んで自分の主張を表現していこうとする姿勢の表れである。ともすれば，自分の意見をはっきりと言わない，主体性に欠けた言語行動と評価されることがあるが，むしろ，相手との協同作業で会話を進めていこうとする態度の表れであり，あいづちを頻繁にするという前述のことと共通している。

●あいさつ

日本人はあいさつをよくすると言われる。確かに朝起きてから夜寝るまで，日常生活のさまざまな場面で決まって用いられる定型的なあいさつ言葉も豊富である。ただ，あいさつを交わすのは，何らかの意味で仲間うちと見なした相手にだけであって，例えば公園を散歩していて会った見知らぬ人，乗物で同席しただけの人などにはよほどのことがないかぎり言葉をかけることはまれである。彼らがその場では部外者・ヨソ者だからである。日本人が閉鎖的と評されるひとつの原因だろう。

Japanese Verbal Signals

● Conversational Counterpoint

When two Japanese are talking, the listener not only listens but also nods along and voices various counterpoint phrases—much like counterpoint in music—to keep the rhythm of the conversation going. This custom of interspersing such "*aizuchi*" injections as *Hai* (yes) and *Eh, sō desu ne* (yes, quite right) was recently the subject of a statistical study which found that such *aizuchi* are interjected once every few seconds in the typical conversation. However, not all *aizuchi* express agreement with the speaker. People often use quasi-interrogative expressions such as *Ah, sō desu ka* (is that right?) and *Sō iu koto mo aru no desu ka* (can that be true?) to merely affirm that they are listening.

These "yes, I'm listening" *aizuchi* can cause considerable confusion in cases where a non-Japanese speaker misconstrues them as signs of agreement. Conversely, a Japanese speaker can get confused and disconcerted when a non-Japanese listener fails to provide the appropriate *aizuchi* responses. Even though the listener is probably being very attentive, the Japanese speaker begins to wonder if his audience has not gone to sleep on him.

● Indirect Expression

Even though the speaker might have strong opinions on something, he usually avoids such direct statements as "this is what I think" or "this is my opinion." Instead, the typical Japanese will use indirect phrases such as "don't you think so?" or "this is how it would seem to me, but what do you think?"—those roundabout, tentative phrases that are generally considered more appropriate for polite conversation. By using such indirect expressions, the speaker leaves room for the other side to disagree with the idea without having to disagree with the person—as well as leaving room for him to fine-tune his own statements to take account of the other side's opinions and avoid offense. While occasionally criticized as being wishy-washy, these efforts to soften statements of opinion—just like the *aizuchi* mentioned above—all reflect the basic Japanese attitude that conversation should be a cooperative activity.

● A Friendly Word

The Japanese are also fond of salutations and other civilities. From morning to night, the day is filled with a rich variety of pleasantries used for specific situations. However, as a general rule, these words are only spoken to friends and acquaintances, and most Japanese are not given to speaking to strangers in the park or on the train. Instead, such people are regarded as unknowns outside the ken of their concern, and this tendency to restrict sociability to people they already know is one reason why Japanese have acquired a reputation for being anti-social.

22 日本人のジェスチャー(1)

日本人の身ぶりやしぐさの中には、日本人に特有な，あるいは他国文化とその意味・用法が異なるものがある。

• おじぎ　日本人どうしのあいさつでは「おじぎ」をすることが基本である。立ったままの場合は，足をそろえて直立し、上体をかがめて頭を下げる。軽い会釈から，体を90度に折ってするおじぎまで，丁寧さの程度によって頭を下げる角度はさまざまである。畳の部屋では，必ず座ってあいさつする。「正座」の姿勢から身をかがめ，両手を前について頭を下げる。

日本人のあいさつでは体と体の接触はないのが普通で，握手の習慣は伝統的なものではない。日本人も握手をすることがあるが、日本人と外国人，立候補者と選挙民，タレントとファンなどの特殊な関係である場合が多い。

• 座る　学校・会社など一般の生活ではすべていす式になっているが，家庭では日本人は伝統的には畳の上に座る生活を続けてきた。最近では，一般家庭でも居間や食堂は洋間であることが多いので，畳の上に座らない若い世代も増えている。

畳の上での正しい座り方は「正座」で，両ひざをそろえて足を折り，かかとの上にしりを載せる。ふだんの生活で正座に慣れていないと，足がしびれてしまうつらい座り方である。楽な座り方には「あぐら」や「横座り」がある。「あぐら」は足を前で組んでしりを床に落とす。ズボンをはいた女性がまれに「あぐらをかく」こともあるが，これはむしろ例外で，「あぐら」は男性の座り方である。正座の足を少し横にくずした「横座り」は主に女性に見られる。

▽おじぎ (bowing)

Japanese Gestures (1)

There are many gestures which are unique to Japan or which do not mean the same thing in Japan as they do elsewhere.

•Bowing Japanese greet each other by bowing. When bowing from a standing position, it is customary to stand at attention and bow from the waist. There are many levels of bowing, from a simple nod of the head to forming a 90-degree angle, depending on the degree of respect one wishes to convey. In a *tatami* room one always bows from a sitting position with feet tucked under the buttocks and both hands on the floor in front.

Japanese do not customarily touch each other in greeting, and shaking hands is not a traditional practice. When Japanese do shake hands it is usually with a foreigner or under special circumstances such as in the exchange of greetings between a politician and his supporters or a celebrity and his fans.

•Sitting While schools and companies furnished with desks and chairs are the norm today, the Japanese have traditionally sat on *tatami* in their homes. However, many homes today are completely Western style with no *tatami* rooms and an increasing number of young Japanese are unable to sit properly on *tatami*.

The proper method of sitting on *tatami* is to bend the knees 180 degrees, tuck your calves under the thighs, and sit on your heels. This can be a difficult posture to maintain if you are unaccustomed to it because the constant pressure is likely to make your feet go to sleep. Another, more comfortable way of sitting is to cross your legs and sit Indian-style, but this posture is usually reserved for men (although some women might sit this way when they are wearing slacks). Women would usually go from the formal to an informal sitting posture by shifting their feet a bit so that they are not actually sitting on them.

△正座
(proper method of sitting)

△あぐら
(Indian-style sitting)

△横座り
(shifting her feet)

23 日本人のジェスチャー(2)

• **マルとバツ**　日本では，○(マル)と×(バツ)の持つ意味は，明確である。○は「正解」「合格」「勝ち」「OK」などのプラスのイメージを，×は「誤り」「不合格」「負け」「だめ」などのマイナスのイメージを表している。したがって，マルとバツの形状のものはすべてこれらの意味を持つと考えてよい。身ぶりとしては，親指とひとさし指で，あるいは時に両腕を頭上に回して「マル」を，両手のひとさし指，あるいは両腕を交差させて「バツ」を示す。

• **数の数え方**　1～10まで片手だけで数える。1～5は，親指からひとさし指，中指と順に指を折っていく。6～10は反対に小指から順に折り曲げた指を開いていく。性別，年齢，その他にかかわりなく広く使われている。

相手に数を指し示すときには、手のひらを相手に向けて，指を軽く結んでひとさし指・中指・薬指・小指・親指の順で起こしていく。6～10は，残りの片方の手を使って同じ動作を加えていく。

• **手招き**　手のひらを下に向けて軽く開き，手首から先を数回手前に動かす。性別，年齢にかかわらず使われるが，目上に対しては失礼になるので避けられる。

• **自分**　「それは私です」「私？」という意味合いで，ひとさし指で自分の鼻を指す。

• **万歳**　勝負に勝ったり，幸運を得たときに両手を挙げて喜ぶ動作。大勢で「万歳」と唱和して，幸運を願ったり，祝福の気持ちを表すことが多い。

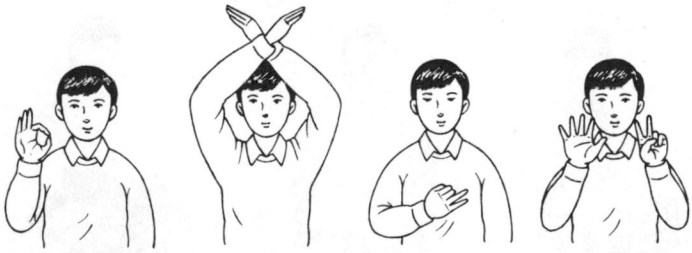

△マル(OK)　△バツ(X)　△数の数え方(counting)　△数の示し方(indicating numbers)

Japanese Gestures (2)

•**Os and Xs** Circles and Xs have clearly defined symbolic meaning in Japan. The circle has such positive associations as correct, passing, winning, and OK. The X, on the other hand, stands for such negative things as mistake, failure, defeat, and rejection. These meanings are conveyed in all circumstances, whether written or as gestures. The circle is often formed with the thumb and forefinger or by holding the arms upraised with the fingers touching to make an O, and the X by crossing the forefingers of both hands or making a big X with the arms.

•**Counting** When counting on their fingers, Japanese use only one hand, starting with the fingers outspread and folding in the thumb, forefinger, middle finger, ring finger, and little finger for one through five; six through ten being the exact reverse as the little finger, ring finger, and so on are unfolded. This is the most commonly used method regardless of sex or age.

To indicate numbers to another person, it is customary to raise one hand with the palm outward and the appropriate number of fingers raised: starting with the forefinger for one and then adding, in order, the middle finger, the ring finger, the little finger, and finally the thumb. To count up to ten the fingers of the other hand are added in the same manner.

•**Beckoning** Japanese beckon with a waving motion with the palm down and the hand flapping up and down at the wrist. This gesture is used by Japanese of both sexes and all age groups, but it is considered impolite to beckon a superior this way.

•**Indicating the Self** Japanese point to their noses with a forefinger to indicate themselves or to ask, "Who, me?"

•**Banzai** This is the cry made while raising both arms high to commemorate a victory or some other auspicious event. It is commonly done in unison by large groups to indicate felicitations toward a person or the success of some venture.

▽手招き (beckoning)

▽自分を示す
(indicating the self)

▷万歳 (banzai)

24 日本語

日本語は，日本人およびアメリカなどの日系移民によって使われており，使用人口の上からでは，世界の言語の中で上位に数えられるが，使用者および使用地域が限定されているため，今まで注目を集めることが少なかった。しかし，近年，国際社会における日本の地位の向上に伴い，日本語も国際語として学習されるようになってきた。

●系統と歴史

日本語の系統についてはさまざまの説が提唱されているが、いまだに決着がついていない。文法上の類似点が多いため，朝鮮語（韓国語），モンゴル語などのアルタイ諸語と関係づけようとする説がある。日本と共通の文化要素が見られる，中国南部からヒマラヤにまで及ぶ照葉樹林帯ないしその周辺の言語(例えばチベット語)の中に同じ系統の言語を求めようとする試みもある。ポリネシア語やドラビダ語と起源を同じくするという意見もある。

日本語の最古の記録は3世紀にさかのぼり，中国の歴史書の日本についての記事に引用された語彙を最初とする。以来，日本語は漢字を借用して表記されてきたが，後に，漢字から発達した音節文字(仮名)によっても表記されるようになった。現在，表意文字である漢字と表音文字である仮名を混用して表示するという正書法が使われているが，この正書法の複雑さが日本語の国際語化を妨げる一因となっている。

●特徴

日本語は日本全国に通用するただ1つの言語であるが，地域，性，社会階層および職種によって顕著な方言差が認められる。特に，地域的方言差はそれぞれが方言で話し合えばほとんど意志の疎通を欠くことがあるほどであるが，東京方言を基礎としたいわゆる標準語が，教育およびマスコミの普及によって広く浸透している。日本語には，音声の長短が有意味である，高低アクセントがある，音節構造が単純であるなどという音声的特徴がある。音節の形式が単純であるから，同音異義語が多く，そのために，表意文字である漢字による表記が廃らないのである。

文化的影響が大きかったため，中国語からの借用が多く，中国語的単語は全語彙の60%以上だと言われる。近年，欧米の文物が導入されると欧米語，特に英語からの借用が顕著である。

その他，日本語の特徴としては，文法的機能が語幹と接辞の結合で表示される，いわゆる膠着語であること，厳密な意味での人称代名詞という文法範疇が存在しない点などが指摘される。

The Japanese Language

Although the Japanese language is used by large numbers of people,* including all of the Japanese in Japan and Japanese immigrants overseas, its relatively isolated position has contributed to keeping it a minor international language. Nevertheless, Japan's increasing importance in the global community has sparked greater study of the Japanese language internationally.

● Origins

There are many theories seeking to explain the origins of the Japanese language, none of which is uncontested. Citing the many grammatical similarities, some scholars have linked Japanese to Korean or to Mongolian and the other Altaic languages. Other scholars seek the language's origins in the ecologically and culturally similar societies from Southern China to the Himalayas. Yet others claim the language's origins are the same as the Polynesian and Dravidian languages.*

The oldest known record of Japanese dates back to the 3rd century, when a Chinese history book entry of Japan contained several words of Japanese vocabulary. Although Japanese has long used Chinese ideograms (*kanji*) for writing, it has also developed its own phonetic *kana* syllabaries based upon representative ideograms. Today the ideograms and *kana* phonetics are used together in standard writing, and the complexity of this *kanji-kana* intermix is another factor keeping Japanese from becoming an international language.

● Characteristics

Although it is the only language used widely in Japan, Japanese varies widely depending upon the speaker's regional identification, sex, social status, and occupation. Regional dialects are so strong as to sometimes impede communication among people from different areas, but these differences have diminished since the educational system and mass media adopted a "standard" Japanese based upon the Tokyo dialect. The sound of Japanese is distinguished by short and extended vowel sounds, with meaning-significant differences between them, pitch accents, and a simple consonant-vowel sound structure. Yet the very simplicity of the sound structure means there are necessarily many homonyms, which is another reason for holding on to the ideographic *kanji*.

Chinese has had a major influence upon Japanese culture and language, and over 60% of all Japanese words are drawn from Chinese. In recent years, however, the increasing access to Euro-American culture has meant greater use of Western languages, especially English.

Other features of Japanese are that it is an agglutinative language* indicating grammatical structure by attaching markers to word stems and that it has no personal pronouns per se.

25 日本人の好きな英雄

読み物，テレビ，演芸などでは繰り返し英雄が取り上げられる。それら日本人の好きな英雄を，３つのパターンに分けることができる。全国制覇の道半ばで倒れた失意の英雄，立身出世した英雄，そして，貴種流離譚に属する身分を隠して流浪する貴人である。これらは互いに重なり合って日本人好みの英雄を形造っていると言える。

●源義経

失意の英雄の代表は源義経である。義経は，12世紀末に武家政治の時代を築いた源頼朝の弟で，頼朝とともに新しい時代を開いた。その後政治的陰謀に巻き込まれ，頼朝の許可なく軍事・警察組織の長である「判官」に任官し，頼朝と不和になり，失脚する。義経は頼朝に追われ，各地を流浪し，最後は東北地方で死ぬのだが，若い悲劇の英雄として伝説化している。さらに，義経には，北海道を経てシベリアに渡り，モンゴルに至ってチンギス・ハンになったという貴種流離譚の形の伝説まで生まれている。

このほか，群雄割拠した戦国時代に全国制覇を目ざしながら倒れていった織田信長，武田信玄，さらに，明治維新の際，活躍しながら新時代を見ずに死んだ坂本龍馬などもこのパターンと言ってよい。

●豊臣秀吉・徳川家康

立身出世物語の典型は，戦国時代の天下統一を成し遂げた豊臣秀吉である。秀吉は足軽の子でありながら，織田信長の家来となり，さまざまな知恵と勇気で，ついに全国を統一する。秀吉に次ぎ天下を治めた徳川家康も，小大名の息子として12年間も人質となり苦労したが，後に天下を取った。徳川300年の治世を開いた人として，その言動が現代の経営者にもてはやされている。

●水戸黄門

貴種流離譚でも源義経がその典型だが，このパターンの変形として，水戸黄門（徳川光圀）がいる。徳川家康の孫に当たる大名で，名君と言われた。引退後，身分を隠して，２人の家来とともに全国を巡り歩いたとするフィクションで知られる。危機が近づくと，自分の身分を示す葵の紋所を示して，悪をこらしめる。権力の持つ悪に対する庶民の批判であり，同時に庶民の権威志向の現れとも言われている。

これらは，もしかしたら自分もそうした英雄となれるかもしれない，自分も英雄の子孫であったらよいのだが，という夢を庶民に与えるものであり，それゆえに，広く支持されてきたとも言えよう。

Popular Heroes

A study of the most popular historical heroes in Japanese literature, on television, and on the stage shows three types: the hero who fails while striving toward some noble ideal, the rags-to-riches hero, and the hero who abandons conventionality to become a lone crusader. Indeed, the Japanese hero is a composite of all three types.

● Minamoto no Yoshitsune

The typical heroic failure is Minamoto no Yoshitsune. Younger brother of the late-12th-century warrior-statesman Minamoto no Yoritomo, Yoshitsune joined with Yoritomo to inaugurate a new era in Japanese history. However, he was later caught up in political intrigues and driven out when he incurred his brother's distrust by accepting appointment as imperial police commissioner (*hōgan*) without Yoritomo's approval. Attacked by Yoritomo, Yoshitsune fled to the Tohoku region, where he died. Yet he remains a popular tragic hero, and stories later arose that he had escaped to Mongolia and reemerged as Genghis Khan.

Other heroes in failure are Oda Nobunaga and Takeda Shingen,* both of whom sought to unite the country and end its prolonged civil wars, and Sakamoto Ryoma* who was an activist in the Meiji Restoration.*

● Hideyoshi and Ieyasu

Toyotomi Hideyoshi's is a rags-to-riches story of his rise from humble birth to ruler of the entire country in the late-16th-century warring states period. Born to a low-ranking family, he became a retainer to Oda Nobunaga and quickly unified the country by dint of his bravery and intelligence. Tokugawa Ieyasu, who succeeded Hideyoshi as ruler of Japan, was born to higher class but as a result spent 12 years in hostage captivity before gaining the freedom to make his bid for power. As the founder of the Tokugawa dynasty which ruled for over 250 years of peace, Ieyasu practiced a single-minded patience which continues to earn the respect of today's captains of industry.

● Mito Komon

The prototype crusader for justice, Tokugawa Mitsukuni (a.k.a. Mito Komon) was a grandson of Ieyasu and a wise fief ruler. After retirement, the story goes, he and two faithful retainers dressed poorly and wandered the land seeking to right social wrongs. In the story, the dangers that they meet in trying to vanquish entrenched evil are often overcome by having Mito Komon reveal his true identity at the crucial point and cow the evildoers into submission. Thus the story is at once a tale of the common man's fight against the abuse of authority and an invocation of authority to rectify such abuses.

These heroes' enduring popularity rests upon the common dream that anyone might himself be such a hero or the descendent of a hero.

26 日本人論の好きな日本人

日本人がいかに日本人論が好きか，それは書店に行けばたちまちにわかる。自分たちのことについて書いた本がこれほど並ぶ現象が，およそ他のどの国で考えられようか。しかも，おかしなことに同国人よりも外国人の書いた日本人論のほうが，よりもてはやされるのである。

●外国人の著した日本人論

外国人による戦後の代表的な日本人論をいくつか挙げると，第1にR. F. ベネディクトの『菊と刀』がある。「日本文化の型」と副題の付いた同書は，今や日本人論の古典と言える。E. O. ライシャワーの『ザ・ジャパニーズ』は駐日大使も務めた著者の日本研究の集大成で，記述は歴史，社会，政治，経済，あらゆる分野に及んでいる。E. F. ヴォーゲルの『ジャパン・アズ・№1』は，そのタイトルが流行語になったほどジャーナリスティックな注目を浴びた。その背景には1980年代前半に醸成された日本大国論がある。

『誤解』はＥＣ高官のE. ウィルキンソンが日欧関係に見る誤解と摩擦を直視，解決への道を探った労作。このほか，『孤立する大国ニッポン』（G. ダンプマン），『縮み志向の日本人』（李御寧），『ひよわな花・日本』（Z. ブレジンスキー），『人は城，人は石垣』（F. ギブニー），『ジャパニーズ・マインド』（R. C. クリストファー），『菊とバット』（R. ホワイティング）等々，日本人論はあらゆる国のあらゆる外国人によって書かれ，枚挙にいとまがない。しかもこうした日本人論のかなりは，著者の国より先に日本で翻訳，出版されている。最大の読者は日本人だからである。

●日本人の著した日本人論

もちろん，日本人の書いた日本人論にも話題作は少なくない。中でも1970年に出版された『日本人とユダヤ人』（イザヤ・ベンダサン）はロングベストセラーで，日本人論ブームの先駆けであり，また『タテ社会の人間関係』（中根千枝）と『甘えの構造』（土居健郎）は，内外の評価も高い，日本人および日本社会研究の名著である。

●日本人論が好きな理由

なぜ日本人は日本人論が好きなのだろうか。まず第一には，日本人がきわめて好奇心の強い民族であること，そして島国であるため外国からの影響に常に敏感であることが考えられる。さらに最近の日本人論の傾向からは，国際社会での日本の役割に，日本人が認識を深めつつあることもうかがえる。

The Japanese Identity Crisis

Any bookstore in Japan provides proof that Japanese love to ponder their national identity. What other people reads so much about itself? And strangely enough, the most popular of these books about the Japanese are those written not by Japanese but by foreign observers.

● Foreign Works on Japan

There have been many important books of this genre since the war. Perhaps best known is Ruth F. Benedict's *The Chrysanthemum and the Sword.* This book, subtitled *Patterns of Japanese Culture,* is considered a classic. *The Japanese* by former U.S. Ambassador Edwin O. Reischauer, is a scholarly collection of studies of Japanese history, society, politics, economics, and many other fields. The title of Ezra F. Vogel's best-seller, *Japan As Number 1,* was so talked about in the popular press that the title became a buzzword in Japan. This book appeared at a time when discussions of things Japanese turned to the notion of Japan as a major world power.

Misunderstanding: Europe vs. Japan is a major work in which author Endymion Wilkinson takes a hard look at the fallacies and frictions that have plagued Japan-Europe relations and searches for solutions. Other popular books on Japan by foreign authors include *2.5mal Japan* by Gerhard Dambmann, *Smaller is Better* by O-Young Lee, *The Fragile Blossom* by Zbigniew Brzezinski, *Japan: The Fragile Superpower* by Frank B. Gibney, *The Japanese Mind* by Robert C. Christopher, *The Chrysanthemum and the Bat* by Robert Whiting, and a host of others by various authors of various nationalities. Perhaps more amazingly, many of these works were published in Japanese translation before being published in the author's own language. Japan is clearly the world's best market for books on Japan.

● Books by Japanese Authors

There are, of course, many books by Japanese authors too. One is *The Japanese and the Jews* written under the pseudonym Isaiah Ben Dassan, a marathon best-seller that helped spark the books-on-Japan boom in the 1970s. Others are *Human Relations in a Vertical Society* by Nakane Chie, and *Anatomy of Dependence* by Doi Takeo—both of which won international acclaim as scholarly sociological studies.

● Reasons for the Fascination

Why do Japanese like so much to ponder their identity? Perhaps the most important reason is that Japanese are typically very curious. Other observers have argued that, as an island people, the Japanese are more sensitive to outside influences. Yet more recently, the current boom in books about the Japanese can also be seen as evidence that the Japanese are trying to come to terms with their role in the international community.

27 日本人と付き合う法

●ウチとソト

日本を訪れた外国人が朝の通勤ラッシュを見て，まず驚くのは，「日本には，日本人ばかりがこんなに大勢いる」ということであるという。日本人と付き合うとき，複雑な多民族国家ではないことが，さまざまな人間関係や行動の基礎になっていることを忘れてはならない。

ほとんど千数百年も血縁集団を中心とした社会が維持されてきた結果，その社会やグループの中では，わざわざ言葉で言わなくてもしぐさ1つで理解しあえるものや，暗黙のうちに前提となっているようなことが多数存在する。それがわかりあえるのがウチ(内)の人間であり，わからない者はソト(外)の人間として，お客様扱いされるのである。

これは外国人に対しても同じで，日本の習慣や風俗を知らない人は，ガイジン(外人)として別格扱いで親切に扱われるが，日本社会に深くコミットする人は変なガイジンと呼ばれる。

●間人主義

欧米で社会の基本は個人主義であるが，日本では“間人主義”であると言う人もいる。独立した人格である個人が作る社会ではなく，常に社会の中で生活する1人として，人と人の間にいることを基本に置いた社会であると言うのである。ある人に意見を聞いても，「みんなはどう言っていますか」と聞き返されることもよくあることだ。

ホンネとタテマエという言葉も日本人の間ではよく使われる。ホンネというのは本音，つまり本当の声であり，タテマエは建前で，表向きの方針である。また，ホンネを個人の論理，タテマエを集団の論理としてとらえることもある。日本人は表向きの方針や集団の論理であるタテマエを優先するが，その奥に本当の声，個人の論理であるホンネが潜んでいることはよくある。

こうした，常に他人や社会を気にしながら生きる日本人の生活の中には，yesでもnoでもない，中間的であいまいな言葉がたいへん多い。「そのうちに」「いずれまた」「考えてみます」「検討してみます」などはいずれもyesでもnoでもない。ある時には上司や関係者の了承をあらかじめ得ておく「根回し」のための仮のyesであったり，ある時にははっきり断わると，相手を傷つけるのではないかとの配慮による婉曲(えんきょく)なnoであったりする。ただ，近年では国際的な商習慣を身に着けたビジネスマンも増えたので，yes, noをはっきりさせる方向には向かいつつある。

Getting along with the Japanese

● Us and Them

Foreign visitors who come to Japan and see the commuter-packed morning rush-hour trains are said to be amazed that there are so many Japanese in Japan. The fact that Japan does have such a high-density homogeneous population governs many of the social customs and personal mannerisms, and makes them different from the way people relate in more heterogeneous societies.

With virtually no major influx of immigrants over the last 1,000-plus years, Japanese society has developed numerous groups each with its own common consciousness and numerous tacit understandings that are reached or conveyed without a word's being said. People who understand are insiders (us) and those who do not are outsiders (them) and treated as company.

The same is true of the reception accorded people from overseas: those who are not attuned to Japanese mores and customs are referred to as *gaijin* (literally outsiders) and treated courteously as company while those who have gotten inside Japanese society and learned the ropes are accepted and called *hen na gaijin* (outsiders who do not act like outsiders).

● Emphasis on the Group

If the individual is the basic unit of Euroamerican society, it is the group in Japan. This is not a society constituted by autonomous individuals but one made up of people who are constantly interacting with society and constantly aware of this interaction. If you ask a Japanese what he thinks, he is very likely to answer by asking what everybody else thinks.

Two very commonly used words in Japanese are *honne* and *tatemae*. *Honne* is the true sound, or what a person really thinks, and *tatemae* is akin to the official position of the group he represents. Thus some people have characterized *honne* as the individual's voice and *tatemae* as the group's voice. Very often, a Japanese will give precedence to the official or group *tatemae* position, but that does not mean that he has entirely abandoned his personal *honne*.

Because the Japanese is always conscious of what other people and the group are thinking, the language has developed a large hedging vocabulary which is neither yes nor no. Among the most common are "I'll do what I can," "Let me get back to you on that later," "Let me sleep on it," and "I'll have to look into that." Sometimes these mean a tentative yes when someone is doing *nemawashi* to touch all the bases and line up support, and sometimes they are definite negatives phrased in a roundabout way to avoid hurting the other person's feelings. Recently, however, there have been more businessmen with international experience who say yes and no loud and clear.

Notes

■1. The Japanese Land and People

location (位置) Japan's territorial rights today extend between the north latitudes of 45°31′ and 20°25′ and between the east longitudes of 153°59′ and 122°56′.

rivers (河川) The Shinano River is the longest in Japan at only 367 kilometers.

●Main mountains, rivers, and lakes in Japan

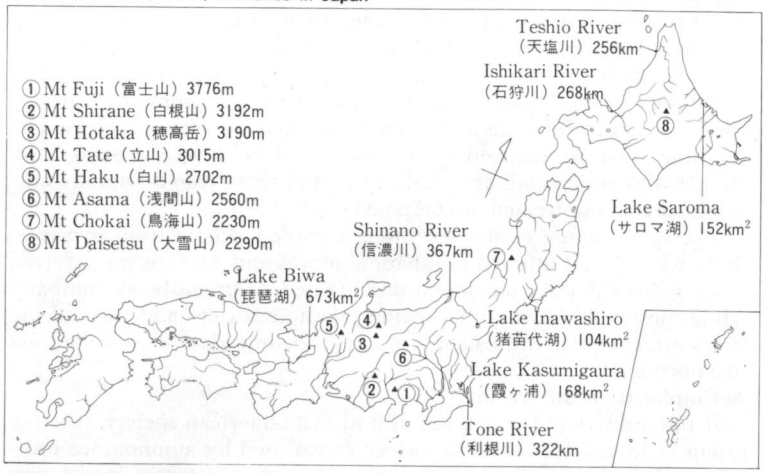

△Jomon pottery

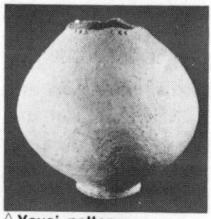

△Yayoi pottery

■2. Japanese History (1)

ritsuryō (律令) A code of laws and ethics evolved in China under the Sui and Tang dynasties and which was widely adopted by Japan and other East Asian countries. This code formed the basis for the early imperial governmental structure in ancient Japan.

Jomon period (縄文時代) So named because of the *jōmon* cord markings found on excavated earthenware from the New Stone Age period. Jomon pottery—probably used for food storage—is a gray, heavy, low-fired ware formed in a variety of shapes and richly decorated with impressed motifs.

Yayoi period (弥生時代) Named after Yayoi-cho in Tokyo where a wheel-thrown pottery of a style distinctive to this period was first discovered. A red ware fired at higher temperatures than the gray Jomon pottery of the preceding period, Yayoi pottery is usually very plain or decorated with only very simple motifs.

Kofun period (古墳時代) The large mounded-earth tombs of this period indicate the emergence of powerful individuals with the ability to control significant groups of people.

keyhole-shaped tomb mounds (前方後円墳) Great tombs of the Kofun period shaped like old-fashioned key holes. The tombs of Emperors Nintoku and Ojin are of this type.

Confucian teachings (儒教) Confucianism offered a system of social organization, and, along with Buddhism, had a profound impact upon Japanese society and thought, forming the basis for feudal ethics.

Prince Shotoku (聖徳太子) (574-622) The son of Emperor Yomei, Prince Shotoku was a brilliant statesman who instituted the *kan'i jūnikai* twelve cap ranking system and the Seventeen-article Constitution and sent Japan's first official emissaries to Sui China. A devout Buddhist, Prince Shotoku sponsored the building of numerous Buddhist temples. His many achievements left a lasting mark on Japanese history.

Taika Reforms (大化の改新) The Taika Reforms were instituted after a coup in 645 which laid the foundation for the establishment of the *ritsuryō* government.

△Keyhole-shaped tomb of Emperor Nintoku

△Prince Shotoku

■3. Japanese History (2)

shōen (荘園) Landed estates belonging to the nobility and shrines and temples which formed the economic foundation of Japan in the Nara period. The last *shōen* was abolished during the time of Toyotomi Hideyoshi.

kōchi-kōmin (公地公民制) The basic foundation for *ritsuryō* government, this was a concept in which all land and people were considered to be the property of the emperor. The right of private ownership and independence was not recognized.

Asuka culture (飛鳥文化) A synthesis of Kofun period culture and the Chinese culture of the Northern and Southern dynasties period (439-589), this culture's artistic achievements are preserved in the temple architecture and sculptures of the Horyuji and other temples of the period. Located in the southern part of the Nara plains, Asuka was the imperial capital for more than 100 years from the late 6th through the early 8th centuries until the capital was moved to Heijokyo in 710.

△Asuka culture (The triad of the Buddha Shaka with two attending bodhisattvas —Horyuji)

△Hakuho culture (The wall paintings—Horyuji)

△Tenpyo culture (*Beauties beneath Trees*—Shosoin in Nara)

Hakuho culture (白鳳文化) A period of cultural flowering under the influence of early Tang culture. Represented by the sculptures of Yakushiji and the wall paintings—partially destroyed by fire in 1949—at Horyuji.

Tenpyo culture (天平文化) In architecture this cultural period is represented by Todaiji, the Shosoin, and Toshodaiji. Well-known Tenpyo paintings include Yakushiji's *Kichijōten* portrait of a goddess of beauty and learning and the six-panel screen, *Beauties beneath Trees*, preserved in the Shosoin. Superb sculptures of the period are to be found in Todaiji's hokkedo (sutra repository) and kaidan'in (ordination hall).

Fujiwara (藤原氏) A powerful court family, the Fujiwara enjoyed wealth and prestige even greater than that of the imperial family at times. The Fujiwara attained their height of power under Fujiwara no Michinaga (966-1027), father of four empresses and grandfather of three emperors, and his son Yorimichi (992-1074).

insei (院政) A system of government in which retired emperors wielded the actual power, *insei* government was institutionalized by Emperor Shirakawa when he abdicated the throne in 1086. *Insei* continued as a practice of the imperial court as late as 1840.

natively inspired art and culture (国風文化) The break with Tang China early in the Heian period provided an opportunity for a truly native Japanese culture to develop. The process of "Japanization" took place in nearly every area of aesthetics and intellectual activity. *Kana*, the syllabary characters evolved from Chinese characters, and Jodo Buddhism are just two examples of the uniquely Japanese achievements of the Heian period.

△Native Japanese culture in the Heian period (Byodoin's Phoenix Hall)

esoteric Buddhist sects (密教) Originating in India in the 7th and 8th centuries, esoteric Buddhism taught that the most sacred teachings of the Buddha should be kept secret. First introduced into Japan by Kukai (774-835) and Saicho (767-822), the esoteric emphasis on chants and incantations appealed to the members of the imperial court and the esoteric Buddhist sects soon became the mainstream of Buddhism in Japan.

Jodo sect (浄土教) The Jodo teachings of other-worldly salvation by such priests as Kuya (903-972), Genshin (942-1017), Honen (1133-1212), Shinran (1173-1262), and Ippen (1239-89) had broad appeal among nobility and commoners alike in an era plagued by constant wars, oppression, and natural disasters.

■4. Japanese History (3)

Minamoto no Yoritomo (源頼朝) (1147-99) A politically astute warrior, Yoritomo succeeded in establishing the supremacy of the warrior class in a single generation. He was cautious to a fault, however, suspicious of everyone around him including close relatives and vassals, and brought about the demise of his brother Yoshitsune, depriving himself of an important and powerful ally in the process.

△Minamoto no Yoritomo

Honen (法然) (1133-1212) Founder of the Jodo sect of Buddhism, Honen taught that simply reciting the *nenbutsu* (*Namu Amida butsu:* I place my faith in the Amida Buddha) was enough to secure one's place in Amida's Pure Land of the West paradise. His teachings had wide appeal, attracting adherents from the nobility, the warrior class, and the common people.

Shinran (親鸞) (1173-1262) A disciple of Honen and founder of the Jodo Shinshu sect of Buddhism, Shinran taught that all that was needed to attain salvation was to have faith. Like his master, he promulgated the recitation of the *nenbutsu*.

Nichiren (日蓮) (1222-82) Founder of the Nichiren sect of Buddhism. Nichiren believed that the true teachings of Shakamuni Buddha were to be found only in the Lotus Sutra (*Hokke-kyo*) and that one could be saved by reciting the *daimoku* (*Namu myō hōrenge kyō:* I place my faith in the Lotus Sutra). His vigorous proselytizing and harsh denouncement of all other Buddhist sects antagonized the authorities and resulted in Nichiren's repeated persecution. Still, Nichiren had great charismatic appeal especially for the lower-class samurai of the Kanto plains region.

early Kamakura sculpture (鎌倉時代初期の彫刻) The early Kamakura period is noted for its fine sculptures of Buddhist deities and revered monks. Among the most famous Kamakura sculptures are those by Unkei (?-1223), his son Tankei (1173-1256), and Kaikei (active in the early 13th century).

Kitayama culture (北山文化) Named after the Kitayama district in Kyoto where the 3rd Ashikaga shogun, Yoshimitsu, built the Kinkakuji or Gold Pavilion in 1397. This culture is marked by the merging of court- and warrior-class aesthetics.

Higashiyama culture (東山文化) In 1489, the 8th Ashikaga shogun, Yoshimasa, built a villa with a small temple, today referred to as the Ginkakuji or Silver Pavilion, in the Higashiyama district of Kyoto which epitomizes the culture of his time. Under the influence of Zen, Higashiyama culture prized simplicity, traditional elegance, and the austerity of *wabi*.

△Early Kamakura sculpture (Statue of Kongo Rikishi in Todaiji by Unkei and Kaikei)

△Kinkakuji

■5. Japanese History (4)

feudal lords (将軍・大名) Shogun is an abbreviation of *seii-tai-shōgun* (barbarian-subduing generalissimo), a title first assumed by Minamoto no Yoritomo when he established his military government in Kamakura. Daimyo are landholding, semi-autonomous lords. Originally officials called *shugo-daimyō* appointed to administer the provinces, the daimyo had become powerful enough by the warring states period in the late 15th and early 16th centuries, to compete for supremacy. In the Edo period (1600-1867) only lords with landholdings valued at 10,000 *koku* or more were classified as daimyo, a *koku* being equivalent to 180.39 liters of rice. There were approximately 270 daimyo in the middle of the Edo period.

bakuhan (幕藩体制) The name given to the government organization of the Azuchi-Momoyama (1576-1600) and Edo periods when Japan was governed by a shogun and daimyo with extensive landholdings called *han*.

Azuchi-Momoyama period (安土・桃山時代) A period noted for its castles which functioned as daimyo residences and governmental headquarters as well as military defenses. Azuchi Castle built by Oda Nobunaga and Osaka Castle built by his successor, Toyotomi Hideyoshi, had a grandeur worthy of their builders. The multi-storied donjon were the main features of the castles of this period. Castle rooms were lavishly decorated and furnished with gold-foil covered *fusuma* doors, walls, and folding screens. Momoyama is where Hideyoshi built his Fushimi Castle.

△Osaka Castle

Oda Nobunaga (織田信長) (1534-82) An intrepid leader who laid the foundation for the unification of Japan in the 16th century. His hegemony nearly assured after numerous battles, Nobunaga built a sumptuous castle in Azuchi near Lake Biwa, but his conquests were brought to an abrupt end by his suicide at Honnoji in Kyoto after a traitorous attack by one of his own vassals.

Toyotomi Hideyoshi (豊臣秀吉) (1536-98) See p. 59.

Tokugawa Ieyasu (徳川家康) (1542-1616) See p. 59.

Osaka (大坂) The original characters used to write the name of the city of Osaka. The present characters 大阪 have been in use since 1870.

△Oda Nobunaga

△Toyotomi Hideyoshi

△Tokugawa Ieyasu

bunjin-ga (文人画) A genre of Eastern painting, these are works painted by scholars, poets, and men of letters.

Dutch learning (蘭学) The study of Western learning through Dutch texts which began in the middle of the Edo period.

terakoya (寺子屋) The fundamentals of reading, writing, and arithmetic were taught at these schools generally established in samurai homes and in Buddhist temples and Shinto shrines.

Meiji, Taisho, Showa (明治,大正,昭和) Era names respectively of the first emperor following the demise of the Tokugawa shogunate, his son, and the current emperor. Historical periods prior to the Meiji era are generally referred to by the name of the governmental seat, e.g., the Nara period and the Edo period.

Sino-Japanese war (日清戦争) (1894-95) Fought over rights to Korea.

Russo-Japanese war (日露戦争) (1904-05) Japan won control over Manchuria and the Korean peninsula.

Taisho democracy (大正デモクラシー) The democratic ideals and movements of the Taisho period in the early 20th century. It was during this period that many of the systems and philosophies of modern Japan were formed.

15 years of war (十五年戦争) The 15 years of war beginning with the Manchurian Incident of 1931, when Japanese forces embarked upon their invasion of northeastern China, and ending with the Pacific War, 1941-45, fought primarily between Japan and the United States.

■7. Sources of Japanese Culture

glutinous paste (もち) In Japan, pounded glutinous rice cakes are a special New Year's food also served on other happy occasions.

tea (茶) The Japanese drink a variety of teas. *Senchu* and *bancha* are the most common types served in the home, while finely powdered *matcha* is reserved especially for the tea ceremony (see p. 255).

konnyaku (こんにゃく) A kind of tuber, *konnyaku* is processed into a tasteless gelatin-like food used by the Japanese in a variety of dishes.

perilla (シソ) Two types of this plant—green-leafed and purple-leafed—are used in Japan, primarily as a condiment and for pickling.

lacquer ware (漆) See p.265.

cormorant fishing (鵜飼い) Cormorant fishing in Japan can still be seen at the Nagara River in Gifu prefecture.

■8. Characteristics of Japanese Culture

kintarō-ame (金太郎あめ) See picture.

■9. Japanese Concepts of Nature

sansui-ga (山水画) Monotone landscape painting was introduced from China near the end of the Kamakura period. The Buddhist monk Sesshu (1420-1506) was a master of this genre and the creator of a powerful Japanese style.

seasonal references (季語) *Kigo* are terms relating to natural phenomena, animals, plants, customs, traditions, and rituals and employed in haiku to set a seasonal tone for the verse.

yūgen (幽玄) Originally meaning something too deeply hidden for human comprehension, this term gradually evolved into an aesthetic concept of mysterious and tranquil beauty.

wabi (わび) Stemming from the word *wabishi*, meaning lonely or sad, this is an aesthetic ideal of tranquility in the midst

△Making rice cakes

△Cormorant fishing at the Nagara River

△*Kintarō-ame*

of poverty. An ambience of *wabi* is essential to the tea ceremony.

sabi (さび) A companion term to *wabi*, this concept was first established as an aesthetic principle in the poetry of Matsuo Basho (1644-94). Like *wabi* it alludes to a sadness locked in one's heart and also has Buddhist connotations of selflessness and complete lack of desire.

■10. Japanese Religion

△New Year's visits to Shinto shrine

visits to Shinto shrines at New Year's (初もうで) Visits to shrines and temples to pray for the safety and good health of the family are customary at the beginning of the year. The Meiji Shrine in Tokyo, Kawasaki Daishi in Kanagawa prefecture, and Naritasan Shinshoji in Chiba prefecture each has more than three million visitors during the traditional three-day New Year's holiday.

trips to Buddhist temples in the spring and fall (彼岸) *Higan* are Buddhist memorial services and visits to family graves are the practice during this seven-day period observed twice a year around the spring and autumnal equinoxes. Literally meaning "the other shore," *higan*, or *o-higan*, refers to the attainment of enlightenment.

△Inari

Inari (お稲荷さん) Formerly a god of cereals worshipped in Fushimi on the outskirts of Kyoto, Inari was later merged with the Buddhist guardian deity Dakini who was generally depicted riding a fox. This and the traditional reverence of the common people for the fox are probably behind Inari's close association with the animal. Miniature Inari shrines marking sacred sites are common. They are distinguished by their smallness, bright red *torii*, and fox figure or figures. Deepfried bean curd, *abura-age*, is thought to be a favorite food of the fox.

△*Dōsojin*

dōsojin (道祖神) Stone markers meant to ward off evil spirits and catastrophes, *dōsojin* are found along village boundaries, in mountain passes, and along country byways. Often these markers take on human form and bear inscriptions. Many *dōsojin* are of an embracing man and woman and are revered as gods of marriage and fertility.

■11. The Japanese Work Ethic

Yamamoto Shichihei (山本七平) (1921-) Founder of the Yamamoto Shoten publishing company.

■12. Relaxing Japanese-style

karaoke (カラオケ) See p.241.

■13. Japanese Aesthetics

△Pachinko

Buddhist feeling (諸行無常) A basic Buddhist tenet which teaches that all things of this world are transient and impermanent. Appealing strongly to Japanese sensibilities, this concept appears repeatedly in Japanese literature, songs, and dramas.

Sen no Rikyu (千利休)(1522-91) Founder of the Sen school of tea. Considered the leading tea master of his time, Rikyu perfected much of the philosophy of the tea ceremony.

masters (宗匠) *Sōshō* are masters and often heads of schools of *waka* and haiku poetry, tea ceremony, flower arranging, and other traditional arts.

Ekuan Kenji (栄久庵憲司)(1929-) One of Japan's most renowned industrial designers.

■14. Views of Life and Death

Jodo Pure Land paradise (極楽浄土) The Pure Land of the West paradise where Amida, bodhisattva savior, is believed to exist.

Hagakure (葉隠) A definitive work on *bushi-dō* written by Yamamoto Jocho of the Nabeshima *han* in Saga, Kyushu, and completed in 1716.

shinjū (心中) This term is also used in reference to multiple suicides such as of parent and child (*oyako shinjū*) and families (*kazoku shinjū*). The term *muri shinjū* connotes a combination murder and suicide.

jōruri (浄瑠璃) Narrative ballads chanted to *shamisen* accompaniment. There were originally several schools of *jōruri*, Kiyomoto-bushi, Tokiwazu-bushi, and Gidayu-bushi, among others, but Gidayu-bushi is the most commonly performed *jōruri* today.

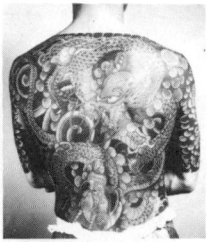

△Tattoo

■15. Groupism

murahachibu (村八分) Ostracism was practiced in feudal Japan, but has been outlawed today.

■16. *Giri* and *Ninjō*

enka (演歌) Popular songs of human frailty and love with a distinctively Japanese melody.

courtesan (遊女) *Yūjo* is an old term no longer in use for prostitutes.

■17. The Japanese Brain

Yukawa Hideki (湯川秀樹)(1907-1981) A theoretical physicist and the first Japanese to win a Nobel Prize.

■19. The Japanese Year

sweet sake (おとそ) Originally an herbal sake thought to exorcise misfortunes and promote long life. (*O-*)*toso* is also the name given to sake served at New Year's.

visit their grandparents (里帰り) Originally *sato-gaeri* referred to a bride's first visit to her former home soon after marriage, but this term is commonly used today to refer to any brief visit to the home of one's birth.

wrap up the year's work (仕事納め) Originally the last day of work in the year for offices, today *shigoto-osame* refers to the last day of work for government ministries and agencies and for private corporations. It is customary to put in only half a day of work at *shigoto-osame*.

toshikoshi-soba (年越しそば) Noodles eaten on New Year's Eve, *toshikoshi-soba* are believed to be especially felicitous for a variety of reasons. One commonly accepted reason is that the long noodles will assure a long and prosperous life.

△*O-toso* set

■24. The Japanese Language

large numbers of people (世界の言語の中で上位) In terms of the number of people who speak it, Japanese ranks sixth after Chinese, English, Russian, Hindi, and Spanish.

Dravidian languages (ドラビダ語) The Dravidian languages, such as Tamil, are spoken in southern India and northeastern Sri Lanka.

agglutinative language (膠着語) A typological classification for languages used along with isolative and inflective. Typology, however, tends to isolate only one or two characteristics of a language in the interest of classification, and linguistic scholars today question its accuracy and meaningfulness.

■25. Popular Heroes

Takeda Shingen (武田信玄)(1521-73) A daimyo of the warring states period, Takeda opposed Oda Nobunaga. He died of an illness in the midst of battle.

Sakamoto Ryoma (坂本龍馬)(1835-67) A samurai from the Tosa domain, Sakamoto was a major proponent of imperial restoration. He was assassinated by a pro-shogunate samurai.

Meiji Restoration (明治維新) Narrowly defined to refer to the 1868 coup d'etat that overthrew the Tokugawa shogunate, the Meiji Restoration more broadly marked Japan's opening to the West and the beginning of modern Japan's drive to industrialize.

Part-2
日本人の生活
LIVING IN JAPAN

1 暮らし

いくつかの指標から日本人の平均的な暮らしぶりを見ていくと，欧米並み，あるいはそれ以上に豊かな反面，非常に前近代的な面も残っていることがわかる。

●白書に見る暮らしぶり

恵まれている面から挙げていくと，1世帯当たりの平均年収は約500万円（1984年）とまずまず。殺人発生率は人口10万人に対して1.5と先進諸国の中で最も低く，世界でも最も安全な国と言える。近代化の1つの目安である電話普及率も人口100人に対して，1982年で世界平均19台の約2.5倍の49.6台で，アメリカ，イギリスには及ばないものの，西ドイツ，イタリアを上回っている。一方，人口1000人当たりの住宅戸数は1983年で309戸と先進諸国の中では最低で，下水道普及率も33%（1982年）と立ち遅れている。社会保障給付費の対国内総生産比も12.8%（1982年）と低い。

日本人自身はそんな自分たちの暮らしをどう見ているのか。総理府が1984年に行った「暮らしの意識に関する世論調査」によると，個人生活の幸福度では「普通よりよい」が64%を占め，「普通より悪い」はわずか4%，現在の日本の社会に対する評価でも「普通よりよい」が65%で，「普通より悪い」は4%に過ぎなかった。日本人はおおむね，自分たちの生活に満足していると言えよう。

次に，具体的に都市と農村における暮らしを見てみよう。

●都市の暮らしと農村の暮らし

日本の都市にはニューヨークやロンドンなどの世界の大都市に劣らないほどの，あらゆる物やサービスがあふれている。都市生活者はホテルのレストランで気軽に世界の料理を楽しみ，数多いデパートで世界の一流品を買うことができる。その都市の暮らしで最も頭の痛いのが住宅問題である。首都圏の地価は1㎡当たり4万9000円（1984年）で，アメリカの約15倍，イギリスの約9倍もするため，マイホームを持つのはたいへん難しくなっている。

情報機関の発達で，物やサービスについては農村と都会との較差はしだいに小さくなっている。農村生活者の悩みは若者の都会への人口流出で，跡継ぎ不足，嫁不足といった現象が出てきていることである。年寄り夫婦だけで田畑を守る家も増え，社会問題化している。

Standard of Living

A variety of indices indicate that the Japanese standard of living, while in many respects on a par with or even exceeding Western standards, still has many sub-standard facets.

● Pluses and Minuses

On the plus side, the average annual household income is a respectable ¥5 million (as of 1984), the homicide rate of 15 per million is the lowest of any major industrial country, Japan is one of the safest places in the world to live, and telephone ownership was 49.6 per 100 population in 1982. On this last index of modernization, the Japanese figure—2.5 times the world average of 19—was considerably ahead of the West German and Italian diffusion rates, though still somewhat behind those for the United States and Great Britain. Negative factors include the lowest house: population ratio of any industrialized nation, at only 309 dwellings per 1,000 population in 1983, and a low sewage installation rate of 33% (as of 1982). Social welfare also lags, accounting for only 12.8% of GDP in 1982.

How do the Japanese view their own standard of living? In answer to a public opinion poll conducted by the Prime Minister's Office in 1984, 64% claimed to be better off than average, and only 4% said they were worse off. Questioned about the quality of contemporary Japanese society, 65% thought it was better, and 4% worse, than average. For the most part, the Japanese people appear satisfied with their lives.

There are, however, some differences between urban and rural life.

● Urban Life vs Rural Life

Japanese cities offer a kaleidoscope of services and products at least the equal of those in any other major country. Urban Japanese can dine on world-class foods at sophisticated hotels and purchase internationally famous brand products at any one of numerous department stores. Housing, however, is a major problem. Urban land in Japan averaged ¥49,000 per square meter in 1984, approximately 15 times the average in the United States and 9 times that in Great Britain. Urban land prices are considerably higher than the national average, making home ownership a near impossibility for most people in urban areas.

The rapid development of transportation and communication networks is gradually narrowing the disparity between urban and rural living standards. Nevertheless, Japanese farming villages are in trouble because increasing numbers of young people are deserting the family farm to migrate to the cities. There are fewer people left to take over the family farm, and the men that stay have difficulty finding brides. With more and more farming households made up exclusively of old people, this situation is developing into a major social problem.

2 生活時間

NHK*の「昭和55年(1980年)国民生活時間調査」によると，睡眠，食事，身の回りの用事などの，いわゆる生活必需時間に約10時間半，仕事，学業，家事などに約8時間半，その他余暇的な行事や移動などの時間に5時間，というのが，平均的な日本人の1日の生活時間である。以下，同調査によってもう少し詳しく，日本人の1日を追ってみよう。

●起床と就寝時間

睡眠時間の国民平均は約8時間で10年来ほとんど変わっていないが，起床・就寝について見ると，日本人は宵っぱりの朝寝坊になってきている。10年前には午前6時までに起床している人が44%だったのが38%に，午後10時までに寝ていた人が44%だったのが，37%にそれぞれ減っている。これはおそらく，農林漁業従事者が減り，都市で働くサラリーマン生活者が増えたためだろう。

●食事の時間

日本人の食事時間は朝昼晩3食合わせても約1時間半と短く，食事のとり方も欧米とはだいぶ違っているようだ。朝食は午前7時から8時の間にとるのが普通だが，最近は朝食抜きの人も増えている。昼食は正午から1時間に集中しているのもきわめて日本的な特徴だ。日本ではサラリーマンが自宅へ帰って昼食をとるという習慣がないだけでなく，ほとんどの会社で昼食時間は正午から1時までと決まっているため，ほとんどの人が会社の社員食堂や，近くのレストランなどで手早く済ませる。オフィス街などにあるレストランでは順番待ちの行列ができるほど，この時間は混雑する。サラリーマン家庭では，父親は付き合いや息抜きなどで外で一杯やりながら夕食を済ませてしまうことも多く，家では母親と子供だけでとることも珍しくない。

●通勤と通学時間

“高・遠・狭”という住宅事情を反映して，通勤・通学などの移動時間もバカにならず，首都圏では往復で平均1時間余りもかかる。日本のラッシュアワーは有名だが，通勤時間が朝7時から9時までに集中しているために，この間，各交通機関は超満員になる。

全体的には，勤労者の仕事時間や主婦の家事時間はしだいに減る傾向にあり，その分，レジャーや読書などの余暇的行動の時間が増えてきている。週休2日制の定着や家事の簡素化によって，自由時間を楽しむようになってきた現れと言える。

The Japanese Day

According to a 1980 NHK* (Japan Broadcasting Corp.) survey of how the Japanese spend their time, approximately 10.5 hours are spent on the "essentials" of eating, sleeping, and bodily hygiene, approximately 8.5 hours at work, at school, or in housework, and 5 hours in leisure activities or commuting.

● Later Hours

The national average time spent sleeping is 8 hours. While this has fluctuated very little over the past ten years, actual sleeping patterns have changed considerably. In short, the Japanese have become night owls and late risers. Ten years ago, 44% of all Japanese were awake and up by 6 a.m.; today this has dropped to 38%. Whereas 44% were in bed by 10 p.m. ten years ago, only 37% go to bed that early now. This trend is probably due to a change in occupations and lifestyles as fewer people are engaged in agriculture and fishing activities and more people are working for companies in the large urban centers.

● Meals

In sharp contrast to the more-leisurely dining in the West, the average Japanese pattern is to spend little more than an hour and a half for all three meals—breakfast, lunch, and dinner—combined. Breakfast is usually between 7 and 8 a.m., but increasing numbers of people have begun skipping breakfast. The custom of having everybody eat lunch from noon to 1:00 p.m. is peculiarly Japanese. Not only do Japanese employees seldom go home for lunch, the fact that everybody has his lunch hour at the same time means company cafeterias and nearby restaurants are too crowded to allow anyone to eat leisurely. Long lines are a common sight at popular restaurants in downtown business districts. Since the Japanese businessman is usually late getting home, eating out with business associates or simply stopping off somewhere for a drink on the way home, mother and the children commonly go ahead and eat without him.

● Commuting

Expensive, distant, and small are the adjectives most commonly used to describe Japanese housing. Commuting to work or school can be quite time-consuming, taking more than an hour round-trip on average in urban centers. The well-known Japanese rush hour lasts from 7 to 9 a.m., during which time all forms of transportation are full to overflowing.

Nevertheless, the trend is toward less time spent at the office and on housework and more time spent on reading and other personal-interest activities. The two-day weekend is taking hold, and housework has been greatly simplified by modern appliances. More and more Japanese are enjoying more and more free time.

3 家庭

欧米先進諸国の例に漏れず，日本でも核家族化は時代の趨勢である。夫婦だけか，夫婦あるいは片親と未婚の子だけの核家族世帯は全世帯の6割にも達し，1940年までは5人台だった平均世帯人数も年々減少して，1980年以降は3.2人前後を推移している。夫婦に子供が1人か2人というのが，日本の一般的な家族構成と言えよう。

●戦前・戦中の家庭

親・子・孫と3世代が同居し，一家の主である夫が家父長として絶対的権威を持っていたのが，戦前の日本の平均的な家庭だった。妻を日本では「家内」とも言うように，一家の主婦は家にいて，夫や夫の両親である舅・姑に仕え，家事・育児一切を切り盛りした。戦中の食糧難時代には，兵隊に出た夫の留守を守って食糧の確保に奔走するなど，家のことでは夫に心配させないというのが，日本的家政学だった。

●戦後・現在の家庭

こうした家庭のイメージも，戦後の核家族化に伴って，だいぶ変わってきている。かつては家風についても子供の教育・結婚についても主導権を握っていた“強い夫”像は後退し，現在では妻や子供の言い分にも耳を傾ける，ものわかりのいい夫が増えている。一方，妻の地位は「戦後，強くなったのは女性と靴下」という言葉が一時はやったほど向上した。夫と同等の立場で自分の意見を言い，特に子供の教育については夫よりも強い決定権を持っているのが，現代の日本の妻たちである。妻の地位が向上した結果，顕在化してきたのが嫁・姑戦争である。嫁が自己主張をするようになったため，姑との摩擦が多くなり，夫は母親と妻の板挟みになって苦労する。

電気製品の普及で家事に時間がかからなくなり，子供が少なく育児に手のかかる期間も短くなった結果，家の中の仕事より生きがいを外に求めて働きに出る主婦も多く，今では主婦の2人に1人は働くに至っている。

しかし，戦後の主婦の地位を最も象徴的に物語っているのは，主婦が一家のさいふを握ったということだろう。欧米では一家の家計を預かるのは夫で，妻は必要な生活費だけを夫からもらうというのが一般的なようだが，戦後は妻が一家の大蔵大臣として夫の給料を管理し，生活のやりくりから貯蓄，財産運用，マイホーム建設資金づくりまでさい配するという家庭が増えている。

The Family

As in the West, the modern Japanese family is small. Some 60% of all Japanese households consist of couples only or a single parent and unmarried children. Back in 1940, the average family had five members. Since then, the number has dropped to 3.2, where it has been since 1980. Thus the average Japanese family is mother, father, and one or two children.

● Pre-1945 Situation

In prewar Japan, three generations (parents, children, and grandchildren) lived under the same roof. The father was head of the household, and his word was law. As one of the Japanese words for wife, *kanai* (lit. inside the home), implies, the prewar Japanese wife's place was in the home, serving her husband and her husband's parents, doing housework, and raising her children. During the war years when food was scarce, the Japanese housewife did everything she could to ensure that the family had enough to eat. She was expected to maintain the household while her husband was at the front, and she was not to burden her husband with the worries of keeping the family fed and intact.

● Changes since the War

However, the Japanese family has changed considerably as the nuclear family became the postwar norm. The father no longer has absolute authority in establishing family rules, governing his children's education, and granting permission for his children's marriages, and increasing numbers of fathers are listening to their wives and children. At the same time, the wife's role is also changing, as aptly illustrated by the once-popular phrase, "The two things that have gotten stronger since the war are women and stockings." The modern Japanese housewife has an equal say with her husband in family matters, and often more say when it comes to the children's education. One manifestation of this improved status for wives is the conflict which has erupted between wives and mothers-in-law. With the wife used to speaking out, there has been increasing friction with the traditional mother-in-law, and the hapless husband often finds himself caught in the middle.

With the time required for household work greatly diminished by modern electrical appliances, and with fewer children to raise, many Japanese housewives are finding fulfillment in work outside the home. Today, one of every two housewives has an outside job.

The most obvious proof of the wife's position is her grip on the family purse strings. In the West it is usually the husband who controls the family finances, giving his wife an allowance to do the shopping with. Yet in postwar Japan it is the wife who handles the money, making all of the major savings, investments, and even home financing decisions.

4 家計

一家のさいふを握っている日本の主婦は，生活のやりくりを上手にするために，まめに家計簿をつけている。こうした各家庭の家計簿を基にして総理府統計局が毎年発表している「家計調査報告」によると，1984年の勤労者世帯1か月の平均実収入は42万4025円，消費支出は28万2716円となっている。

かつては生活費の中で食料費の占める割合であるエンゲル係数か，衣食住などの基礎的支出の割合が消費生活を推し測るものさしだったが，“飽食の時代”にある現在の日本では，このものさしは通用しなくなってきている。具体的には，1970年に32.2%だった勤労者世帯の1か月の食料費は75年30.0%，80年27.8%，84年26.1%と減少の一途，衣食住などの基本的支出の割合のほうも同じく56.0%，53.2%，49.5%，47.8%と，すでに50%を切っている。逆に増えているのが教養娯楽・教育・交際費などの選択的支出である。

●増える教育費

とりわけ，高学歴社会を反映して，教育費のウエートが年々拡大しているのが最近の日本の家計の大きな特徴である。1975年から1984年までの家計支出と教育支出の年平均伸び率を比較した試算によると，家計支出が8%の伸びに対して教育支出は18%と，倍以上の伸び率だった。

これはあくまで平均の数字で，教育熱心な都市部や大きい子供がいる世帯では，それだけ教育費支出の占める割合は高くなる。一例として，1983年に東京都が就学者を持つ都内の452世帯を対象に行った調査を挙げておくと，月平均消費支出29万9309円の21.3%，6万3780円が教育費に充てられており，中には家計の3分の2を教育費に充てている家庭もあった。

●高い貯蓄率

日本人が貯蓄熱心な国民であることはよく知られている。1984年の1世帯平均貯蓄現在高は649万円。可処分所得に占める貯蓄の割合を示す家計貯蓄率は1984年で17.3%で，イタリアが20.3%，カナダ15.5%，フランス11.5%，イギリス7.0%，アメリカ5.2%であるから欧米先進諸国の中でも高いほうである。日本人が貯蓄に熱心なのは豊かさの現れというより，老人福祉がまだ充分でないことへの不安や，なかなかマイホームを持てない住宅事情のためと言えよう。

The Household Budget

It is generally the housewife who holds the family purse strings in Japan, and she keeps a detailed record of household accounts. According to a 1984 annual survey of such household accounts by the Statistics Bureau of the Prime Minister's Office, average monthly household income was ¥424,025 and average expenditures ¥282,716.

Neither the Engel coefficient, used to measure the percentage of household expenditures on food, nor the percentage spent on the basic necessities of food, shelter, and clothing, is an adequate indicator of the quality of consumer life in today's affluent Japan. Food accounted for 32.2% of the wage-earner household's monthly expenditures in 1970, but the ratio has decreased steadily since then, to 30.0% in 1975, 27.8% in 1980, and 26.1% in 1984. The same downward trend is evident in the food-shelter-and-clothing figure: 56.0% in 1970, 53.2% in 1975, 49.5% in 1980, 47.8% in 1984, and continuing below the 50% mark ever since. In contrast, there has been a marked increase in family spending on recreation, entertainment, and education.

● The Growing Cost of Education

Reflecting the Japanese people's strong belief in the benefits of a good education, Japanese household spending on education has grown sharply in recent years. Indeed, spending on education increased 18% per annum between 1975 and 1984—a figure more than twice the 8% growth rate for total household expenditures.

These are averages, of course, and educational spending has gone up even more in the highly education-conscious urban household and homes with older children. According to a 1983 survey of 452 Tokyo households with school-age children, spending on education averaged ¥63,780, or 21.3% of the average total household spending of ¥299,309, per month. Some families earmarked nearly two-thirds of their total monthly expenditures for their children's education.

● High Savings Rate

The Japanese have long been known for their high savings rate. The average household savings balance was about ¥6.5 million and the household savings rate (the percentage of disposable income saved) 17.3% in 1984. This compares favorably with the average savings rates in other industrialized nations: 20.3% in Italy, 15.5% in Canada, 11.5% in France, 7.0% in Great Britain, and 5.2% in the United States. However, the Japanese propensity to save is often attributed not so much to affluence as to the extremely high cost of owning one's own home and the need to save for a rainy day in a society lacking adequate welfare for the aged.

5 住宅

かつて「ウサギ小屋」と評されたことのある日本人の住居であるが，これは必ずしも的を射た表現ではない。国連の「統計年鑑」と建設省の「建設統計要覧」による住宅水準比較でも，日本の新築住宅の1戸当たり床面積は93.9m²で，アメリカの136.1m²，スウェーデンの103.2m²には及ばないものの，西ドイツの98.8m²とほぼ並び，フランスの77.1m²をはるかに上回っている。

●根強いマイホーム志向

総理府が5年ごとに発表している「住宅統計調査」の1983年調査によると，空き家などを除いた住宅3475万戸のうち，「持ち家」が2164万戸で62.3%，「借家」は1290万戸で37.1%。「持ち家率」は，58年の71.2%から73年の59.2%まで調査ごとに低下傾向にあったが，60.4%で上昇に転じた前回に続き，今回もその割合を伸ばし，マイホーム志向が強いことを表している。建て方別では，「一戸建て」が2237万戸で全体の64.4%。ついでマンションなどの「共同住宅」932万戸となっており，前回調査と比べると「一戸建て」が6.7%増なのに対して，「共同住宅」は17.1%増と急激な伸びを示した。

●大都会の住宅事情

日本の大都市圏での住宅事情を表す表現に“高，遠，狭”というものがある。「ウサギ小屋」という言葉は，おそらく東京，大阪といった大都市の住宅を指したものだと思われるが，日本と欧米の住宅で最も違うのは，むしろ“高，遠”である。今回の調査でも，サラリーマン2307万世帯のうち，通勤時間「30分から59分」が29.2%で最も高く，「1時間以上」も16.1%を占めている。前回調査との比較でも「30分から44分」が30.9%増と目だって伸び，「1時間以上」も増加傾向にあって，住まいと会社の間がますます遠くなっている。

●変化する住まい観

従来の日本の住まいと言えば，木造に瓦屋根，戸内をふすまや障子で区切った，いわゆる日本家屋が主だった。が，今回の調査にもあったように，最近，鉄筋コンクリートのマンション志向派が急激に増えている。これは，便利さ重視のライフスタイルを好む若い世代が増えたこと，本当は一戸建て志向ながら，なかなか持てない現状から妥協住宅としてのマンションが見直されたことなども要因としてはあるが，根本的な理由は，家イコール家族という戦前の住まい観が，家は人が住む単なる器とする考え方に変わったためである。

Housing

"Rabbit hutches," a term once used to describe Japanese houses, is not an entirely accurate description. As shown in the United Nations *Statistical Yearbook* and Ministry of Construction surveys, Japan's present housing situation compares favorably with that in other countries. While the average Japanese home's 93.9m^2 of floor space is not as spacious as in the United States (136.1m^2) or Sweden (103.2m^2), it is on a par with West Germany's 98.8m^2 and considerably larger than France's 77.1m^2.

● Current Statistics and Issues

The Prime Minister's Office's latest housing survey, conducted every five years, counts 34,750,000 dwellings nationwide in 1983. Of these, 21,640,000 or 62.3% are resident-owned and 12,900,000 (37.1%) rented. The percentage of resident-owned housing had dropped from 71.2% in 1958 to 59.2% in 1973, but rose again to 60.4% in 1978, indicating the Japanese people's strong desire to own their own homes. Single-family dwellings numbered 22,370,000 (64.4% of the total), followed by condominiums* and other multi-family housing at 9,320,000. Compared to the 1978 results, there were only 6.7% more single-family dwellings but 17.1% more multi-family dwellings.

● Urban Housing

Housing in Japan's principal metropolitan areas is often characterized as expensive, distant, and small. The earlier reference to "rabbit hutches" was most likely made with the Tokyo-Osaka situation in mind. The factors which best distinguish Japanese housing from its Western counterparts are its high cost and distance from the wage-earner's place of work. According to the 1983 survey, 29.2% of 23,070,000 salaried worker households were within 30-59 minutes' commuting time, while 16.1% had to commute for an hour or more. The most conspicuous difference from the 1978 results were the 30.9% increase in the 30-44 minute commuting time range and the increase in housing requiring a commute of an hour or more.

● Changing Attitudes

While Japanese homes were formerly wooden buildings with tile roofs* and sliding-door partitions* inside, the most recent housing survey points up the sudden popularity of reinforced concrete condos. In part, this reflects the growing number of young households and their concern with convenience, but it also means many people are opting for multi-family housing in lieu of the single-family homes they would prefer but cannot afford. Even more basic, however, is the changing concept of the family, from the prewar oneness of the home and family to the contemporary view of the home as nothing more than a place where the family lives.

6 耐久消費財と日本的家具

●耐久消費財

経済的繁栄を象徴するように，日本の家庭には電気製品があふれている。昭和30年代(1955～64年)の家庭電化ブームのはしりに目標とされた洗濯機・冷蔵庫・掃除機などは，経済企画庁の1984年の調べによると，それぞれ98.4%，98.7%，96.7%の普及率で，ほぼ全戸に1台ずつ行き渡っている。その後の目標となったのが“3C”，すなわちカラーテレビ・クーラー・車などの高級品だが，これらも同調査では99.2%，49.3%，64.8%と，日本の家庭では決してぜいたく品でなくなっていることを示している。全般に，同じ品物でもより機能性の高いものや普及途上にある高級品などで普及率の伸びが高くなっているのが特徴で，現在欧米でも人気を呼んでいるビデオは，1981年に5.1%だった普及率が1984年には18.7%で5軒に1台の割になるなど，急速に広まっている状況である。日本人は，欧米並みかそれ以上の近代的な暮らし方をしていると言えよう。

●日本的家具

その一方で日本人は，畳，布団，風呂，こたつといった日本の伝統的な家具類にも強い愛着を持っている。

• **畳**　畳は，日本住宅の床上に敷くもので，欧米で言えばじゅうたんのようなものに当たる。わらで作った厚床の上にい草などで織った畳表を付けたもので，畳の上では靴，スリッパなしで歩く。住まいの洋風化が進み，居間や子供部屋などは欧米流に板床かじゅうたん敷きにしていても，まだまだ畳敷きの和室も多い。

• **布団**[*]　欧米のベッドに当たる日本の寝具が布団で，畳んで押[*]し入れなどに入れておき，寝るときに畳の上に敷いて使う。折り畳みができるので，ベランダなどに干すと，新品のようにふっくらとして寝心地よくできるという良さが布団にはある。

• **風呂**　日本人の風呂好きは有名だが，欧米のシャワーと違って，日本では大きな湯舟にたっぷり湯を張って，ゆっくりとつかる。

• **こたつ**[*]　こたつは冬季に下半身を暖めるための日本独得の生活用具である。炭火や電気などの熱源を四角い櫓(やぐら)の中に置き，熱が逃げないようにその上に布団を掛けたものだが，こたつを囲んで家族が団らんするというのが，きわめて日本的な冬の光景になっている。

こうした日本的家具に対する関心は欧米でも高まっているようで，日本旅館が外国人観光客に人気を呼んでいる。

Consumer Durables

● Consumer Durables

The Japanese home is full of electrical appliances, symbols of the nation's prosperity. The main stars in the electrical appliance boom of 1955-64 were the washing machine, refrigerator, and vacuum cleaner, and soon there was one of each in nearly every home (a 1984 survey by the Economic Planning Agency finding that 98.4% of all Japanese households had a washing machine, 98.7% a refrigerator, and 96.7% a vacuum cleaner). Interest next shifted to the "three Cs" of color television sets, air conditioners, and cars, and these have also achieved everyday status in the typical Japanese home (diffusion rates being 99.2% for color television sets, 49.3% for air conditioners, and 64.8% for cars). As a result, the demand is now for superior replacement models and wider ownership of other high-priced products. Popular in the United States and Europe as well as in Japan, video recorders, for example, have jumped from a 5.1% diffusion rate in 1981 to 18.7% in 1984 (the equivalent of one unit for every five households). Overall, the Japanese lead very modern lives with a standard of living at least as high as that in the other industrialized countries.

● Japanese-style Furniture

In seeming contrast to the demand for state-of-the-art consumer durables, the Japanese have a nearly equal passion for such traditional Japanese furnishings as *tatami*, *futon*, the Japanese bath, and the *kotatsu*.

Tatami are sturdy straw mats used for flooring in the typical Japanese home, comparable to Western carpeting. Made of a thick layer of bundled straw covered with a finely woven rush matting, *tatami* are meant to be walked on barefoot. Shoes and slippers alike are removed before entering a *tatami* room. Western trends in housing dictate carpeted floors for the living room and children's bedrooms, but many families still have rooms floored in *tatami*.

The *futon** is the Japanese bedding. Thick quilts folded and put away in a closet* during the day, they are laid out on the *tatami* at night as bedding. Light and easy to handle, *futon* are often aired to keep them fresh, soft, and comfortable.

The Japanese propensity for bathing is well known, and in contrast to the Western preference for a quick shower, the Japanese enjoy the luxury of a long soak in a deep tub full of clean, hot water.

The *kotatsu** is a unique Japanese heating device used in the winter months. With charcoal or an electrical heating unit placed under its four-legged frame and a *futon*-like quilt over it to hold in the heat, the *kotatsu* is a central piece of furniture in the winter as the whole family gathers around to talk and warm their feet under the quilt.

Along with the growing Western interest in Japanese furniture, Japanese inns are increasingly popular with visitors from overseas.

7 洋服と着物

日本女性の着物姿はどの国へ行っても珍しがられるそうだが，日本国内においても，そうした事情はあまり変わらなくなってきている。女性に限らず現代の日本人は洋服が一般的で，着物を日常的に着るのはお茶，お花といった日本の伝統芸能のお師匠さんや，水商売の女性，力士などの特殊な職業の人に限られ，あとは，結婚式・成人式・正月などの儀式に着る装飾的なものになってしまっているためだ。したがって，自分で着物を着られる人も少なくなり，着物の着方を教える「着付け教室」に通うことが，若い女性の“嫁入り修業”の1つになっているほどである。

●着物の変遷

洋服に対して在来の日本の衣服，つまり和服を総称して着物と言うが，一般的には羽織やコートを除いた，いわゆる長着（前でかき合わせて帯で締めるワンピーススタイルの現在の着物）を指すことが多い。長着の型が成立したのは奈良時代のことだが，平安時代のころまでは下着として着用されたものだった。その後，ズボン式の袴と合わせて着る表着となり，室町時代に男女とも袴が省略されて，今の着流しが一般的になった。江戸時代に入ると，着物は，特に男性の場合，封建社会の身分制と結び付き，さまざまな規制を受けるようになる。例えば，白無垢の肌着は大名でも嫡男だけにしか許されず，一般武士でも綸子は着てはいけないことなどである。一般民衆は麻か木綿を常用した。しかし，町人の経済力が増すにつれて江戸時代末期から徐々に服装の自由化が進む。明治に入ると，皇族，軍人，官公使，学生と順を追って洋服化が進み，一般にも普及した。

●洋服の普及

男の着物が身分制に縛られていたのに，女性の場合は，袖の長い振袖は娘の着るもので結婚すれば詰め袖という程度でそれほど厳しくなかったったため，大正期ごろまでは着物生活が続いたが，女性も自我に目覚めだした昭和になって，急速に洋服が広まった。

以来，男性の場合でさえ1世紀余の短い日本人の洋服の歴史だが，現在では，若い女性が世界の一流デザイナーのプレタポルテを身に着けることが特別でないほど，すっかり洋服は定着している。その需要の高さから，ファッションショーの舞台も，パリ，ニューヨークから東京へ移りつつあると言われるほどで，森英恵，三宅一生，山本寛斎といった日本人デザイナーも，世界的に活躍するまでになった。

Clothing and Kimono

The young Japanese woman attired in kimono* is becoming as rare a sight in Japan as it is overseas. Both Japanese men and women prefer Western clothing for their daily attire, and about the only people who wear Japanese-style attire every day are teachers of such traditional Japanese arts as the tea ceremony and flower arrangement, bar nightclub hostesses, and sumo wrestlers.* For most Japanese, the kimono is reserved for weddings, coming-of-age rites, the New Year's holidays, and other special occasions. Few can successfully dress themselves in the elaborate kimono, and many young ladies attend "kimono school" to learn this social grace before they get married.

● The Kimono's Evolution

While kimono is the generic term for Japanese-style clothing (*wafuku*), as opposed to Western-style, it more specifically refers to the long single garment overlapping in front and tied with a broad, stiff sash called an *obi*.* This long kimono traces its origins back to the Nara period, but it was simply an undergarment until the Heian period. Later it evolved into an outer garment worn by both men and women in combination with a *hakama** (long pantaloon-like skirt), and in the Muromachi period it finally reached its modern form without the *hakama* In the hierarchical Edo period, the type and make of kimono was strictly regulated according to social rank, especially for men. For example, only the official heir to a fief lord could wear pure white ; ordinary samurai were forbidden to wear satin; and the common people could only wear flax and cotton. As the commercial class gained economic clout, the restrictions on dress were gradually relaxed toward the end of the Edo period. After the shogunate's downfall in the late 19th century, Western clothing spread to the imperial family, the military, the civil service bureaucracy, students, and finally to the general public.

● Spread of Western Clothing

Whereas the kimono had indicated rank for men, for women it generally symbolized marital status, unmarried lasses wearing colorful *furi-sode** kimono with long flowing sleeves and changing to the more work-like *tsume-sode* after they married. Kimono continued to be worn as daily wear by women through the beginning of this century until heightened consciousness sparked a change to Western dress after World War I.

It is only a little more than a century since the Japanese chose to adopt Western dress, but already young Japanese women wear leading designer fashions with ease. The fashion center of the world is shifting from Paris to New York to Tokyo, and Japanese designers such as Hanae Mori, Issey Miyake, and Kansai Yamamoto are internationally recognized as among the best there are.

8 食生活

●食生活と高度経済成長

戦後の日本，とりわけ，高度経済成長時代に入った1950年代後半以降に，日本人の生活は大きく変わった。それは，国民所得が大幅に増大したり，テレビ・洗濯機・冷蔵庫・炊飯器といった電化製品が普及したために，日本人の生活が非常に便利になると同時に，生活を楽しむゆとりができてきたからである。

当然，食生活においてもその影響が現れた。例えば食生活の考え方である。かつては「男子厨房に入るべからず」という言葉があった。これは，家庭内において料理を作るのは女性の役目で，男性がする仕事ではないという意味であるが，換言すると，男性が食事に興味を示すのは女々しいこととされていた。現在では，この言葉は死語のようになり，男女を問わず，食事に関心を持つ人が多くなった。

また，台所の環境も一変した。以前は，家の間取りから見て条件の悪い位置に置かれることが多かったが，現在では，調理設備を整えるだけでなく，採光や通風など好条件の場所に配置したり，インテリアにも十分配慮している家庭が多い。

●多様化する食生活

1日の食事回数は朝昼夕の3回で，最も重点が置かれているのは夕食である。戦前までは多くの家庭が日本食中心で，米を主食に魚や野菜などの副食，それにみそ汁と漬物という組み合わせが一般的であったが，戦後になって学校給食の影響でパン食が普及したり，肉類，卵，乳製品も多く取り入れられるようになった。

食事の内容は経済成長とともに多様化してきている。現在のほとんどの家庭では，日本食だけでなく，洋食，中華とバラエティーに富んだ食事が食卓に並ぶ。それに，インスタントラーメンをはじめとする即席食品，半調理品，調理済み食品のようなひと手間かけるだけで食べられる食品が数多く出回っている。

街に出れば，すし，てんぷら，そば，うどんなどの多くの日本食とともに，中国料理やフランス料理をはじめ，イタリア，ドイツ，ソ連，インドなど世界の各国料理が楽しめるし，フライドチキンやハンバーガーなどのファーストフードもお好みしだいである。

さらに，一部では，健康食としての自然食品，ダイエット食，手作り料理が人気を博している傾向もある。とにかく現在の日本は飽食の時代にあると言う人もいるくらいなのである。

The Japanese Diet

● Recent Changes

Japanese lifestyles changed drastically in the decade of rapid economic growth which began in the late 1950s. As the nation's GNP soared, television sets, washing machines, refrigerators, and electric rice cookers proliferated, making life considerably more convenient and increasing leisure time.

These changes have naturally had an impact on the Japanese diet and attitudes toward food and eating. In the past, the kitchen was off limits to men and *danshi chūbō ni hairubekarazu* was the byword, a custom which not only indicated that cooking was women's work but that even expressing an interest in food and cooking was somehow unseemly for a man. Today, this no longer holds true, and men and women alike are interested in what they eat and how it is prepared.

The kitchen has also changed. Whereas it was once given the worst location in the house, it is now often seen as one of the most important rooms, completely equipped and bright and airy.

● Wide Choice

Three meals a day are the norm, with the evening meal usually the largest. Before World War II, everyone ate the traditional Japanese meal of rice supplemented by fish, vegetables, *miso* soup,* and pickles. After the war, however, bread became a mainstay of school lunches and this influenced dietary habits in society at large. People have also begun to eat more meat, eggs, and dairy products.

The Japanese diet has diversified as the nation has prospered. In the typical home today, Western and Chinese dishes are as likely to appear on the table as are more traditional Japanese foods. There has also been a phenomenal increase in instant foods such as instant *rāmen*, semi-processed and processed foods which require very little effort to prepare, and what can only be called junk foods.

△ Restaurant menu display

Eating out is common, and one can choose from among all kinds of foods—Japanese foods such as sushi,* tempura,* *soba*,* and *udon** as well as Chinese, French, Italian, German, Russian, Indian, and many more international cuisines. Fast food chains serving fried chicken, hamburgers, and the like are also widespread.

Health-conscious Japanese are also accomodated by a variety of natural foods, diet foods, and restaurants specializing in home cooking. Japan is today a virtual paradise for gourmet and gourmand alike.

9 日本食と材料

●欧米型の食事と日本食

近年，日本食は栄養面からあらためて見直されてきている。特に外国ではダイエット食として注目され始め，理想的な食事の1つとして評価する人もいる。

確かに，欧米型の食事と日本食とを比べてみた場合，欧米型の食事は肉類，乳製品などを中心とした高カロリー，高脂質であるのに対して，日本食はてんぷらを別にすれば，油を使った料理が少なく，低カロリー，低脂質であり，かつ栄養のバランスもよい。

●主食と副食

日本人の食生活には，伝統的に主食と副食という考えがある。主食は米で，普通は七分ないし精白についた*うるち米を水といっしょに炊いて常食にする。日本人の米食の歴史は古く，すでに弥生時代から食されているが，現在と同じようなご飯が登場するのは平安時代と言われている。

副食は，日本列島が四方を海に囲まれているだけあって，魚介類が中心で，重要な動物性たんぱく源になっている。魚介類の調理法は，焼く，煮る，蒸すなど多彩である。中でも「さしみ」はごく新鮮な魚介類を包丁さばきひとつで調理するもので，生で食べる日本独特の料理である。肉食も古くから行われていたが，仏教の普及によって禁忌されるようになり，どうしても魚介類に頼らざるをえなかった。

魚介類と並んで重要なのは，大豆加工食品である。これには，豆腐，*油揚げ，納豆などがあり，貴重な植物性たんぱく源として日本食には欠かせない。そのほか野菜類もよく使われ，煮物，あえ物，酢の物，*おひたしなど野菜料理は豊富である。

●調味料の王様しょうゆ

日本食を語るとき，これらの主食や副食以上に忘れてならないのは，調味料のしょうゆ，みそである。特にしょうゆは調味料の王様と言ってよいくらい優れたもので，つけじょうゆ，かけじょうゆ，調味にとほとんどの料理に合う。日本食がここまで発展したのも，このしょうゆという調味料に負うところが大きい。中国のしょうゆ，東南アジアの魚じょうゆもあることはあるが，これらと日本のしょうゆは味，香りとも全く異なる。みそはしょうゆほどではないが，みそ汁を始め，焼き物，あえ物などの調味料として重要である。

Japanese Food

● Western vs Traditional Diet

The traditional Japanese diet is gaining renewed acceptance both in Japan and overseas for its nutritional balance. Overseas, traditional Japanese foods are looked upon as ideal diet foods.

As many people have noticed, the meat- and dairy-product-based Western diet is much higher in calories and cholesterol than the Japanese diet which uses little oil or fats except for a few dishes such as tempura, is low-calorie, and yet is highly nutritious.

● Staples and Side Dishes

The traditional Japanese meal consists primarily of rice as a staple supplemented by a number of side dishes. The rice is usually a non-glutinous rice,* partially or completely polished before being boiled. The Japanese have been rice-eaters since as far back as the Yayoi period, and rice as it is eaten today first appeared in the Japanese diet in the Heian period.

Seafood is an invaluable source of protein for the island nation of Japan. Side dishes of grilled, boiled, and steamed seafood are common, and *sashimi* (very fresh fish and shellfish eaten raw) is an especially popular and uniquely Japanese dish. While the ancient Japanese also ate meat, the introduction of Buddhism and its injunctions against killing brought about a greater dependence on seafood as a source of protein nutrition.

△さしみ(*sashimi*)

Soybeans and soybean products are another important food in the Japanese diet. These include *tōfu* (bean curd), *abura-age** (deep-fried *tōfu*), and *nattō* (partially fermented soybeans), all of which are rich in vegetable protein. Numerous other vegetables are also eaten, boiled, mixed with soybean paste or other flavorings, vinegared, or seasoned with soy sauce.*

● Seasonings

Shōyu (soy sauce) and *miso* (a soybean paste) are the primary flavorings used in Japanese cooking. *Shōyu* in particular is used in nearly all Japanese dishes, as a dip, as a sauce, and for seasoning, and it has played a major part in the development of Japanese cooking. Although other countries also have soy-based sauces, Japanese *shōyu* differs from its Chinese and Southeast Asian counterparts in both taste and fragrance. Although not used as much as *shōyu*, *miso* is a primary ingredient in soups, in flavoring fish or meat for grilling, and mixed with boiled vegetables as a flavoring.

10 伝統的な日本食

●五味五色五法の日本料理

日本食には，家庭での日常の食事だけでなく，伝統的な行事食や宴席料理などがあり，依然として，現代の日本人の生活の中に生きている。諸外国ではすし，てんぷら，すき焼きなどが代表的な日本食として知られているが，日本食の特徴という点から言えば，むしろ，伝統的な行事食や宴席料理のほうがその色彩が濃い。

昔から，日本食を「五味五色五法の料理」と言って，その特徴を表現する。「五味」とは，甘・酸・辛・苦・鹹(塩辛い)のことを，「五色」とは，白・黄・赤・青・黒のことを，「五法」とは生・煮る・焼く・揚げる・蒸すという調理法を指す。つまり，日本食とはこれくらいデリケートな料理だということである。素材の持ち味を生かしながら，味・香り・色をだいじにし，春夏秋冬の季節感をも重視する。材料の旬(最もおいしい時季)にも気を配る。さらに，料理を盛り付ける器も，料理によってあるいは季節によって，色・形・材質について配慮するのである。

●伝統的な日本食

伝統的な日本食に次のようなものがある。

- **本膳料理**　室町時代に武家の礼法とともに定められたもてなしの形式が基になった料理。現在では，冠婚葬祭などの儀礼的な料理としてわずかに残っているだけであるが，ほかの伝統的な日本食の形式や作法上の基本になっている。
- **茶懐石**　茶の湯で茶を出す前に供する簡単な料理。懐石とは，温めた石を懐に抱いて腹を温めるのと同じくらいに，空腹をしのぐという意味である。懐石料理とも言う。
- **会席料理**　本膳料理よりもずっと形式ばらず，くつろいだ形の宴席料理。言うなれば日本のパーティー料理である。現在の日本料理店で供する宴席料理の多くがこれである。
- **精進料理**　魚介類や肉類を用いずに，大豆加工品や野菜，海草などの植物性食品だけを使った料理。これには，仏教の禅宗に伝わる精進料理と，黄檗山万福寺に伝わる普茶料理がある。
- **おせち料理**　正月の祝い料理で，五段重ねの漆塗りの重箱に各種の料理を詰めて出すもの。昔は，特別の行事の日に，神に供える料理のことを言っていた。

Traditional Japanese Dishes

● The Three Fives

Japanese cuisine is rich in variety, encompassing everything from the simplest home-cooked meal to special meals for ceremonial occasions and fabulous banquets. Japanese food popular overseas includes sushi, tempura, and sukiyaki, but these have fewer traditional elements than do ceremonial and banquet menus.

The Japanese diet is commonly said to consist of five flavors, five colors, and five basic methods of preparation. These are the five flavors of sweet, sour, hot, bitter, and salty; the five colors of white, yellow, red, green, and black; and the five preparations of raw, boiled, grilled, deep-fried, and steamed. Japanese foods are prepared to retain as much of their natural flavor as possible, and great importance is placed on the delicacy of color, fragrance, and taste. Seasonality is also stressed, with foods being served at their peak season. Serving dishes play an important role; their color, shape, and material being carefully matched to the food and season.

● Traditional Japanese Cooking

While there are far too many kinds of traditional Japanese cooking to list them all, some of the best-known ones are:

• ***Honzen-ryōri**** Originally a formalized method of presenting food to guests in the samurai homes of the feudal Muromachi period, *honzen-ryōri* is served today only on such ritual and ceremonial occasions as weddings, funerals, and other formal occasions. Still, *honzen-ryōri* remains a basic influence in all traditional Japanese cooking styles and manners.

• ***Cha-kaiseki**** This is a simple meal served to guests before serving tea. The term *kaiseki* referring to the warmed stones that Japanese people used to put next to their stomachs to ward off hunger, the name connotes a frugal meal. This is also called *kaiseki-ryōri.*

• ***Kaiseki-ryōri**** This is a much more relaxed and informal banquet style than *honzen*, and may be thought of as the typical Japanese party menu. Much of the food served at the modern Japanese-style restaurant is in the *kaiseki* mode.

• ***Shōjin-ryōri**** Abstaining entirely from the use of any meat or fish, *shōjin-ryōri* is an all-vegetarian diet of soybean products, vegetables, seaweed, and rice. The two best-known schools are the *shōjin-ryōri* of Zen Buddhism and the *fucha-ryōri* served at the Zen Obakusan Manpukuji.

• ***O-sechi-ryōri**** This is the festive food eaten at New Year's, and it is often served in a five-layer set of lacquer boxes.* In olden times, *o-sechi-ryōri* was used to refer to the food prepared as offerings to the gods on special occasions.

11 結婚・離婚

厚生省の「人口動態統計」によると，1984年に結ばれたカップルは73万9993組(43秒に1組)で，前年より約2万3000組減り，人口1000人当たりの婚姻率は6.2と，統計開始以来最低を記録している。一方，離婚は17万8758組(2分57秒に1組)となっている。1964年以来上昇を続ける離婚率は人口1000人当たり1.50に達し，アメリカ(5.30)，スウェーデン(2.42)には及ばないものの，フランス(1.59)，西ドイツ(1.56)と肩を並べた。日本では，夫婦になれば“ともに白髪の生えるまで”添い遂げるというのが結婚についての考え方だったが，うまくいかなければ別れたほうがいいという欧米型の結婚観に，急速に変わりつつあると言える。

●見合い結婚

結婚に際してきわめて日本的なものに「見合い」がある。見合いというのは，本人どうしの自由恋愛によって結ばれるのではなく，「仲人」と呼ばれる仲介者が結婚したいと思っている男女を紹介し，当人どうしが気に入れば結婚まで世話をするというしくみである。たいていの場合，適齢期の息子や娘を持った親が，当人のスナップ写真や「釣り書」という結婚のための経歴書を添えて，仲人に相手探しを頼む。適当な相手が見つかったところで双方の親も同席して，顔合わせの見合いとなる。この見合いで趣味や家庭についての抱負などを語り合って，自分の結婚相手にふさわしいかどうかを判断するのである。戦後の民主化によって，恋愛結婚が増えている中でも，見合い結婚は相変わらず支持されていて，挙式後1年以内の中堅企業のサラリーマンを対象にしたある調査では，恋愛8割見合い2割という傾向は，ここ数年変わっていない。ちなみに同調査では新郎の平均年齢は27歳，新婦24歳だった。

●ブライダル産業

挙式からハネムーン，新居の手当てなどにかかる結婚総費用が，日本では500～600万円が相場となっている。ホテルで豪華結婚式を挙げ，ハネムーンはハワイ，グアムなど海外へというカップルが増えているためだ。その結果，一大産業になっているのが，結婚式場・貸衣裳・旅行会社などのブライダル産業。最近では，独身の男女を会員とし，それぞれの基本的データをコンピューターに入れ，理想の相手を紹介する結婚情報サービス業も新ビジネスとして登場し，たいへんな人気を呼んでいる。

Marriage and Divorce

According to the Ministry of Health and Welfare's *Population Statistics*, 739,993 couples got married in 1984 (one every 43 seconds). This was approximately 23,000 fewer couples than in 1983 as the marriage rate fell to 6.2 per 1,000 population—the lowest ever recorded. On the other side of the ledger, 178,758 couples got divorced (one every 2 minutes and 57 seconds). After climbing every year since 1964, the divorce rate now stands at 1.50 per 1,000 population. While still far less than in the United States (5.30) and Sweden (2.42), this is on a par with the figures for France (1.59) and West Germany (1.56). The Japanese ideal used to be that husband and wife, once joined in matrimony, would stay together till death did them part, but this has recently been changing toward the Western better-to-get-a-divorce-if-things-don't-work-out view of marriage.

● ***Miai***

Arranged marriages are very Japanese. The arranged marriage starts not with love between the young man and woman but with an introduction by a go-between who thinks they would make a good couple. If they find they hit it off, the go-between sees them through to marriage. Often a young man or woman's parents will take their child's picture and a brief personal sketch (a *tsuri-gaki*) to a go-between and ask him/her to look for a suitable match. Once a suitable person has been found, the young people are introduced at a formal meeting (the *miai*) with their parents present. At the *miai*, they usually talk about personal interests, the kinds of families they want, and other generalities in an effort to see how compatible they are. Even with the rapid increase in non-arranged "love" marriages that accompanied the postwar democratization, the *miai* system still has a strong following. Surveys of first-year newlyweds at leading Japanese companies have found a consistent ratio of 8:2 in favor of non-arranged marriages in recent years. For what it is worth, the same surveys have found the average groom to be 27 years old and the average bride 24.

● **The Wedding Industry**

When everything is taken into account—including the wedding,* the honeymoon, the costs of moving into a new apartment, and everything else—getting married costs ¥5-6 million on average in Japan. If this seems expensive, it is because increasing numbers of people are having lavish receptions at big hotels and honeymooning in Hawaii, Guam, or some other overseas resort. As a result, the people who provide the wedding halls, clothes rental agencies, travel agents, and assorted other purveyors catering to newlyweds have flourished. Another thriving addition to the wedding industry recently has been companies which sign up young singles and then try to computer-match them with the perfect partner.

12 死の儀式

日本には国教と言えるような特定の宗教がないので，故人の宗教やその遺志などによって，葬儀・告別式の方法も仏式，神式，キリスト教式，無宗教式といろいろある。身内に不幸があった場合，遺族の代表として死亡から葬儀までの中心となる喪主と，喪主や遺族に代わって実務的な仕事を取りしきる世話人とを決めるまでの段取りはすべて共通だが，その後の葬儀・告別式のやり方はそれぞれの方式によってだいぶ違ってくる。ここでは最も一般的な仏式を中心に紹介しておく。

●仏式の葬儀と告別式

キリスト教・新教の納棺式に当たるのが通夜で，死者を葬る前に家族・親戚（しんせき）・友人など，故人にゆかりの深い人々が夜通し棺の前で守る。祭壇は葬儀社に頼んで飾り付けるが，経験豊かで，「○○式」と告げるだけで，その方式どおりに最後まで式次第の世話をしてくれるのが，日本の葬儀社の特徴である。次に僧侶を呼んで読経してもらい，死者の死後の名前である戒名（*）を付けてもらう。その後，参列者が焼香（*）し，軽い酒食をとりながら故人をしのぶのがしきたりになっている。昔は遺体を寝かせたまま通夜を行い，その後に納棺したが，最近は衛生的配慮から，通夜の前に納棺を行うようになった。

死者を弔う葬儀と，死者に会葬者が最後の別れを告げる告別式は引き続き行われるのが普通だが，場合によっては遺族や近親者だけで葬儀を行い，一般会葬者は告別式にだけ参列するとか，公葬にするためにすぐ葬儀が行えないようなときには，死後2，3日以内に，取りあえず近親者だけで密葬を行い，後日，正式の葬儀，告別式を行うこともある。キリスト教の献花の代わりに，仏式では祭壇で合掌し，焼香して死者に別れを告げる。告別式の後，火葬場に行き火葬，骨上げを済ませ，遺骨とともに帰宅して翌日，埋葬（納骨）をする。墓地が正式に決まらない場合や，遠くてすぐに行けないような場合には，寺院の納骨堂にいったん遺骨を預け，後日，埋葬することもある。

●法要

キリスト教の場合，昇天記念日に礼拝や追悼ミサを行うように，仏式でも故人の死後，冥福（めいふく）を祈って読経する法要という行事がある。死後7日目の初七日，同様に四十九日，百か日。命日に行う一周忌，三回忌，七回忌などの年忌法要もある。盆や，春秋の彼岸にも墓参りをして，死者をしのび，供養する。

Funerals

Because there is no state religion in Japan, there are many different types of funeral services, including Buddhist, Shinto, Christian, and secular, depending upon the deceased's religion or last wishes. Most people handle the business of making funeral arrangements in much the same way—one family member is chosen as "chief mourner" and this person, sometime with help from outside the family, makes the arrangements—but the services themselves vary widely from family to family. Nonetheless, Buddhist rites are the most common in Japan.

● Buddhist Wakes and Funerals

Like many Christian and other funerals, Buddhist funerals include a wake at which family, relatives, and close friends mourn beside the coffin. Buddhist wakes begin with the preparation of the funeral altar by a professional mortician. Japanese undertakers have extensive experience with all manner of services, and one has only to specify the type to have everything taken care of from start to finish. Next, a Buddhist priest arrives to chant sutras and give the deceased a posthumous Buddhist name.* After the posthumous naming, it is customary for the people attending the wake to burn incense* before reminiscing about the deceased over a little food and drink. In the past, the body lay outside the coffin until the end of the wake, but it is now more common for the body to be encoffined before the wake.

Although the wake is usually followed directly by the funeral, in some cases the funeral is attended by close friends and family only and a separate memorial service is held for a wider group of mourners. At times, a small private funeral soon after the death may precede a large public funeral several days later. Instead of presenting flowers as is done in Japanese Christian funerals, Buddhist mourners pray before the funeral altar, burn incense, and pay their last respects to the deceased. After this, the mourners proceed to the crematorium for the cremation rites, including placing the deceased's ashes into a cinerary urn, and the mourners take the urn home with them to keep until the burial rites the next day. If no cemetery has been selected yet, or if it is too far away to reach right away, the urn may be kept at a local temple's cinerarium until it can be properly buried.

● Memorial Services

Just as Christians hold church services or memorial masses on the anniversary of a loved one's death, Buddhists also meet after the funeral to recite sutras and pray for the deceased's soul. In Japan, these services are held primarily on the seventh, forty-ninth, and one-hundredth days following the death and on the first, second, and sixth anniversaries. In addition, people visit family graves during the summer *bon* season and the spring and autumn *higan* seasons to remember the dead and to leave offerings of flowers, food, and drink.

13 正月・盆

●正月

日本人の1年の生活を区切る節目が，正月である。正月期間は，官庁も民間企業も学校も休みになって，国民こぞって新しい年の初めを祝う。正月は陰暦の第1月，つまり1月を指し，年頭に当たって家々の祖先の霊を迎えて，その年の実り豊かなことを祈願するのが本来の意味であった。しかし，一般的には1月1日から7日までの松の内を言い，その意味も単に新年を祝うというものに変わってきている。

正月準備は前年の暮れに始まり，各家庭では大掃除をして家の内外を清め，祖先を迎える門松を門前に立てたり，正月に食べる雑煮用のもちやおせち料理を用意したりで，主婦はてんてこ舞いになる。俗に民族大移動と言われる大移動が始まるのもこのころで，故郷へ帰る人，旅行に出る人で各交通機関は連日大混雑となる。旧年最後の大晦日（12月31日）の夜には，翌年も細く長く生きられますようにと，そばを食べて年を越すのが習わしである。

明けて1月1日から3日までの三が日，あるいは門松を取る7日までの松の内の間に，新年のさまざまな行事が行われる。最も正月行事らしいのが，「初もうで」と「年始回り」で，たいていの人が近くの神社や寺に参拝して1年の無事を祈り，親戚や職場の上司など，日ごろ世話になっている人々の家へ新年のあいさつをして歩く。ふだんは洋服が多い日本女性が髪を結い，着物で着飾って歩くのもこの正月期間である。書面で年始回りに代えるものとして発達した年賀状も，正月には欠かせないもので，もらった年賀状の多寡がその人の社会的地位を物語るような一面もある。子供たちの中には凧上げ，独楽回し，羽根つきなど昔からあった正月の遊びをして過ごす子もいる。正月の小遣いである「お年玉」をもらうのも，子供の大きな楽しみである。

●盆

正月に次いで，日本の年中行事の大きなピークとなっているのが盆で，釈迦の16弟子の1人が，7月15日に，地獄に落ちて苦しむ亡母をねんごろに供養して救ったという仏教説話に基づいて，7月13日から15日（地方によっては1か月遅れ）までの間，仏壇に供物を供えて，祖先の霊を祭る。盆には，広場に大きな櫓を組み，近所中集まって，笛や太鼓に合わせてみんなで踊る盆踊りが，各地で開かれる。

Shōgatsu and *Bon*

● *Shōgatsu*

For the Japanese, *shōgatsu* serves to punctuate life with an annual beginning and end. *Shōgatsu* is a time when government offices, private companies, schools, and everyone else takes a few days off to celebrate the arrival of a new year. The Japanese word for January, *Ichigatsu* (first moon), reflects *shōgatsu*'s original significance as the beginning of the lunar year, a time when families paid their respects to their ancestors and prayed for successful crops. Nowadays, however, the first week of January* is generally referred to as *shōgatsu* and is celebrated as simply the start of the new year.

Come late December and Japanese homes are abuzz with activity as housewives clean the house and garden, set traditional pine ornaments called *kado-matsu** outside the front door to welcome ancestral spirits, and prepare holiday foods such as *o-sechi-ryōri*, *zōni*,* and *mochi*. Just prior to the new year's arrival is the big urban exodus—a period of several days during which every transportation artery is clogged with people leaving the city to return to their ancestral village or to take a vacation trip. On New Year's Eve it is common to eat *soba* noodles to symbolize long lives and continuity across the years.

Many special events take place during the first week of the new year, and especially during the first three days. The two most typical are the first visit to a shrine or temple where people gather to pray for good fortune during the year ahead and the formal New Year's calls paid on relatives, company superiors, and anyone else to whom you have become indebted during the past year. It is also during this week that Japanese women, most of whom ordinarily wear Western clothing, take the trouble to put their hair up* and wear traditional kimono. New Year's calls have to some extent been replaced by *nengajō** (New Year's cards), an indispensable part of *shōgatsu* if only because receiving large numbers of *nengajō* is an indication of high social status. Children spend *shōgatsu* flying kites, spinning tops, playing Japanese battledore, and enjoying other traditional pastimes. Another treat for the children is *otoshidama*—small gifts of money from parents and relatives.

● *Bon*

After *shōgatsu*, the other big holiday of the year is *bon*, based on the Buddhist legend describing how on the 15th day of the seventh month one of Buddha's 16 disciples made a generous offering to save his mother from torment in hell. Today *bon* is observed between July 13 and 15 in Tokyo (and one month later in most other parts of Japan) by placing offerings on *butsudan* (small Buddhist altars) and by otherwise seeking to please the ancestral spirits. Communities all over Japan erect scaffolding in the squares for musicians playing flutes,* and drums* to accompany everyone in special *bon-odori** dances.

14 子供の年中行事

いずれも子供の無事な成長を祝う，日本の年中行事である。

●ひな祭り

ひな祭りは3月3日に行われる女の子の節句で，正しくは「桃の節句」と言う。女の子が将来いい伴侶に恵まれて幸わせな結婚ができますようにと，内裏びな，三人官女，五人ばやしなどのひな人形を段飾りに飾り，白酒や紅白のあられで祝う。いつまでも飾っておくと縁が遅れるという言い伝えから，3月3日を過ぎたらすぐしまい込むのがしきたりになっている。娘の嫁入り道具の1つとして，ひな人形一式を持たせる習わしも残っている。桃の節句が女の子の節句として広まったのは明治以降のことで，もともとは男女を問わず，子供たちが野外へ出て野遊びをする日であった。これに，桃の節句とは関係なく，平安時代の貴族の子女たちの間で楽しまれていたひな遊びとが江戸時代に結び付いて，しだいに女の子のお祝いになったと言われている。

●端午の節句

3月3日の桃の節句に対して，5月5日の端午の節句は男の子のお祝いである。この日はまた「こどもの日」として国民の祝日にもなっている。男の子のいる家庭ではよろい・かぶとなどの五月人形を飾り，屋外にこいのぼりを立てて，菖蒲やかしわもちで，その子の立身出世を祈る。この端午の節句も，古くは災厄を避けるために，菖蒲などの薬草や鳥獣を捕る薬猟の日だった。菖蒲は尚武(武事を尊ぶこと)に通じることから，室町時代から，紙製のかぶとに菖蒲の花を飾るようになり，江戸時代になって，武者人形やこいのぼりが現れた。広く定着したのは，やはり明治に入ってからのことである。

●七五三

七五三は，数え年3歳と5歳の男児，3歳と7歳の女児に，晴着を着せて宮参りをする祝いで，11月15日に行われる。江戸時代の武家社会のしきたりが一般化したもので，当時，武家の子女は3歳で男女とも初めて髪を伸ばす「髪置きの儀」を行い，その後，男児は5歳になると初めて袴を履く「袴着の儀」，女児は7歳で初めて，それまでのひもを解いて本式の帯を用いる「帯解きの儀」を行った。

どの祝いも，メーカーやデパートの商魂にあおられて，年々華美になってきており，こうした風潮に対する批判も一部にはあるが，子供たちの成長を祈る親心のほうが勝っていると言えよう。

Children's Festivals

Hina Matsuri, *Tango no Sekku*,* and *Shichi-go-san* are all annual events celebrating children and praying for their sound development.

● *Hina Matsuri*

Celebrated on March 3, *Hina Matsuri* (Doll Festival), formally known as *Momo no Sekku* (Peach Festival), is for girls. It is a time when girls pray for a good marriage, set out tiered platforms decorated with *hina-ningyō** (*hina* dolls usually including emperor and empress, three court ladies, and five musicians), and enjoy treats such as *shiro-zake* (sweet sake with rice malt) and red and white candies. Leaving the *hina* dolls out too long is said to delay marriage, and it is customary to put them away soon after March 3. Traditionally, the *hina* doll collection has been part of a new bride's dowry. *Momo no Sekku*'s popularization as *Hina Matsuri* occurred only since the Meiji period; earlier it had been a picnic festival for both boys and girls. The Doll Festival has its roots in the ceremonies and rituals involving dolls performed by the daughters of the Heian nobility, and it was only later, during the Edo period, that these dolls came back into fashion and gradually evolved into a Girl's Day tradition connected with *Momo no Sekku*.

● *Tango no Sekku*

May 5 is a day for boys. Long the *Tango no Sekku*, it has been officially renamed Children's Day and made a national holiday. Families with sons buy armored* samurai dolls and miniature helmets,* hang out *koi-nobori*,* buy irises and *kashiwa-mochi*,* and pray for their sons' success in life. *Tango no Sekku* used to be a day for hunting game and gathering medicinal herbs, such as iris leaves. *Shōbu* in Japanese, the iris has a homonym meaning "military spirit," from whence came the Muromachi custom of decorating paper helmets with iris leaves. Samurai dolls and *koi-nobori* first appeared in the Edo period, but it was not until the Meiji period that these customs became popular nationwide.

● *Shichi-go-san*

Literally, 7-5-3, this celebration falls on November 15 and is a time for boys who have reached their third or fifth birthday* and girls who have reached their third or seventh to dress up and pay their respects at the local shrine. A popularization of various rituals observed by the Edo-period samurai class, *Shichi-go-san* originally included various rites of passage: boys and girls aged three were permitted to begin growing their hair long, boys aged five could start wearing *hakama* (a divided skirt worn by men), and girls aged seven were given *obi* instead of rope to tie their kimono.

As doll manufactures, department stores, and other merchants vie for profits, these celebrations are becoming more lavish every year, and some people now say they should be abandoned or at least purged of this ostentation. Yet the festivities are likely to continue as outlets for parental affection and the desire to see their children succeed.

15 七夕・クリスマス

もともとは伝統的な祭りではないが，商魂たくましいデパートや商店街の巧みな客寄せ作戦に使われ，すっかりお祭り化した行事に，七夕とクリスマスがある。

●七夕

七夕は奈良時代に中国から渡って来た星祭りの1つで，天の川を隔てて向かい合っている牽牛星と織女星が，陰暦の7月7日に，年に一度の逢瀬を楽しむという「牽牛織女」の伝説に基づいている。この日，中国では織女星を祭って，女性が裁縫の上達を祈る風習があったことから，日本でも五色の短冊に願い事を書き，色紙や折りづるなどといっしょに庭に飾った笹竹につるして，習字や手芸などの上達を祈ることが行われるようになった。

織女星を日本では「棚機津女」と言ったため，陰暦の7月7日と，その日に行われる行事を「七夕」と総称するようになったものだが，地方によっては太陽暦の7月7日や，1か月遅れの8月7日ごろに行うところもある。

いずれにしても七夕は，家庭や，子供を教育する，昔で言えば寺子屋のようなところで，こぢんまりと行われた夏の風物詩だった。それが，いつのころからか下火になり，その代わりに盛んになったのが，商店街の七夕である。大きな飾り玉や，人気者の人形などを軒並みにつるし，お祭りムードを盛り上げて客足を呼ぼうというわけである。宮城県仙台市や神奈川県平塚市の七夕はそのはでさで全国的に有名で，観光の目玉の1つにさえなっているほどである。

●クリスマス

キリストの降誕を祝うクリスマスも，本来，キリスト教国でない日本では無縁のものだったが，これも，デパートなどが商戦の一環として宣伝に努めたため，今ではすっかり日本人に定着した行事となっている。さすがにクリスマス休暇はないが，イブには小さなツリーを飾り，みんなでケーキを食べたりプレゼントを贈ったりすることが，多くの家庭で行われる。各デパートでは，12月に入ると，大小さまざまのツリーを店内に飾り付け，このときが稼ぎ時とばかり，「クリスマス・ギフト・セール」と銘打って，華々しい客取り合戦を展開する。

2月14日のバレンタインデーも年ごとに盛んになっているが，その行事が持っている宗教的な意味合いとは全く無関係に行われているところが，いかにも特定の宗教がない日本らしい。

Tanabata and Christmas

Although not traditional festive occasions in Japan, Tanabata and Christmas have both recently been seized upon by department stores and other merchants and developed into major commercial attractions.

● Tanabata

The Tanabata Festival came to Japan from China during the Nara period and is based on the folk legend of the Cowherd Star (Altair) and the Weaver Star (Vega), two lovers whose celestial paths cross but once a year—on the seventh day of the seventh month of the lunar calendar. In ancient China, Tanabata was a time when women prayed to the Weaver Star for sewing skills, and this custom was transformed in Japan into one in which prayers for academic proficiency and such cultural arts as *shūji** are written on multicolored streamers of paper* attached to bamboo poles along with origami cranes and other decorations for display in the family garden.

The Japanese name Tanabata, written with the characters for "seven" and "evening," is a phonetic writing of *Tanabatatsume*—the Japanese pronunciation of the Chinese characters for "the Woman Weaver"—and reflects the timing of the festival on the seventh day of the seventh month. For most Japanese, this day is July 7 on the Julian calendar, although in some areas Tanabata is still observed on August 7 in keeping with the older traditions.

In either case, Tanabata used to be a time when people gathered at home or at *terakoya* schools to enjoy a warm midsummer evening. This custom eventually yielded to the lavish, commercialized Tanabata Festivals held in shopping districts. Festival sponsors draw crowds of potential customers with parades of oversized prayer poles, dolls resembling popular singers and actors, and other displays conducive to a festive mood. The Tanabata Festivals held in Sendai and Hiratsuka have won national fame for their gaudiness, and they attract tourists from far and wide.

● Christmas

The religious celebration of the birth of Jesus was observed by almost no one in this non-Christian nation until merchants saw it as a sales opportunity, and Christmas celebrations are now quite popular among Japanese. Christmas is not an official holiday in Japan, but most families observe the day by gathering on Christmas Eve to decorate a small Christmas tree, eat decorated cakes, and exchange presents. In early December, department stores begin decorating their floors with ornament-laden Christmas trees while vying to attract shoppers with advertisements for special Christmas sales.

St. Valentine's Day is another celebration that has become very popular in Japan in a form absolutely devoid of any religious connotations—a twist which is only natural in this secular nation.

16 日本の祭り

日本ほど祭りの多い国も珍しい。各地に根付いた伝統的な祭りから，近年，民間で始められた「浴衣祭り」や「温泉祭り」まで，多彩な祭りがあって，毎日，日本のどこかで祭りが行われていると言っても言いすぎではない。

もともと日本の祭りは，農耕儀礼に由来する農村の春の豊作祈願祭や秋の収穫祭が中心で，その後これに，悪霊，疫病を払うための都市の夏祭りが加わった。いずれも神々をもてなして，祭りの担い手である，その土地の居住者の繁栄と結束を願うものだったが，江戸時代以降，しだいに形骸化し，祭りは日々の暮らしに区切りをつける一種のレクリエーションとなった。昭和，とりわけ戦後に入ってからはその意味合いさえ薄れて，すっかり観光化した祭りも少なくない。数ある祭りの中から有名なものをいくつか紹介すると——

- **青森・ねぶた祭り**　8月1日の夜から7日にかけて行われる青森の夏の風物詩。木や竹の骨組みに紙を張り，これに『三国志』の英雄や加藤清正のトラ退治などの勇壮な絵を書いて作った，縦横数メートルの灯籠が，何台も町々を練り歩き，最後にその灯籠を海に渡して祭りは終わる。「ねぶた流し」と言って，眠けを払って，祖先の霊を慰める盆を迎えるための祭りである。
- **東京・三社祭り**　江戸の町に夏の到来を告げた浅草神社の例祭。5月中旬の土曜と日曜，町内から数10体のみこしが繰り出し，びんざさらと呼ばれる古い楽器を鳴らしてにぎやかに踊る「びんざさら舞い」という珍しい舞いが奉納される。下町情趣あふれる庶民の祭りだ。
- **京都・祇園祭り**　京都には，「賀茂の競馬」や「葵祭り」など，古都ならではのみやびやかな祭りが多いが，最も豪華なのが；7月1日から1か月間も行われる「祇園祭り」だ。なかでも15，16日の宵山は圧巻で，散在する鉾から祇園ばやしの鉦の音が流れ，鉾町一帯は不夜城となる。
- **福岡・博多どんたく**　5月3，4日に行われる民間の港祭り。しゃもじを叩きながら歌う博多松ばやしや，仮装行列で，全市が一大歓楽境と化す。

こうした各地の代表的な祭りを一同に会して，毎夏，東京では「日本の祭り」という催し物が行われ，東京に住む人や外国人観光客などでたいへんにぎわう。

Japanese Festivals

Japan is a land of festivals. Not only are there numerous festivals based on age-old traditions, there are also many newer theme festivals such as *yukata** festivals, and hardly a day passes without some sort of festival somewhere.

Japanese festivals originally centered on agrarian rituals such as spring prayers for bountiful rice crops and autumn harvest celebrations. These were later joined by the urban summer festivals for driving away evil spirits and plagues. All of these festivals were intended to placate the gods and ensure the community's continuing solidarity and prosperity, and it was not until the Edo period that festivals began to be popularized as diversions from everyday life. In recent decades, and especially since the end of the war, festivals have grown even more devoid of meaning, and many now exist mainly as tourist attractions.

• **Nebuta Festival*** **(Aomori)** This celebration of summer takes place from the evening of August 1 through August 7. Enormous floats depicting famous warrior-heroes from ancient China* or Japan's famous samurai such as Kato Kiyomasa*are lit from within so that they glow as they are paraded throughout the city and, at the end of the festival, set adrift on the sea. This closing ceremony, called *nebuta-nagashi*, symbolizes the dispelling of sleep in order to usher in the *bon* season when ancestral spirits are welcomed and entertained.

• **Sanja Matsuri*** **(Tokyo)** This festival began as a parade to herald the arrival of summer. Every year on a mid-May weekend, scores of *mikoshi** are carried through the streets to Asakusa Shrine, accompanied by *binzasara** percussion instruments which set the beat for a wild dance called *Binzasara no Mai*. Held in the traditionally working-class *shitamachi* part of Tokyo, the Sanja Matsuri has a very plebeian mood.

• **Gion Festival*** **(Kyoto)** Kyoto, the nation's capital for many centuries, hosts a large number of traditional festivals, among them the Kamo no Kurabeuma*and the Aoi Matsuri,*but grandest of them all is the Gion Festival which begins on July 1 and lasts throughout the month. The highlight of the Gion Festival is on July 15 and 16, when floats with *gion-bayashi* musicians playing bells and other instruments light up the nighttime streets.

• **Hakata Dontaku*** **(Fukuoka)** The Hakata Dontaku festival is held in Fukuoka on May 3 and 4 every year. Featuring singers beating rice paddles* as well as a procession of numerous people wearing colorful costumes, Hakata Dontaku makes the whole city of Fukuoka come alive with merriment.

While these festivals are rooted in local customs, representatives from all of the major festivals come together each summer in a Tokyo "Festivals of Japan" exhibition delighting residents and visitors alike.

17 消費生活

●消費のしかた

アメリカの主婦は，食料や日用雑貨などは1週間に1度ぐらい車でスーパーなどに出かけて，まとめ買いするのが一般的なようだが，日本では，買い物は主婦の大事な日課である。たいがい，毎日夕方4時，5時ごろに近所のスーパーや肉屋，魚屋，八百屋に出かけて，その日の夕食分と翌日分ぐらいをこまめに買う。日本では魚，野菜類を多くとる食生活が長かったため，鮮度をとても大切にしてきた。そうした習慣から，多少めんどうでも，なるべく新鮮なものを求めて，毎日買い物をするのである。

その代わり，衣類や日用品など鮮度に関係のないものについては，日本の主婦もまとめ買いをする。それも安い時を見計らって買う。デパートやスーパーのバーゲンセール会場の光景は，おそらく日本独得のものだろう。安売りがあると，日本の主婦は開店前から店の入り口で行列を作る。店が開くと我先にと売場に殺倒し，少しでも安くていいものを買おうとして会場のあちこちで小競り合いを演じる。その熱気たるや，とても世の亭主族の及ぶところではない。一家のさいふを預かる日本の主婦にとっては，普段着とか雑貨などはなるべく安く上げるのが，やりくりの腕の見せどころなのである。

金額の張るものや耐久消費財などを買うときは，ローンが利用される。アメリカには及ばないものの，日本も今「クレジット時代」と言われ，若い女性がローンを利用して毛皮のコートを買ったり，気軽に海外旅行へ出かけたりしている。

●消費傾向の変化

かつては衣食住が消費の中心だったが，今では衣食住以外の，いわゆる選択的支出が消費の過半数を占めるに至っており，このような傾向は今後ますます強まるだろうことが予測されている。経済企画庁では，2000年の消費生活がどのようになるかを展望している。それによると，高齢化社会の到来，自由時間の増大，女性の社会進出，消費者自身の価値観の多様化などの社会・経済的変化によって，医療サービス，個人年金，老人ホームなどの分野や，教育，文化，健康産業，託児所，家事代替業などが，それぞれ消費拡大するだろうとされている。物もサービスもますます多様化し，それとあいまって，各人の消費生活自体もより個性化していくと言えそうだ。

The Japanese Consumer

● Shopping

Unlike the typical American housewife, who drives to the supermarket about once a week for food and other supplies, the typical Japanese housewife goes shopping nearly every day. Most Japanese shoppers step out around four or five in the afternoon to go to the supermarket or the local meat, fish, and produce shops, buying just enough for that night's dinner and the morrow's breakfast and lunch. The Japanese table has traditionally included a large variety of fish and vegetables, and freshness is very important. Troublesome though it is, Japanese housewives still shop daily to get their food at its freshest.

When freshness is not a factor, as with clothing and other everyday articles, Japanese try to stock up when things are on sale. And, of course, they take advantage of seasonal clearance sales. In fact, Japanese women flock to department-store and supermarket sales with a fervor that is probably unmatched anywhere else in the world. Stores holding big sales often have lines of eager customers waiting at their doors well before opening time. Once the door is open, the shoppers scramble to snap up even the smallest bargain, and there are inevitably a number of minor skirmishes. It is difficult for men to comprehend the intensity that women bring to these events. Taking their budgetary responsibilities seriously, Japanese housewives recognize bargain sales as opportunities to prove their budget-stretching skills by getting everyday items at the lowest possible prices.

Japanese consumers use loans for time payments and durable goods. Although not as card-using as Americans, many young Japanese women use their credit cards quite casually to buy fur coats or pay for vacations abroad.

● Changing Consumer Trends

The Japanese household budget has traditionally focused on food, shelter, clothing, and other basic necessities, but non-essentials have recently come to account for more than half of all consumer spending. This trend is expected to continue. An Economic Planning Agency report on Japan's consumer trends predicts that social and economic changes as a result of the graying of the population, more leisure time available, the social advances achieved by women, and more diversified and individualized consumer preferences will mean expanded spending for medical services, private pensions, retirement facilities, social and educational services, day-care centers, and household help by the year 2000. In sum, there will be a greater variety of goods and services, and Japanese consumers will become even more individualistic in their preferences.

18 贈答

日本人は贈り物が好きな国民だとよく言われる。結婚祝いや誕生祝いといった他の国にもある贈り物はもちろん，ちょっとした訪問にも手土産を持参して，敬意や好意を表わすというのが，日本的な習慣になっている。かつてレーガン政権の国家安全保障担当補佐官だったR.アレン氏が，日本の出版社から取材の謝礼として，1000ドルの現金小切手と腕時計を受け取っていたことを申告し忘れて，辞任する騒ぎがあった。日本では，取材の際に若干の金品を贈ることは珍しくないが，アメリカでは，政府の高官，補佐官などは，いかなるプレゼントも黙って受け取ることは禁じられている。アレン事件は，そうした贈り物に対する日米の習慣の違いを象徴するものと言えるだろう。

●中元・歳暮

さまざまな贈り物の中でもきわめて日本的なものが，中元，歳暮である。中元は暑中見舞いを兼ねて6，7月ごろに，歳暮は1年の感謝を込めて年末に，ともに，日ごろ世話になっている人たちに贈る季節の贈答で，ひところ近代的な合理主義者から，「虚礼廃止」といった批判があったにもかかわらず，個人どうしでも企業間でも，相変わらず盛んに行われている。デパートの商戦も年々激しくなり，最近では自宅やオフィスから電話で注文できる「ファクシミリ・オーダー」や，指定の日時に届く「アポイント便ギフト」など，新しいサービスで勝負するデパートが増えてきた。

●その他の贈答

引っ越しそばも欧米にはない習慣で，引っ越し先の近所にそばを配りながら，自己紹介と「今後よろしく」というあいさつをして回る。そばの代わりに手ぬぐいとか菓子を配ることもある。

そのほか子供の七五三，入学，進学，成人式，会社関係者の栄転祝い，病気の治癒を祝う快気祝いなど，実に多様な贈り物があり，家計を預かる主婦にとって，交際費捻出（ねんしゅつ）は頭の痛い問題になっている。そんな主婦の苦労を見込んで登場したのが，「贈答品買い取り業」。同じような品物が集まって，家庭で使われもせず山積みになっている頂き物を安く買い取り，それをまた安く売るというもので，主婦の間で重宝がられている。

一見，実に非合理的に見えるこうしたやり取りの中に，合理主義では割り切れない人間関係の機微を求める日本的贈答習慣のエッセンスがある。

Gift-giving

Japanese love to give gifts. While it is common in all countries to give gifts for birthdays, weddings, and other special occasions, in Japan people paying even a casual visit often bring a gift as a token of respect or affection for the host. A few years ago, Richard Allen, then President Reagan's National Security Advisor, had to resign because he had failed to report a $ 1,000 check and a watch given him by a Japanese publishing company in gratitude for his granting them an interview. In Japan, it is not at all unusual to give gifts to people who consent to interviews and otherwise provide information, but in the United States government officials at all levels are required to report any gifts they may receive. As such, the Allen incident illustrates how much Japanese and American gift-giving customs differ.

● ***Chūgen* and *Seibo***

Most typical of Japan's many customary gifts are the *chūgen* and *seibo* gifts. The *chūgen* (mid-year) gift often serves in lieu of the greeting in the hot summer months to inquire after the health and well-being of friends and work associates, and the *seibo* (year-end) gift stems from the custom of giving someone a gift as a token of gratitude for everything he has done for you during the past year. Despite the efforts of modern-minded critics to do away with such "empty formalities," seasonal gifts are still regularly exchanged among individuals and among companies. For their part, department stores are contriving ever-more ingenious ways of promoting gift-giving, including such new services as accepting gift orders by facsimile and delivering gifts on a specified date and hour.

● **Other Gift-giving**

Hikkoshi-soba (moving-in noodles) is another uniquely Japanese custom by which someone who has just moved into a new neighborhood goes from door to door handing out *soba* noodles as gifts to the new neighbors while at the same time introducing himself and generally expressing the hope that they will become good neighbors. Sometimes people give small towels* or sweets instead of *soba*.

A large variety of gifts are given on a number of happy occasions, such personal milestones as the 7-5-3 festival, starting or graduating from school, becoming an adult, getting a promotion at work, and recovering from an illness; and it is a real headache for many housewives to find money in the household budget for all of these gifts. However, a new business has appeared in response to this problem—used-gift companies who buy up piles of unopened and unwanted gifts at low prices and resell them at a discount—a service that has been welcomed by budget-beleaguered housewives.

Gift-giving, like many other typically Japanese customs, seems quite illogical on the surface, yet somehow it makes sense in the context of human relations which themselves defy logical explanation.

19 新聞

日本は新聞王国と言える。全国紙，地方紙約165社が，毎日(朝・夕刊合わせて)5000万部近い新聞を発行している。これは人口の2人に1紙という普及率で，ソ連，アメリカ，イギリスなどの3人に1人の普及率をしのぎ，世界一新聞の好きな国民であることを示している。

●新聞の歴史と信頼度

日本には100年以上の歴史を持つ新聞社が少なくない。こうした新聞社は，日本が近世(江戸時代)から近代(明治)に突入した時代，自由民権運動という言論自由化の中から生まれ，世論(オピニオン・リーダー)として高い社会的信用を得ている。「新聞は社会の木鐸(ぼくたく)」という言葉がまだ生きているし，期待されてもいる。アメリカの調査では，新聞を信頼すべき情報源と思っていない人，テレビにより信頼を置く人が増えているが，日本では今のところ，新聞の優位性は失われていない。しかし，高い信用ゆえに権力主義に陥りやすく，政治権力に抱き込まれやすい欠点を持っていることを，日本の賢い読者たちは過去の歴史から学んでおり，数紙を購読して読み比べたり，購読紙を変更したり，一種の牽制(けんせい)を働かせている面がある。したがって，各社の発行部数は常に流動的である。

●新聞の発行部数と現状

最大発行部数の新聞社は，1874年設立の読売新聞(従業員7700人)で，毎日1350万部を発行している。これは1社としては世界最大の発行部数で，共産圏のソ連の『プラウダ』(1000万部)，中国の『人民日報』(700万部)をもしのぎ，自由主義国の民営商業紙としては驚異的な数字である。アメリカ最大の発行部数は，『ウォール・ストリート・ジャーナル』の192万部，『ニューヨーク・デイリー・ニュース』の150万部。また，イギリスでは『ザ・サン』385万部，というところだが，日本には『読売新聞』以外にも『朝日新聞』(従業員8500人)1200万部，『毎日新聞』(同5600人) 650万部，『サンケイ新聞』『日本経済新聞』などがあり，これら全国五大紙が圧倒的に強いのが特徴である。アメリカには1756社もの多数の地方紙があって，ローカルニュースを前面にした新聞作りが伝統だったが，『ニューヨーク・タイムス』や『ウォール・ストリート・ジャーナル』などが全国紙への進出作戦を開始しているなど，日本とはおおいに事情を異にしている。

Newspapers

Japan can be called a land of newspapers. There are about 165 national and local newspaper companies in Japan, printing a total of almost 50 million copies a day (including morning and evening editions). This means that roughly half the Japanese population buys a newspaper every day—compared to 1/3 in the Soviet Union, the United States, and Britain—making the Japanese by far the world's most avid newspaper readers.

● History and Credibility

There are a number of Japanese newspapers that go back over 100 years. Established during the free-speech reforms made as part of Japan's Freedom and People's Rights Movement following the downfall of the feudal system and the rise of the Meiji government, these newspapers gained the public's trust and developed into opinion leaders. Even today, Japanese still expect newspapers to act as the national conscience.* While U.S. surveys have shown that increasing numbers of people trust television more than newspapers as a source of information, newspapers are still the most-trusted medium in Japan. However, the Japanese have learned from history that newspapers can easily abuse this trust and slip into authoritarianism or political intrigue. Thus many people subscribe back and forth among several papers for comparison and to maintain perspective. A check on the press, this also causes considerable fluctuation in circulations.

● Circulation

Yomiuri Shinbun, established in 1874 and employing 7,700 people, has a daily circulation of 13,500,000. This makes the *Yomiuri* far and away the most widely read newspaper in the world, surpassing even socialist papers such as *Pravda* in the Soviet Union (10,000,000) and the *People's Daily* in China (7,000,000)—a remarkable achievement for a privately owned newspaper in a democracy. The best-selling newspaper in the United States is the *Wall Street Journal* (1,920,000) followed by the *New York Daily News* (1,500,000). In Britain, it is *The Sun* (3,850,000). Yet these figures pale in comparison with not only the *Yomiuri* but also other leading daily Japanese newspapers such as *Asahi Shinbun* (8,500 employees and 12,000,000 circulation), *Mainichi Shinbun* (5,600 employees and 6,500,000 circulation), and others such as *Sankei Shinbun* and *Nihon Keizai Shinbun*. These five leading newspapers together dominate the Japanese newspaper industry. By contrast, the United States has a far greater diversity of coverage in its 1,756 newspapers, most of which are local newspapers devoted mainly to local news. Although some newspapers such as the *New York Times* and the *Wall Street Journal* have been trying to establish themselves as national newspapers, the situation remains quite different from that in Japan.

20 テレビ・ラジオ

●高い普及率と視聴率

日本でテレビ局が開設され，放送が開始されたのは1950年代のことである。以来急速に各家庭にテレビが普及し，現在では普及率は99%になっている。また一家で２台，３台のテレビを持つ家庭も増えている。

ＮＨＫが調べた「国民生活時間調査」(1980年)によると，国民１人がマスコミと接触している時間は，１日(平日)４時間32分。そのうち断然長いのがテレビで，日本人は１日３時間はテレビを見ている。次いでラジオ(30分)，新聞(15分)の順である。

ラジオも普及率93%でやはり根強い人気がある。特に若者はラジオが好きで，ラジオの深夜ＤＪ，ＦＭの音楽番組が好まれている。

●多くの局

日本のテレビ・ラジオ局には，カナダやイギリスのように受信料で経営する公共放送局(ＮＨＫ)があり，全国に同じプログラムを流している。ほかはすべて受信料なしの民間テレビ局で，１県に２～５局，全国では約100局のＶＨＦ局がある。それらのほとんどがラジオ局をも併設している。ＵＨＦ局もほぼ１県１局の割合で作られつつあり，現在約20局となっている。

東京には，日本テレビ(読売新聞社系)，ＴＢＳテレビ(毎日新聞社系)，フジテレビ(サンケイ新聞社系)，テレビ朝日(朝日新聞社系)，それにテレビ東京(日本経済新聞社系)のキー局があり，全国の地方テレビ局と系列配信をしている。

●多彩な番組

テレビは，各局とも朝６時から深夜まで１日中放送している。放送内容はニュースなどの報道，ドラマ・歌・クイズなどの娯楽，学校放送・美術などの教養から成っていて，民放各局では娯楽に力を入れている。朝のニュースとスタジオトークショー，昼のニュースとメロドラマ，夕のニュースと子供向けのアニメーションなどは，各局がほぼ同じように流し，深夜には映画とかポルノっぽいものが目につく。

ＮＨＫの教育テレビは小学校から大学までの教育，成人(社会)教育を補充する幅広い番組を制作し，１日中放送している。この番組の中では語学講座に人気があり，英・独・仏・露・中国語などのほか，最近韓国語も加わった。

Radio and Television

● Popularization

Japan's first television stations were started in the 1950s. Television quickly found its way into nearly every home, and the diffusion rate is now 99%, including a number of 2- or 3-set homes.

A 1980 NHK report on how people spend their time found that the average person spent four hours and 32 minutes a day (on weekdays) in contact with some form of mass media. Most of this time is spent in front of the TV—the average daily viewing time being about three hours. The average person also spent 30 minutes a day listening to the radio and 15 minutes reading the newspaper.

An abidingly popular medium, radios can be found in 93% of Japanese homes. Young people are particularly avid listeners, and there are numerous FM music programs and late-night disc jockey programs catering to the youth audience.

● Many Stations

Like Canada and the United Kingdom, Japan has a national network (NHK) financed by viewer levies and providing uniform programming throughout the country. In addition, there are private broadcasters which do not receive any public money. With stations in every prefecture, there are over 100 VHF stations, many of them affiliated with local radio stations. This VHF coverage is now being supplemented with new UHF stations being licenced one to a prefecture, with about a score already in operation.

In Tokyo, viewers have a choice of NHK's general-programming channel 1, NHK's educational channel 3, Nihon Television (4, affiliated with the Yomiuri Shinbun), Tokyo Broadcasting (6, Mainichi Shinbun), Fuji Television (8, Sankei Shinbun), Television Asahi (10, Asahi Shinbun), and Television Tokyo (12, Nihon Keizai Shinbun), all of which are the flagship stations for nationwide networks.

● Richly Varied Programming

All of the stations start at 6:00 a.m. and run until the wee hours of the morning (except NHK, which signs off at midnight), providing a wide variety of news and information; dramas, songs, quiz programs, and other entertainment; and educational and other cultural programs —although the private networks tend to stress entertainment. The typical day sees news and talk shows in the morning, news at noon, early-afternoon soaps, late-afternoon children's programs, more news, and then prime-time entertainment. Late-night shows tend to old movies and soft-core pornography.

NHK's educational network offers a full curriculum of programs throughout the day for students at the elementary through university levels as well as general adult-level educational programming. Foreign-language courses—in English, German, French, Russian, Chinese, and, recently, Korean—are also very popular.

21 出版

●出版王国

出版統計の取り方は世界各国まちまちだから正確な比較は困難だが，日本が有数の出版王国であることはまずまちがいない。ユネスコの統計によると，自由世界の中で出版点数の最も多いのはアメリカで約7万7000点，以下西ドイツ5万9000点，イギリス4万3000点，日本4万2000点，フランス3万7000点の順になっている。

英語やスペイン語のようなグローバルな言語ではないが，それを使う人が小さな島国に1億2000万人も住んでいる。しかもその民度は高く，知的活力に満ちており，高校進学率は約94％と高い。したがって出版産業にとっては非常に恵まれた肥沃（ひよく）なマーケットである。特に戦後の大衆社会化現象の過程で，出版産業は急速に膨張した。

●本好きな日本人

日本人は通学や通勤の電車の中でよく本や雑誌を読む。もちろん諸外国でも似たような光景は見られるが，日本の場合はその傾向が特に強い。文庫（※）本とか新書（※）判と言われる小さなサイズのペーパーバックスに人気があるのは，その車中読書という習慣と密接につながっている。もちろん価格が安いということは言うまでもないが……。

そうした日本人はいったいどのくらいの本や雑誌を読むのか。1年間の本の推定発行部数は約5億冊，月刊誌は約21億冊，週刊誌は約14億冊，つまり大ざっぱに言って，人口1人当たり1年間に4冊の本を読み，30冊の雑誌を読んでいる勘定になる。ただし学校教育における教科書は含まれていない。そして，本と雑誌を合わせた販売額は約1兆6000億円に達している。つまり1人当たり年間1万円余りを本や雑誌のために支出していることになる。その1兆6000億円産業を支えている出版社の数は約3000社に上る。社員が1000人を超す大出版社から1人の零細出版社まで企業規模の格差は大きい。

メガネをかけた日本人というイメージは，日本人の本好きを象徴している。それは近代以前は中国の書物から，近代以降は欧米の書物から貪欲（どんよく）に知識を取り入れてきた歴史によるものと言えるかもしれない。今日も翻訳出版は盛んで，年間3000点（児童書・学習参考書を除く）に上っている。その半分近くが文学書だというところに，洋風化した日本人の生活ぶりをうかがうこともできるだろう。そして出版物の輸出入は輸出が260億円，輸入が301億円で，近年輸出が着実に伸びている。

Publishing

● Publishing Power

Although the different statistical methodologies make any exact international comparison impossible, Japan is clearly one of the world's major powers in publishing. According to UNESCO figures, the United States is the Free World's top publisher with 77,000 titles yearly, West Germany is second with 59,000, Britain third with 43,000, Japan fourth with 42,000, and France fifth with 37,000.

While Japanese is not an international language like English or Spanish, there are over 120 million Japanese-language readers concentrated in Japan alone. What is better from a publisher's point of view, these people are affluent, curious about the world they live in, and well-educated (94% having had some high school education), making Japan a rich market. Little wonder publishing has flowered in the postwar era's mass-consumption culture.

● Book-loving People

Japanese often read on the train to and from work and school. Of course, this is also true of other peoples, but it seems to be even truer of Japanese, and such in-train reading accounts for much of the popularity of the pocket-sized *bunko-bon** and *shinsho ban* books* although the fact that they are inexpensively priced certainly does not hurt any.

It is estimated that there are about 500 million books, 2,100 million monthly magazines, and 1,400 million weekly magazines published in Japan every year. This works out to about four books and 30 magazines per person per year, not counting the many textbooks which students read in school. All together, publishing is a ¥1.6 trillion market in Japan. On a per-population basis, this means that the average Japanese spends over ¥10,000 a year on book and magazine reading alone. On the other side of this ¥1.6 trillion market are Japan's approximately 3,000 publishers—ranging from giant firms with over 1,000 employees to tiny one-man operations.

The international stereotype of the bespectacled Japanese attests to the Japanese love of reading. Some people have explained this as part of the Japanese appetite for foreign learning, first from China and more recently from the industrialized West. Even today, the publishing of translations is big business in Japan, and there are about 3,000 foreign titles translated every year (not counting children's stories and academic texts). It is indicative of the Westernization of Japanese lifestyles that about half of these are fiction. In international trade, publishing accounts for exports of ¥26 billion and imports of ¥30.1 billion, with the export figure rising steadily in recent years.

22 道路網

●車社会日本

日本は急速な車社会の時代を迎えている。日本の自家用乗用車保有台数は1965年に132万台であったものが，1984年には2403万台と，約18倍になった。全国的には公共交通の発達しなかった地域に急速な車社会化が見られ，１世帯に１台という県もある。

欧米では1920年代から自動車が普及し，道路も整備されていったが，日本で自動車が普及したのは戦後になってからである。しかし，その後の急成長ぶりは目覚ましい。特に，1950年代後半以降の高度経済成長時代に入ってから，貨物輸送が飛躍的に増大し，自動車工業の発達で性能のよい自動車が次々に生産されるようになり，鉄道の斜陽化もあって，自動車は陸上輸送の花形となった。

●急ピッチで進む道路整備

車社会になるとともに，道路への依存度が大きくなるのは当然であるが，日本の道路はまだ十分とは言えない。道路の総延長は112万kmであるが，舗装されているのは60%ほどである。しかし，道路整備は重要国策として取り組んでおり，舗装率は1945年にはわずか1.2%であったことから見ても着実に成果を上げてきていると言えよう。とりわけ，高速道路の建設はめざましく，急ピッチで進んでいて，現在は青森と鹿児島間のほとんどが結ばれている。

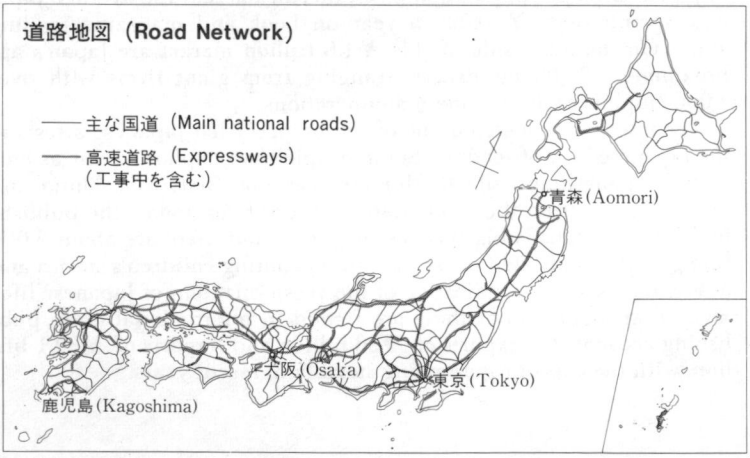

Roads

● Automotive Japan

In a relatively short time Japan has become an automotive society. In 1965 there were 1.32 million passenger cars, but by 1984 this number had gone up more than eighteenfold to 24.03 million. Regions with little public transportation have taken the lead in automobile ownership, and some prefectures average one car per household.

In the U.S. and Europe automobiles appeared on the roads in the 1920s, stimulating the construction of extensive highway networks. In Japan, the automobile did not come into common use until after the Second World War, but its dissemination was especially rapid in the years of fast-paced economic growth which began in the latter 1950s, when trucks became a major means of transporting goods. As a result, automobiles have come to dominate overland transport, the railroads slipping into decline as advances in automotive technology have led to more functional and more attractive vehicles.

● Road Construction

The phenomenal increase in automobile transport has made Japan's roads more important than ever. The present road network is far from sufficient. Though there are 1,120,000 kilometers of roads, only about 60% are paved. Road construction, paving, and maintenance are thus a primary concern for the national government, and, as evidenced by the fact that this 60% figure is up from only 1.2% in 1945, considerable progress has been made. A particularly strong effort has been made in expressway construction, and today most of the distance between Aomori and Kagoshima is linked by expressways.

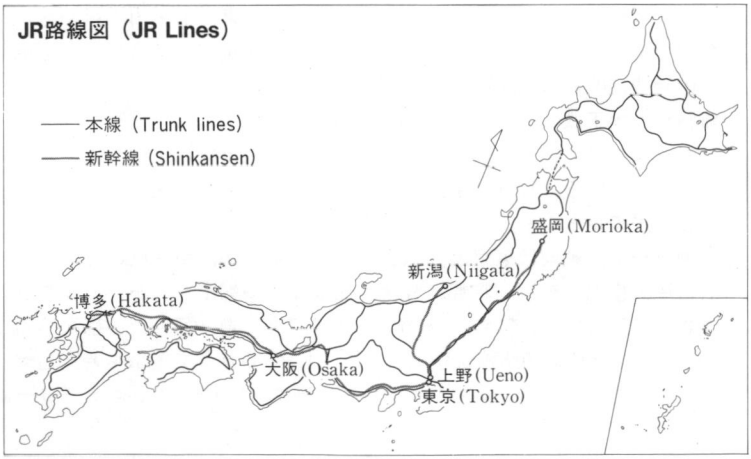

23 鉄道網

日本の鉄道網は，全国を結ぶＪＲ線（旧国鉄）と，大都市に発達した私鉄・地下鉄網から成っており，日本各地を旅行するのにはＪＲ線，大都市生活には私鉄・地下鉄が便利である。

現在，鉄道は２万6600㎞を営業しているが，この大部分を占めていた旧国鉄は，旅客・貨物とも自動車や飛行機に圧迫され，新幹線と大都市の一部の路線を除いて，ほとんどの路線が赤字となり，これまでに累積した赤字額は16兆円にも上った。このため国鉄は1987年４月に６ブロックに分割され，それぞれ民営鉄道として再スタートを切った。したがって，日本の鉄道は一部公営を除きほとんどが民営となった。

●新幹線

「夢の超特急」と呼ばれた新幹線は旧国鉄が開発したもので，1964年10月，営業時速210㎞で，東京―新大阪間を走りはじめた。国鉄の安全技術をフルに駆使した新幹線は，以来20年間日本の大動脈として成長し続けた。乗客の死傷事故は１度もなく，世界で最も安全な鉄道と言われている。現在の路線は，東京―新大阪間の東海道(552.6㎞)をはじめ，山陽(新大阪―博多間623.9㎞)，東北(東京―盛岡間535.3㎞)，上越(大宮―新潟間303.6㎞)に増えた。この20年間に新幹線が走った距離は，延べ地球を約２万周した計算になり，利用客も1984年春で20億人を超えている。

各線とも，各駅停車の特急，限定停車の超特急の２種類の列車が走り，「こだま」「ひかり」（東海道・山陽新幹線）など，それぞれ独特のニックネームがつけられている。1987年から，東海道・山陽新幹線の車両を全面的にモデルチェンジする方針で，実現すればスピードも現在の時速210㎞から230㎞にアップする。

●私鉄と地下鉄

私鉄は主に大都市と近郊都市を結び，また地下鉄は大都市内で縦横に発達している。私鉄は全国で4700㎞営業しており，運転本数も多く，都市住民の足となっている。

地下鉄は，戦前は東京と大阪にしかなかったが，現在はこのほかに名古屋，横浜，神戸，京都，札幌，福岡などの都市が加わり，営業キロ数は417㎞に上っている。とりわけ，1927年に走り始めた首都東京の地下鉄は，公私営10路線が縦横に走り，１日600万人を運ぶ主要交通機関となっている。その営業キロ数は総延長で，199㎞あり，ニューヨーク，ロンドン，パリに次いで世界第４位。

Rail Transport

Japan's rail system is comprised of the JR network (the post-privatized Japanese National Railways or JNR) with lines throughout the country and private railways and subways in the major urban areas. The JR is especially convenient for travel to or in outlying areas, while the private lines and subways are important commuting links in the cities.

The JR, which accounts for most of the 26,600km of track in Japan, has lost a large percentage of its passenger and freight custom to automobiles and airlines, and the only lines that are operating in the black are the shinkansen and certain urban lines. At the time it was privatized, the JNR was ¥16 trillion in the red. With privatization, the system has started over again, split up (into six regional passenger companies, plus a special company for the shinkansen and a number of service companies) and turned over to private management. As a result, there are few public-sector rail lines left in Japan.

● Shinkansen

Since the inauguration of service between Tokyo and Osaka in October 1964, the 210-kph shinkansen "dream express" service has been one of Japan's main transportation arteries. It is arguably the world's safest rail line, without a single major accident in more than 20 years.

Today, shinkansen service has expanded to include not only the 552.6-km Tokaido line between Tokyo and Osaka but also the 623.9-km Sanyo line between Osaka and Hakata, the 535.3-km Tohoku line between Tokyo and Morioka, and the 303.6-km Joetsu line between Omiya and Niigata. In their first 20 years, shinkansen trains served two billion passengers and collectively traveled far enough to circle the globe nearly 20,000 times.

Each line includes two types of trains—locals which stop at every station and expresses which stop only at the main stations—each distinctively named. On the Tokaido and Sanyo line, for example, the local is called the Kodama (echo) and the express the Hikari (light). The Tokaido and Sanyo lines are scheduled to get a completely new model of shinkansen train in 1987 which will have a cruising speed of 230km/h—or 20km/h faster than the present model.

● Private Lines and Subways

Numerous private rail lines link Japan's cities to their suburban satellites while the subways provide inner-city transportation. There are 4,700 km of private lines throughout the country with trains running at frequent intervals.

Before the war, only Tokyo and Osaka had subways, but today there are also subways in Nagoya, Yokohama, Kobe, Kyoto, Sapporo, and Fukuoka—with 417 kilometers of subway track in all. Tokyo's subway system, which went into operation in 1927, now consists of a total of 10 public and private lines carrying six million people per day. With 199 kilometers of subway track, Tokyo ranks fourth worldwide after New York, London, and Paris.

24 日本の治安

●治安優良大国日本

日本のように治安がよく安心して市民生活の営める国はほかにないのではないだろうか。海外に出たことのある日本人ならだれでもそう思うようだ。アメリカの都会のようにドアにいくつもの鍵(かぎ)をつけなくてもいいし，本物のピストルにお目にかかることも子供の誘拐を心配することもまずない。そして何より，日本の街は女性が夜でも１人歩きできる。これは日本の治安のよさを示すいちばんのバロメーターだ。ニューヨークの地下鉄に，深夜女性が乗ることなど考えられないが，日本の地下鉄では，深夜１人でも不安を感じることはない。

●低い犯罪発生率と高い検挙率

最近，犯罪の多発に悩んでいるアメリカなど諸外国の警察は，さかんに日本の警察の研究をしている。どうしたら日本の警察のようによい状態を維持できるのだろうか。実際，犯罪の認知件数ではアメリカが最も多く，1982年では1286万件，片や日本はその８分の１だった。また，10万人当たりの犯罪発生率は同年，アメリカ，イギリス，西ドイツ，フランスともに6000件前後だったのに対し，日本はその５分の１である。また，犯罪増加率(10年間)も他の先進国が1.5～２倍なのに，日本は1.2倍程度。さらに，日本の犯罪の検挙率は全体で60％で，この成績のよさはアメリカの３倍である。犯罪の中でも殺人，強盗，婦女暴行という凶悪犯はアメリカの100分の１ほどだし，それらの検挙率は殺人97.3％，強盗77.6％，婦女暴行88.7％でアメリカの1.5～４倍の好成績だ。

●派出所・駐在所制度

こうした数字が日本の治安のよさを物語っているが，この秘密は日本独特の「派出所・駐在所制度」にあるのではないかと，最近，アメリカやアジアの警察でまねをするところが出てきている。

「派出所，駐在所」は「署」と違い，街の角々に設けられ，そこを中心に警官が受け持ち区域を常にパトロールして回るシステムで，そこには住民の調査票があり，常に不審な動きを牽制(けんせい)している。また万が一事件が起きたときも，すぐに現場に駆けつけられるし，警戒網を瞬時に敷くこともできる。事件発生からの初動捜査の強みは，全国津々浦々に散在している派出所，駐在所なくては考えられない。ちなみに，派出所，駐在所は「交番」と呼ばれる。日本の交番は江戸時代から続いている日本の犯罪防止の知恵である。

Public Order in Japan

● A Safe Place to Live

Perhaps nowhere else in the world can city dwellers live as free from fear of crime as in Japan—that is the impression among Japanese who have traveled abroad. Unlike Americans, Japanese urbanites do not have to multi-lock their doors, worry about getting shot, or cringe at the thought that their children may be kidnapped. In fact, Japan's streets are safe enough for women to walk alone at night—an impressive indication of public peace and order. While few women would even think of riding a New York subway alone at night, unescorted women routinely board Japanese subways late at night without a second thought.

● Crime Low, Arrests High

Law enforcement officials from the United States and other high-crime countries have been studying the Japanese system in an attempt to discover the secret behind Japan's enviable record in public order. In 1982, the number of crimes reported in Japan was only 1/8 the American figure of 12.86 million. On a per-population basis, Japanese crime was only 1/5 the approximately 60 per thousand people in the United States, Britain, West Germany, and France. Likewise, crime rose by 20% in Japan as opposed to the 50-100% increase in the other industrialized nations. Japan's arrest rate is about 60%, roughly three times that in the United States. At the same time, there are only 1/100 as many serious crimes such as murder, robbery, and rape in Japan as there are in the United States, and the Japanese arrest rates are 97.3% for murder, 77.6% for robbery, and 88.7% for rape—in some categories four times higher than the comparable American figures.

● *Hashutsujo* and *Chūzaisho*

Much of the credit for these impressive statistics goes to such distinctively Japanese institutions as the *hashutsujo* (police box) and *chūzaisho* (live-in police box)—commonly called *kōban**—and these are now being studied and adopted by police anxious to reduce crime rates in other Asian nations and the United States.

Unlike large central police stations, street-corner *kōban* put the patrolmen right in the middle of their assigned beats. *Kōban* officers patrol their beats regularly, have a register of local residents, and keep an eye out for anything that looks suspicious. When a crime does occur, they are close enough to move quickly to the scene and call in a dragnet if necessary. Japanese recognize the *kōban* as a sine qua non for effective policework, and they would not dream of being without them. Interestingly, the *kōban* tradition dates back to the days of the shogunate.

25 公害問題

日本でも近代化とともに公害問題が発生し，明治20年代に栃木県・足尾銅山の鉱毒問題などが世論を沸かせたが，各地で本格的に問題となったのは，戦後1960年代の日本経済の高度成長期になってからである。しかし，市民運動，新聞のキャンペーン，公害防止法の制定などにより，公害問題は改善されつつある。かつて病死者を出した水質汚染，大気汚染などのように急性の公害は消えたが，じわじわと河川・湖沼の水質汚染が進むというように，慢性で緩い環境破壊が現在問題とされている。

●公害惨禍と反対運動

1960年代の公害で代表的なものに，海に垂れ流しになった工場排水中の有機水銀が海の魚を汚染，魚を食べた人に中毒患者が発生した熊本県・水俣の有機水銀中毒事件がある。マスコミにも大きく取り上げられ，世間の注目を浴び，裁判にも持ち込まれて会社は敗訴した。このほか，富山県のイタイイタイ病，四日市ぜんそくなどがあいつぎ，いずれも裁判に持ち込まれて被害者が勝利した。

反公害キャンペーンでは，新聞社の果たした役割が大きいが，アメリカの1960年代平和反戦運動の中から出てきた環境運動，反公害運動の影響も大きく，日本の革新政治団体が大きな役割を果たした。神奈川県，東京都など公害問題が大きかった地域で，革新政権が誕生したり，このころから強力な消費者運動が始まったのも，そうした影響による。

●公害の教訓

厳しい体験に学んだ企業は，公害防止設備に投資するなど自己規制を強めた。また大気汚染，水質汚濁など代表的7公害について公害対策基本法が制定され，守るべき排出基準が定められたため，公害は急速に減少した。車の排気ガス問題も光化学スモッグの原因として大問題だったが，無鉛ガソリンの使用などで急速に改善され，家庭用洗剤による河川・湖沼の汚染問題も，無リン洗剤の普及などで改善されつつある。

現在，環境問題として浮上しているのは，家庭雑排水による湖沼の富栄養化，都市生活の中の騒音公害，ゴミやし尿の処理問題など，市民の責任によるものである。一方，住宅や観光開発による自然破壊も大きな問題となっている。

Pollution

In Japan as in most countries, industrialization has been accompanied by increasingly serious pollution. Although there was considerable outcry around the turn of the century over the pollution from the Ashio copper mines in Tochigi prefecture, pollution did not become a real national problem until the rapid economic growth of the 1960s. Since then, the situation has been considerably improved as a result of public pressures, newspaper campaigns, and the passage of anti-pollution legislation. People are no longer hospitalized or killed by water pollution, air pollution no longer triggers acute illnesses, yet pollution remains a persistent and chronic problem as Japan's waters are steadily fouled by effluent.

● Public Outcry against Pollution

Perhaps the leading pollution case in the 1960s was the Minamata disease in Kumamoto prefecture where local people got gravely ill after eating fish which had ingested organic mercury from local industrial effluent. The mass media played this up very big and an aroused citizenry supported the victims' suit against the company. Other major cases involved the Itai-itai disease in Toyama prefecture and the industry-caused asthma in Yokkaichi. All of these cases went to court, and the courts consistently found for the victims.

While the Japanese press played a major role in heightening public awareness of pollution's dangers, the anti-pollution campaign was led by the progressive political parties and influenced by the environmental campaigns which had grown out of the 1960s anti-war movement in the United States. Reformist governors were elected in Kanagawa prefecture, Tokyo, and other areas with serious pollution problems. This same momentum also gave birth to a revitalized consumer movement.

● Pollution's Lessons

Having learned from bitter experience, industry invested heavily in pollution prevention and otherwise sought to clean up its act. In addition, the Basic Law for Environmental Pollution Control set maximum permissible levels for air pollution, water pollution, and five other areas. As a result, pollution has abated rapidly. Photochemical smog, which used to be a major problem caused by automotive exhausts, has now been largely eliminated with the switch to non-leaded gasolines; and the polluting of rivers and lakes from household laundry detergents has been considerably slowed with the widespread use of phosphorus-free detergents.

The main problems remaining now are individual-generated pollution such as the explosive growth of algae feeding on household effluent nutrients in rivers, high noise levels in urban areas, and the difficulty of safe disposal of household waste. At the same time, tourism and development are seen as major threats to Japan's natural heritage.

26 社会保障

日本の社会保障は公的扶助(生活保護)，社会福祉(障害者・老人・児童福祉など)，社会保険(年金・健康保険・労働災害補償保険など)，公衆衛生および医療(伝染病予防・保健所・公害対策など)の4本柱から成っている。社会保障制度が確立されたのは第2次世界大戦以後で，当初は公的扶助や公衆衛生の比重が高かったが，1950年代後半以降の高度成長期には社会福祉が，そして高齢化社会を迎えた現代は社会保険，特に年金制度と医療保険に力が注がれている。

社会保障への財政支出も戦後一貫して伸びている。しかし，日本の社会保障費給付額が国民所得に占める割合は13%にすぎず，スウェーデンの33%，イギリスの21%，アメリカの15%に比べ，まだまだ低い(1980～82年度)。

●国民に浸透する医療保険

国民すべてがなんらかの健康保険に加入しており，よく発達している。その現れとして，1973年には70歳以上の老人医療無料制度ができたが，財政負担が大きく，1982年に一部患者負担(軽微)となった。

健康保険にはサラリーマン，日雇，公務員などの被用者保険と，そうでない人のための国民健康保険があり，その加入比率は6対4である。被用者保険は雇用主(企業)が保険の掛け金を約半分負担するのに対し，国民健康保険は国が半分の掛け金を負担してくれるが，医療費給付の自己負担分は被用者保険が10%なのに国民健康保険は30%と差があり，現在この格差解消が問題となっている。

●制度の確立が急がれる年金制度

老年人口は9.9%(1984年)で，平均寿命は女80.2歳，男74.5歳となったため，老後の年金制度確立が急務となっている。老齢年金(60歳以上)には被用者の厚生年金(雇用主半額負担)と国の国民年金がある。日本でも2000年には老年人口が15.6%になると同時に受給者の割合も28.3%に増えて，社会保障費が国民所得の23%を占め，欧米並みになると見られている。けれども，欧米における社会保障の完備が生み出す，労働意欲の減退や財政負担の増大，それらによる個人および社会の活力低下の傾向を，ヨーロッパ病と自戒的にとらえ，そのような結果を招かないよう，日本的な新たな道を模索中である。

Social Welfare

The four mainstays of social welfare in Japan are public assistance for the indigent; welfare for the handicapped, elderly, and other disadvantaged; social security including pensions, health insurance, and workers' compensation; and public health care including vaccinations, health centers, and environmental policies. Most of these policies came into being only after the end of the war. At first, the emphasis was on assistance for the indigent and public health policies, but the rapid economic growth beginning in the late 1950s prompted a greater concern for society's disadvantaged members and the prospect of population aging has lent new urgency to social security, especially health insurance and pensions, for senior citizens.

Expenditures on social welfare have increased steadily over the last four decades. Although welfare-related transfers now account for 13% of Japanese national income, this is still less than Sweden's 33%, England's 21%, or even the United States' 15% (1980-82 figures).

● Medical Insurance

All Japanese are covered by some form of health insurance, and the system is highly developed. Typical was the move in 1973 to provide cost-free treatment for everyone 70 or older, although burgeoning costs meant that this system had to be modified in 1982 to levy a token charge on elderly patients.

Most health insurance is provided by employees' insurance for salaried workers, day laborers, civil servants, and other employees and their families and by national health insurance for the other 40% of the people. While employers pay approximately half of the premiums for employees' insurance, it is the government which pays that half in national health insurance. Yet the two systems are perceived as unequal because the insurance covers 90% of costs for heads of households on employees' insurance and only 70% for people on the national scheme.

● Pensions

With 9.9% of the population 65 or over in 1984 and with life expectancies of 80.2 for women and 74.5 for men, there is an urgent need to devise pension schemes appropriate to this new era. Like health insurance, pension plans for people 60 or older divide into employees' plans (with the company paying half) and the national pension plan. As Japan ages, it is expected that 15.6% of the population will be 65 or older by 2000, that 28.3% of the people enrolled will be receiving benefits, and that welfare transfers will rise to 23% of national income (putting it on a par with the other Western countries). Looking ahead, Japan needs to find a way to flesh out its social welfare provisions without inducing the "Eurosclerosis" of a permanent dole, soaring entitlement costs, and the rest of the social debilitation that has accompanied welfare statism elsewhere.

27 教育制度

戦後，日本の教育制度は大きく変わった。それまでの6・5・3・3制に代わって小学校6年，中学校3年，高等学校3年，大学4年の，いわゆる6・3・3・4制が導入されたが，これはアメリカ占領行政の一環であった。これに伴い，義務教育も6年から9年に延長され，男女共学も一般化した。今日の就学率100%，文盲率0%という数字は日本が世界に誇るものである。高校は義務教育ではないが，進学率は90%を超え，特に都市部では事実上全員入学に近い。4年制大学は最古の*東京大学をはじめとする国立大学が95，東京都立大学など公立大学が34，さらに早稲田大学，慶応義塾大学など私立大学が331ある。大学進学率はアメリカの50%には及ばないが，30%を超える。

●日本の大学

日本の大学の外国と比較しての最大の特色は，入学試験の厳しさだろう。かつて“四当五落”なる流行語が生まれたが，これは，「睡眠時間を5時間も取っては合格はおぼつかない。4時間で合格」という意味で言われたものだ。現在，国立大学の入試は全国一斉に行われる共通1次と，各大学が個別に行う試験との併用である。希望者の殺到する有名国公私立大学への門は依然狭い。学部では医学部の人気と難度が群を抜いている。このため医大への裏口入学を巡る話題が例年，入試シーズンともなると後を絶たない。希望大学へ入るための*浪人も一般的であり，予備校は教育産業として立派に成り立っている。

新しいタイプの大学として，1985年から放送大学が学生を募集している。イギリスの放送大学にならって，ラジオ・テレビ放送と通信教育を組み合わせた教育を行うもので，運営費の約7割は国庫補助金という準国立大学である。受講対象者は，88年までは専用電波の届く東京とその周辺地域の居住者に限られるが，将来は全国規模になる予定である。

●教育制度の改革

第2次中曽根内閣は，行革とともに教育改革を最重要課題とした。21世紀を目指した世界的日本人づくりを主眼に，臨時教育審議会を諮問機関として，6・3・3・4制の見直しをはじめ受験教育偏重是正，道徳教育の充実，非行化対策，教師の質の向上等々が俎上（そじょう）にのっている。アメリカ的民主教育が日本の戦後の発展の原動力になったことは疑いないが，戦後も約40年，1つの検討期にさしかかっていることも，また，確かと言える。

The Japanese Education System

Japan's educational system underwent major reform after World War II. Under the Occupation, the old 6-5-3-3 system was changed to a 6-3-3-4 system (six years of elementary school, three each of middle and high school, and four of college). In addition, compulsory education was extended from six years to nine and most schools went coed. Japan boasts one of the world's best-educated populations, with 100% enrollment in compulsory grades and zero illiteracy. While not compulsory, high school enrollment is over 90% nationwide and nearly 100% in the cities. At the university level, there are 95 national universities, of which the oldest is the University of Tokyo,* 34 other public universities, and 331 private universities. Over 30% of all high school graduates go on to college, which is low only in comparison to the 50% figure for the U.S.

● Japanese Universities

What most distinguishes Japanese universities from their foreign counterparts is the difficulty of their entrance examinations. A few years ago, the term *yontō-goraku* (four-pass, five-fail) came into vogue with its warning that anyone getting more than four hours of sleep a night will fail the university entrance exams. Today, the entrance exam process for the national universities has two parts: a standard exam which everyone takes on the same day and the university-specific exam administered by each school. The competition to get into the elite universities is very stiff. Admission to medical school is much prized, and the papers run stories every year of people who try to bypass the examination and bribe their way in. Because students who fail to get into the school of their choice commonly study full-time as *rōnin** for a year or two until they pass the exam, cram schools have developed into a major industry.

In 1985, a University of the Air was inaugurated as a new kind of university. Patterned after the British Open University, it features a combination of radio and television broadcasts plus correspondence courses. With a 70% government subsidy, it is a quasi-national university. Although limited to the Tokyo-and-environs broadcast area until 1988, this experiment in education intends to go national after that.

● Educational Reform

The Nakasone Administration has made education a top second-term priority, and the Ad Hoc Council on Educational Reform is looking into revising the 6-3-3-4 system, downplaying the emphasis on entrance exams, beefing up moral education, countering delinquency, upgrading teaching-credential requirements, and making various other changes to give students a 21st-century internationalist perspective. While agreeing that American-style education contributed to Japan's postwar development, many people feel this is a good time for retrospection and review.

28 学校生活

日本の小・中・高校生の学校生活は進学問題に大きく左右されている。進学問題は今日，子供を持つ家庭の最大の関心事である。有名受験校では高校3年間のカリキュラムを2年間で終えてしまう所が少なくないが，これも最後の1年間を，受験勉強に集中させるためである。よい高校とは，しばしば大学への進学率，それも一流校へのそれがよい高校と同意義となっている。

学期は4月から始まり，授業時間は世界の中でも長いほうに属する。休みは夏休みが40日余り，正月休みと春休みがそれぞれ10日前後あるだけで，2か月を超す長い夏休みやイースター，クリスマスと，何かにつけて休暇の多い欧米とたいへんな違いだ。しかも日々の勉強は厳しく，宿題も付き物で，最近，日本企業の海外進出で増加している海外帰国子女の中には，この学校教育の違いにカルチャー・ショックさえ覚える者もあり，一部では深刻な教育問題にもなっている。

●多彩な学校行事

とはいえ，受験重視の一方ではバラエティーに富んだ，また，いかにも日本的な催しも少なくない。中でも春，もしくは秋(あるいは両方)に行われる遠足，それに修学旅行は日本ならではのものである。遠足は主として小学校で行われる日帰り旅行で，行き先は動物園から名所旧跡までさまざまだが，いずれも社会科の課外授業の一環であることが特徴だ。修学旅行は主として中学，高校の最終学年で，文字どおり修学(学を修める)の意味で行われる。日数は1週間前後，行き先は古都・京都を中心とする関西方面が多いが，九州・北海道・東京，それに昨今はアメリカなど海外に行く学校もある。男女とも全員制服姿でバスなどを連ね，集団移動する修学旅行は，外国人の目には，まさに集団主義の象徴に見えるようである。

このほか，体育の成果を競う運動会，劇や合唱・演奏などを披露する学芸会・文化祭などの年中行事が，主に春と秋に催されている。また，日ごろの課外活動として，スポーツ・音楽・文芸・美術・科学などのクラブ活動も授業の後の放課後を利用して行われている。

●自由な大学生活

皮肉なことに，受験競争から解放された大学生活こそ，生涯を通じ，日本人のいちばん自由な期間かもしれない。休みは長い。宿題も文化系では(欧米と比べれば)ないも同然だ。学生運動こそ衰退したが，サークル活動に，アルバイトに，選択の余地は広い。

Student Life

Japanese elementary, junior high, and senior high school students' lifestyles are largely determined by their academic aspirations. Educational advancement is topic number one in families with school-age children. Many of the best high schools compress the 3-year senior high school curriculum into two years so that the final year can be devoted to preparing for college entrance exams. A "good" school is one with a high percentage of students who not only go on to university but are able to enter the prestigious schools.

The school year begins in April, and Japanese spend perhaps more time in the classroom than students anywhere else. Vacations are only about 40 days in the summer and around 10 days each for spring and the New Year's holidays; much less than the months-long summer, Easter, and Christmas breaks enjoyed by students in Western countries. In addition to the long hours, Japanese course work is often very difficult and homework common. The children of Japanese assigned overseas are often bowled over by "culture shock" when they return to Japan and start attending Japanese schools. For many, the transfer back to the highly competitive Japanese system is nearly impossible.

● School Events

Even though the education system concentrates on preparing students for entrance examinations, there are many events throughout the year to help alleviate the pressure. Among the most popular, and perhaps the most peculiarly Japanese, are the school trips in spring, autumn, or both seasons. Outings at the elementary level are usually day trips to zoos, historical sites, or the like as part of the social studies curriculum. Junior high and senior high students make more extensive school trips in their third years. Known as *shūgaku-ryokō*, trips to cultivate learning, these are usually about one week. Kansai, especially Kyoto, is extremely popular, but trips are sometimes made to Kyushu, Hokkaido, Tokyo, and even overseas. For many foreigners in Japan, the busloads of uniformed students on their school trips epitomize the Japanese group spirit.

Other annual events include athletic meets, show-and-tell days of musical and theatrical performances, and *bunka-sai* with student-run booths offering everything from food to entertainment. Extracurricular club activities are also very popular, from sports to music, literature, visual arts, and even science.

● College Life

Ironically, after the extremely competitive pressure to get into a good university, the student who gets in then has the freeest four years of his life. Vacations are long and homework, at least in the liberal arts, is virtually nil by Western standards. Despite the decline in political activism the typical student still has a broad selection of activities to choose from, including school clubs and part-time work.

29 塾

日本の子供は，勉強という点では，世界で最も忙しい生活を送っているのではないだろうか。理由は言うまでもなく，学習塾の存在である。よい就職のためには一流大学へ，一流大学へ入るには有名高校へ，そして有名中学へ，と世界一厳しい受験戦争を勝ち抜くためである。東京周辺では夜8時，9時の電車にトレードマークのカバンを肩から掛けた子供たちの姿を見かけることが少なくない。同じ塾帰りの生徒たちである。

東京の有名な進学塾では，親も塾に通う。子供に家庭で教えるため，親は一歩先を予習する。まさに一家総がかりだ。と同時に，塾の学習レベルの高さの証左でもある。算数など，一流中学にパスするには，高校レベルまで消化できなければおぼつかない，とまで言われている。有名進学塾に入るには入塾テストがあり，「入試より難しい」とは，笑えぬ冗談である。当然ながら，このような塾通いを中心とする教育費は多額になり，白書に見るごとく，家計を圧迫している。

●乱塾時代

今日，塾の数は10万とも20万とも言われる。数字がこのように概数にならざるを得ないのは，小は主婦の内職程度から，大は全国に支部を持つマンモス塾まで，多岐にわたるからだ。文部省によれば，塾に通う小学生は150万人，中学生は200万人にも上り，学習塾産業の売り上げは，年間4900億円という巨額である。このため最近では，商社や大手電鉄会社などの塾経営への参入も目立つ。電鉄会社には駅前ビルを持っているところも少なくないので，不動産利用の塾経営である。まさに乱塾時代とも呼べる現状だが，注目すべきは，これら塾のすべてが必ずしも進学塾だけではないことで，補習専門の塾や，落ちこぼれ対象と銘打った塾さえある。いずれにしても，今日の教育に占める塾の存在は大きい。

有名進学塾でトップクラスを占める子供たちは，「学校は息抜きの場」と言う。授業が易しすぎるからで，彼らには塾こそ真に学力を発揮しうる場所なのである。一方，落ちこぼれ組にとっても塾は不可欠となっている。

塾はともすれば否定的テーマとして語られがちだが，このように今日の学校教育を，いわば補充する存在として学習塾産業が成長してきた現実は無視できないだろう。なお塾にはそろばん，習字などもあり，水泳・ピアノ・バイオリンなどの稽古(けいこ)をする子供も多く，小学生の半数が何らかの形で塾・稽古通いをしているというデータもある。

Cram Schools

Japanese children are probably the world's hardest-studying. This situation has spawned a whole industry of special private tutoring schools called *juku*. You cannot get hired by a good company unless you have graduated from a good university, which you cannot get into unless you have graduated from a good high school, which you... and so on with rigorous examinations at every level. Thus the *juku*. Identifiable by the book-bags slung from their shoulders, *juku* students are a common sight on the late-evening commuter trains in and around Tokyo.

Some of Tokyo's more famous *juku* are attended by both students and their parents—the parents keeping one step ahead so they can coach their children at home. Getting the kids through the right schools is a project for the whole family. These *juku* generally offer course work far in advance of the standard curricula for each grade, and it is said that students have to know high school math to pass the entrance exam to a top-notch junior high school. The best *juku* have their own entrance exams—which are sometimes even harder to pass than the ones they help students study for. These *juku* have helped push education costs up and up, creating serious problems for many families.

● The *Juku* Boom

It is estimated there are between 100,000 and 200,000 *juku*. The precise number is difficult to gauge because the *juku* industry includes everything from one-room schools run by housewives in their homes to giant *juku* corporations with branches nationwide. According to the Ministry of Education, there are 1.5 million elementary-school children attending *juku*, and at the junior-high-school level this figure is up to 2 million—all supporting an industry that takes in ¥490 billion a year. Some of the big trading companies and railroads have recently made news by going into the *juku* business themselves. Owning real estate in front of the stations, private railroads are now using these assets for *juku* income. *Juku* are bursting out all over. Yet not all of these *juku* offer advanced exam-preparation course work. Some offer refresher courses or even remedial courses for school "dropouts." *Juku* are clearly a major part of education in Japan today.

For the top students at the better *juku*, regular school is a place to relax. For them, regular school courses are old hat, and it is only at the *juku* that their academic abilities are truly tested. At the other end of the spectrum, *juku* are indispensable for the dropouts.

While the *juku* are often criticized, they indisputably fill an educational need not being met by the regular school system. Half of all elementary-school students are said to be taking some kind of extracurricular lessons, including everything from *soroban* (Japanese abacus) and penmanship to swimming, piano, and violin.

30 観光

日本はここ数年，旅行ブームに沸いている。ストレス解消型からゆとり型へという娯楽観の変化を反映して，余暇開発センターが発表した「レジャー白書」(1984年)でも，外食，ドライブなどの手軽で安上がりなレジャーに次いで，旅行もベスト3に食い込んでいる。

●海外旅行

とりわけ，国内観光が景気の低迷の影響を受けてしだいに伸び悩みの傾向を見せているのに対し，海外旅行だけは年々増加の一途をたどっていることが，総理府の「観光白書」(1984年)でわかっている。白書によれば，1年間の宿泊を伴う国内観光の1人当たり年間消費額は，交通費などの値上がりで4万5000円と，前年に比べ実質5％増えたものの，延べ旅行者数1億4000万人(国民1人当たり平均1.17回)，延べ宿泊数2億6900万泊(同2.26泊)で，神戸ポートアイランド博覧会が開かれた1981年を除けば，ともに横ばい。

これに対して，海外旅行者のほうは前年比4％増の423万人で，史上最高を記録。この数字は，海外旅行者が増え始めた十数年前の4.5倍に当たる。人気のある旅行先はハワイ，台湾，韓国，香港などで，この4か所で過半数を占めている。以前は，日本人旅行者というと，諸外国の新聞，雑誌などで劇画的に描かれたように，カメラを首や肩にぶら下げてにぎやかに練り歩く年輩者の団体旅行が多かったが，20歳代の若い女性の比率が高くなっているのが，最近の特徴だ。新婚旅行で海外へ出かけるカップルも目だって増えている。

●旅行の風習

庶民の間で旅行が一般的となったのは江戸時代のころだが，その始まりは「代参講」という講にある。村落外にある他所の神社や仏閣に参拝するために何人かが寄り合って懇親する社会集団で，講中で講金を集め，くじ引きで決まった代参者を講の代表として寺社に派遣した。神社を中心とした*伊勢講・*熊野講・*富士講，仏閣を中心とした*身延講・*成田講など，枚挙にいとまがないほど多くの講があり，しだいに代参者を派遣するだけでなく，講員それぞれがお金を積み立てておいて団体でお参りするようになったのが，今日の旅行の原型である。こうした講は，今でも年輩者の間では根強い人気がある。

年輩者や所帯持ちはバスや鉄道で国内旅行，独身貴族の若者は飛行機で気楽に海外へというのが現状のようだ。

Tourism

Japan is enjoying a travel boom. Just as modern life has changed, the reasons for traveling have changed from "getting away from it all" to "intellectual broadening." According to the Leisure Development Center's 1984 *White Paper on Leisure*, travel is the third-most popular form of recreation today, ranking behind the cheaper and more spur-of-the-moment alternatives of dining out and going for a drive.

● Overseas Travel

The Prime Minister's Office's 1984 *White Paper on Tourism* reported that overseas travel is growing every year, even though the sluggishness in the economy has hurt domestic travel. The *White Paper* noted that domestic travel has grown very little in recent years, with the one exception of 1981's blip induced by Kobe's Portopia Expo. In 1983, the average Japanese spent ¥45,000 on domestic travel involving at least one night's hotel lodging (up 5% in real terms from 1982 due chiefly to higher transportation costs). All told, Japanese took 140 million such trips (1.17 per person), and spent 269 million nights at inns (2.26 nights per person).

By contrast, the total 4,230,000 Japanese traveling abroad represented a 4% increase over 1982 and set an all-time high. This is 4.5 times as many people as went overseas before foreign travel fever became popular a dozen or so years ago. The four most popular destinations—Hawaii, Taiwan, South Korea, and Hong Kong—receive the lion's share of these travelers. While Japanese tourists have been caricatured in the foreign press as happy herds of middle-aged or elderly people with cameras, overseas travel has increasingly been dominated by young women in their 20s. There has also been a very visible rise in the number of young Japanese honeymooners abroad.

● Travel Customs

Travel first spread among ordinary Japanese during the Edo period when it was promoted primarily by religious associations called *kō*. Collecting money from all of the members and then drawing lots to see who would go on behalf of the group, these associations served both as social organizations and as a way for everyone to have the chance to make pilgrimages to distant shrines and temples. Innumerable *kō* sprung up, the most prominent being Shinto groups such as the Isekо,* Kumanoko,* and Fujiko* and Buddhist groups such as the Minobuko* and Naritako.* Later the *kō* not only sent proxy pilgrims but also organized pilgrimages for members who had saved up enough money to make the trip themselves, and these groups were the forerunner of today's tourist groups. Even now, such groups remain very popular among many older Japanese.

The current pattern in Japanese travel is for older people and families to take the train or bus to domestic destinations while young singles fly off to foreign lands.

31 温泉巡り

●最もポピュラーな旅

日本で最もポピュラーな旅は，*温泉を巡る旅である。老夫婦が老後の楽しみに名所旧跡を訪ねる旅で，彼らが好んで泊まるのは温泉のある日本旅館だし，職場の社員旅行でも，たいてい近県の温泉が旅の目的地に選ばれる。日中は温泉の近くにあるゴルフ場や釣り場などのレジャー施設で存分に汗を流し，温泉にゆっくりつかって一息入れた後，宴会場にみんなで集まって一献酌み交わしながら社員どうしの親睦を図るというのが，おおかたのパターンである。若者たちは概して年輩者ほどには温泉好きではないが，それでも，スキーや登山などのついでに温泉につかる，あるいはグループで秘湯や露天風呂を訪ねるというケースが，最近では増えてきている。

●湯治の習慣

そもそも温泉巡りは，湯治の習慣に始まった。温泉に含まれるさまざまな成分の薬効によって病気の治療をする湯治は西欧にもあり，主に飲用法によって病人・傷兵の治療に使われていたようだ。しかし，素朴な山奥の秘湯からいくつもの宿が並んだ温泉郷まで2000余もの温泉に恵まれている日本では，湯治はもっぱら入浴法によるもので，しかも持病の治療というだけでなく，日ごろの疲労回復をも兼ねて気軽に出かけられる，最も庶民的なレクリエーションの１つだった。

湯治宿はたいてい自炊だったから，農閑期になると，農民は米・みそ・しょうゆから布団まで持って近隣の湯治場へ集まり，毎日ゆっくり湯につかることを日課にしながら，１週間，１か月と長逗留をして体を休めたのである。その湯治自体は，近代医療の発達とともにめっきり少なくなったが，日本人の温泉好きだけは相変わらずというわけである。

●人気の名湯

どの温泉にもそれぞれ特徴があるが，非常に人気のあるのは伊豆の熱海温泉。眼前に海を見下し，背後に緑濃い坂の町が広がる風情から，東洋のリビエラとも言われ，芸者が多いことでも有名だ。日本最古の湯と言われるのが，神戸の六甲山中腹にある有馬温泉。歴史があるだけに付近に名所旧跡が多く，清少納言の『枕草子』にも，「湯は*ななくりの湯，有馬の湯，*玉造の湯」と，その名湯をうたわれている。別府・浜脇・亀川など別府八湯からなる大分の別府温泉郷も，1000余軒もの宿がある世界一の大温泉都市として知られ，その夜景の美しさで多くの観光客を呼んでいる。

Japan's Hot Springs

● Widespread Popularity

The most popular outings in Japan are trips to hot springs.* Retired couples visiting famous historical sites usually stay at traditional inns (*ryokan*) with hot-spring baths, and these same inns are also popular with groups of workers on company outings. Most of the company groups spend the day at nearby leisure facilities golfing or fishing and return to the *ryokan* for a relaxing soak before gathering in the banquet room to eat, drink, and reaffirm friendships. Young people are generally not as fond of the hot-spring resorts, but more and more young people have been staying at hot-spring inns or indulging in open-air baths while on skiing or mountaineering trips.

● Health Spas

The Japanese hot-spring habit began as medical therapy. Many of the minerals in hot-spring waters are said to be good for what ails you. Although hot-spring water has often been drunk in Western Europe, Japan's hot springs are generally only bathed in—and not just by the sick but also by the healthy and hard-working for relaxation. There are now over 2,000 hot-spring inns throughout Japan, ranging from small inns near tiny hot springs deep in the mountains to rows of large hotels near major hot-spring arteries.

It used to be that hot-spring inns offered very inexpensive lodgings to guests who did their own cooking, and farmers would pack up everything from food to *futon* to spend the off season at the local hot-spring inns where they could enjoy the luxury of several weeks of treating tired muscles to daily hot-spring baths. While this custom declined with the advent of modern medicine, today's Japanese are no less fond of visiting hot springs.

● Famous Spas

Each hot-spring resort has something different to offer, but one of the most popular resorts is Atami on the Izu Peninsula near Tokyo. Nicknamed the Riviera of the Orient, Atami is blessed with a view of the Pacific, a backdrop of lush green hills, and a large contingent of geisha. Japan's oldest hot-spring resort is Arima spa, located part way up Mt. Rokko near Kobe. There are many historic sites in that area, and Arima spa is mentioned, along with the hot springs at Nanakuri* and Tamatsukuri,* in the Heian-period classic *Makura no Sōshi* (Pillow Book) by Sei Shonagon. The city of Beppu in Kyushu's Oita prefecture, home of eight famous hot springs including Beppu, Hamawaki, and Kamegawa, is known as the hot-spring capital of the world with over 1,000 hot-spring inns and a nighttime charm that attracts large numbers of tourists.

32 花見・紅葉狩り

●花見

春を表す日本の古い言葉に，「桜時」というのがある。昔から，桜の花に特別の愛着を持っている日本人ならではの言い方だが，その桜の花を心ゆくまで眺めて春をめでようというのが，日本の花見である。

格式の高いところでは，「観桜会」といって，皇室や内閣総理大臣が各界の著名人や各国の大使など数千人を招いて行う盛大なものもあるが，一般に行われる花見は，家族や町内，職場の気の合った仲間どうしで楽しむ，もっと庶民的なものである。庶民の花見に付き物なのが宴会で，枝ぶりのよい桜の木の下にござやビニール風呂敷を敷いて陣取り，料理や酒やカラオケを持ち込んで，飲めや歌えや踊れの大騒ぎとなる。東京の上野公園のような桜の名所となると，その宴席を確保するための陣取り合戦がまたたいへんで，各グループの先発隊が前日から乗り込み，眺めのいい場所を巡って「こっちが先だ」「いや，こっちだ」と小競り合いを演じる狂騒ぶりである。

花見の歴史は古く，平安時代の812年に宮中で行われた桜の花宴がその始まりとされている。豊臣秀吉が1598年に京都の醍醐寺で開いた「醍醐の花見」は，その豪華さで史上最も有名だが，花見が庶民の行事となったのは江戸時代に入ってからのことで，葛飾北斎の「富嶽三十六景」には，花見に興じる江戸町民の様子が鮮やかに描かれている。

桜の名所として有名なのは，日本一の誉れ高い奈良県・吉野山。俗に「吉野千本桜」と呼ばれるたくさんの桜が山すそから頂上まで植えられ，春には満山花で埋まる。京都の嵐山や，世阿弥作の謡曲「桜川」で知られる茨城県・桜川なども多くの花見客でにぎわう。

●紅葉狩り

春の花見に相当する秋の行事が，紅葉狩りである。日本は秋が長く，楓や紅葉など秋に紅葉する樹木が多いため，山紫水明の風土とあいまって，世界で最も紅葉の美しい国の1つとされている。日本人は桜の花を見て春をめでたように，紅葉の名所へ行き，その景観美を眺めて秋を感じるのである。

花見と同様，紅葉狩りも，もともとは宮中で行われる宴だったが，しだいに紅葉を求めて遠出をするようになった。紅葉の美しいのはやはり京都で，桜の名所でもある嵐山，谷が一面の紅葉となる嵯峨野近くの栂尾，人里離れた秋の風情が楽しめる大原などに人気がある。

Cherry-blossom and Maple-leaf Viewing

● ***Hana-mi****

An old Japanese word for spring is *sakura-doki* or "cherry blossom time"—an indication of the age-old Japanese passion for cherry blossoms and the special delight felt in viewing them at *hana-mi* (flower-viewing) parties each spring.

In addition to the lavish high-society *hana-mi* parties attended by thousands of guests including the imperial family, the Prime Minister and his cabinet, celebrities, and members of the diplomatic corps, there are more plebeian parties at which families, neighbors, or co-workers supplied with food, drink, and groundcloths* stake out a claim under a blossoming cherry tree, perhaps singing along to taped accompaniment as the evening progresses in a revelry of drinking, singing, and dancing. At the more popular sites, Tokyo's Ueno Park for instance, advance parties begin arriving a full day ahead to lay claim to good locations, and territorial disputes sometimes flare up among the more aggressive strategists.

The *hana-mi* tradition is a long one, originating in the Heian period when *hana-mi* parties were held at court. In 1598, Toyotomi Hideyoshi held a *hana-mi* party at Kyoto's Daigoji temple which is remembered as the most opulent ever. It was not until the Edo period that *hana-mi* parties spread to the commonfolk, but such parties are depicted in the famous "36 Views of Mt. Fuji" series of woodblock prints by Katsushika Hokusai.

Among Japan's famous *hana-mi* sites, the most highly regarded is Mt. Yoshino in Nara prefecture. Known as the mountain with 1,000 cherry trees, Mt. Yoshino is graced from top to bottom with cherry trees so that the entire mountain seems to blossom in spring. Kyoto's Arashiyama and Ibaraki prefecture's Sakuragawa (made famous by a popular poem of the same name by Zeami) also draw large numbers of *hana-mi* enthusiasts.

● ***Momiji-gari***

Autumn's counterpart to spring's flower-viewing is *momiji-gari* (maple-leaf viewing). Japan's long autumn season hosts a variety of colorful maple leaves such as the *kaede* and *momiji* varieties, painting gorgeous mountain landscapes and making Japan's autumn colors among the world's most beautiful. Just as Japanese love spring for its beautiful cherry blossoms, so do they travel wide and far to drink in the beauty of famous maple landscapes.

As with *hana-mi*, *momiji-gari* began with the court nobility and gradually became a custom whereby people traveled to renown *momiji-gari* sites. Today's most popular spots for *momiji-gari* include Kyoto's Arashiyama, mentioned earlier for its beautiful cherry blossoms; Toganoo near Sagano; and Ohara, a reserve of autumn beauty far removed from human dwellings.

33 野球

今や野球は日本人の国民的スポーツである。するスポーツとしても見るスポーツとしても，本家アメリカの人気を凌駕(りょうが)するほどだ。

●高校野球

アマチュア野球の人気のトップは毎夏開かれる「甲子園大会」(全国高等学校野球選手権大会)だろう。北海道から沖縄まで全国の予選を勝ち抜いた代表校の球児たちが日本一をかけて甲子園で熱戦を繰り広げる。このときばかりは日本人も郷土意識に燃えて応援し，テレビの中継放送は高視聴率を記録する。活躍した球児たちがマスコミの人気者になるのは言うまでもない。甲子園大会は戦前から行われ，1985年ですでに67回を数え，参加校は3791校に上った。春には同じ甲子園で「選抜大会」が開かれている。

●プロ野球

高校野球の人気は春と夏に限られるが，1年を通じて広いファンの関心を呼んでいるのがプロ野球である。サラリーマンは昼となく夜となく野球談義に花を咲かせ，人気チームや上位チームどうしの対戦の中継放送は高視聴率を記録する。プロ野球が始まったのは，野球が日本に伝えられてから60年ほどたった1934年だが，今日のような隆盛は戦後からである。わけても伝統チーム「読売ジャイアンツ」の長島茂雄*と王貞治*はプロ野球の生んだ国民的ヒーローで，王選手は1977年にはホームラン756本を打ち，ハンク・アーロンを抜いて世界記録を樹立，1980年に引退するまで通算868本のホームランを記録した。外国人選手もいわゆる助っ人として参加しているが，しばしばカルチャー・ギャップが取りざたされるのは日米文化比較の点で興味深い。

現在セントラル，パシフィックの2リーグ，各6球団，計12球団があり，シリーズの終わりには両リーグの覇者が日本一を決める。

●アマチュア野球

大学野球は，今日では人気の点では高校野球に譲るものの，東京六大学*はじめ，東都，首都，関西大学など各リーグ戦が春秋行われ，ファンを沸かせている。1985年で14回になる日米大学野球も日米で交互に開催され，近年人気が高まっている。

ノンプロの「都市対抗野球大会」は企業の野球チームが代表となって戦うもので，甲子園大会が郷土意識の発露とすれば，都市対抗は企業意識のそれであり，いずれも野球の日本的適応と言えるだろう。このほか，リトルリーグ，草野球なども広く人々に親しまれている。

Baseball

Baseball is Japan's most popular sport. Both a participatory sport and a spectator sport, baseball is probably even more popular in Japan than in its birthplace, America, and Japan's love of baseball has been likened to Europe's passion for soccer.

● Summertime Highlight

The top amateur baseball event is the All-Japan High School Baseball Championship held each summer at Koshien Stadium—commonly referred to as simply "Koshien." Regional playoff winners from Hokkaido to Okinawa battle it out for the national pennant as Japanese nostalgically root for teams from their home prefectures. Koshien broadcasts always score very high ratings, and the best players become instant celebrities. Now in its 67th year, the tournament drew a total of 3,791 teams in 1985. In spring, Koshien Stadium hosts the National Invitational High School Baseball Championship.

● Professional Baseball

High school baseball attracts fans in spring and summer Koshien tournaments, but professional baseball is followed all year round by millions. Workers spend their lunch hours and evenings talking baseball, and the leading teams' televised games consistently have high audience ratings. The first Japanese pro team was formed in 1934, almost 60 years after baseball was introduced to Japan, and it is only since the war that the sport has flourished. One of the oldest teams, the Yomiuri Giants, has produced Japanese baseball's two "national heroes"—Nagashima Shigeo* and Oh Sadaharu.* In 1977, Oh Sadaharu hit his 756th home run, breaking the world record set by Hank Aaron in the U.S., and by the time Oh retired in 1980, his home-run total was 868. Foreign players have also signed up with Japanese teams, but many are put out by the cultural gap.

Japanese professional baseball has two leagues of six teams each (Central and Pacific). Each season ends with League Championships and the Japan Series match between the two league champions.

● Amateur Baseball

Although college baseball still trails high school baseball in popularity, the collegiate leagues, including the Tokyo Big Six League,* the Toto League, the Shuto League, and the Kansai Daigaku League, attract a growing number of fans in the spring and autumn. The Annual Japan-United States College Baseball Championship, an event held alternately in Japan and America, had its 14th year in 1985, and this event has grown in popularity in recent years.

Other amateur baseball events include the Intercity Baseball Championship Tournament dominated by company teams. Just as the Koshien tournaments rekindle hometown fervor, these Intercity Tournaments are excellent morale-boosters. In addition, Little-League baseball and sandlot baseball are also very big in Japan.

34 ゴルフ・テニス・釣り

日本人のスポーツ志向は，この数年急速に高まりを見せ，中でもゴルフ・テニス・釣りは野球・スキーと合わせて「5大スポーツ」と言ってよい。いずれもファッション化が目覚ましく，関連産業は国内需要ばかりでなく，輸出産業の面でも活力を見せるというメリットを生み出している。

●ゴルフ

かつて戦前の日本では，ゴルフと言えばごく一部の上流階級のお遊びとされていたが，戦後，とりわけ1960年代ごろから爆発的に普及し，現在のゴルフ人口は1200万人と言われている。15歳以上の人口比で見ると，実に13人に1人がゴルフをする計算になる。ゴルフ場の数は，狭い国土に1400か所もあり，ほとんどが民間経営である。最近は女性も目だって増えてきたが，料金が外国に比べてかなり高い点が泣きどころ。大都市周辺のゴルフ場では，休日料金が平日よりも50%前後高いのが普通で，大衆化はしたものの，日本では依然として金のかかるスポーツである。各種スポーツの年間支出平均の中でも，ゴルフは10万円と群を抜いて高い。プロゴルフも隆盛を極め，世界的プレーヤーとして青木功，岡本綾子などを生み出し，トーナメントの賞金総額は年間15億円を超えている。

●テニス

ゴルフに負けず劣らず人気のあるのがテニス。皇太子ご夫妻の仲を結び付けるきっかけがテニスだったこともあって，テニス人口は急速に増え，現在では500万人にも上る。民間のテニスクラブは全国で1000を超えるが，テニス人口が多いため，いつでも，どこでもできるというわけにはいかない。

もともと1970年代後半から急成長したスポーツで，ここ数年で成熟期に入ったと言われており，それにつれてテニスウエアなどの関連産業も巨大化し，売り上げは年間総額で500億円を上回っている。このテニスブームは都市から地方に広がり，観光地近くでは農家が畑をつぶして，貸しコートを造る例も少なくない。

●釣り

釣りブームは20年ほど前から高まり，現在の人口は1500万人と言われている。海に囲まれ，至る所に川や湖，池がある日本だけに，釣りブームはむしろ当然のことと言える。それに業界が次々に質のよい釣り具を開発したことも，ブームに拍車をかけた。釣りは完全にスポーツとして定着した。

Golf, Tennis, and Fishing

Golf, tennis, and fishing have joined baseball and skiing as the "big five" sports which have enjoyed increasing popularity in recent years as the Japanese have become more sports-minded. All of these sports are strongly fashion-oriented and offer major domestic as well as export markets for sports equipment and sportswear manufacturers.

● Golf

In prewar Japan, golf was a game for the very rich. Since the 1960s, however, golf has spread rapidly to become a game for the masses, and there are now about 12 million golfers in Japan. That means one in every 13 Japanese above the age of 14 plays golf, this in spite of the fact that golf is much more expensive in Japan than elsewhere. So far, 1,400 golf courses, most of them private, have been squeezed into Japan's modest land space. There has recently been a sharp increase in the number of female golfers. Golf courses near major cities often charge weekend and holiday premiums that make course fees up to 50% more expensive than on weekdays. Golf has indeed become a mass-consumer sport, but it remains a very expensive one. The average golfer spends ¥100,000 a year on the game, making golf by far the most expensive popular sport in Japan. With world-class players such as Aoki Isao and Okamoto Ayako, and with about ¥1.5 billion in prize money awarded each year at tournaments, professional golf has also made it big in Japan.

● Tennis

Neck and neck with golf in popularity is tennis. A mutual passion for tennis helped tie the wedding knot for Crown Prince Akihito and Crown Princess Michiko, and the increasingly popular game is regularly played by about five million Japanese. There are now over 1,000 private racquet clubs in Japan. With so many tennis players, though, getting a court is often still a problem.

Tennis began to boom in Japan in the late 1970s and is only now leveling off. With this growth has come equally rapid growth for manufacturers of tennis equipment and accessories, and these items now enjoy sales of over ¥50 billion a year. The tennis boom began in the cities and spread to countryside resorts, and quite a few enterprising farmers have converted the fields to better-paying tennis courts.

● Fishing

Fishing began to jump in popularity about 20 years ago, and there are now about 15 million sport fishermen in Japan. It is only natural that fishing should be popular in Japan, a nation not only surrounded by the sea but full of rivers, lakes, and ponds. The intense competition among fishing-equipment manufacturers and the high-quality equipment that they have developed has further propelled sport fishing's popularity.

35 相撲

日本の国技である相撲は，日本人ばかりでなく近年は外国人の間にも人気を博している。単なるスポーツ以上に，歌舞伎などに通じる日本的魅力が土俵にはあると言うのである。

●相撲の歴史

起源は遠く神代にまでさかのぼり，『古事記』や『日本書紀』にその記述が見られる。初めは豊作を占う神事相撲の要素が強かったが，しだいに見せるスポーツとして発展し，江戸時代には職業力士が登場した。1909年には初めて国技館が建てられ，1925年には東西に分かれていた相撲協会が合併，財団法人大日本相撲協会が誕生した。昭和期前半は不世出の大横綱双葉山の人気を中心とした黄金時代だが，敗戦を経て，戦後も勝るとも劣らない隆盛を迎えた。この間，1958年からは「年間6場所(1場所は15日)制」，1965年からは「部屋別総当たり制」を採用するなど改革に取り組んだ。また1985年には新国技館が完成，さらに新しい相撲発展時代を迎えようとしている。なおアマチュアスポーツとしても盛んに行われている。

●競技方法

直径4.55mの円形の土俵の中で力士2人が技を競う。力士はまわしを締めただけの姿で登場し，勝負に入るまでの制限時間(幕内で4分)内に古式にのっとり，四股を踏み，また清めのための塩を土俵にまく。土俵上の力士の行為にはすべて意味と由来があり，長く受け継がれた一種の儀式である。外国人が相撲に日本の伝統を見いだすのも，この辺に一因があるのだろう。勝負の決まり手は70手あるが，実際には寄り，押し，突きが全体の半数を占める。15日間の成績で地位は上下する。最高位の横綱は過去60人足らずしか誕生していない。

●人気の変遷

相撲のラジオ放送は1928年から，テレビ中継は1953年から行われ，特にテレビが相撲大衆化に果たした役割は大きい。名力士の輩出も相撲人気の大きな要因である。戦後は千代の山・鏡里・吉葉山・栃錦(とちにしき)・若乃花ら強豪が続出，中でも栃若時代，それに柏戸，大鵬(たいほう)の柏鵬時代は相撲史に残るものである。またハワイ出身の力士，高見山の活躍は相撲人気を国際化した点で特筆される。今や大相撲は来日外国人の必見コースであり，外国人ファンクラブや英文の相撲専門誌まである。日本に帰化した高見山は引退後は親方を襲名した。

Sumo

Japan's national sport, sumo, counts not only Japanese but increasing numbers of non-Japanese among its fans. Indeed, sumo is more than just a sport, and the sumo ring* has the same sort of distinctively Japanese appeal as, for example, the kabuki theater.

● History

Sumo has existed since ancient times, and there are accounts of sumo bouts in Japan's earliest extant records. Originally an oracular ritual connected with prayers for the harvest, sumo gradually evolved into a spectator sport. Professional sumo appeared in the Edo period. Sumo's main arena, the Kokugikan, was built in 1909 and is the home of the Japan Sumo Association formed in 1925. World War II killed sumo's golden age led by the popular *yokozuna** (grand champion) Futabayama,* but sumo regained its former splendor as Japan recovered from wartime defeat. In 1958, the number of 15-day tournaments was upped to six a year. Other reforms, such as round-robin competition among stables, were initiated in 1965. The 1985 inauguration of a new Kokugikan has ushered in a whole new era in the evolution of this age-old sport. Today, sumo is widely practiced as an amateur sport too.

● Techniques

In sumo, two wrestlers face off in the middle of a *dohyō* (ringed platform) measuring 4.55 meters in diameter. Clad only in *mawashi*,* they first engage in pre-bout ritual* such as striking fearsome poses and scattering purifying salt on the ring (four minutes at most for upper-division wrestlers), all of which actions are part of sumo's ancient tradition. This ritual is one of the aspects that particularly appeals to foreign fans. Although there are 70 different ways to win a bout, about half are won using the most common *yori-* , *oshi-* , and *tsuki-* techniques. Wrestlers are reranked after each tournament on the basis of their won/lost record. The top rank of *yokozuna* has been conferred upon fewer than 60 men in the history of sumo.

● Renewed Popularity

With radio broadcasts beginning in 1928, and especially with the television coverage beginning in 1953, sumo's audience rapidly grew to include the general public, and this renewed popularity led to the appearance of a number of great wrestlers, including such *yokozuna* as Chiyonoyama, Kagamisato, Yoshibayama, Tochinishiki, and Wakanohana. The late 1950s are recalled as the Tochinishiki-Wakanohana era and the 1960s as the Kashiwado-Taiho era. The 1960s also saw Takamiyama, a wrestler from Hawaii whose achievements did much to internationalize sumo's appeal. Now sumo is on every foreign visitor's must-see list, and there are even foreign fan clubs and English-language sumo magazines. Upon retirement, Takamiyama became an *oyakata** (stable master).

36 柔道

「柔よく剛を制す」。柔道の原理はこの諺(ことわざ)に象徴されていると言っても過言ではない。「柔(やわら)」とは「柔らか」の意味。その柔の道，それが柔道であり，日本の生んだスポーツである。

●柔道の歴史

柔道の源は古代の武術，「柔術」にさかのぼるが，これを「柔道」と命名，明治時代初期にその基礎を確立したのは，当時東京大学の学生だった嘉納治五郎である。嘉納は柔術に関心を抱いて多くの流派を学んだが，これに教育的意義を見いだし，1882年講道館を設立，柔道の研究，指導に励んだ。嘉納によれば，柔道とは「心身の力を最も有効に使用する道であり，攻撃，防御の練習によって身体，精神を練磨修行し，その道の真髄を体得すること」である。柔道に限らず剣道，弓道，空手道など日本古来の武術がいずれも「道」なのはきわめて示唆的だ。つまり，それは単に勝負を競うスポーツではなく，道を求めての精神修行も兼ねた人間形成，それこそが柔道の究極目標なのである。

1951年に国際柔道連盟が発足，日本は1952年に加盟した。今日，国際柔道連盟には120を超す国が加盟，柔道人口は世界で500万とも言われる。1964年の東京オリンピックからは五輪種目になったほか，世界柔道選手権など各種国際大会も行われている。

●競技の方法

講道館柔道の規定によれば，試合者は柔道着を着用しなければならない。試合場は14.55m四方とし，その中央に9.1m四方(畳50枚)の場内を設け，互いに組み合って技を競う。柔道の技は投げ技，固め技，当て身技の3種類がある。ただし，当て身技は相手の急所を突いたり打ったり蹴る方法で，普通の試合・練習には用いず，形として練習する。練習は「形」と「乱取り」の2形式がある。形は一定の順序，方法に従って行い，乱取りは自由に技を競う。

力量は「段」と「級」で表され，最高は10段で最低は初段，それ以下が級となる。1級を最高に5級まである。段と級は帯の色で区別し，10，9段は紅，8～6段は紅白，5～初段が黒，1～3級は茶，4級～初心者は白色である。

重量による階級別のほか無差別級があり，無差別級制覇が真のチャンピオンと見なされている。常に礼儀作法を重んじ，「礼に始まり礼に終わる」という言葉は有名である。

Judo

Softness controls hardness. This ancient wisdom is a fundamental principle of judo. The *jū* (*yawara*) in judo means softness and the *dō* (*michi*) means way or method, hence the name *jūdō* meaning "the way of softness."

● History of Judo

Judo's roots go back to the ancient *jūjutsu*, but it was not until early in the Meiji period that Kano Jigoro, a Tokyo University student, created and named judo as we know it today. Adept at many *jūjutsu* techniques, Kano saw judo as a tool for physical education. Believing that judo makes most effective use of both mental and physical faculties with offensive and defensive techniques practiced to cultivate the whole person and achieve mastery of the discipline, Kano established the Kodokan school of judo in 1882. This holistic orientation is typical not only of judo but also of *kendō* (way of the sword), *kyūdō* (way of the bow), *karatedō* (way of the empty hand), and the many other *dō* (ways) that are collectively called *budō* (way of the warrior, i.e. martial arts).

The International Judo Federation was established in 1951, with Japan becoming a member in 1952. Today, the International Judo Federation has over 120 member nations, and there are an estimated five million judoists worldwide. Judo has been an Olympic event since the 1964 Tokyo Olympics and judo championships and other international competitions are held all over the globe.

● Competition

Kodokan rules require that wrestlers be dressed in regulation uniforms. The floor space must be 14.55 meters square, with a 9.1 meters square center area on which the contestants wrestle. There are three categories of *waza: nage-waza* (throwing), *katame-waza* (grappling), and *atemi-waza* (attacking vital points). However, the *atemi-waza*'s sharp blows are not normally used except in formal shows. Practices are either formal or free-form. While prescribed techniques are used in a prescribed order in formal practice, judoists are free to use whatever techniques they like in free-form practice.

Wrestlers are ranked according to ability in a system of *dan* (ranks) and *kyū* (classes), the highest rank being 10th *dan* and the lowest *shodan* (beginners). Below *shodan* are the *kyū* with 1 the highest and 5 the lowest. There are different color belts for different ranks: red for 9th and 10th *dan*, red-and-white stripes for 6th through 8th *dan*, black for *shodan* through 5th *dan*, brown for 1st through 3rd *kyū*, and white for 4th *kyū* through unranked novices.

Matches are both by weight class and in a single ungraded class, but the winner of the all-weight class is considered the true champion. Decorum is heavily stressed in both practices and matches, as shown in the famous axiom that judo starts and ends with decorum.

37 剣道・弓道・空手道・合気道

●剣道

剣道は日本古来の剣術からスタートしたもので，もともと剣術は武士が戦闘技術をマスターするための訓練手段だった。20世紀に入って呼称が剣道と改められ，剣道を通じて心身を鍛える点に主眼が置かれるようになり，やがて戦後は新しい格技形式のスポーツとして変身した。現在では中学，高校の教育課程にも取り入れられているほか，各地に道場も多い。

1970年には国際剣道連盟が創立されて，国際的スポーツとして認知されるようになった。現在の剣道人口は700万人。有段者は技術の発達によって進級するが，現在は110万人。最高位の10段は過去５人いたものの，今は１人もいない。女性の参加もこのところ増えている。

●弓道

弓道も古代から伝わる武道の１つで，弓術とも言う。ほぼ完全にスポーツ化した武道の中にあって，いまだに古い形式を残す数少ない伝統武道で，戦後一時衰えを見せたものの，現在は再び盛んになっている。弓道場は全国に2500か所あり，弓を射る人口は50万人，うち有段者が40万人いて，その20%は女性，それも若い女性が多い。

●空手道

空手は武器を一切使わない，徒手空拳の武技である。中国の唐時代に始まった中国拳法が沖縄に伝わり，「手」，「唐手」として発達したと言われている。武器の携帯を許されなかった庶民が，護身の術としてひそかに技を磨くという，独特の歴史によって発展したものである。

日本の空手は４大流派に大別できるが，各々多くの派があり，空手人口は，外国も含めて2300万人に上るという。うち有段者だけで100万人余，その10%が海外と言われるぐらい，柔道と並んで外国人に人気があるスポーツとなっている。

●合気道

合気道も日本伝来の武道の１つだが，現代武道の中では唯一ゲーム化していない特異な存在である。守りの武道とも言われるように，心身の鍛練を基本とし，あくまでも守りに徹する武術で，攻撃技はない。相手を制する技には投げ技，押さえ技がある。歴史は浅く，大正年間に合気道の名で成立，現在は合気会により組織的に統轄されている。全国の道場数は約500か所，合気道人口は国内60万人（うち女性20万人），海外20万人で約50か国に愛好者がいる。

Kendō, *Kyūdō*, Karate, and *Aikidō*

● ***Kendō***

Swordmanship was vital to the samurai of ancient Japan and *kenjutsu* was their primary means of practice. By the early 20th century, it had evolved into a martial art with equal emphasis on moral and spiritual training and was known as *kendō*. After the Second World War, *kendō* was established as a major sport in Japan, growing to become part of the regular curricula of junior and senior high schools. There are also numerous training centers, called *dōjō*, throughout the country.

The founding of the International Kendo Federation in 1970 firmly established *kendō* as an international sport, and there are some seven million practitioners worldwide today. Within this seven million, people are ranked in *kyū* and *dan* by level of proficiency. Of the 1.1 million rankholders, however, none holds the highest rank of 10th *dan*—a rank held by only five people in history. More and more women are taking part in this traditional sport.

● ***Kyūdō***

Also known as *kyūjutsu*, archery is another ancient Japanese sport. Of all the martial arts that have evolved into sports, *kyūdō* has stayed very close to its original form. The sport declined somewhat after the Second World War, but it is now enjoying a revival. There are 2,500 archery *dōjō* in Japan with some 500,000 archers. Of the 400,000 who hold ranks, 20% are women, many of them young women.

● **Karate**

This martial art for unarmed combat originated in Tang China and was further developed in Okinawa, where it was originally called 'karate' (lit. "Tang hand"). Karate is different from the other martial arts in that it was secretly practiced by the common people who were not allowed to bear arms.

There are four main schools of karate and innumerable subschools, with a total of 23 million karate enthusiasts worldwide. Over 10% of the million rankholders are foreigners, and karate has joined judo as another Japanese sport gone international.

● ***Aikidō***

Another uniquely Japanese martial art, *aikidō* is purely defensive and does not lend itself to contests. Largely a spiritual exercise, it relies on throws and holding techniques to protect from attack and has no offensive techniques. Sharing its origins with *jūdō* and other traditional martial arts, *aikidō* is actually relatively new, not having been organized and named until the 1920s. Today there are approximately 500 *aikidō dōjō* in the Aikido Federation. There are 600,000 *aikidō* practitioners in Japan (200,000 of them women) and around 200,000 in half-a-hundred countries overseas.

38 映画

戦後の日本映画の歩みは，大まかに３つの段階に分けられる。

●第１期

再興期とも言うべき第１期は，1945年の敗戦からＧＨＱ占領時代を経て，現在の自民党単独政権の因となった1955年の保守合同までの10年間で，価値観を喪失した世相をそのまま反映した，社会性の高い映画が数多く世に出た。戦前から，性的差別に苦しむ女を描いて秀逸な作家，溝口健二は，無実の姦通の罪に陥れられた人妻が，束縛の中で生きるより磔刑（たくけい）に処せられるほうを選ぶまでを描いた「近松物語」(1954年)などで，封建性に対する鋭い批判を打ち出し，日本人独特の情緒を重んじた一連の小津調作品で知られた小津安二郎は，老後の相談をするために子供たちを訪ね歩く老夫婦を描いた「東京物語」(1953年)で，民法改正に伴って崩壊していく家族の悲劇を世に問うた。後に「七人の侍」「用心棒」などで世界的評価を得る黒沢明も，武士夫妻襲撃事件の真相を巡って関係者の証言が対立する裁判劇を描いた「羅生門」(1950年) で，溝口，小津とはまた違った視点から人間存在そのものへの問いを投げかけた。この作品は1951年ベニス国際映画コンクールで「国際映画大賞」に輝き，黒沢はその名声を高めることになった。

●第２期

日本が高度経済成長時代に入った1960年までの第２期は娯楽性に重点が移され，この間，日本の映画界は隆盛を極める。その転換点となったのが，石原慎太郎原作の「太陽の季節」(1956年)である。朝鮮特需に伴う資本主義の復興によって退廃したブルジョアの子弟を描いたこの映画は，戦後映画史に残る大ヒットとなり，以後，スピード，セックス，酒を扱った，いわゆる太陽族映画が続出し，観客動員数は58年には11億人にも達した。

●第３期

しかし，ブームに乗った粗製濫造の安易さがやがて客を遠ざけ，1960年以降，映画は衰退の一途をたどる。ヤクザ，ロマンポルノと各社とも独自路線を打ち出したが，それでも映画離れに歯止めはかけられず，63年には観客動員数５億人と全盛時の半分。石油危機を経て，77年以降は１億6000万人前後と低迷を続けている。そんな中で，唯一健闘したのが山田洋次の「寅さんシリーズ」で，三十数作を数えるヒットとなっている。

Films

The postwar development of Japanese film can be broadly divided into three periods.

● First Period

This is a decade of revival starting with Japan's surrender in 1945, running through the Occupation years, and ending in 1955 when the conservative parties merged to form the Liberal Democratic Party (LDP) and begin its domination of Japanese politics. These years saw the production of socially conscious films portraying the plight of a postwar society bereft of values: Mizoguchi Kenji, noted for his prewar films depicting women as victims of sexual discrimination, did a number of films critical of Japanese feudalistic thought patterns, including *Chikamatsu Monogatari* (1954) about a woman unjustly accused of adultery who chooses to be crucified rather than continue to lead a life of restriction; Ozu Yasujiro continued to direct films which were very Japanese in their emotions, such as *Tokyo Story* (1953) depicting democratization's erosion of the traditional family structure as seen in an aging couple's trip to visit their children in Tokyo; and Kurosawa Akira, later to consolidate his international reputation with *Seven Samurai* and *Yōjinbo*, questioned human existence from a different angle in his classic *Rashōmon* (1950) about the conflicting stories told by the witnesses to an attack on a samurai couple. In fact, Kurosawa first won major recognition in Japan and abroad when *Rashōmon* won the Grand Prix at the Venice Film Festival in 1951.

● Second Period

The second stage in the Japanese industry's postwar development was between 1956 and 1960, as the emphasis switched to pure entertainment and the industry prospered. This era was ushered in with Ishihara Shintaro's *Taiyō no Kisetsu* (1956) depicting the decadence of bourgeois youth under the material affluence generated by the Korean War. This was a major hit and prompted a genre known as *taiyō-zoku* (day in the sun) films dominated by sex and violence. By 1958 movie attendance had climbed to 1.1 billion.

● Third Period

Audiences soon tired of the simplistic hedonism, however, and the film industry began to decline in the 1960s. While the film studios responded with gangster* films and soft-core porn flicks,* they were unable to stop the industry's decline. By 1963 movie attendance had dropped to 500 million, less than half of attendance at the height of the industry's Golden Age. Since the first oil crisis in the early 1970s, movie attendance has tapered out at 1977's 160 million. The one bright spot in all of this has been the "Tora-san" series developed by Yamada Yoji, as the more-than-30 films in this series have all been winners with the public, with the critics, and at the box office.

39 碁・将棋・マージャン

●碁*・将棋*

碁も将棋も2人で勝ち負けを争う室内ゲームである。

碁は，361目の盤上に交互に白と黒の碁石を置き，最終的にどちらが広く地域を占めたかを競う，きわめて頭脳的な要素を持つゲーム。小学生から年寄りまで，幅広いファンがあり，囲碁人口は1000万人に上る。日本棋院，関西棋院の2つの組織があり，囲碁を職業とするプロ棋士は約500人(うち日本棋院400人)いる。

将棋はチェスの東洋版と考えればいい。盤面で，王将を中心とした各20個の駒(こま)を交互に動かし，相手の王将を捕えた側が勝ちとなる。古くから大衆ゲームとして広まり，現在でも盛んに行われ，将棋人口は2000万人と言われている。日本将棋連盟に加わるプロ棋士は4段以上で約170人(うち退役は約30人)，新聞社などが主催する主なビッグゲームは10を超える。

碁も将棋も，遣唐使や入唐僧などによって中国から伝えられたものとされ，特に将棋はインドが発祥と言われている。江戸時代には，幕府が専門の棋士を抱えていたほか，町人にも碁や将棋を大いに奨励した。おそらく，庶民の頭脳訓練の手段として考えたのだろう。

碁盤と碁石，将棋盤と駒は，全国どこででも売っていて，数百円という安いものから，数十万円という高級品までが並んでいる。また，古い家庭には先祖伝来という碁盤や将棋盤がよくあり，家宝になっているケースもある。

●マージャン*

マージャンも中国からの伝来。4人で楽しむ複雑なゲームで，骨材と竹材を組み合わせたものに彫刻が施された牌(はい)が中心。さまざまな種類の牌合わせて136個を使い，親を決めた後，それぞれが順番に牌を取捨し，規定の組み合わせを早く完了したほうが勝ちというルールである。組み合わせはいくつもあって，それにより点数が違う。

日本には1920年ごろに伝わり，比較的後発の伝来遊戯である。最近でこそやや下火となっているが，依然マージャン熱は盛んで，マージャン屋は全国で3万，マージャン卓は約18万卓に上っており，その総売上げは160億円と言われている。

Go, *Shōgi*, and Mahjong

● *Go** and *Shōgi**

Both *go* and *shōgi* are two-player board games. *Go* is played with black and white stones on a 19 x 19 grid board with 361 intersections. The players alternate in placing stones on intersections and the player who captures the most territory wins. With the nearly infinite variations of moves possible, *go* is a highly intellectual game enjoyed by 10 million Japanese of all ages from grade school children to retirees. Professionally the game is played under the auspices of two organizations, the Nihon Kiin and the Kansai Kiin. Today there are approximately 500 professional *go* players in Japan, 400 of them in the Nihon Kiin.

Shōgi is an Oriental version of chess. Each player has 20 pieces, and the object of the game is to capture the opponent's king. Widely played since ancient times, *shōgi* remains popular today with an estimated 20 million adherents of the game in Japan alone. As with *go*, *shōgi* players are ranked by skill level. The Japan Shogi Association is made up of around 170 professional *shōgi* players of the fourth rank and above (approximately 30 of them retired). There are about a dozen major *shōgi* tournaments each year, primarily sponsored by the newspaper companies.

Both *go* and *shōgi* are believed to have been introduced into Japan in ancient times by Japanese emissaries and monks to China. *Shōgi* traces its origins back all the way to India. In the Edo period, the Tokugawa shogunate established *go* and *shōgi* masters and encouraged the playing of these games among the common people as intellectual exercises.

Shōgi and *go* sets are sold throughout Japan and range in price from a few hundred yen to hundreds of thousands of yen. Older households are likely to have *go* and *shōgi* boards that have been passed down from generation to generation, many of them treasured as family heirlooms.

● Mahjong*

A complex game played by four players using 136 tiles made of ivory and bamboo, mahjong is played with each player alternating in drawing and discarding tiles. Whoever accumulates a complete "hand" of one of the many possible combinations of tiles possible wins the game. A player's score depends on what combination of tiles he has.

Mahjong was not introduced into Japan until the early 1920s, but it has remained extremely popular ever since. Though this popularity seems to be waning somewhat, there are still at least 30,000 mahjong parlors in Japan with a total of 180,000 playing tables and combined total turnover of around ¥16 billion.

40 公営ギャンブル

●公営ギャンブルの種類

日本では，ギャンブルは法律で禁止されている。ルーレットやダイスなどをギャンブルとして楽しむ場所は，日本にはない。ただし，地方公共団体などが行う競馬・競輪・競艇・オートレース・宝くじは特別に許可されていて，人気を集めている。

•競馬　日本では古代から，神社の祭事あるいは宮廷の儀式としての競馬というものはあった。その姿を現在までとどめているのが京都・上賀茂神社の「賀茂の競馬（くらべうま）」と言われている。しかし，近代競馬は，19世紀後半に横浜在住の外国人が始めたのが最初である。日本政府も近代競馬が日本馬の改良に役だつことに着目して認めるようになった。日本にはギャンブルを罪悪視する気風があったため非難もあって，レジャーとして人気を得るようになったのは戦後になってからである。欧米の競馬がイギリスの貴族・王室を中心に発達し，上流階級色の強いものであるのに対し，日本の競馬は庶民のギャンブルとなっている点が特徴である。

現在，中央競馬と地方競馬に分かれて開催されており，1984年の売り上げは合わせて2兆1000億円，入場者数は2100万人となっている。

•競輪　プロ選手の自転車競走。戦後の日本経済の復興と，自転車産業の振興を図ることを目的として1948年から行われた競輪は，一時は公営ギャンブルの王座を占めたほどの人気があった。獲得賞金がプロスポーツ選手として初めて1億円を超えた中野浩一というスターを，競輪は生み出している。

•競艇　モーターボート競走で，日本では後発の公営ギャンブル。女子選手も登場している。

•オートレース　自動2輪車および自動4輪車の競走。

•宝くじ　番号を記入した抽選券を発売し，抽選に当たった券を当選金と引き換える。宝くじ1枚の当選金最高額は，宝くじ発売価格の20万倍と決められている。江戸時代には「富くじ」と呼ばれる同形式の宝くじが流行していた。

●パチンコの隆盛

ギャンブルとは言えないが，大衆遊戯として定着している「パチンコ」は，公営ギャンブルをおびやかす勢いである。バネで鋼鉄の玉をはじき，穴に入れると玉がたくさん出てくる日本独特のゲームで，玉を景品に換えることができる。

Legalized Gambling

● Legalized Gambling

Most gambling is illegal in Japan, and there are no casinos where you can play roulette or shoot craps for entertainment. However, there is legalized gambling sponsored or sanctioned by various local governments, including racing (horses, bicycles, motorboats, motorcycles, and cars) and lotteries.

• Horse Races Japan has a horse-racing tradition going back to the ancient shrine festivals and court ceremonies, and these practices are still to be seen in the Kamo no Kurabeuma at Kyoto's Kamigamo Shrine. Modern horse racing was introduced into Japan in the late 19th century by the foreign community in Yokohama, and it was quickly approved by the Japanese government in the hope that it would contribute to improving the breed for Japanese horse ranches. Yet it was not until after the war that racing became widely popular, even though there was still considerable criticism from people who saw gambling as a vice. In contrast to the aristocratic air which pervades horse racing in the United States and England from its association with the British nobility, Japanese racing is decidedly a gambling pursuit for the average man.

With separate associations for metropolitan circuits and rural circuits, horse racing grossed ¥2.1 trillion in 1984 from a total gate of 21 million.

• Bicycle Racing Powered by professional bicyclists, bicycle racing was started in 1948 to stimulate Japan's economic recovery and promote the bicycle industry, and it caught on to become the top gambling sport at one point. Indicative of the sport's popularity, Nakano Koichi, the first Japanese professional athlete to win over ¥100 million, is a professional bicycle racer.

• Other Racing Motorboat racing is a latecomer to the world of Japanese gambling, but it has made considerable strides, and there are now women racers competing for rich purses. In addition, Japan has both motorcycle and automobile racing.

• Lotteries Lotteries in Japan sell tickets, each with a different number, and the holders of the lucky numbers win prizes. At present, lotteries are not allowed to give a top prize more than 200,000 times the price of a ticket. Vestiges of the *tomi-kuji* under the Tokugawa shogunate, these lotteries are just as popular now as they ever were.

● Pachinko

Although not strictly a form of gambling, pachinko has eclipsed many kinds of gambling in popularity. Sometimes referred to as Japanese pinball, pachinko has a spring mechanism to shoot a small steel ball and vertical board with holes in it. Any ball that goes into a hole wins more balls for the player, who can then exchange the balls for cigarettes or other merchandise on the way out.

41 子供の遊び

●現代の遊び

日本の子供たちがしだいに外遊びをしなくなっていることが，文部省が小学6年生を対象に実施した「児童の日常生活に関する調査」(1984年)で明らかになっている。それによると，家での1日の勉強時間は「1時間ぐらい」が33.1%で最も多く，家に帰って友達とどれくらい遊ぶかでは「ほとんど遊ばない」が男子30.6%，女子46.6%でいずれもトップ。さらに，遊び場所については「家の外」50.5%，「家の中」49.3%で約半々となっている。

つまり，半数の子供たちが家の中に閉じこもっているわけだが，その最も大きな原因はテレビで，1日3時間以上テレビを見ている子供が6割もいる。次いで多いのが，ここ数年都会の子供たちを中心に流行しているゲームウォッチである。時計や電子計算器にゲームが組み込まれたものだが，男子で92.1%，女子で76.8%もの子供たちが「7回以上遊んだことがある」と答えている。ゲームウォッチでは飽き足りず，街のゲームセンターにある電子ゲームや，電気店，デパートなどのマイコン売り場でマイコンゲームに打ち興じる子供たちも結構多く，中には小遣いをためたり親にねだったりして，自分専用のマイコンを持っている子供たちさえいる。日本の現代っ子たちが，いかにブラウン管などによる間接的な遊びに熱中しているかがわかろう。

●昔の遊び

昔は，子供どうし誘い合って家の外で体を動かすことが遊びだった。男の子なら，歴史上の英雄や漫画の人気者が書かれた丸や四角のボール紙をお互いに地面に置いて，自分のもので相手のものを裏返したりはじき飛ばしたりする「*メンコ遊び」や，小さな模様付きのガラス玉を，これも相手のものにぶつけて取ったり取られたりする「ビー玉遊び」。女の子なら，目隠しをした子の周りを歌を歌いながら輪を作って回り，歌が終わったときに後ろに来た子の名を当てて遊ぶ「かごめかごめ」，鬼を1人決めて，みんなは鬼に捕まらないよう逃げ回る「鬼ごっこ」などをして過ごすのが常だった。家の中での遊びには「*あやとり」や「*お手玉」などもある。こうした友達との遊びを通じて，子供は子供なりにルールを守ることや，人との付き合い方を学んだのである。

しかし，こうした昔ながらの遊びは，今ではお正月にする「凧(たこ)上げ」とか「*羽根つき」ぐらいになり，遊びながら学ぶという遊びの原点が忘れられつつある。

Children's Games

● Modern Games

Children's games are increasingly an indoor activity. This was the conclusion reached by the Japanese Ministry of Education in its 1984 *Jidō no Nichijō Seikatsu ni kansuru Chōsa* (Survey of children's everyday lives) report on sixth-grade elementary-school children. Asked how much time they spent on homework every day, a strong plurality (33.1%) said "about an hour." By contrast 30.6% of the boys and 46.6% of the girls said they spent "almost no time at all" playing with friends after school. When asked whether they usually play indoors or outdoors, the responses were roughly equal, with 50.5% saying outdoors and 49.3% indoors.

In other words, half of the children prefer to stay shut up indoors, and the primary reason for this is that 60% watch at least three hours of television a day. The second most important reason has been the popularity (especially among urban children) of "game watches"—watches or calculators with built-in game programs. Indeed, the survey found that 92.1% of the boys and 76.8% of the girls said they had played such video games at least seven times. Many children, not satisfied with the simple game watches, turn to video arcades or to the many computer games on display at electrical appliance stores and department stores; and some children have managed to save up enough money, or to hit their parents for enough, to buy their own computers and game programs. Today's children seem to be more interested in playing vicarious games in front of cathode-ray tubes than in playing outside with their friends.

● Old-fashioned Games

Play used to be something physical that kids got together to do outdoors. One of the games boys played is *menko*,* in which two or more opponents would lay out small circular or square pieces of cardboard decorated with paintings of popular historical heroes or cartoon characters and each boy would throw his pieces (*menko*) down on the ground to create a gust which would flip his opponent's over. Many other boys shot marbles. Girls' games included *kagome-kagome*, in which several girls dance and sing in a circle around a blindfolded girl who tries to guess who is behind her when they stop. Another was tag (*oni-gokko*) with the *oni* being "it" and trying to catch the others. *Ayatori*,* cat's cradle, and *o-tedama*,* a form of juggling, were also popular indoor games. In all of these activities, the games helped the children learn how to follow rules and get along with other people.

Nowadays, the traditional games are very seldom played, except for a smattering of kite-flying and Japanese battledore* at New Year's, and the basic point of playing—socialization through games—is gradually being forgotten.

Notes

■2. The Japanese Day

NHK Japan's national broadcasting system. It is the only public broadcasting company in Japan, and it is supported solely by subscriber fees paid by television owners. NHK has two AM stations, one FM station, and two television stations —one for general broadcasting and another for educational programming. It also handles Radio Japan's international broadcasts.

■5. Housing

condominiums (マンション) *Manshon* is a generic term referring to reinforced concrete multi-unit dwellings. *Manshon* can be either rented or purchased. While more impressive-sounding than apartment, *manshon* does not have the same meaning of a large, impressive residence that mansion has in English.

tile roofs (瓦屋根) The traditional Japanese home is built of wood and has a tiled roof.

sliding-door partitions (ふすまや障子) *Fusuma* are sliding doors separating rooms in a traditional Japanese home. Made of wooden frames covered on both sides with paper or cloth, *fusuma* slide along grooves cut into wooden beams in the ceiling and floor. *Fusuma* are usually decorated with pictures and patterns. *Shōji* are gridded sliding doors covered with a single layer of paper on one side. Some *shōji* are partially fitted with glass instead of paper. In contemporary Japanese homes, which usually have both Japanese- and Western-style rooms, *shōji* are only used in the Japanese-style rooms, where they fulfill the same function as curtains or blinds.

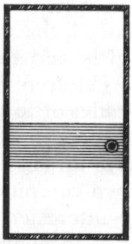

△*Fusuma*

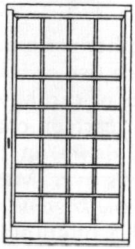

△*Shōji*

■6. Consumer Durables

closet (押し入れ) A closet in a typical Japanese-style room. A recess with its *fusuma* door flush with the wall, the *oshiire* is used to store bedding during the day and other things year-round.

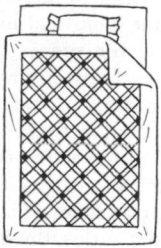

△*Futon*

△*Kotatsu*

■7. Clothing and Kimono

sumo wrestlers (力士) The *rikishi* is also called a *sumō-tori*.

obi (帯) A broad sash worn over a kimono. There are several variations, and men and women wear distinctly different styles of *obi*.

●Kimono

hakama (袴) A pleated, skirt-like garment worn over a kimono. Worn by men on formal and highly ceremonial occasions. Worn by some women only upon graduation from a school.

furi-sode (振袖) Kimono with sleeves between 95 and 115 cm deep. Worn by unmarried women as a wedding dress, for coming-of-age ceremonies, upon graduation, and on other such special occasions. Usually decorated with vibrant, colorful motifs.

■8. The Japanese Diet

***miso* soup** (みそ汁) A soup made of *miso* stock with vegetables, fish, and other ingredients. *Miso* is a bean paste made of steamed soybeans and a fermenting agent, and is a basic flavoring in Japanese cooking.

soba (そば) Fine noodles made of buckwheat flour kneaded with wheat flour, grated yam, and egg. Eaten either steeped in a hot broth or cold with a soy sauce-based dip.

udon (うどん) Thick white noodles made from wheat flour.

△Soba (mori-soba)

△Udon

△Sushi

△Tempura

■9. Japanese Food

non-glutinous rice (うるち米) This is different from the glutinous rice pounded into *mochi* rice cakes.

abura-age (油揚げ) A common food, *abura-age* is often an ingredient in *miso* soup. *Inari-zushi* is *abura-age* cut in half to form small pouches which are stuffed with vinegared rice.

seasoned with soy sauce (おひたし) This is a simple side dish of boiled greens, usually a leafy green vegetable such as spin-

△Inari-zushi

ach, seasoned with soy sauce and topped with *katsuo-bushi* dried bonito flakes.

■10. Traditional Japanese Dishes

△*Honzen-ryōri*

△*Cha-kaiseki*

△*Kaiseki-ryōri*

△*Shōjin-ryōri*

△*O-sechi-ryōri*

△A set of lacquer boxes

■11. Marriage and Divorce

△Shinto-style wedding

wedding (結婚式) Three types of marriage ceremony are common in Japan: Shinto, Buddhist, and Christian. The choice of ceremony depends less on a couple's religious inclinations than on which ceremony they find most attractive. The marriage ceremony is usually followed by an elaborate reception.

■12. Funerals

posthumous Buddhist name (戒名) *Kaimyō*, a posthumous Buddhist name, is usually based on the deceased's social status and quality of life. *Kaimyō* are commonly purchased, the larger the payment the more illustrious the name. The *kaimyō* is engraved on the gravestone and the deceased's tablet kept in the home altar.

■13. *Shōgatsu* and *Bon*

△Burning incense

first week of January (松の内) *Matsu-no-uchi* is the period of time around New Year's during which pine decorations are displayed. Formerly 15 days, *matsu-no-uchi* is today usually observed for only seven days.

zōni (雑煮) A soup with *mochi* as its main ingredient, *zōni* is prepared in many different ways according to regional and family custom.

nengajō (年賀状) The post office stocks New Year's cards mailed in late December and delivers them during the first days of the year. Many people use special *nengajō* issued by the Post and Telecommunications Ministry and printed with lottery numbers. In 1984, 3.15 billion *nengajō* of this type were issued.

△*Kado-matsu*

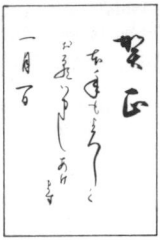

△*Nengajō*

△Traditional Japanese hair styles

bon-odori (盆踊り) Originally these were dances to console departing spirits, but today *bon-odori* are simply enjoyed as entertainment.

■14. Children's Festivals

sekku (節句) Originally days marking seasonal changes, there were five officially recognized *sekku* in the Edo period. Only the March 3 *Momo no Sekku* (Doll Festival) and May 5 *Tango no Sekku* (Children's Day) are still observed today.

armor (よろい) A suit of armor usually made of metal or leather strips sewn together with silken cords.

koi-nobori (こいのぼり) Made of paper or cloth, these are streamers made to look like carp and strung on poles outside of the house. Because the carp will swim upstream and jump waterfalls to get to its spawning grounds, it is considered a symbol of perseverance and valiant effort.

kashiwa-mochi (かしわもち) A *mochi* rice cake wrapped in an oak leaf.

birthday (数え年) *Kazoe-doshi* is an arcane method of counting age by which a child is considered one year old at birth and a year is added every New Year's instead of on the child's actual birthday.

△Flute and drum

△*Koi-nobori*

△ *Hina-ningyō*

■15. Tanabata and Christmas

shūji (習字) The practice of penmanship, primarily calligraphy executed with a brush.

multicolored streamers of paper (短冊) Thin strips of paper used to write haiku, *waka*, and other forms of poetry.

△ Rice paddle

△Binzasara no Mai

■16. Japanese Festivals

yukata (浴衣) *Yukata* is an informal cotton kimono worn in the summer. White *yukata* with stenciled patterns are common.

famous warrior-heroes from ancient China (三国志) Heroes from the Chinese historical novel, *Sanguo zhi yanyi* (Romance of the Three Kingdom).

Kato Kiyomasa (加藤清正) (1562-1611) A daimyo of the Azuchi-Momoyama and early Edo periods, Kato Kiyomasa led both of Hideyoshi's invasions of Korea and later served under Tokugawa Ieyasu.

mikoshi (みこし) A portable shrine carried in festivals.

binzasara (びんざさら) A long, rattle-like percussion instrument made by stringing numerous wooden clappers together.

Kamo no Kurabeuma (賀茂の競馬) A horse race held annually at the Kamigamo Shrine in northern Kyoto on May 5.

Aoi Matsuri (葵祭り) An annual joint festival of the Kamigamo and Shimogamo Shrines in Kyoto held on May 15.

△Nebuta Festival

△Sanja Matsuri

△Gion Festival

△Hakata Dontaku

△ *Hachimaki*

■18. Gift-giving

small towels (手ぬぐい) A rectangular piece of cotton cloth (about 30 × 80cm). In addition to functioning as a towel, the *tenugui* is also sometimes worn on the head (*hachimaki*) in different styles especially during festivals and by craftsmen and workers in various fields.

■19. Newspapers

national conscience (木鐸) *Bokutaku* is a bell with a wooden clapper used in ancient China to summon people whenever a new decree or law was to be announced. It is often used in Japanese as a simile for a leader who guides the people.

△*Kōban*

■21. Publishing

bunko-bon (文庫本) A popular paperback book size, 105 × 148 mm.

***shinsho-ban* books** (新書判) Another paperback book size, usually for non-fiction works, standard size 105 × 173 mm.

■24. Public Order in Japan

kōban (交番) See picture.

■27. The Japanese Education System

University of Tokyo (東京大学) Japan's oldest national university, the University of Tokyo is considered an elite school and its entrance examinations are extremely difficult.

rōnin (浪人) Originally meaning masterless samurai, *rōnin* today is used to refer to someone who failed to get into the school (or company) of his choice and is devoting himself to another try next year.

■30. Tourism

Iseko, Kumanoko, Fujiko (伊勢講,熊野講,富士講) The Iseko traveled to Ise Shrine; the Kumanoko to the shrines of Kumano Hongu Taisha; and the Fujiko to Mt. Fuji.

Minobuko, Naritako (身延講,成田講) The Minobuko visited the temple of Kuonji on Mt. Minobu and the Naritako went to Naritasan Shinshoji.

△University of Tokyo

■31. Japan's Hot Springs

Nanakuri and Tamatsukuri (ななくりの湯,玉造の湯) Nanakuri is now known as the Sakakibara hot springs in Mie prefecture and the Tamatsukuri hot springs in Miyagi prefecture.

△Hot springs

■32. Cherry-blossom and Maple-leaf Viewing

groundcloths (ござ,ビニール風呂敷) The *goza*, a mat of woven rush reeds, is commonly used as a groundcloth, as are plastic *furoshiki*. The *furoshiki* is a square cloth used to wrap and carry things. Called a *furoshiki* because it was originally a cloth used to stand on after getting out of the bath.

■33. Baseball

Nagashima Shigeo (長島茂雄) (1936) Nagashima joined the Yomiuri Giants in 1958. Known as Mr Giants up to his retirement in 1974, Nagashima was a flamboyant and highly popular player. He also managed the Giants for several years.

Oh Sadaharu (王貞治) (1940-) A Tokyo-born and -bred Taiwanese, Oh is famous for his home-run records. He became manager of the Yomiuri Giants in 1983.

Tokyo Big Six League (東京六大学) Hosei, Keio, Meiji, Rikkyo, Tokyo, and Waseda.

△*Hana-mi*

■35. Sumo

sumo ring (土俵) A raised dais of packed earth with a ring of sand in the middle.

yokozuna (横綱) The highest rank in sumo, a *yokozuna* is so-called because of the twisted rope (*yokozuna*) he is priviliged to wear.

△*Furoshiki*

● **Pre-bout ritual**

Futabayama (双葉山) (1912-68) *Yokozuna* Futabayama is credited with winning a record 69 bouts.

oyakata (親方) Retired sumo wrestlers who remain active in the sport even after they retire are called *toshiyori*. The term of address for a *toshiyori* is *oyakata*.

■38. Films

gangster (ヤクザ) Originally a name for gamblers and thugs, *yakuza* is used today in reference to gangsters and their organizations. The gangster movies of the mid-sixties had as their heroes an old-fashioned breed of "honorable" *yakuza*. While these films appealed to some, they were also widely criticized for their romanticization of violence and lawlessness.

soft-core porn flicks (ロマンポルノ) A series of films put out by the Nikkatsu production company with sexually explicit scenes.

■39. *Go*, *Shōgi*, and Mahjong

△*Go*

△*Shōgi*

△Mahjong

■41. Children's Games

△*Menko* △*Ayatori* △*O-tedama* △Japanese battledore

GAKKEN's Best-Selling Japanese Language Materials

楽しく学べる学研の日本語教材

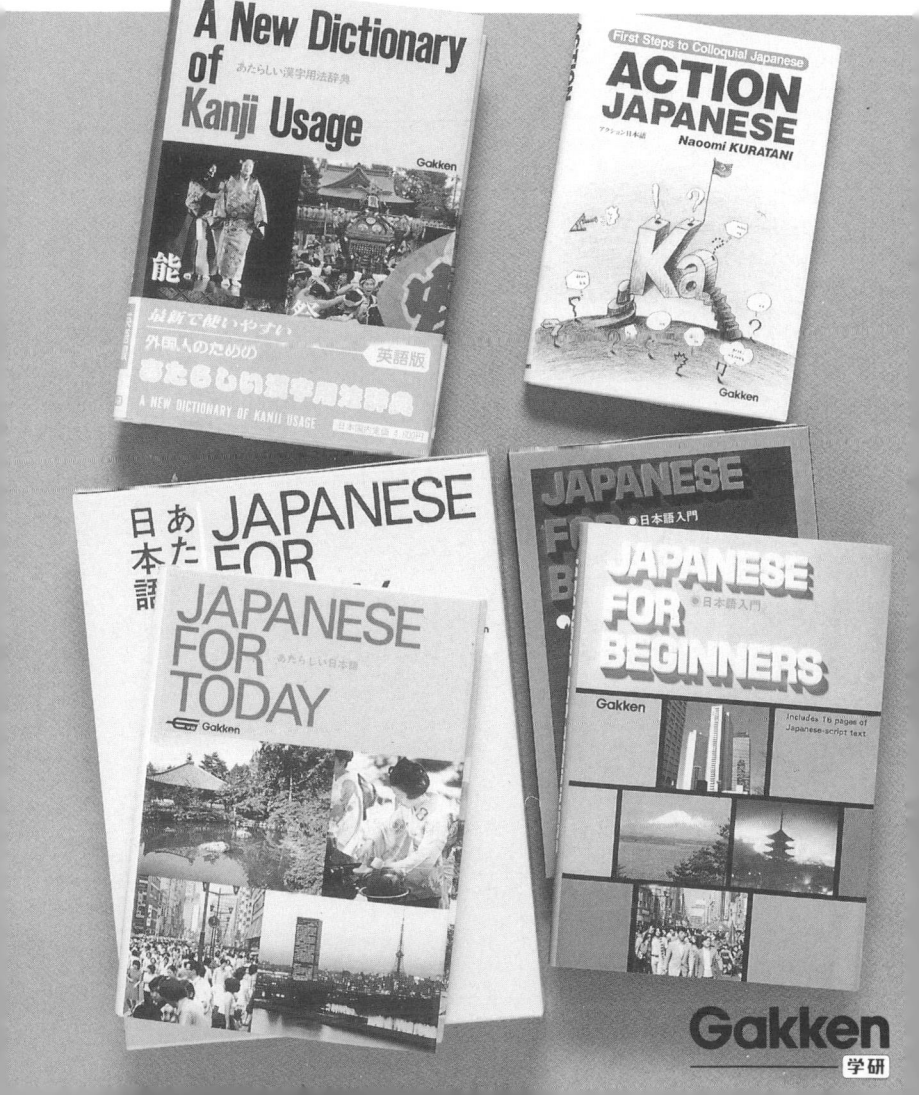

Gakken
学研

ACTION JAPANESE

アクション日本語　　倉谷直臣 著

First Steps to Colloquial Japanese
by Naoomi Kuratani

Here at last is a delightful introduction to the Japanese language that entertains as well as instructs. Full of rich anecdotes and creative drawings, ACTION JAPANESE provides engaging insights into Japan's culture and provides a firm basis for more advanced linguistic study.

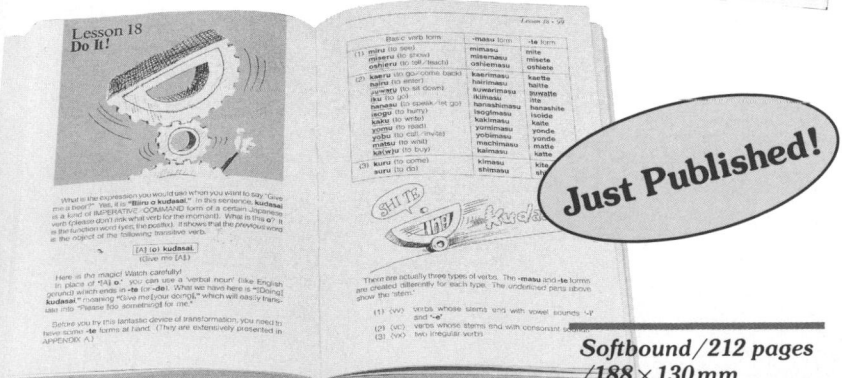

Softbound/212 pages
/188×130mm
Price in Japan: ¥1,600

JAPANESE FOR TODAY

あたらしい日本語　吉田弥寿夫 著　by Yasuo Yoshida

Widely adopted for classroom and self-study use. Available with 8 cassette tapes.

Hardbound/400 pages/216×150mm/
Price in Japan: ¥3,500/cassette tapes: ¥23,000

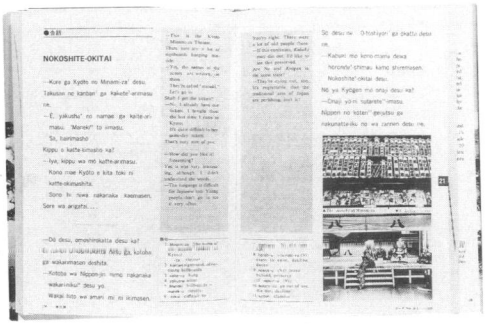

JAPANESE FOR BEGINNERS

日本語入門　吉田弥寿夫 著　by Yasuo Yoshida

The perfect start for those with no background in Japanese language. Available with 2 cassette tapes.

Hardbound/208 pages/216×150mm/
Price in Japan: ¥2,000/cassette tapes: ¥6,500

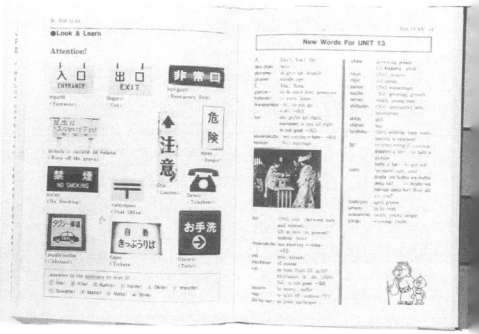

A New Dictionary of Kanji Usage

あたらしい漢字用法辞典　吉田弥寿夫 著　by Yasuo Yoshida

Contains the 2,000 kanji characters necessary to read modern Japanese.
"MUST" for the Japanese learner.

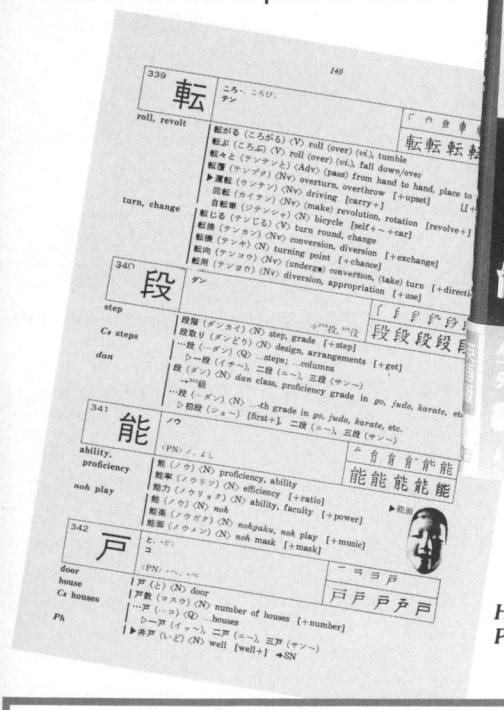

Hardbound/504 pages/216×150mm/
Price in Japan: ¥4,800

全国書店の洋書売場、ホテル売店でお求め下さい。
(または、最寄の書店か小社に直接お申込みも可)

Available at major bookstores, hotel bookstalls and Narita Airport.
To order, please contact nearest bookstores or call us directly.

For more information and details, please contact:

Gakken Co., Ltd., International Division
4-28-5, Nishi-gotanda, Shinagawa-ku, Tokyo 141, Japan
Phone: 03-493-3353/Fax: 03-493-3338/Telex: GAKKENSB J 27771/Cable: GAKKENCOL TOKYO

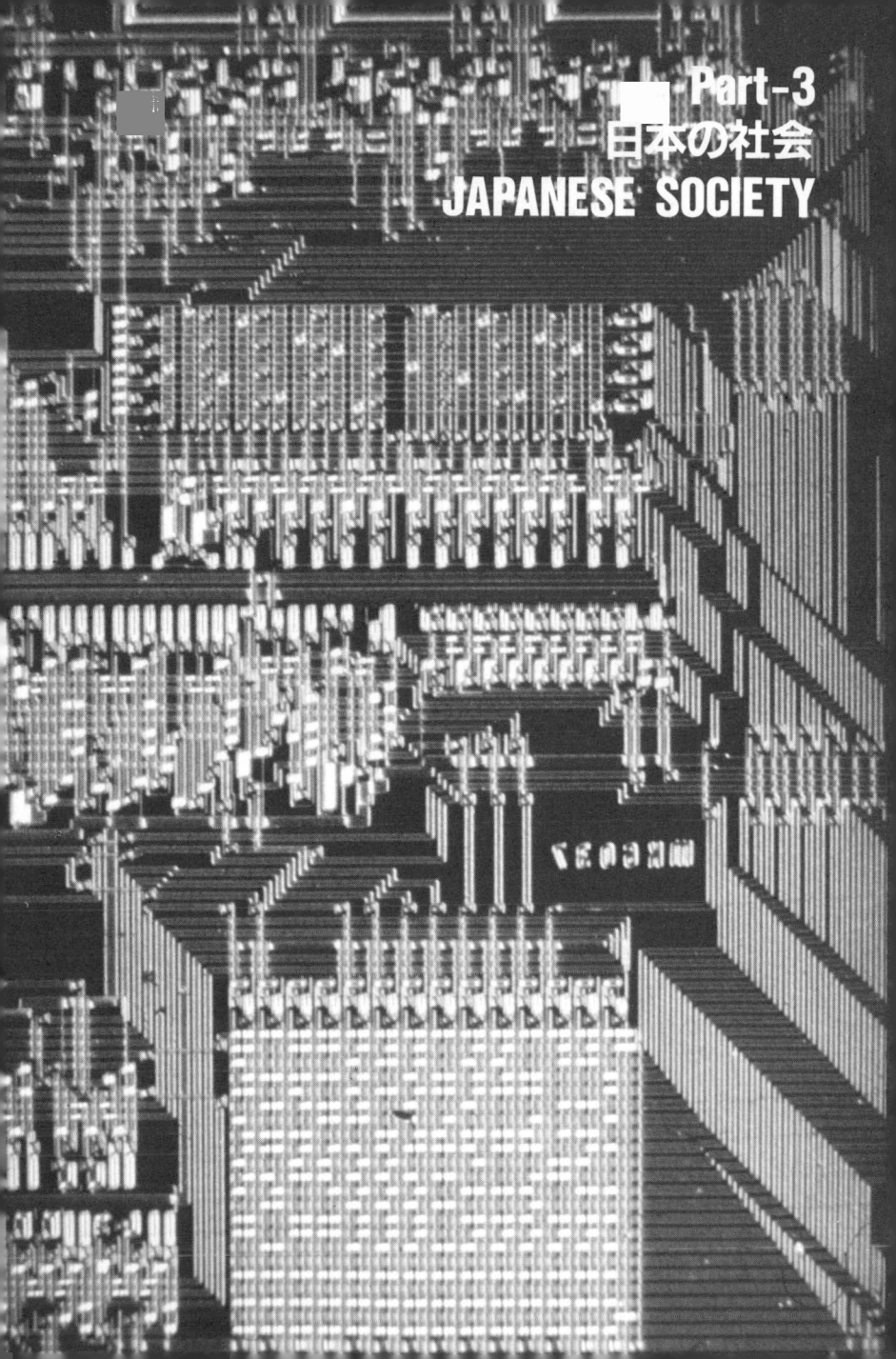

Part-3
日本の社会
JAPANESE SOCIETY

1 統治のしくみ

●日本国憲法の特色

日本の政治のしくみは，1947年*5月3日に施行された日本国憲法(新憲法)によって規定されている。日本国憲法は，第2次世界大戦に敗れた日本が，連合国の占領下に，さまざまな分野で民主化が行われていく中で，制定されたものである。その特徴は，①主権在民　②平和主義(戦争放棄)　③基本的人権の尊重　である。

主権在民，基本的人権の尊重などは今日の世界の国々では当然のことと考えられているが，日本国憲法が施行される以前の大日本帝国憲法(1889年2月11日施行)では主権は天皇にあったため，国民の人権は一定の法律の枠内だけでしか認められていなかった。このため国民にとって新憲法は旧憲法に比べて画期的な意義を持つものであった。

平和主義は，第9条で，「国権の発動たる戦争と，武力による威嚇又(また)は武力の行使は，国際紛争を解決する手段としては，永久にこれを放棄する」とうたっており，さらに，「前項の目的を達するため，陸海空軍その他の戦力は，これを保持しない。国の交戦権は，これを認めない」としている。

主権者は国民であるが，天皇が「日本国の象徴であり日本国民統合の象徴」(第1条)とされていることも日本国憲法の特色であり，天皇は憲法改正の公布や国会の召集などの国事行為を内閣の助言と承認により行うことになっている。

●三権分立

このような日本国憲法の下で，立法，司法，行政の三権分立を明確にしている。立法府としての国会は民選による定数512の衆議院と定数252の参議院との二院制で，国会議員の中から首相を指名する議院内閣制をとっている。行政府の内閣は，議会で指名された総理大臣が，各行政官庁の長である大臣を任命して，内閣を組織する。司法府である裁判所は，地方(または簡易)，高等，最高の三審制である。

国民の政治参加は，投票によって国会議員を選ぶこと，最高裁判所裁判官の国民審査のほか，地方自治体の首長の選挙・罷免，議会議員の選挙，さらに憲法改正の際の国民投票への参加(各議院の3分の2，国民の過半数の賛成により改正)などが行えることになっている。

Government

● Constitution of Japan

The basic framework of government in Japan is defined by the Constitution of Japan, which went into force on May 3,* 1947. Drawn up at the same time as postwar Japan was undertaking democratization in a number of fields under the tutelage of the victorious Allied powers, this Constitution is distinguished by its (i) vesting sovereign power in the people, (ii) including a pacifist renunciation of war, and (iii) pledging respect for fundamental human rights.

While popular sovereignty and respect for fundamental human rights are now the legal norm worldwide, the earlier Meiji Constitution (in force from February 11, 1889, until it was superseded in 1947) vested sovereign power in the Emperor and recognized popular civil rights only within narrow legal limits. As a result, the postwar Constitution represents a radical departure from prewar Constitutional principles.

The Constitution's renunciation of war is in Article 9, which states, "(T)he Japanese people forever renounce war as a sovereign right of the nation and the threat or use of force as means of settling international disputes.

"In order to accomplish the aim of the preceding paragraph, land, sea, and air forces, as well as other war potential, will never be maintained. The right of belligerency of the state will not be recognized."

While sovereign power rests with the people, Article 1 provides that the "Emperor shall be the symbol of the State and of the unity of the people." This is also a distinguishing feature of the postwar Constitution, and the Emperor is empowered only to perform certain matters of state with the advice and approval of the Cabinet, including promulgation of constitutional amendments and convocation of the Diet.

● Division of Powers

Governmental power under the Constitution is clearly divided among the legislative, judicial, and executive branches. The legislature is the bicameral Diet with its 512-member House of Representatives and 252-member House of Councillors. A parliamentary body, the Diet designates the Prime Minister from among its members. The executive is headed by the Cabinet appointed by the Prime Minister to preside over the various Ministries and Agencies. The judiciary includes district courts, high courts, and the Supreme Court.

The people participate in politics through voting in elections to elect Diet members, approve or disapprove of Supreme Court judges, elect local officials, and decide national referendums on amendments to the Constitution (passage requiring the approval of two-thirds of each house of the Diet and a majority of the popular votes cast).

2 戦後政治の流れ

●ＧＨＱの介入と吉田内閣誕生

日本を占領した米軍の占領政策は，戦前の日本を否定することから始まった。アメリカの狙いは，日本が再び世界に脅威を与えないことにあり，そのため，非軍事化と欧米的民主主義制度の導入を，最重要政策に掲げた。まず行ったのは，極東国際軍事裁判で，*東条英機元首相ら戦時中の指導者の戦争責任の追及を通して，日本の戦前までの歴史的価値観を悪として断罪した。と同時に，憲法改正に着手，非武装中立の思想を盛り込もうとした。具体的な政策では旧日本軍の解体，天皇の神格化の否定，思想犯の釈放，大地主からの農地解放などを，日本政府を通して実施させた。

米軍政は当初社会党の育成を目指し，社会党政権が実現したものの，政権担当能力に欠けていたうえ，汚職事件を引き起こし，つぶれた。これに代わって登場したのが，*吉田茂の率いる保守系の自由民主党の前身である自由党だった。吉田は外交官出身で，戦時中，戦争を批判したとして憲兵隊に逮補された。こうした経歴から，総司令官のマッカーサー元帥の信頼を得た吉田は，巧みな政治手腕で，戦後日本政治の指導的地位を確立していった。

●「講和条約」締結と「安保」闘争

アメリカは朝鮮戦争を契機に日本をアメリカの安全に役だたせるという立場から，日本に自衛力保持を認めるなど占領政策をしだいに変更，その比重を革新派から保守勢力に移していった。1951年，講和条約が締結されたが，ソ連圏諸国がこの調印に加わらなかったため，左翼勢力が講和条約に反対し，保守勢力との対立が激化した。この講和条約を巡って革新陣営内で分裂もあったが，やがて統一に向かった。保守陣営も革新側の統一に刺激を受け，1955年，保守系政党が糾合，保守合同政党として現在の自由民主党が誕生した。与野党の対立は1960年，日米安全保障条約の改定を巡って再び激化，訪日が決まっていたアイゼンハワー米大統領の来日が中止になるなど，日本列島は大揺れに揺れた。

一方日本経済は，その前後から高度成長期に入り，自由民主党はしだいにその基盤を固めていった。しかし，革新陣営は「安保」の敗北と高度経済成長に伴う社会構造の変化に対応する政策を打ち出すことができず，活気を失った。これに引き替え，石油危機を巧みに乗り切った自民党政権は，結党以来政権を維持し続けている。

Postwar Politics

●SCAP and the Yoshida Cabinet

Postwar occupation policy toward Japan was predicated on rejection of prewar Japanese systems. Determined not to allow Japan ever again to threaten world peace, the United States pursued demilitarization and Western-style democratization as its top priorities. The first concrete step was the convening of the Tokyo Military Tribunal to fix responsibility for the war on former Prime Minister Tojo Hideki* and other wartime leaders and hence to make a clean break with wartime values. At the same time, work was begun on Constitutional reform and a policy of unarmed neutrality propagated. More specifically, the occupation disbanded the Japanese military, had the Emperor renounce his divinity, freed political prisoners, redistributed agrarian land from large landholders to tenant farmers, and guided the Japanese government through other reforms.

At first, the U.S. Occupation authorities tilted toward the Japan Socialist Party(JSP), but that collapsed when the JSP proved itself unable to govern and corruption-ridden. In its stead came the conservative Liberal Party (forerunner of today's Liberal Democratic Party(LDP)) led by Yoshida Shigeru* A former diplomat, Yoshida had been arrested during the war for opposing government policies, credentials which won him the trust of General MacArthur and SCAP. Once in office, Yoshida proved himself an adroit politician as he consolidated his position in postwar Japanese politics.

●Peace Treaty and Security Treaty

With the outbreak of war on the Korean peninsula, SCAP reversed field in its Occupation policies and sought to make Japan a useful ally, including urging Japan to create a defense force and tilting politically from the progressives to the conservatives. While the San Francisco Peace Treaty was signed in 1951, the Soviet Union's refusal to participate in the signing threw Japanese leftists against the treaty and squarely in conflict with the conservatives. Although this treaty split the progressive forces, the rift was soon healed. Meanwhile the conservatives, alarmed at the leftist union, merged themselves in 1955 to form the LDP. The clash between the government and opposition parties came to a head in 1960 over revision of the U.S.-Japan Security Treaty, and the ensuing riots rocked society and forced the cancellation of President Eisenhower's visit to Japan.

About this same time, the economy entered an era of rapid growth which helped the LDP consolidate its hold on power. Despondent at their defeat over the Security Treaty and their inability to respond to the social changes wrought by rapid economic growth, the progressives have seemingly lost heart. By contrast, the LDP skillfully rode out the oil crises to hold the reins of government continually since its founding.

3 天皇と皇室

●憲法上の天皇の地位

日本にはイギリスの王室のように皇室があり，第2次世界大戦後の新憲法では，天皇は日本国の象徴という位置付けをしている。憲法は第1条から8条までに，天皇の地位，その世襲制，国事行為，財産授受などについて定めているが，第1条で，その地位は「日本国民の総意に基づく」とありながら，廃位などの規定が全くないことなど，不明確な点が多い。

敗戦処理に当たって，欧米諸国は日本の天皇制をどうするか大問題だったということだが，結局，天皇の戦争責任を追及せず，政治の一線から引退させて，名誉ある地位を保つ形に落ち着いた。戦前の天皇は現人神(あらひとがみ)と呼ばれ，神格化され，日本国という大家族の家長のように扱われていたから，その絶対的な存在をなくしてしまえば，日本にはパニックが起こる。精神のかなめとして天皇が必要とされたと言われるけれども，新憲法は法の下の平等，国民主権の原理を明らかにしながら一般国民と異なる身分を持つ天皇と皇族を継承したことは，現代日本の民主主義に非常に微妙な点を残している。

●天皇制の歴史

天皇は権力であり権威であった。また，時には，実質上の権力に利用されながら，歴史上存続してきた。日本の歴史は天皇の歴史，天皇と新しい時代の権力者との政治史であると言える。その1つの証拠に，日本には元号*という天皇の時代ごとの年号の数え方がずっと続いている。武士の時代(鎌倉時代～江戸時代)には天皇は不遇な存在だったが，下級武士が革命を起こした明治維新では，天皇はおみこしのように担ぎ出されて強力に復活した。

天皇は時代の中で浮き沈みしながら，権力や権威の度合いを強めたり弱めたりして存続してきたが，その本質は，宗教的な起源と関係がある。明治以降，日本には神道が国家宗教のように強力となったが，天皇はもともと神官で，農業生産のための神事を行うという原始的宗教と密接な存在だった。祈ることが国の方向を見極めていくというきわめて原始的な国家の長だったわけで，このなごりは現在の天皇でも，水稲の田植えや稲刈りを宮中神事として行っていることなどに現れている。日本の天皇のこうした宗教的色彩は，その地位をローマ法王などと同様の根強いものとしている。

The Imperial Institution

● Constitutional Position

Japan's imperial family is somewhat like the British royal household, and the postwar Constitution states that the "Emperor shall be the symbol of the State." Articles 1 through 8 of the Constitution concern the Emperor, including his status, dynastic rules, involvement in matters of state, and imperial property. While Article 1 of the Constitution states that the Emperor derives his position from the will of the people, it leaves many points such as deposition vague.

The handling of the imperial institution was a major issue for the victorious Allies after World War II, yet they finally decided not to indict the Emperor as a war criminal but to transform his position into a ceremonial office at arm's length from government. This decision to retain the Emperor as a psychological anchor for the people stemmed from fear that his elimination would trigger chaos, especially since the prewar Emperor had been worshipped as an earthly incarnation of the gods and respected as the head of the extended family which was Japan.The fact that the Emperor and imperial family were retained and set above the man in the street even as the new Constitution proclaimed popular sovereignty, equality before the law, and democratic government poses ticklish questions for Japanese democracy.

● History

The imperial institution has come down through history as sometimes a wielder of power, sometimes an authority figure, and sometimes a pawn of more powerful interests; but always a survivor. Japan's history is thus the history of the imperial institution and how it interacted with the new political powers that arose in every age. Illustrative of this is the fact that Japanese historical eras are named for the reigning emperor.* Although the emperor was seen as an anachronism in the centuries of military rule (from the Kamakura period through the Tokugawa shogunate), the Meiji Restoration's coup d'etat by lower-ranking samurai in 1868 justified its grab for power as an effort to restore the emperor to his rightful place.

The imperial institution has flowed with history, its political power waxing and waning, yet it has remained an essential religious force. Although State Shinto became an increasingly dominant force beginning with the Emperor Meiji, the emperor's Shinto identification is rooted in his having originally been a priest performing primitive religious rites to ensure agricultural productivity. Later, this supposed power to influence the state's fortunes with his prayers was expanded to make him the head of state. These agrarian origins are retained even today as the emperor performs symbolic planting and harvesting of rice. In terms of his religious significance, the emperor's position in the religion of Japan is somewhat like the pope's in the Catholic church.

4 内閣

●首相の選出と組閣

日本の内閣はイギリスなどと同じように，議院内閣制を採っている。首相は国会議員の中から国会によって指名される。その際，与野党ともそれぞれ党員を立候補させて，投票によって決めるが，自由民主党は結党(1955年)以来，過半数を割ったことがなく，したがって，自民党の党首が常に首相に指名されている。

指名された首相は直ちに組閣に入り，首相以外の閣僚を任命するが，閣僚の過半数は，国会議員でなければならない。閣僚のポストは法務・外務・大蔵・文部・厚生・農林水産・通商産業・運輸・郵政・労働・建設・自治・総務・防衛・経済企画・科学技術・環境・国土・特命事項担当・官房の20となっている。上述のように閣僚は過半数を割らなければ，議員以外でも採用できるのだが，議員以外の人が閣僚になるのは例外で，全員が議員から任命されるのが恒例である。1983年の総選挙で，自民党は過半数すれすれまで議席数を減らした。このため自民党から分党した新自由クラブと連立内閣を組閣，新自由クラブから1人が入閣した。しかし，1986年の総選挙で自民党は圧勝し，再び単独政権となった。

●組閣の背景

自民党の組閣の方法は，まず国会が首相を指名した後，党の副総裁，幹事長，総務会長，政務調査会長の党幹部を参謀に閣僚人選に入る。首相は閣僚任命に当たって，常に「適材適所で人選した」と述べるが，党内の派閥の大きさによって閣僚ポストが配分され，その中から当選回数を基準に選ばれる。このうち衆議院議員は18(首相を含む)で，残りの3ポストは参議院議員から選ばれるのがこれまでの例である。これは「派閥均衡，派閥順送り」の人事と呼ばれ，組閣のたびに批判を受けているが，いっこうに改められていない。これは，自民党内閣が党内の派閥の力関係によって成立していることに起因している。閣僚の任期は特に定まっていないが，在職期間は平均1年と短くなっている。これも1人が何年も閣僚を続けていると，派閥内部の閣僚希望者の閣僚になるチャンスが少なくなり，派内の不満が高まるからである。

内閣の寿命は佐藤内閣の7年，吉田内閣の6年，中曽根内閣5年，岸内閣3年，池田内閣3年を除いて，平均2年である。

The Cabinet*

● Formation

Just as with the British system, the Japanese Prime Minister is selected by the Diet from among its membership and serves at the Diet's sufferance. Generally, all the parties nominate their presidents and the issue is decided by vote. Since the Liberal Democratic Party has consistently had a majority ever since its formation in 1955, LDP presidents have regularly been named Prime Minister's

Once elected, the Prime Minister appoints the other ministers of state to form his Cabinet. Over half of the Cabinet must be appointed from the Diet membership. The score of ministerial posts are justice, foreign affairs, finance, education, health and welfare, agriculture, forestry and fisheries, international trade and industry, transport, posts and telecommunications, labor, construction, home affairs, management and coordination, defense, economic planning, science and technology, environment, national land use, special portfolio, and chief cabinet secretary. Although it is possible for non-Dietmembers to be appointed to the Cabinet so long as they are not a majority, it is unusual for such appointments to be made, and most commonly all Cabinet members hold Diet seats. In 1983, the LDP came very close to losing its majority in the Diet, and as a result the New Liberal Club (which had splintered off from the LDP earlier) joined with the LDP to form a coalition government, one NLC Dietman being appointed to the Cabinet. However, the NLC disbanded in the wake of the LDP's 1986 landslide election victory and Japan returned to one-party government.

● Selection Process

Once a Prime Minister is elected, he huddles with the LDP Vice President, Secretary General, Policy Affairs Research Council Chairman, and Executive Council Chairman to select Cabinet members. While the Prime Minister always claims that this is a process of choosing "the right man for the right job," Cabinet posts are actually allocated among the party factions in proportion to their sizes, and usually go on the basis of seniority. So far, the pattern has been for 18 of the Cabinet members (including the Prime Minister) to come from the House of Representatives and the other three from the House of Councillors. While this "factional-balancing, wait-your-turn" process comes in for criticism every time a Cabinet is formed, it persists as a means of satisfying the power balance within the LDP. Although there is no set term of office for Cabinet ministers, the average incumbency has been only about one year—since having people hold their posts for too long would deprive other aspirants of the chance to serve in the Cabinet and frustration would thus build up within the factions.

Except for Sato's seven years, Yoshida's six years, Nakasone's five years, and Kishi and Ikeda's three years, the Prime Minister's average term of office has been two years.

5 政党

●各政党の概要

日本には現在主な政党として自由民主党，日本社会党，公明党，民社党，日本共産党，社会民主連合がある。

「自由民主党」は1955年に，それまであった自由党と日本民主党の保守政党が合同して結成された政党である。結党以来選挙では常に過半数を超える議席数を獲得し，政権を握っている。「社会党」は終戦直後に，戦前の社会主義政党が一本化され，結成された社会主義政党である。「公明党」は*日蓮正宗の信徒の団体(創価学会)を母体としてできた政党である。創価学会は信徒数約1700万人という日本最大の信徒団体で，他の宗教団体に先駆けて政界に進出した。宗教団体のため団結力が固く，選挙の際，支持者である創価学会員は100%近くの投票率を示すが，一般票への浸透は弱い。「共産党」は戦前に結党された古い政党であるが，戦前は非合法政党で，公然と活動を始めたのは戦後である。終戦直後の選挙では議席数をかなり伸ばしたが，占領軍によるレッドパージと過激な活動が裏目に出て一時衰退した。最近の支持率は6%前後と落ち着いている。「民社党」は社会党の右派が社会党と別れて，1959年に結成した政党である。その基盤は同盟系の労組と中小企業経営者で，防衛問題については自民党に近い主張をしている。「社会民主連合」は，社会党左派に批判的なグループが1978年に結成した。

●政権政党

このように日本には多くの政党が存在しているが，政権を担当したのは，終戦後間もなくの短期間の社会党政権を除くと，すべて保守政党である。特に自由民主党は結党して以来ずっと政権政党である。同党は一部にウルトラ・コンサーバーとして批判を受けているが，その政策は幅が広く，しかも時代に対応する姿勢は野党各党よりもある。こうした政策への柔軟性のほかに，党内には政権を目ざす派閥が，競い合って選挙を戦うため，選挙では野党を常に圧倒している。自民党の基盤はここ当分緩みそうにない。

各政党のここ10年来の支持率は社会22%，公明8%，民社，共産各6%であり，同党による一党支配は，ここ当分は続くものと見られる。

Political Parties

● Party Differentiation

The main political parties in Japan are the Liberal Democratic Party (LDP), Japan Socialist Party (JSP), Komei Party, Democratic Socialist Party (DSP), Japan Communist Party (JCP), and United Social Democratic Party (USDP).

The LDP was formed with the 1955 merger of the two main conservative parties, the Liberal Party and the Japan Democratic Party. It has consistently won more than half of the seats in every national election, and hence held the reins of government since its formation. The JSP was formed right after the war as a coalition of socialist-leaning prewar parties. The Komei Party was formed by the Soka Gakkai religious organization (followers of the Buddhist Nichiren sect*). With about 17 million devotees, Soka Gakkai is the largest of Japan's religious groups and the first to go into politics. Although highly organized and enjoying virtually 100% voter turnout among its supporters, the Komei Party has little appeal to ordinary voters. The JCP is an old party, dating back from before the war, but it was banned before the war and has only been openly active since the war's end. After making strong electoral gains right after the war, the party fell prey to the Occupation's "red purge" and went into temporary eclipse as a result of its radical activisim. In recent elections, JCP support has held at about 6%. The DSP was formed in 1959 when the right wing of the JSP broke off. With strong support among Domei unionists and small-business people, the DSP position on defense is very similar to the LDP's. Finally, the USDP was formed in 1978 by a group critical of the leftist JSP.

● The Government Party

While political parties abound in Japan, the conservatives have reigned throughout the postwar period, except for a brief fling with socialist rule immediately after the war. This is especially true of the LDP, which has been in power ever since its formation. Although the LDP is criticized for being ultra-conservative, its policies are wide-ranging and sometimes more responsive to circumstances than the opposition parties are. In addition to this policy flexibility, the LDP also benefits at election time from the fierce campaigns waged by LDP factions as each tries to win legitimacy in its bid for party leadership, and the LDP's base seems secure.

With the other parties' lower approval ratings, JSP 22%, Komei 8%, and DSP and JCP 6%, one-party government will be the norm for some time.

6 選挙

選挙は，国政選挙と地方選挙に大きく分けることができる。国政選挙は衆議院選挙と参議院選挙，地方選挙は，都・道・府・県・市・町・村・区の地方首長選挙とその地方自治体の議会選挙である。

衆議院は定数512，130選挙区，１名単記で行われる。被選挙権は衆議院議員と地方議員が25歳から，参議院議員は30歳から，選挙権は20歳以上の男女に与えられている。日本の衆議院議員選挙の特徴の１つに，選挙区の定員がある。１選挙区１人でなく，定員が２～６の中選挙区制を採用していることである。参議院は定数252，選挙区は日本全国を１選挙区とする拘束名簿式比例代表制と各都道府県を１選挙区とし定員１～４の選挙区に分かれている。1983年までは全国区は候補者への直接選挙だったが，選挙法が改正され，政党に投票する比例代表制が導入された。

任期は参議院が６年，ほかは４年。地方議会はリコールなどによるほかは任期いっぱいで改選される。ただ衆議院議員は，任期いっぱいの４年で自然解散するのはむしろ例外で，平均２年半で解散選挙が行われている。選挙の時期は，解散のある衆議院を除くと，参議院が３年ごとの半数改選で７月，地方選挙は４年ごとに，４～５月に集中的に行われる。これは「統一地方選挙」と呼ばれている。投票率は各選挙とも最近の若者たちの選挙離れを反映し，年々減少の傾向にある。平均は60％ぐらいで，このうち都市部は50％前後と低く，農村部は高くなっている。

衆・参両院議員は一部の例外を除いて，政党に所属しているが，地方議員は所属政党を明確にするのを避ける傾向にある。特に首長選挙の場合はその傾向が強い。それは「県民党」「市民党」と名乗るほうが幅広く支持者を集められ，選挙に有利だからである。しかしその大多数は自由民主党系の保守派であって，野党は少ない。

選挙に金がかかることは日本も例外ではなく，こうしたことから新人が出ることはしだいに難しくなってきている。日本の選挙では“地バン，看バン，カバン”の“三バン”が，当選の必要条件であると言われている。地バンは地方社会と密着していること，看バンは知名度，カバンは金である。このため最近では議員になるのは官僚出身者か議員の二世が多くなってきている。衆議院ではすでに官僚と二世議員が半数近くも占めている。

Elections

Elections may be broadly divided into national elections for the Houses of Representatives and Councillors and local elections for town, city, prefectural, and other local government councils.

While all Japanese adults (20 or older) can vote, candidates must be at least 25 years old for the House of Representatives and local councils and 30 or older for the House of Councillors. The House of Representatives has 512 members elected from 130 election districts, each voter voting for a single candidate. One feature distinguishing Japanese elections is that 2-6 candidates are elected to the House of Representatives from each district. The House of Councillors has 252 members elected both in a nationwide contest with votes cast for the parties' binding candidate lists and in prefectural contests electing 1-4 Councillors per prefecture. The use of binding lists and vote-proportional representation was part of the Election Law's 1983 revision. Until then, national candidates had been subject to direct election.

Terms of office are six years for the House of Councillors and four years for all other offices. Unlike local councilmembers, who usually serve their full terms except for citizen recalls or the like, members of the House of Representatives typically find their terms interrupted by House dissolution and general elections, and the average has been two and a half years or so. Except for the House of Representatives, which can be dissolved and new elections called any time, the House of Councillors elects half its members every three years, usually in July, and local council elections are every four years, usually concentrated in April and May. With the growing political apathy among young people, voter turnout has been slipping at all levels. Today, the average turnout nationwide is about 60%—about 50% in urban areas and higher in the countryside.

Almost all members of the National Diet belong to one of the major parties, but there is a tendency to downplay political affiliation in the local elections, especially at the prefectural level. Instead, local politicians prefer to cast themselves at the head of "citizen parties" for broader appeal. Yet even so, most of these "independent" candidates are actually conservatives aligned with the Liberal Democratic Party, and the opposition remains largely in opposition at local levels as well.

Japanese elections, like elections everywhere, cost money, and this makes it very difficult for unknown candidates to compete against incumbency. To succeed, the candidate needs a base of support, a famous name, and a trunkfull of money. As a result, many of the more successful candidates have been people from the bureaucracy or from political families, and these people now account for nearly half of the members of the House of Representatives.

7 派閥

日本では，３人集まると派閥ができると言われている。派閥とは，仲間を作って特定の利益を追求するというのがその定義である。仲間を作る場合，出身地・出身校・縁戚（えんせき）によるケースが多く，それは「藩閥」「学閥」「門閥」とそれぞれ呼ばれている。このうち「藩閥」「門閥」はほとんどなくなっているが，「学閥」は残っている。例えば高級官僚のほとんどが東京大学の出身者であるため，各省庁は“東大閥”で占められている，と言われている。しかし現代の日本では，派閥と言うと自由民主党内のグループを指す場合が多い。

●党内派閥の成り立ち

自由民主党内には竹下登首相が率いる竹下派，安倍晋太郎の安倍派，宮沢喜一の宮沢派，中曽根康弘前首相の中曽根派，河本敏夫の河本派の５つの派閥があり，最大の派閥が竹下派である。グループは政策を研究し，それを政治に反映させることを目的としているが，その政治活動の大半は，派閥の長，親分を党首＝総理大臣にすることに置かれている。

自民党内に派閥ができたのは，日本の選挙区制が原因だと言われている。選挙区の定員が１名の欧米諸国と相違して，日本は２～６人の中選挙区制を採っている。したがって常に過半数を目指す自民党は同一選挙区に同党の候補者を複数，選挙区によっては定員いっぱい立候補させている。このため必然的に選挙では党員どうしがライバルとなり，同じ党員どうしが激しい選挙を戦うことになる。そこで党首を目ざす党内の実力者は，自分の勢力を拡大するために系列化し，系列に入った立候補者に資金援助するなどして支援する。候補者は当選するとその派閥の所属議員として，派閥の親分の政権実現のために努力する。

●派閥の功罪

議員が派閥に入るのは，選挙の資金援助のほか，政務次官や大臣のポストを得るために大いに役だつからである。というのは自民党内の内閣は派閥の連合内閣であり，閣僚のポストはその派閥の大きさによって配分されているからで，無派閥議員が閣僚になることはきわめて難しい。

派閥は人材登用の大きな障害になることや党内の政争を激化させる要因であることなどから，常に派閥解消が唱えられるが，これまでに１回も実現されていない。それはやはり選挙区制度が原因で，それが改善されないかぎり，派閥解消の実現は難しいのが現状である。

Political Factions

There is an old saying in Japan that three people make a faction—defined as a gathering of people to press for special interests. Many factions are formed of people from the same city, the same school, or with blood ties. Although geographical and blood alliances have become less important recently, old school ties retain their strength. For example, because almost all of the top government bureaucrats are University of Tokyo graduates, "the U of T clique" is said to dominate the government. However, the term faction in modern Japan most commonly calls to mind the political factions within the ruling Liberal Democratic Party (LDP).

● Formation of Factions

The five main factions in the LDP are those led by Prime Minister Takeshita Noboru, Abe Shintaro, Miyazawa Kiichi, former Prime Minister Nakasone Yasuhiro, and Komoto Toshio. The largest one is the Takeshita faction. Although these groups' official raison d'etre is to study policy issues and have an impact on public policy, most of their efforts seem directed at getting the faction leader (referred to as "the old man") elected LDP President and hence Prime Minister.

Japan's electoral system is said to be at least partly responsible for the factions' existence. Whereas most Western countries elect one person from each district, Japanese voters return 2-6 people per electoral district. Any party (such as the LDP) hoping for a majority in the Diet must therefore run more than one candidate in every district, sometimes fielding as many candidates as there are seats available. As a result, candidates from the same party end up competing with each other for votes, and established politicians vying for the party presidency contribute endorsements and money in the expectation that successful candidates will return the favor later. Once a candidate is elected, he teams up with his patron and works to help "the old man" become Prime Minister.

● Pros and Cons

The main advantage of belonging to a faction is that it promises electoral support as well as a better shot at vice minister and ministerial posts. Because LDP Cabinets are basically coalitions among the various LDP factions, Cabinet posts are distributed proportional to each faction's strength, and it is very difficult for a non-aligned politician to become a Cabinet minister.

Because the factions tend to block the promotion of capable non-faction people as well as to exacerbate political infighting within the party, the LDP regularly calls for their dissolution—always in vain. With the factions a natural outgrowth of the electoral system, it is difficult to see how they can be dissolved unless the system is changed.

8 官僚

日本では官僚という場合は，中央省庁の高級公務員，国家公務員上級職試験・外交官試験・警察官上級職試験を通った行政のテクノクラートを指すのが普通である。

●官僚制度の歴史

日本の官僚制度は非常に古い。千数百年前，大和(やまと)朝廷(政権)が中国から導入した律令(りつりょう)制が，時代とともに整備され，それに伴って官僚も育っていった。特に江戸時代は，戦乱のない平和な時代が二百数十年の長期にわたって続いたため，武士たちは，しだいに行政テクノクラートとなり，官僚制度はいっそう成熟していった。明治になって日本は，欧米の思想・技術を積極的に取り入れ，急速に近代化したが，その原動力となったのが，武士出身の行政官たちだった。彼らはこれまでの官僚組織を基礎に，欧米の行政制度を巧みに導入する一方，国立大学を設立，官僚の養成を図った。特に中央省庁の高級官僚養成を目的とした東京大学には，全国から優秀な学生が集まった。こうした伝統が今も生きており，現在の中央省庁の官僚の大部分は東京大学出身者で占められている。

●官僚制度の功績

官僚と言うとどこの国でも融通のきかない，杓子(しゃくし)定規，冷たいというイメージが持たれている。日本もその例外でなく，「官僚的」と言えば形式的で独善的の同義語として使われている。しかし日本の官僚の場合，その能力は高く評価されている。例えば近年欧米の学者やジャーナリストたちの間で，日本研究が盛んになっているが，彼らが「日本の繁栄と奇跡的な高度成長」の秘密を語るとき，例外なく挙げるのが官僚の功績であり，官僚機構である。

日本の官僚制度がうまく機能している理由は，①優秀な人材が集まっている　②政策立案に大幅な権限を持ち，かつ積極的である　③民間との関係が密接である　などが挙げられる。ちなみに戦後の総理大臣だけでも，その大半が官僚出身であり，国会に提案される法案の100%近くが，官僚たちが立案したものである。また，官民の密接な関係を示す例として，「日本株式会社」という言葉がある。これは外国人の研究者が官民一体を株式会社にたとえたものである。また，官僚の指導力を示す言葉として，「悪名高き通産省」というのがある。戦後の日本産業を諸外国に対抗できるよう強力に指導した通産官僚に，外国企業が付けたニックネームである。

The Bureaucracy

In Japan, "the bureaucracy" usually refers to government technocrats who have passed the qualifying examinations for high-level posts in the central government offices, diplomats, and police officials.

● History

Japan has a long history of bureaucracy. Well over 1,000 years ago, the Yamato Court adopted rules of government patterned after the Chinese model. With time, a bureaucracy grew up to service these regulations. This was especially conspicuous during the Edo period when peace prevailed for 250 years and the warrior class gradually metamorphosed into a bureaucracy. Although Japan modernized rapidly with the introduction of Western thinking and technology in the late 19th century, the driving force behind the state remained these warrior-scion bureaucrats. Building upon the indigenous Japanese government structure, these people grafted on Western administration and founded national universities in an effort to build a strong bureaucratic corps. The University of Tokyo, for example, founded to train elite bureaucrats for the government in Tokyo, drew outstanding students from throughout the country. This tradition lives on even today, and most of the top government bureaucrats are University of Tokyo graduates.

● A Successful System

Worldwide, bureaucrats are perceived as uptight and unfeeling people who rigidly go by the book. Japan is no exception, and the adjective "bureaucratic" is synonymous with paperwork and arbitrariness. Yet the Japanese bureaucracy is also perceived as highly capable. Western scholars and journalists have recently done considerable research on Japan, and without exception they give much of the credit for Japan's prosperity and miraculous economic growth to the skilled bureaucracy.

Among the reasons Japan's bureaucracy has worked so well are that it has attracted outstanding people, it has considerable authority in drafting policy, and it enjoys the trust of the private sector. The caliber of its people is shown by the fact that, for what it is worth, most of Japan's postwar prime ministers started their public careers in the bureaucracy. Policy-wise, nearly all of the bills submitted to the Diet for consideration are drafted by the bureaucracy. And the close ties between government and business is hinted at by the term "Japan, Inc." In fact, foreign students sometimes tend to think the two are working hand in glove. Another term indicative of the bureaucracy's leadership position is "the notorious MITI"—the nickname foreigners have given MITI in recognition of its postwar efforts to revive Japanese industry and enable Japan to compete in world markets.

9 裁判

日本の裁判制度は，戦後大幅に変わったものの１つである。戦前は天皇の裁判所であったが，戦後は国民の裁判所として，行政，立法とともに三権の１つとしての地位を確立した。日本の司法は戦前まで「ドイツ法」の影響が強かったが，戦後は「英米法」の制度が導入された。しかし陪審制度の採用は見送られた。

●司法の組織

裁判所には最高裁判所，高等裁判所，地方裁判所，家庭裁判所，簡易裁判所がある。裁判は三審制で，地方裁判所が一審，高等裁判所が二審，最高裁判所は最終審である。家庭裁判所は離婚などの裁判，簡易裁判所は地方裁判所の下部機関で，交通違反などの軽い犯罪を扱う。最高裁判所は判事と長官を含め15人，全判事で裁判を行う大法廷と，３人の判事で構成する小法廷がある。通常は小法廷で扱われるが，大きな問題のときは大法廷が開かれる。最高裁判所はこうした裁判のほか裁判官の人事など全裁判所の司法行政事務の最高機関でもある。高等裁判所は全国で８か所，地方裁判所は50か所にあり，それぞれ刑事，民事の裁判を行っている。

●裁判の方法

まず，裁判は一審を担当する地方裁判所で争われる。刑事犯罪に例を取ると，検察官が起訴，不起訴を決め，起訴が決まると裁判が始まる。

通常の場合，地方・高等裁判所は，裁判長と陪席判事２人の計３人の裁判官と検事，弁護士で構成する。証拠調べの後，検事の求刑，弁護人の最終弁論，そして裁判官の合議で判決が下される。見解が分かれたときは多数決で決まるが，少数意見は明らかにされない。高等裁判所の裁判は，一審裁判に不満を持った被告，あるいは検察官の控訴によって行われる。裁判の方法は一審と同じだが，書面審理の比が大きくなる。最高裁判所は，憲法にかかわる問題と重大な事実誤認が明らかになったとき法廷が開かれる。

最高裁判事は内閣の任命によるが，任命された新しい判事は次の衆議院選挙の際と10年ごとに国民投票で審査を受ける。また裁判官の不正などが明らかになったとき，国会の裁判官弾劾裁判所（国会議員で構成）で裁判にかけられ，不適と判断されると罷免される。

The Japanese Judicial System

The judicial system is one of the Japanese institutions that changed most after the war. In place of the prewar imperial courts, popular courts were established (along with the executive and the legislature) as one of the three main pillars of authority in Japanese society. The prewar court system had been strongly influenced by German law, but now it is closer to the Anglo-American system, albeit without juries.

● Structure

The judicial system consists of the Supreme Court, high courts, district courts, family courts, and summary courts. The appeals process has three levels, the 50 district courts having first jurisdiction, the eight high courts acting as appellate courts, and the Supreme Court the court of last appeal. Family courts handle such things as divorce cases while summary courts handle only such minor cases such as traffic violations. The Supreme Court is made up of 15 justices, including a chief justice, and is divided into the grand bench consisting of all supreme court justices and petty benches of three justices each. Most cases are decided by the petty benches, but the grand bench may be convened for especially important cases. In addition, the Supreme Court is responsible for administering the judicial system, including personnel appointments, and is the highest judicial administrative body.

● Procedures

Cases go first to the district courts. In criminal offenses punishable by imprisonment, the case begins in the district court when the public prosecutor decides to indict the defendant.

Ordinarily, cases in the high courts and district courts are tried by three judges, one of whom presides, with prosecution and defense attorneys present. After the judges have heard the evidence, they hear the prosecution's sentencing recommendations and the defense's final argument and hand down their verdict. When the judges are divided, the majority opinion is adopted and no dissenting opinion announced. The high courts try cases which have been appealed, by either the defendant or the prosecution, after a previous trial. Procedures are similar to those in the district court, except that record of the previous trial also plays an important part. The Supreme Court considers Constitutional questions and other matters deemed important enough to require the highest court's attention.

Supreme Court justices are appointed by the Cabinet subject to popular approval in the first general election following appointment. The Diet Court of Impeachment is empowered to investigate allegations of malpractice and dismiss any justices deemed incompetent.

10 税制

日本の税制は，欧米諸国と比較すれば，間接税を主体とする欧州各国とは異なり，アメリカの税制に類似している。所得税，法人税などの直接税を主とし，酒税，関税など間接税を従としているからである。その比率は，直接税が70%，間接税が30%になっている。

●税の徴収方法

税制の基本的な原則は「公平にして公正」であり，申告納税を土台にしている。担税力(税を負担する能力)によって税率格差を設けており，所得に応じた累進税率が適用されている。ただ，サラリーマンなど勤労者は，毎月の給料から「天引き」で税が徴収され(源泉徴収と言う)ている。このため税の捕捉は，サラリーマンは100%に近い。ところが自営業者などは自己申告制であり，申告しない人もいて，申告内容にも必要経費などの面で裁量が効く。このため自営業者は半分程度，農民の場合は30%程度しか所得が捕捉できないのが実情。これを「トーゴーサン(10・5・3)」などと言っている。

●歳入に占める税収の割合

国の歳入に占める日本の税収は，1985年度の場合で，71%であった。本来，国の財政は100%を税収，または納付金など「税外収入」によるべきだが，1973年の第1次石油危機以降，景気後退などから税収不足が慢性化してしまった。このため日本でも他の先進国同様に，歳入不足を補うために国債を発行して財源の穴埋めを続けている。税収の主なものは所得税（全税収の40%），法人税（同33%）で，このほか間接税として酒税，揮発油税，物品税などが体系化されているが，所得税，法人税とも個人，企業の税負担率が高くなっている。特に，諸外国に比べて所得税の累進税率は高い。

●税制改正の問題点

一方，税務当局(大蔵省)では，国債発行(1985年3月末で残高は120兆円）を減らし，財政を健全にするために増税や新規税制の導入などを検討，中期的には大型間接税の導入によって，税収増加を図りたい考えである。これは欧州各国型で，間接税の比重を高めて税収の安定を狙ったものだが，国民のコンセンサスが得られにくいのが現状である。これら国税のほか，地方税(住民税や事業税など)があり，国民所得に対する租税負担率は24%である。なお，税制改正については，首相の諮問機関である税制調査会が決める形式になっているが，政治家や役人の介入があり，各国同様に「税は政治そのもの」となっているのが実情である。

Taxes

Compared with taxes in the other industrialized countries, Japanese taxes do not have European taxes' reliance on indirect taxation and are more like U.S. taxes. In Japan, the main thrust of personal income taxes, corporate taxes, and other direct taxes is supplemented by such indirect taxes as the liquor tax and the customs tariffs in a 70:30ratio.

● Tax Collection

The guiding principle is that of "fair and equitable taxes," and the system relies upon self-reporting. Tax rates are progressively graduated by ability to pay. However, because office workers and other salaried personnel have their taxes withheld (i.e., deducted at the source) every month, the collection rate on these people is nearly 100%. By contrast, self-employed people are expected to file their own returns, and some of them either fail to file or claim excessive deductions. As a result, it is felt that self-employed entrepreneurs pay only half of their real taxes and farmers only 30% of the rightful amount—in what has been called a 10:5 : 3 payment pattern.

● Tax Revenues

In 1985, tax revenues accounted for 71% of the national government's total income. Although tax and non-tax revenues should provide for all of the government's funding, there have been chronic shortfalls ever since the recession in the wake of the first oil crisis (1973). As a result, Japan, like the other industrialized countries, moved to offset this revenue shortfall by issuing government bonds. The main categories of tax revenue are personal income taxes (40% of the total), corporate taxes (33%), and then such indirect taxes as the liquor tax, gasoline tax, and excise tax. Yet the tax burdens on individuals (income tax) and companies (corporate tax) have gotten steadily heavier, and income tax schedules are high by international comparison.

● Issues in Tax Reform

At the same time, the tax authorities (Ministry of Finance) have been studying raising taxes or levying new taxes to boost revenues and cut back on government bond issues (¥120 trillion outstanding as of March 31, 1985), and the government is considering major new indirect taxes as revenue enhancers over the medium term. Although the European countries have stabilized revenues by emphasizing indirect taxation, no consensus has gelled on this yet in Japan. In addition to these national taxes, there are also local taxes (e.g., residence taxes and enterprise taxes), and taxes now account for 24% of national income. The Tax Adjustment Council (a panel advising the prime minister) is supposed to have the final word on tax reform, but politicians and bureaucrats are bound to intercede and there is a widespread feeling that "taxes are what politics are all about."

11 外交

日本の外交が戦後本格的にスタートしたのは1951年，サンフランシスコで講和条約が調印されたときからである。講和条約を締結するに当たって，ソ連圏を含めた関係諸国のすべてと締結する全面講和論と，とりあえず欧米諸国だけとの講和をするという多数講和論が激しく対立，国論も二分された。当時の吉田内閣は多数講和を選択したが，現在もこれが，日本外交の原点となっている。すなわち日本外交の基軸はまず「日米友好」であり，西側の一員として，欧米民主主義諸国と協調を図りながら，外交を展開するという現在の外交方針が，このとき確立したのである。これに対して野党側，とりわけ社会党，共産党は，欧米諸国，特にアメリカとオーバーコミットすることに反対，ソ連，アメリカとは「等距離外交を採るべきだ」と主張してきた。

●日米関係

日米関係はこれまで大きなトラブルもなく推移してきたが，近年アメリカの対日貿易赤字が膨大になるにつれ，自動車・鉄鋼・農産物を中心とした貿易摩擦，また防衛問題で，日本の防衛力整備がアメリカの希望どおりに進んでいないことなど，日米間に摩擦が起きている。しかし日本の外交の中で，日米間の友好は最優先で，毎年明らかにされる政府の外交青書では，「日米安全保障条約に基礎を置く，アメリカとの友好協力関係は，日本外交の基軸であり，政治・経済・防衛をはじめ，広範な分野にわたり，アメリカは日本の重要なパートナーである」と強調している。

●アジア諸国との関係

日米関係とともに日本が重視しているのは，韓国，中国，ASEAN諸国である。韓国との関係は隣国でありながら，必ずしもスムーズな外交関係が確立されているとは言えなかった。しかし，中曽根内閣になって，中曽根首相・全斗煥大統領の首脳どうしの公式訪問が実現し，日韓関係を修復した。中国，ASEAN諸国へは日本の首相は在職中必ず歴訪しており，その友好関係に心を砕いている。

●日ソ関係

日ソ関係については，まだ平和条約が締結されていない。これはハボマイ，シコタンなど，北方領土の返還問題が解決していないためである。日本側は「経済，文化の交流を維持しながら，粘り強く北方領土の返還を求める」としているが，ソ連が北方領土返還にはかたくなな態度を崩しておらず，平和条約の締結が早急にできる見通しはない。

Foreign Policy

Japanese postwar foreign policy was shaped in 1951 with the signing of the San Francisco Peace Treaty. At the time, Japanese public opinion was split between advocates of waiting for a comprehensive peace treaty including the Soviet Union and all other principals and advocates of going ahead with a partial peace treaty signed by the Western powers. By establishing the basic orientation of a foreign policy premised upon friendship with the United States and Japan's membership in the Western community of nations and building cooperation with the other Western democracies, the Yoshida government's decision to go with the partial peace determined Japanese foreign policy to this day. On the other side of the aisle, the opposition parties, especially the Socialist Party and the Communist Party, charge that Japan is overcommitted to the United States and should adopt a foreign policy more equidistant between America and the Soviet Union.

● U.S.-Japan Relations

U.S.-Japan relations have been largely trouble-free so far, but there has been increasing trade friction recently in automobiles, steel, agricultural products, and other items as the U.S. trade deficit with Japan has soared and defense friction as the Japanese build-up has not been as fast as the United States would like. However, friendship with the United States remains Japan's highest foreign policy priority, the *Diplomatic Bluebook* has annually emphasized that the relations of friendship and cooperation with the United States based upon the security arrangements are the cornerstone of Japanese foreign policy, and the two countries are important partners in a wide range of political, economic, defense, and other areas.

● Relations with the Countries of Asia

Japan also emphasizes its relations with the Republic of Korea, China, and the Association of Southeast Asian Nations (ASEAN) countries. Although Korea is right next door, Japan-Korea relations have not always been the smoothest. However, relations were normalized in 1965 and further improved in 1983-84 with the exchange of official visits by Prime Minister Nakasone and President Chun Doo Hwan. Major efforts have also been made to strengthen Japan's friendly relations with China and the ASEAN countries, and these areas are musts for Prime Ministers traveling overseas.

● Relations with the U.S.S.R.

Given the yet-unresolved status of Habomai, Shikotan, and the other Northern Territories, Japan and the Soviet Union have yet to sign a peace treaty. Japan is pushing tenaciously for the Territories' return even as it maintains economic and cultural relations with the Soviet Union, but the Soviet Union has been unrelenting on this issue and there is little likelihood of a peace treaty's being signed soon.

12 防衛

●専守防衛と安全保障条約

日本の防衛政策は，各国に比べてきわめて大きな制約を受けている。憲法第９条に，戦争放棄，戦力の不保持と交戦権の否定に関する規定があること，核については「持たず，作らず，持ち込ませず」という非核三原則があるからである。したがって，日本の防衛は専守防衛を基本的な方針として，自衛隊を創設，その整備を推進し，運用を図ってきた。

専守防衛という言葉についての確定された定義はないが，①相手から武力攻撃を受けたとき，初めて防衛力を行使する　②その行使は必要最小限度にとどめる　③装備も攻撃的なものでなく，自衛的な武器に限る　など「受動的な戦略である」と日本政府は説明している。具体的には，性能上，もっぱら他国の国土の壊滅的破壊のためにのみに用いられる兵器，例えばICBM，長距離戦略爆撃機などは持てない。また武力行使の目的を持って武装した部隊を他国の領土・領海・領空に派遣する海外派兵は，「必要最小限度」をはるかに超えるものとして許されない。このためその防衛力を補うため，日本は米国と安全保障条約を結んでいる。つまり，核を含む米国の軍事力のプレゼンスが日本の防衛力の大きな柱となっているのである。

●自衛隊と防衛力の拡大

自衛隊については，当初国民の中に「憲法に違反している」としてかなり強い反対があったが，現在は国民の80％以上が自衛隊の必要性を認めている。自衛隊の規模は，陸上が普通師団12，機甲師団１，高射特科群８，隊員の計は16万人。海は４艦隊を基軸に，対潜水艦艇約60隻，潜水艦16隻，航空機220機。空はＦ４ファントム，Ｆ15イーグルを主力とする10飛行隊を中心に約430機となっている。世界で８位の軍事力と言われるまでに整備されてきているが，現在も軍隊を駐留させているアメリカは，「日本の防衛力はまだ不十分」として，さらにその整備を求めている。

防衛力の整備をするに当たって，日本政府は防衛力大綱を作り，それに基づいて充実を図っているが，その上限をＧＮＰ１％としていた。しかし装備費，人件費の上昇で，１％の枠を守るのはしだいに困難になってきて，1987年度の予算で１％の枠を超えた。アメリカは日本周辺の領海の防衛を日本に担当させ，太平洋にシーレーンを設けることを，日本政府に強く要望している。

Japanese Defense Policy

● Defense-orientation and the Security Treaty

Japanese defense policy operates under many more restrictions than exist in most other nations. Article 9 of the Japanese Constitution is a declaration that "land, sea, and air forces, as well as other war potential will never be maintained" and a renunciation of the right of belligerency of the state. Added to this is the government's Three Nonnuclear Principles which state that Japan will not produce, possess, or allow the entry of nuclear weapons. Japan's stance is thus purely defensive, and the establishment and maintenance of the Self Defense Forces (SDF) has been in line with this fundamental policy.

Although Japan's defense strategy has no official definition, it is said to a reactive policy in that (1) Japan will employ its self-defense capability only when attacked, (2) such a response will be limited to the absolute minimum force required, and (3) all weapons will be defensive weapons only. More specifically, weapons capable of being used in an attack on a foreign nation, such as ICBMs and long-range strategic bombers, will not be maintained. In addition, any deployment of armed SDF units on foreign soil, waters, or airspace clearly goes beyond the "absolute minimum" required for defense and will not be allowed. Given these constraints, the security arrangements with the United States providing for Japan's protection through an American military presence that includes America's "nuclear umbrella" are an important mainstay of Japanese defense policy.

● Growth of the SDF

Although the establishment of the SDF was at first strongly opposed on the grounds that it violates Article 9 of the Constitution, Japanese public opinion has gradually changed, and over 80% now acknowledge the SDF necessary. The SDF are made up of 12 ground force divisions, 1 armored division, and 8 anti-aircraft units with a combined troop strength of 160,000; a four-fleet maritime force including a 60-ship anti-submarine fleet, 16 submarines, and 220 aircraft; and a 430-aircraft air force including 10 squadrons of F-4 Phantoms and F-15 Eagle fighters. Although Japan is already the world's eighth largest military power, the U.S. forces in Japan continue to contend that this is inadequate and that Japan's defense capability must be further beefed up.

In building up Japanese defenses, the government has formulated a defense outline for scheduling and prioritizing defense budget increases within the 1%-of-GNP ceiling. However, rising personnel and equipment costs made this ceiling increasingly difficult to maintain, and in the fiscal 1987 budget the 1% figure was exceeded. The United States has expressed a strong desire to have Japan defend nearby waters and Pacific sea lanes.

13 経済協力

●経済協力

自由世界ではアメリカに次いで第2位の国民総生産を持つまでに成長した日本は，現在，世界各国への経済協力を要請されている。

実質国民総生産では，1970年を1とすると，1983年で，日本は1.8倍の成長を示した。これに対し，アメリカ，イギリス，フランス，西ドイツ，イタリアが1.3倍前後である。一方，1人当たりの国民所得を見るとアメリカ，カナダをはじめ，スイス，ノルウェーなど主な西欧，北欧諸国よりやや低い地位にある。そのうえ，社会資本や住宅・土地など個人資本が貧しい日本では，政府予算でも家計でもその約3割が借金しながら資本を蓄えている——というのが，日本の経済の実力である。

しかし，失業者の増大など不況色を強める欧米諸国や，低成長のなかで債務累積問題に悩まされている開発途上国などの世界経済にあって，日本は世界の保護貿易化を防ぐため，自らの市場解放を行う一方，政府開発援助(ODA)に積極的に取り組んでいる。日本は，ODAの新中期目標(1981～85)の援助総額を214億ドル以上とした。1983年実績では，前年より24.4%増の37.6億ドルとなり，各国比では，アメリカ，フランスについで第3位となった。

外務省は1981年1月，経済協力評価委員会を設置し，こうした援助の統轄管理や評価活動を行うなど本腰を入れてきている。協力の内容としては，無償資金協力の分野では，医療が全体の3分の1を，分野別の事業借款実績では，陸運関係が4分の1を占めているのが特徴である。

●研究技術協力

技術の国際協力は1982年，83年のサミットの重要課題でもあり，現在22の協力事業を行っているが，日本はこのうち20に参加，太陽光発電，光合成，先端ロボット，軽水炉の安全研究の4事業ではリーダー役を務めている。

また，先進国とは2国間協定が締結されているほか，発展途上国の経済・社会の開発に欠かせない人材養成のための研修生の受け入れ，専門家の派遣，機材の供与などの協力を推進している。1983年には途上国に4.6億ドルの技術援助を行った。これはフランスの4分の1，アメリカの3分の1であるが，日本は西ドイツに次いで第4位となり，着実に進展している。

International Economic Cooperation

● Economic Cooperation

Having grown into the second-largest market economy (after the United States), Japan has a responsibility to cooperate with the rest of the world economically.

Japanese growth has been particularly rapid. There was, for example, 80% growth in Japan's net national product (NNP) between 1970 and 1983. By contrast, the United States, United Kingdom, France, West Germany, and Italy had NNP growth of only about 30%. In terms of per-capita income, however, Japan lags somewhat behind the United States, Canada, Switzerland, Norway, and most of the other countries of Europe and Scandinavia. Moreover, lacking social infrastructure or such personal assets as land and homes, the Japanese government and family alike rely upon borrowing for about 30% of their operating capital even as they work on asset formation.

Nevertheless, faced with mounting protectionism arising from the persistent unemployment and recession in the West, the accumulated external debt burdens and other problems facing the developing countries, and other difficulties in the world economy, the government has sought to stay this deteriorating climate by further facilitating access to the Japanese market and instituting a vigorous program of official development assistance (ODA). The ODA target for the five years of the New Medium-term Plan (1981 through 1985) is over $21.4 billion. In 1983, total ODA disbursements were up 24.4% over the previous year to $3.76 billion, making Japan the world's third-largest donor country (led only by the United States and France).

In January 1981, the Ministry of Foreign Affairs set up an Economic Cooperation Evaluation Committee to assess and coordinate Japanese assistance. As things stand now, about one-third of all grant capital aid is medical assistance, and about one-fourth of the project credits are for overland transport.

● Science and Technology Cooperation

Research cooperation was an important concern at the 1982 and 1983 summit conferences of industrialized states. Of the 22 cooperative international projects in this field, Japan is participating in 20 and taking the lead in the four of solar cells, photosynthesis, advanced robotics, and light-water reactors.

In addition to bilateral cooperative projects with the other industrialized countries, efforts are also being made to supply experts, provide equipment, and provide training to help the developing countries with their economic and social development. Japan's $460 million in technical cooperation for the developing countries in 1983 placed Japan fourth—one-fourth the figure for France, one-third that for the United States, and slightly less than that for West Germany—and Japan is fast expanding its efforts in this field.

14 戦後日本経済の復興

戦後の日本経済は通常，1945～55年の戦後復興期，それに続く高度成長期，そして1973年の石油危機以降の安定成長期に大別される。

●経済の民主化

戦後の日本経済は，占領軍による経済の民主化によって新たな出発の基盤が作られた。この経済の民主化とは，「財閥解体」「農地改革」「労働改革」を言う。

財閥解体は，三井，三菱，住友，安田など戦前の大財閥の解散を言い，これにより財閥一族による人的・資本的支配が一掃され，財閥一族以外の少壮経営者が大いに企業者精神を発揮しうるようになり，また企業間の競争も活発化することになった。また，農地改革により，小作地の81%が自作地として解放され，地主制が解体した結果，新たに自作農となった人たちによる農業の近代化が進展した。さらに，労働者については，労働三法(労働組合法，労働関係調整法，労働基準法)が制定され，労働運動の合法化をはじめ，労働者の地位が大幅に改善されて，勤労意欲の向上や労使関係の安定化に寄与した。

●インフレからデフレへ

他方，産業面では1947年から石炭，鉄鋼へ資材，労働力，資金を集中的に投入する「傾斜生産方式」が採用され，1948年から日本経済はインフレを伴いつつも，復興の軌道に乗った。しかし，1949年に特命全権公使として来日したJ．ドッジは，「日本経済は両足を地に着けずに竹馬に乗っているようなものだ。片足はアメリカの援助，他方は国内の補助金であり，竹馬の足をあまり高くしすぎると，転んで首を折る危険がある」と述べ，厳しい財政，金融の引き締めを勧告した。これの実施により，日本経済は深刻なデフレに突入した。

「安定恐慌」と呼ばれたこの時期，一般大衆は貯蓄を強いられ，その資金は大企業に向けられた。そのため，大企業のその後の成長には寄与したものの，中小企業の倒産，失業が増大し，社会不安が高まった。そうした折，1950年6月，朝鮮戦争が勃発し，その特需によって日本の生産活動は飛躍的に拡大した。そして，早くも1951年度の実質国民総生産は戦前水準(1934～36年平均)に達した。

1951年9月，対日講和条約が成立し，占領時代は終わった。折から朝鮮戦争も終わり，産業界は一時，動乱ブームの反動不況に陥ったものの，それは次の高度成長期への小休止であった。

Japan's Postwar Economic Recovery

The postwar economy is usually divided into the three periods of postwar recovery from 1945 to 1955, the subsequent rapid-growth era through 1972, and the period of slower but stable growth in the wake of the 1973 oil crisis.

● Economic Democratization

It was the Occupation's economic democratization policies—zaibatsu dissolution, agrarian land reform, and labor reform—which laid Japan's postwar economic foundations.

Dissolution of the zaibatsu, meaning the breaking of the Mitsui, Mitsubishi, Sumitomo, Yasuda, and other wartime financial cliques' control over management and capital, made it possible for non-zaibatsu businessmen to exercise their entrepreneurial talents and sparked renewed market competition. Agrarian land reform promoted agricultural modernization by abolishing landlording and distributing 81% of the tenant-farmed land to the people who tilled it. In labor reform, the Occupation enactment of the Trade Union Law, Labor Relations Adjustment Law, and Labor Standards Law legalized union activities, vastly improved the status of working people, and contributed to motivating workers and stabilizing labor relations.

● From Inflation to Deflation

While this was going on, industry was investing massive amounts of materials, manpower, and capital in the coal and steel industries under the priority production system, and the economy was put on the road to recovery, albeit with inflation, by 1948. In 1949, however, Joseph Dodge came to Japan as financial advisor to the Occupation and, commenting that, "Far from having both feet firmly planted on the ground, the Japanese economy is like a man on stilts*—one American aid and the other domestic subsidies—yet if these stilts are too high the economy is likely to fall and break its neck," he recommended sharply tighter fiscal and financial policies. These policies plunged the Japanese economy into rapid deflation.

This period of "controlled recession" was one of forced savings with the capital made available to the big companies. Although this contributed to the big corporations' growth, it also meant more small business bankruptcies, higher unemployment, and enhanced popular dissatisfaction. Yet the outbreak of the Korean War in June 1950 sparked an explosive expansion in Japanese production to meet American military procurement needs. By fiscal 1951, Japanese real GNP had regained its prewar (1934-36 average) level.

In September 1951, the San Francisco Peace Treaty was signed and the Occupation officially ended. The Korean War ended soon afterward, and the economy fell into a post-boom recession which, as it turned out, was but a brief interlude before the rapid-growth era.

15 高度成長から安定成長へ

●高度成長期

「もはや『戦後』ではない。我々は異なった事態に直面しようとしている。回復を通じての成長は終わった。今後の成長は近代化によって支えられる」と1956年度の『経済白書』が指摘したように，日本経済は1950年代後半から高度成長時代に入った。すなわち，1955年からの10年間の実質平均成長率は９％，続く1965年からの10年間のそれも８％と，ほぼ４分の１世紀ほどの長期にわたって，日本の経済は世界に冠たる高い成長を続けた。ちなみに，1955～73年のアメリカ，イギリスの年平均成長率は３％前後，西ドイツ，フランス，イタリアのそれは５，６％であった。また，1955年には自由主義国第７位であった日本のＧＮＰは，12年後の1967年には第２位となり，かつて「中進国」と言われた日本は，「経済大国」と言われるようになった。

この間に，工業生産は著しい拡大を見た。例えば1973年において，ラジオ・テレビ・船舶・商業車が世界のシェアで20％を超え，粗鋼・精銅・亜鉛・紙・レーヨン・合繊・セメントなどが10％を超え，アルミ・ガラス・時計など５％を超えたものも数多い。消費水準も大幅に向上し，実質消費は1955年から1970年までの15年間に２倍となった。その結果，テレビ・冷蔵庫・洗濯機をはじめ，主要な耐久消費財の普及率はほぼ飽和状態となったほか，1949年ごろには，日本では生産は無意味であるとも言われていた乗用車も，急速に普及した。

●高度成長の要因

この高度成長の要因については多くの議論があるが，大約，次のような要因が挙げられている。①戦後の民主化改革　②企業の積極的投資　③豊富な優れた労働力　④高い貯蓄率　⑤積極的な技術導入　⑥高い教育水準　⑦小さい軍事負担　⑧労使関係・社会・政治の安定　などである。なお，これらに加えて，「先進国に追いつけ，追い越せ」といった人々の心意気も無視できない。

●安定成長

さて，よく知られているように，1973年10月に生じた産油国の石油値上げ(第１次石油危機)により，日本経済も減速を余儀なくされた。かくして，さしもの高度成長にも終止符が打たれ，以後，日本の経済は安定成長期へと移行した。1975年から1983年までの実質平均成長率も４％強という水準になっている。だが，経済は沈滞してはおらず，先端技術産業の台頭，サービス経済の拡大など，安定成長の内側にはダイナミックな動きも見られる。

From Rapid Growth to Stable Growth

● Rapid Growth

"The postwar period is over. The era of growth through recovery has ended, and we face a new situation. Future growth will be sustained through modernization." So said the 1956 *White Paper on the Economy* in pointing out that the Japanese economy had entered a period of rapid economic growth in 1955. For the 10 years 1955-64, the average annual growth rate in real terms was 9%. For the next decade, it was 8%. By contrast, the average growth for the years 1955-73 was only 3% for the United States and Great Britain, and 5-6% for West Germany, France, and Italy. For nearly a quarter of a century, Japan had one of the highest economic growth rates in the world. The seventh-largest GNP in the free world in 1955, Japan had climbed to second place in 1967. Once a minor developing nation, Japan quickly developed into a major economic power.

Industrial production expanded significantly during the period of rapid economic growth. In 1973, Japan accounted for over 20% of the world demand for radios, television sets, shipping, and commercial vehicles. Japan also took over 10% of the world's blister steel, copper, zinc, paper, rayon, synthetic fiber, and cement and over 5% of its aluminum, glass, and watches. In the 15 years from 1955 to 1970, consumption increased 2-fold in real terms. Domestic markets for durable household goods such as television sets, refrigerators, and washing machines attained near-saturation, and domestic passenger car production, considered "unnecessary" as recently as 1949, showed phenomenal growth.

● Contributing Factors

Amid the debate about the actual cause of this rapid economic growth, there is broad agreement on the importance of, inter alia, (1) postwar democratization, (2) aggressive private-sector investment, (3) abundant availability of high-quality workers, (4) high savings rate, (5) ready adoption of advanced technologies, (6) uniformly high educational standards, (7) minimal defense spending, and (8) social, political, and labor-relations stability. In addition, many people would cite Japan's strong motivation to catch up with and surpass the other industrialized nations.

● Deceleration

Yet the oil crisis of October 1973, when the oil-producing nations hiked crude oil prices sharply, put an abrupt end to this dramatic growth. Since then, Japan's economy has stabilized at about 4% real growth between 1975 and 1983. While growth has slowed, the economy is by no means in recession. Advances in the high-technology industries and expansion in the service industries indicate that there is still considerable dynamism in the economy even in this period of slower growth.

16 産業構造の変遷

産業の栄枯盛衰はきわめて激しい。戦後の経済復興の立役者であった石炭産業は，今や全く寂れてしまった。また，かつての花形産業であった繊維・造船・化学・鉄鋼・アルミなども，今や斜陽産業のレッテルをはられている。代わって，電機・自動車・エレクトロニクスなどが花形産業となっている。大学生に人気のある就職先は，そのほかに銀行，損保，商社などがある。流通部門では，スーパーをはじめとするディスカウント店が急速に増えた。それやこれや，斜陽産業と新興産業の交代劇の例は枚挙にいとまがない。

●著しい就業者構成の変化

一般に産業構造を表す指標としては，産業を第1次産業(主に農林漁業)，第2次産業(主に建設・製造業)，第3次産業(卸小売，金融，運輸通信，サービス業，公務など)に分け，それぞれの就業者数の割合(全就業者を100として)＝構成比が用いられる。

日本の1955年の就業者構成比は，第1次産業41%，以下，第2次23.5%，第3次35.5%であった。つまり，この時期ではまだ農業就業者がいちばん多かったわけである。言い換えれば，まだ製造工業がさほど発展していなかったとも言える。だが，10年後の1965年には，第1次24.6%，第2次32.0%，第3次43.3%となり，第1次産業の就業者が大幅に減少し，その分，第2次，第3次の就業者が増えた。つまり，高度経済成長が本格化し，製造工業が拡大するに伴って，農村の労働力が工業に吸収されていったのである。

そしてさらに10年後の1975年になると，第1次13.9%，第2次34.1%，そして第3次は52%となった。ここで目だつのは，第1次は10%台にまで低下した一方，第3次が50%を超えたことである。実は，第3次の数字は，すでに1973年に50%台に達したのだが，このことは，全就業者の半分が物(財)ではなく，サービスの生産に携わるようになったことを意味している。また，この年には，第3次産業の生産高も全産業の50%を占めるようになっており，生産の面でも全生産高の半分をサービスの生産が占めるようになったのであった。

こうして経済のサービス化が本格化し，1984年には，第3次産業の就業者比は56.9%にまで高まっている一方，第1次のそれは8.9%と10%を切っている。また，第2次産業の就業者比は1980年代に入って漸減傾向にあり，1984年は34.2%であった。

Changes in the Industrial Structure

The ups and downs of industry can be extreme. The coal industry, for example, once a major pillar of Japan's postwar recovery, is today relegated to a minor role. Likewise, such once-leading industries as textiles, shipbuilding, chemicals, steel, and aluminum are now in decline, rapidly being replaced at the forefront of Japanese industry by electrical machinery, automobiles, electronics, and the like. The other business sectors most popular with job-seeking university graduates are banking, non-life insurance, and international trade. In the distribution sector, supermarket and discount store chains have mushroomed. Every field has its declining sunset industries and its ascending sunrise industries.

● Changes in Employment Patterns

A nation's industrial structure is conventionally divided into three sectors—primary (agriculture, forestry, and fisheries), secondary (construction and manufacturing), and tertiary (retail and wholesale trade, finance, transport, communications, services, and civil service). The employment index for each sector (total 100 for all employees in all sectors) is an indicator of that sector's importance within the total industrial structure.

In 1955, the employment ratios in Japan were 41% primary, 23.5% secondary, and 35.5% tertiary. As may be seen, a plurality of Japan's work force was in agriculture, and secondary-sector manufacturing was still immature and undeveloped. Ten years later, however, in 1965, the ratios had changed to 24.6% primary, 32.0% secondary, and 43.3% tertiary. The primary sector was down sharply, its place taken by the secondary and tertiary sectors. With the rapid economic growth, manufacturing had expanded and much of the labor force had moved from farm to factory.

Within the next decade, to 1975, the ratios further shifted to 13.9% primary, 34.1% secondary, and 52% tertiary. While primary-sector employment had dropped to under 20%, tertiary employment exceeded 50%. This shift in the employment structure was already evident in 1973 when tertiary employment first topped 50%—more than half of Japan's workers being involved in producing and selling services rather than things. At the same time, tertiary production accounted for 50% of all production by value.

The growth in the service industries continues today. In 1984 employment in tertiary industries accounted for 56.9% of all Japanese workers. By contrast, the primary sector had dropped to 8.9%. Employment in secondary industries has also decreased since 1980, declining to 34.2% in 1984.

17 産業組織

●主要な企業集団

戦前型の財閥は解体されたが，代わって銀行を中軸に据えた企業の集団化が定着している。現在の日本の主要企業集団は，次の6グループになる。

①三井グループ（月曜会）…三井銀行を中心とし，三井物産，東レ，東芝，トヨタ自動車，三井石油化学工業，王子製紙，三越など。

②三菱グループ（金曜会）…三菱銀行を中心に，三菱商事，麒麟麦酒，三菱レイヨン，三菱電機，三菱重工業，三菱自動車工業など。

③住友グループ（白水会）…住友銀行を中心に，住友商事，住友化学工業，住友金属工業，日本電気など。

④芙蓉グループ（芙蓉会）…富士銀行を中心に，丸紅，大成建設，サッポロビール，昭和電工，日本鋼管，日立製作所，日産自動車など。

⑤三和グループ（三水会）…三和銀行を中心に，日商岩井，帝人，宇部興産，神戸製鋼所，日立製作所，シャープ，ダイハツ工業など。

⑥第一勧銀グループ（三金会）…第一勧銀を中心に，伊藤忠商事，旭化成，川崎製鉄，富士通，いすゞ自動車，清水建設，富士電機など。

●産業組織の特色

さて，日本社会はよく「*タテ型社会」と言われるが，以上の企業集団はいわばヨコ型金融系列を成し（ワンセット主義とも言われる），それぞれ独立した企業の横断的な緩やかな結合関係を成している。もっとも，日本には新日鉄グループとかトヨタグループといったようなタテ型の集団も存在していて，親会社・子会社といったかなり緊密な結合関係になっている。

以上のように，タテにヨコに複雑に入り組んだ関係（ネットワーク）が見られるのが，日本の産業組織の大きな特色となっている。こうした企業集団は，一種の共同体的性格を強く持っており，ある部品を調達するときには，極力同一集団内の企業から購入するなど，集団内の取引を優先したり，また集団内での情報交換を密にする等々のことを行っている。例えば，自動車会社は部品生産をもっぱら集団内の部品メーカー，あるいはタテ系列の子会社，下請会社に委ねているので，内製化率はアメリカの自動車会社に比べると著しく低い。このことは，ある意味で分業化が進んでいることでもあり，それが日本企業の活力を維持する重要な要因となってもいるようである。

Japan's Industrial Structure

● Main Industrial Groups

Although the prewar zaibatsu were broken up after the war, there has been a distinct trend toward *keiretsu* regrouping centered around the banks. The six main corporate groups and their leading members are:

1. Mitsui Group (Getsuyokai): Mitsui Bank (leader), Mitsui and Co., Ltd., Toray Industries, Inc., Toshiba Corporation, Toyota Motor Corporation, Mitsui Petrochemical Industries, Ltd., Oji Paper Co., Ltd., Mitsukoshi, Ltd.
2. Mitsubishi Group (Kin'yokai): Mitsubishi Bank (leader), Mitsubishi Corp., Kirin Brewery, Mitsubishi Rayon, Mitsubishi Electric, Mitsubishi Heavy Industries, Mitsubishi Motors
3. Sumitomo Group (Hakusuikai): Sumitomo Bank (leader), Sumitomo Corp., Sumitomo Chemical, Sumitomo Metal Industries, NEC Corp.
4. Fuyo Group (Fuyokai): Fuji Bank (leader), Marubeni, Taisei, Sapporo Breweries, Showa Denko, Nippon Kokan, Hitachi, Nissan Motors
5. Sanwa Group (Sansuikai): Sanwa Bank (leader), Nissho Iwai, Teijin, Ube Industries, Kobe Steel, Hitachi, Sharp, Daihatsu Motors
6. Dai-Ichi Kangin Group (Sankinkai): Dai-Ichi Kangyo Bank (leader), C. Itoh & Co., Asahi Chemical Industry, Kawasaki Steel, Fujitsu, Isuzu Motors, Shimizu Construction, Fuji Electric

● Organizational Characteristics

While Japanese society is commonly referred to as a vertical society,* these corporate groups are horizontal financial affiliations of independent companies spanning the entire range of industrial activity. In addition, there are also vertically affiliated groups, such as the Nippon Steel Group and the Toyota Group, with closely knit parent companies and their subsidiaries in a particular industrial field.

The complex *keiretsu* networks of vertical and horizontal group affiliations are a major characteristic of Japan's industrial organization. The members of a *keiretsu* share a distinct group consciousness and sense of solidarity. In many cases, a corporation will purchase from a *keiretsu* affiliate, and the corporations within an affiliate group are in close communication with each other. In the automobile industry, for example, the Japanese automaker purchases almost all of the parts it needs from its affiliated parts manufacturers, subsidiaries, and subcontractors. As this very low internal sourcing ratio suggests, there is a high degree of specialization, and this specialization is probably one of the main reasons for Japanese industry's vitality.

18 産業政策

●独占禁止政策

従来，産業政策とは，独占行為や不当な競争など，自由かつ公正な競争を制限する行為を禁ずる政策を指した。日本ではそれを，「独占禁止法」(独禁法)に基づいて，「公正取引委員会」(公取)が担当している。1965年前後，日本では大型合併が相次いだが，特に1968年には当時の鉄鋼業界の上位2社，つまり八幡製鉄と富士製鉄の合併が発表された。当然，公取はこれを審査し，その間，経済学者の多くが合併反対のキャンペーンを行った。結局，合併は承認され，「新日本製鉄」が誕生したのだが，これはこれまでに公取が扱った最も大きな事件であった。

カルテルは，もちろん独禁法で禁じられている。しかし，不況業種の場合，価格の低落を防ぐ意味で不況カルテル(主に価格カルテル)が行われ，日本ではこれを独禁法の適用除外として認める場合が多い。また，産業界からは常に独禁法の適用緩和が望まれており，他方にはそれを警戒し，公正競争を守ろうとする経済学者グループがいるなど，この意味の産業政策はなかなかに緊張をはらんでいる。

●日本的産業政策

産業政策は，狭義には，産業界の投資調整，勧告操短(減産の指示)など，通産省による行政指導を指す場合が多い。より広義には，特定の産業に対する振興・助成(典型的なのは戦後復興期の傾斜生産方式)，さらには産業再編成などを言い，もちろん通産省が関係する。明治時代に国が中心となって行った殖産興業の伝統が官民協調方式として続いているのが，特に外国人の目から見ると，日本は官民の癒着が目だつようであり，そこに日本独自の秘密めいた産業政策が成立しているとして，「日本株式会社」といった見方をされたりもした。

1963年に，貿易・資本の自由化(外圧)対策として，欧米大企業に対抗しうる規模の企業作りを策した「特定産業振興(臨時措置)法」(特振法)を通産省は国会に提出した。これには，さすが産業界も官僚統制を恐れて反対し，国会に3度提出されたが成立しなかった。しかし，先の大型合併の続出の背景には，こうした産業政策思想があったと言える。他方，公害防止，省エネ，先端技術等々の面でも，日本の官庁はかなりキメの細かい指導を行っており，「日本株式会社」という指摘も，的外れとは言いがたい。

Industrial Policy

● The Anti-monopoly Act

The purpose of Japanese industrial policy has been to promote fair and free competition by outlawing monopolies and other unfair trade practices. This is the responsibility of the Fair Trade Commission under the Anti-monopoly Act. In the 1960s, several large-scale corporate mergers took place in Japan, the most prominent being the 1968 merger of the nation's top two iron and steel companies, Yawata Iron & Steel and Fuji Iron & Steel. Although many economists spoke out publicly against the merger, the Fair Trade Commission, in one of the most important cases it has ever handled, approved the merger to create the Nippon Steel Corp.

Industrial cartels are obviously prohibited by the Anti-monopoly Act. However, anti-recession cartels (especially price-support cartels) have been allowed in several particularly depressed industries to keep prices from falling too low, and many companies have been granted such special exemptions from the ant-trust laws. As might be expected, there is a constant stream of companies requesting immunity from the Anti-monopoly Act, and an opposing army of economists lobbying against any weakening of the Act.

● Japanese-style Industrial Policy

In the narrow sense, Japan's industrial policy is one of guidance by the Ministry of International Trade and Industry (MITI) on such matters as investment adjustments and production curtailment, and in a wider sense it is one of promoting and supporting designated key industries (as was done under the priority production system during the postwar rehabilitation period) and otherwise encouraging industrial restructuring. The cooperation between Japan's public and private sectors continues a tradition that began in the nation-building policies of the Meiji-era governments, yet the good relations between the two sectors have led some foreign observers to charge that a "Japan, Inc" government-industry complex runs the country.

For example in 1963, MITI proposed that the government's decision to institute capital and trade liberalization be mitigated by a special law to protect designated industries from overwhelming Western competition. However this was opposed by private-sector interests wary of bureaucratic regulation, and, though proposed three times, it never passed the Diet. Nevertheless, MITI's industrial policy did have some success with the large-scale mergers discussed earlier, and the "Japan, Inc" characterization is somewhat substantiated by the government's very detailed administrative guidance in such areas as pollution prevention, energy conservation, and high-technology development.

19 貿易構造と貿易摩擦

●貿易構造の偏り

資源に乏しい日本が経済大国と言われるまでに発展したのは，貿易に負うところがきわめて大きいことは言うまでもない。実際，今日の日本は輸出入大国ともなっている。例えば，自由経済圏において，日本の食料輸入はアメリカ，西ドイツに次いで第3位，木材・繊維原料・金属鉱などの原料輸入は圧倒的に第1位，原油などの燃料輸入はアメリカに次ぐ第2位だが差は小さい。他方，カラーテレビをはじめとする電気機器，自動車，船舶，鉄鋼，カメラ・時計などの光学・精密機器については，今や日本は世界一の輸出国となっている。まとめて言えば，日本は食料・原材料の輸入が断然多く，製造工業品の輸出が世界のトップということになる。

これはまさに加工貿易の優等生といったパターンではあるが，このことは，極端に言えば，世界の中で日本だけが工業国で，ほかは食料・原料供給国といった，きわめて偏った貿易構造になっているとも言えるわけである。

●激化する貿易摩擦

こうした輸出入構造であってみれば，当然，他の工業国から不平が生じる。つまり，日本は自国の工業製品を売りつけるばかりで，こちらの工業製品を買ってくれないという不満である。特に1970年代の前半には，日本の製品輸出は「集中豪雨的」と形容され，欧米のひんしゅくを買った。こうして貿易摩擦が本格化した。

特に日米貿易は，近年，日本が一貫して黒字である上，日本がアメリカから買うものと言えば，食料・飼料が主であるのに対して，日本からは繊維が，次いでカラーテレビが，さらには自動車がなだれ込んでいくのだから，アメリカとしても黙ってはいられない。こうして，日米貿易摩擦は激化の一途をたどってきたのである。

とにかく日本の工業品輸出攻勢が問題にされただけでなく，工業品の輸入が少なすぎる点にも，欧米の非難の目が向き始めた。日本は，何か特別な輸入抑制措置を設けているのではないか，という疑惑の目で見られるようになった。少なくとも日本は，ガットに反するような輸入規制は行ってはいないのだが，わずかに残っている輸入制限（特に米）の自由化が強く求められているのも，上のような状況があるからである。しかし，欧米人にとっては，日本への製品売り込みは苦手であるということも事実のようである。

Trade Structure and Trade Friction

● Japan's Unbalanced Trade Structure

Resource-poor Japan's rise to economic-superpower status obviously owes much to international trade. Japan is a giant in both exports and imports. For instance, Japan ranks third in the free world (after the United States and West Germany) as an importer of foodstuffs, is by far the world's biggest importer of raw materials such as wood, textile materials, and metals, and is a close second behind the United States as an importer of crude oil and other fuels. On the other side of the ledger, Japan is currently the world's biggest exporter of color TV sets and other electrical appliances, automobiles, ships, steel, and high-precision optical and electronic products such as cameras and timepieces. Japan, more than any other country, has prospered by importing food and raw materials and exporting manufactured goods.

It has done brilliantly with its processing-trade structure. Yet when taken to its logical conclusion, this structure posits Japan as the world's sole supplier of manufactured goods and relegates all other countries to being sources of food and raw materials. This is clearly an untenable imbalance.

● Trade Friction

This lopsided trade orientation has naturally led to charges of unfairness, and Japan stands accused of being interested only in selling its own products and not in buying other nations' manufactured goods. In the early 1970s, Japan was criticized by the United States and Western Europe for "flooding" their markets with exports, and trade friction became a major international issue.

Friction is especially evident in Japan-U.S. trade, where Japan has consistently recorded surpluses in recent years, and this problem is compounded by the fact that Japan's imports from the United States are centered on such items as food and feed while its exports are concentrated in textiles, color TVs, and automobiles. Over the years, Japan-U.S. trade friction has gotten progressively worse.

Europeans and Americans are blaming Japan not only for its aggressive exports of manufactured goods but also for its failure to import more manufactured goods, and they suspect Japan of actively restricting imports. Although Japan is in conformity with the GATT (General Agreement on Tariffs and Trade) rules and regulations enjoining against import barriers, the persistent imbalances have led to strong calls for liberalization in the few fields where residual import quotas exist (particularly rice). Whatever the institutional arrangements, the other industrialized nations continue to have difficulty exporting to Japan.

20 農林水産業

●農業

昭和30年代(1955～64年)末期までは順調に拡大していた日本の農業だが，高度経済成長が進展する中で，1963年ごろからほぼ一貫して生産高，就業者数とも低下を続けている。農家人口に占める65歳以上の老人の割合が高まる一方，1960年には600万戸あった総農家数も，1984年では450万戸にまで減少し，総農家の34％を占めていた専業農家は13％台に低下している。この農家数の減少テンポは最近はやや鈍ってきているが，農家人口の高齢化，後継者難は深刻な問題となっている。

また，食用農産物の自給率も，米は90％台を保っているが，昭和30年代には40％台にあった小麦の自給率は10％前後まで落ち込んでいる。そのため，日本は食料輸入大国となっている。したがって，ひとたび外国の穀物生産に異変が生じたときには，日本の穀物需給，ひいては国民の食卓にも，大きな影響が生じることになる。

一方，牛肉，オレンジに関しては，日本は国内生産者保護のために輸入制限を行っている。そのため，再度にわたってアメリカから強い自由化要請の圧力を受けている。

●林業

日本の木材需要は，近年は7000万㎥前後で推移しているが，そのざっと55％ほどが輸入によって賄われてきた。ちなみに，1960年では，それは12％にすぎなかった。なお，日本の林野面積2500万haは，国有林が約31％，都道府県市町村などの公有林が12％，私有林が57％となっている。

木材のほぼ67％は製材用であり，次いで合板用16％，木材チップ用(13％)に用いられているが，ともかく外材に押されて国内の林業は振るわない。そのため政府は，1980年に新しい林業構造改善事業10年計画を開始した。

●水産業

日本の漁獲量は1980年に1000万tの大台に乗り，世界第1位の座を保ってはいる(以下，ソ連，中国，アメリカ，チリ，ペルー，ノルウェー)。だが，200カイリ設定国の増加に伴い，遠洋漁業(特に北洋での)漁獲量は減少傾向を強めている。これに伴って水産物の輸入が増加し，かつての水産国日本も，今では世界一の水産物輸入国となっている。

Farming, Forestry, and Fisheries

● Farming

Japanese farming developed smoothly after the war until 1963, when it was derailed by rapid economic growth and began its current downward trend in both productivity and manpower. As more and more people are drawn to work in urban-based industries, an increasing percentage of the farming population is 65-and-over. At the same time, the number of farming households dropped from nearly six million (of which 34% were full-time farmers) in 1960 to 4.5 million (only 13% full-time) in 1983. Although this decline has slowed in the past few years, the older average age in farming communities and the lack of successors for many family farms still pose serious problems for the future.

In terms of agricultural food self-sufficiency, Japan is still over 90% self-sufficient in rice but has declined from 40-50% self-sufficiency in wheat in the late 1950s and early 1960s to about 10% at present. As a result, Japan has become one of the world's biggest agricultural food importers, and Japanese dietary patterns are very vulnerable to the ups and downs in world food supplies.

While importing vast quantities of other foods, Japan has placed import quotas on such products as beef and oranges to protect domestic producers. This practice has led to insistent demands from the United States for further liberalization.

● Forestry

Japan's annual demand for lumber has been estimated at about 70 million cubic meters. Close to 55% of this demand is now met by imports—up from only 12% of the total in 1960. Japan has a total of 25 million hectares (about 62 million acres) of forest land, of which 31% is owned by the national government, 12% by local governments, and 57% by private individuals or companies.

Almost 67% of Japan's lumber is used for wood products, 16% for plywood, and 13% for wood chips; and strong foreign competition has depressed the Japanese forestry industry across the board. As a result, the Japanese government moved in 1980 to establish a ten-year plan for restructuring the domestic forestry industry.

● Fisheries

Japan's fish catch topped 10 million tons in 1980, underscoring Japan's position as the world's top fishing nation (followed by the Soviet Union, China, the United States, Chile, Peru, and Norway in that order). However, as an increasing number of nations have established 200-nautical-mile economic zones, Japan's deep-water catches have necessarily fallen off, especially in northern waters. As a result, Japan has had to turn increasingly to imports, and this once-proud fishing nation is now the world's biggest importer of marine products.

21 主要製造業

●鉄鋼業

1980年に1億1140万tを生産し，アメリカを抜いた日本の粗鋼生産は，82，83年と1億t台を割ってはいるが，ソ連に次ぐ世界第2位の地位にある。日本の代表的な鉄鋼会社は，新日本製鉄（1982年度粗鋼の生産シェアは28.1%），日本鋼管（同11.9%），川崎製鉄（同10.8%），住友金属工業(同10.7%)，神戸製鋼所(同6.4%)で，「高炉5社」と呼ばれている。このうち，新日本製鉄は世界最大の鉄鋼会社である。

●電子機器・電機産業

現在の花形産業の1つである。特にカラーテレビ・VTR・オーディオ機器など民生用電子機器と，通信機器を中心とした産業用電子機器を擁する電子機器産業は，いわゆる「エレクトロニクス革命」の担い手として脚光を浴びている。カラーテレビの普及率はすでに飽和点に達しているが，新たに*AV時代を迎え，これまで普及の伸びの鈍かったVTRの急速な需要増とあいまって，新型テレビへの買い替えが活発化している。また，*マイコン，*ワープロの普及も著しい。さらに，OA，FAの進展等々，まだまだ新しい成長製品の登場する可能性を秘めている。民生用機器の代表メーカーである松下電器産業，ソニー，通信機器の代表メーカーである日本電気，富士通など，有力メーカーの数は多い。また，日立製作所，東芝などの重電機メーカーも，家電部門に早くから進出しており，音響機器などにも力を注いでいる。

●自動車産業

粗鋼生産がアメリカを追い抜いた1980年には，自動車の総生産台数も1000万台を突破し，アメリカを抜いて世界第1位となった。乗用車だけを見ても，日本は世界のトップに立っている。100万台に達したのが1963年のことであるから，20年間で10倍に成長したことになる。それには内需だけでなく，輸出が大きく寄与している。これは電機の場合も同様で，それだけに，当然ながら外国からの風当たりも強く，電子機器，電機と自動車産業とは貿易摩擦の台風の目となっている。トヨタ自動車と日産自動車の2大メーカーは，アメリカのGMとともに世界の3大メーカーとなったが，マツダ，本田技研の2社も，年産100万台を生産しており，日本では年産100万台のメーカーが4社となっている。ただ，世界の自動車戦争はさらに激化が予想され，今後，国際的な提携の強化，国内メーカーの再編成などが進みそうである。

Japan's Principal Manufacturing Industries

● Steel

In 1980, Japan's steel industry produced 111.4 million tons of crude steel, surpassing the United States in steel production. Even though Japanese crude steel production fell below 100 million tons per year in 1982 and 1983, Japan was still the world's second-largest producer of steel (after the Soviet Union). The "Big Five" Japanese steelmakers are Nippon Steel (which produced 28.1% of the nation's total crude output in 1982), Nippon Kokan (11.9%), Kawasaki Steel (10.8%), Sumitomo Metal Industries (10.7%), and Kobe Steel (6.4%). Japan's biggest steelmaker, Nippon Steel is also the world's largest.

● Electronics

Japan's electrical and electronic equipment industries are among the nation's most successful. In both mass-market electronic equipment such as color televisions, video tape recorders, and audio equipment and telecommunications equipment and other industrial-use products, these companies are in the spotlight as leaders in the electronics revolution. Although color TV ownership has reached the saturation point, sales are being revitalized as people turn to more modern equipment in keeping with the upturn in previously slow sales of video tape recorders for the audio-visual age.* Likewise, more and more Japanese are buying microcomputers* and word processors,* and the advances being made in OA (office automation) and FA (factory automation) equipment hold the promise of many new types of growth products soon. Japan boasts a large number of leading electronics companies, including Matsushita Electric Industrial and Sony in mass-market electronic equipment and NEC and Fujitsu in telecommunications equipment. Close behind them, Hitachi, Toshiba, and others in heavy electrical machinery have moved quickly into household electronics with a major push in audio equipment and other areas.

● Automobiles

In 1980, the same year that Japan surpassed the United States in crude steel production, Japanese automobile production topped the 10-million mark to overtake the United States as the world's No.1 automaker. Japanese passenger car production reached the million mark in 1963 and has risen rapidly in the two decades since then with growth in both domestic demand and exports. However, as in electronics, export success has triggered trade friction. Two Japanese companies (Toyota and Nissan) are among the world's three top automakers (the other being General Motors of the United States). Two other Japanese firms, Mazda and Honda, also produce more than a million a year. Yet as the global "car wars" grow fiercer, there will be increasing need for more international joint-venture efforts and continued restructuring within the Japanese industry.

22 先端技術製品

1960年代には数多くの新しい成長製品が商品化されたが，その後，新技術，新製品の開発がやや途絶え気味であった。そうした折，1973年秋に起こった石油危機は，ある意味で新技術，新商品の開発を急がせる大きなインパクトとなったと言えよう。

●エレクトロニクス産業

1970年代に入ってからの新技術，そしてそれの実用化の中核を成してきたのはエレクトロニクス産業であり，「エレクトロニクス革命」が本格化した。特に，ＩＣ，ＬＳＩなどの半導体技術の進歩により，マイコンがさまざまな機器に応用されるようになった。パソコン・ワープロ・ファクシミリなどのＯＡ機器，産業用ロボットなどのＦＡ機器，そしてＣＡＤ／ＣＡＭは急ピッチで普及しつつある。産業用ロボットの設置台数(1982年)は，合成樹脂工場(6240台)，自動車工場(5240台)，電機機器工場（4660台）などを中心に合計で２万4000台ほどに達し，世界第１位となっている。

マイコンは，デジタル方式の導入とあいまってテレビ・オーディオ・カメラなどにも広く応用され，機器の性能の向上に大きな役割を果たしている。コンピューターについては，現在の超ＬＳＩに基づく第４世代コンピューターに続くものとして，自ら問題を推理，解決していく機能を備えた第５世代コンピューターの開発が，通産省を中心とした官民協力による財団法人「新世代コンピューター技術開発機構」(1982年４月設立)によって10年計画で進められている。また，日本電信電話株式会社も，高度情報通信システム(ＩＮＳ)に関連して，第５世代コンピューターと同様の新しいコンピューターの開発に着手している。

●新素材産業・ライフサイエンス産業

エレクトロニクス技術の発達は，新半導体をはじめとする新素材産業の発展を促している。この産業ではほかに，アモルファス合金，ニューセラミックス，スーパー繊維と言われるアラミド繊維等々の新製品がそう遠くない将来に実用に供されようとしている。

他方，糖尿病の治療薬インシュリン，抗ガン剤のインターフェロンなど，これまで量産が困難であったものが，遺伝子工学，あるいはバイオテクノロジーの発達に伴い，量産の見通しがついたと言われる。この分野はライフサイエンス産業とも言われ，そこではまた，光合成促進剤の実験も始まっている。これが実用化されれば，いろいろな農産物の増産に大いに寄与すると言う。

High-technology Products

In the 1960s, Japanese industry experienced a shift in emphasis toward the commercial development of new high-growth products, yet as the decade closed, the pace of development slowed. However, the oil crisis of 1973 had a major impact in speeding up progress in several new technologies and products.

● Electronics Industry

The 1970s became host to the electronics revolution, and the electronics industry formed the nucleus for many new technologies and commercial applications. This was particularly true as advances in integrated circuits (ICs), large-scale integrated circuits (LSIs), and other semiconductor technologies yielded a whole new variety of microcomputer applications, including office equipment such as personal computers, word processors, and facsimile machines; factory automation equipment such as industrial robots; and increasingly popular computer-aided design and manufacturing (CAD/CAM) systems. Approximately 24,000 industrial robots had been installed in Japanese factories by 1982, with most of them being used to help make synthetic resins (6,240 units), automobiles (5,240), and electrical products (4,660).

The widespread introduction of digital electronic designs in televisions, audio equipment, cameras, and other products brought improved product quality based on microcomputer technology. In computers, the Institute for New Generation Computer Technology was established in April 1982 with support from MITI and other governmental agencies to carry out a 10-year plan for developing fifth-generation machines featuring artificial-intelligence inferential and analytical functions to supplant the present state-of-the-art fourth-generation models based on VLSI (very-large-scale integrated circuit) technology. Nippon Telegraph & Telephone Corp., Japan's largest domestic telecommunications company, is doing similar research and development in connection with its INS (Information Network System) project.

● New Materials and Life Sciences

Advances in electronics generally stimulate advances in the new materials industry which includes semiconductors and other electronic components. Other new-materials-industry technologies expected to be commercialized in the near future include amorphous alloys, fine ceramics, and "super-fabrics" such as aramids.

In other areas, products which have traditionally been extremely difficult to mass produce—including insulin to treat diabetes and interferon to fight cancer—will soon enter mass production as a result of advances in genetic engineering and biotechnology. These new technological fields, collectively called the life sciences, also include photosynthesis accelerators—an experimental substance that will sharply increase agricultural yields if it can be commercialized.

23 物価と流通産業

●物価

日本の消費者物価(指数)は，1973年の第1次石油危機のときには，前年上昇率が24.5%(1974年)，1979～80年の第2次石油危機でも8.0%(1980年)を示したが，1974～83年の平均上昇率は7.6%であった。同期間の先進主要国の消費者物価は，イギリス23.3%，フランス17.2%，カナダ13.5%，アメリカ11.3%，西ドイツ5.5%という上昇率であったので，日本は西ドイツに次いで物価上昇率の低い国であったことになる。さらに，1982年以降，物価は急速に鎮静化し，1983年，84年といずれも2%内外という低い上昇率を示している。今や，第1次石油危機後のインフレ体質が克服されたと言ってよいだろう。

しかし，消費者の実感としては，物価は高いとする人が多い。これは，公表される消費者物価指数が家計の支出のすべてをカバーするものでないこともあるが，値上りした商品には敏感だが，値下りしたものには注意がいかないことによるものと思われる。

ちなみに各品目の小売価格を世界主要都市と東京とで比較してみると，食料品，ことにバター・牛乳・牛肉・米の価格が割高になっている。反対に，比較的安価な品目は，ワイシャツ・テニスシューズ・オートバイ・小型乗用車などの工業製品，アパート賃貸料・ホテル料金・クリーニング代・パーマ料金などのサービス料金の一部である。

●流通産業

日本には，1982年で43万の卸売店と170万の小売店がある。170万の小売店のうち，デパート・スーパーなど法人組織のものは25%にすぎず，残りは零細規模の個人商店である。この個人商店の販売額は，近年低下している。それは大型店舗，コンビニエンスストアの増加の影響によるもので，今後は経営的にもますます苦しくなるのではないかと思われる。

1970年代後半から小売業全体の年間販売額の伸び率は鈍化しているが，特に1980年代に入ってからは停滞が強まり，大型小売店といえども販売額は伸び悩み，上昇率はGNPの伸びを下回っている。消費支出の伸びも鈍化しているが，それをかなり上回って小売業全体の販売額が鈍化している。それは，小売を介さない消費支出，特に教育，旅行，稽古(けいこ)ごとなどへのサービス支出の増加(モノ離れと言われる)と関係があるようである。

Prices and Distribution

● Prices

Although there were sharp price increases sparked by the two oil crises (24.5% over the previous year in 1974 and 8.0% in 1980), Japan's consumer price index increased 7.6% per annum on average over the decade 1974-83. Given that the average per-annum price increases in the other industrialized countries for the same decade were 23.3% in the United Kingdom, 17.2% in France, 13.5% in Canada, 11.3% in the United States, and 5.5% in West Germany, Japan's record was the second-lowest of any major country. Prices have been especially stable in Japan since 1982, with 1983 and 1984 both showing increases of only about 2% over the previous year, and the economy has apparently shaken off the inflationary propensity that infected it during the first oil crisis.

Nevertheless, many consumers still feel that prices are high. While part of the problem is that the official consumer price index figures do not cover everything a family buys, it is also partly because consumers are quick to feel the pain when prices go up and tend not to notice when they go down.

Looking at consumer prices in Tokyo in comparison to some of the world's other major cities, prices in Tokyo are higher for such foodstuffs as butter, milk, beef, and rice but lower for manufactured goods such as clothing (dress shirts and tennis shoes), consumer durables (motorcycles and compact cars), and such service-sector items as room rents, hotel rooms, dry cleaning, and hairdressing.

● Distribution

As of 1982, there were 430,000 wholesale dealers and 1,700,000 retail outlets in Japan. Of the retail outlets, only 25% were such corporate entities as department stores and supermarkets, and the other 75% were small unincorporated mom-and-pop stores. Yet the percentage volume handled by these corner operations has been declining in recent years under the onslaught from the superstores and convenience shops, and they are expected to face continued rough sailing in the years ahead.

Although total retail sales growth has been gradually slipping since the latter half of the 1970s, this stagnation has been especially pronounced since the turn of the decade. Even the giant superstores have been hurt, and consumer spending has failed to keep up with the growth in GNP. The trend is even more pronounced within consumer spending as retail sales have in turn failed to keep up with consumer spending overall. This change in Japanese patterns of consumption would seem to indicate that people's values are less material-oriented and that there has been a priority shift to spending on education, travel, hobby interests, and other services not found at your local supermarket.

24 日本の原子力利用

●原子力の平和利用

世界で唯一の原子爆弾被爆国である日本では，原子力利用はもっぱら平和利用に限られ，特に原子力発電のウエートが高い。原子力発電は，準国産エネルギーとして供給の安定性が高く，そのうえ経済性にも優れているので，現在では，日本の石油代替エネルギーの中核的存在に位置付けられている。

日本で本格的な原子力発電の火がともったのは，1966年7月，茨城(いばらき)県東海発電所が営業運転を開始してからであり，以後原子力発電の開発は急速に進んだ。その結果，1984年末には全国で28基，1986万kW（キロワット）（電源設備の12%）の原子力発電設備が運転されるようになっている。こうして日本は，アメリカ，フランス，ソ連に次いで世界第4位の原子力発電国となった。

●原子力発電の利用率

1983年度に日本の原子力発電所が発電した電力量は1140億kWh（キロワットアワー）に達し，全発電電力量の18.5%を占めている。これは，ほぼ5軒に1軒の割合で原子力による明かりがともっていることを意味している。また，発電電力量を電源別に見ると，原子力は石炭，水力，ＬＮＧをしのぎ，石油火力(39%)に次いで第2位となっている。さらに，原子力発電所の年間設備利用率は1982年70.2%，83年70.0%，84年72.3%と，3年連続して70%台となった。これは日本の原子力発電所が年に3，4か月の定期点検を課せられていることから見て，実質的には100%稼働に近く，世界的に見ても，きわめて良好な成績と言える。

●原子力発電の未来

1983年11月の長期需給見通し（電気事業審議会）によれば，原子力発電量は1990年度には1900億kWh（全発電電力量の28%），1995年度には2850億kWh（同35%）と着実に伸びていく見込みである。また，電源別シェアで見ても，1990年度までに石油火力を抜き，以後，首位を占めると予想されている。

しかし，日本の原子力発電をよりいっそう定着させるためには，安全性の確保と環境保全に万全を期するとともに，発電所建設地の地元住民をはじめ，国民全体の理解と協力を得ることが必要であることは言うまでもない。また，それと同時に，建設費のいっそうの低減，安全行政の充実，そして自主的な核燃料サイクルの確立などの必要性が強まっている。

Japan's Nuclear Power Industry

● Peaceful Uses

Japan, the only nation in the world to have suffered an atomic bomb attack, has developed a large nuclear power industry to put the power of the atom to peaceful uses. Because nuclear power is economical and is not subject to world market fluctuations, Japan has made nuclear power its chief alternative (non-oil) energy source.

Japan's nuclear power industry moved into high gear in July 1966, when the Tokai nuclear power plant in Ibaraki prefecture went into operation, and the industry has grown rapidly ever since. As of the end of 1984, there were 28 nuclear power plants in operation with a combined capacity of 19.86 million kilowatts—12% of the nation's total electric power capacity. Japan is thus the fourth-largest generator of nuclear power (after the United States, France, and the Soviet Union in that order).

● Operating Rates

The amount of electricity actually generated by Japan's nuclear power plants in 1983 came to 114 billion kilowatt-hours, or 18.5% of the nation's total electric power output. This means that nearly one of every five homes in Japan was lit by nuclear power. Nuclear power has thus surpassed coal, hydroelectric power, and liquified natural gas (LNG) to become Japan's second-most important energy resource, led only by oil-fired power plants at 39% of the total 1983 output. Nuclear capacity utilization was 70% or better for three consecutive years: 70.2% in 1982, 70.0%, in 1983, and 72.3% in 1984. Given that regular inspections shut plants down for three or four months each year, this means close to 100% utilization exclusive of these regular maintenance shutdowns. Japan's nuclear power plants are clearly among the most productive in the world.

● Outlook for the Future

According to the November 1983 long-term electric power demand forecast made by the Electric Utility Industry Council, the amount of electric power supplied by nuclear plants is expected to increase to 190 billion kilowatt-hours (28% of the nation's total output) in 1990 and 285 billion (35% of the total) in 1995. This means nuclear power plants will match oil-fired plants in importance by 1990 and surpass them thereafter.

Yet developing Japan's nuclear power industry will obviously require a thorough regard for plant safety and environmental protection as well as the understanding and cooperation of communities adjacent to plant sites and of the nation as a whole. In addition, there will be a growing need to reduce construction costs, to beef up safety regulations and their enforcement, and to estabish an independent Japanese nuclear fuel cycle.

25 意思決定のしくみ

日本における意思決定の方法は，欧米のそれとはかなり異なる。欧米がトップ・ダウンであるのに対し，日本は次のようなボトム・アップ方式で決定がなされている。

●集団主義と意思決定者の役割

最終的な意思決定は，意思決定者の責任においてなされるが，最終結論がなされる過程では，決定事項を遂行する関係者全員が参加し，検討し合う。その間，意思決定者はそれぞれ参加者の意見を聞き，最善の結論へと導くとともに，最終的判断を下す。したがって，意思決定者は，参加者の意見を調整し，全員のコンセンサスを得るようにまとめていくことも重要な役割であり，そうした能力を要求される。

こうしたボトム・アップ方式による意思決定では，実行段階で予想されるあらゆる問題の発生に対しても検討が加えられる。つまり，最終的な決定というのは，その目的を達成するための遂行上の問題に対する対応策まで含んだものなのである。こうした意思決定の方法については，確かに決定までに相当の時間を要するという欠点もあるが，結論については最善の選択ができることや，実行段階に移ったときには実行当事者全員が組織的に目的達成に向かって素早く対応できることなど，長所も多い。ただ，全員の検討段階では，依然としてむだも多く，その効率化が叫ばれている。

●代替案の作成

ボトム・アップによる意思決定では，必ずしも欧米的な，いくつかの選択肢から最適なものを選ぶといったことではない。起案に対する検討やいくつかの素案を検討，調整することによって，初めの案とは別の代替案を作成する場合も多い。これも，遂行を含めた最善の方法を取るための当然の結論である。

●稟議（りんぎ）制

ボトム・アップによる意思決定が，経営慣行となったのが，稟議制である。下役が起案した文書を関係各部所に回し，協議し，上司の決済を仰ぐという一連の手続きを言う。この方式は，何人もの目を通るため，安全かつ確実な方法であるが，決定に至るまでに時間がかかること，また，責任の所在があいまいになることなど，批判も多いので，簡単な事務処理についてはかなり改善が進められている。

The Japanese Decision-making Process

The Japanese decision-making process differs from the Western process in that decisions in Japanese organizations are not made from the top down but, as described below, are gradually arrived at from the bottom up.

● Group Identification and the Decision-maker

Although the final formal responsibility for a particular decision may rest with the nominal decision-maker in Japan, the actual decision-making process itself is a cooperative effort with the cooperation of everyone involved in or affected by the decision's implementation. The good decision-maker is one who listens to everyone and leads the group toward a consensus coalescing around the idea with the broadest support. Accordingly, the Japanese decision-maker needs to be skilled not so much in problem-analysis as in people-analysis and negotiating a consensus among differing viewpoints.

This Japanese bottom-up approach to decision-making also includes consideration of all the many problems that might arise in the plan's implementation, and the final plan thus includes contingency thinking taking account of these difficulties to facilitate implementation and fulfillment of the new policy. While this process can be very time-consuming, it does have several distinct advantages, among them that the final choice is widely recognized within the organization as the best one and that everyone involved is already oriented to the decision's smooth implementation. Yet even granting these advantages, it is widely acknowledged in Japan that the decision-making process still needs to be streamlined.

● Drafting Alternatives

The bottom-up decision-making process entails more than just choosing the best of a number of plans. With several competing plans and many variations of each plan under consideration at the same time, the final result is often an amalgam of elements from many different sources. As might be expected, this amalgamation is done to ensure the best possible decision and the smoothest possible implementation.

● The *Ringi* System

The *ringi* system has become a very common way of making bottom-up decisions in Japanese companies. Basically, this *ringi* system is one in which someone, usually a lower-level manager, writes up a proposal for something and this proposal is then passed up within the organization, people discussing and revising it as they sign on. This system, which makes for safe decisions with input from a broad spectrum of people, is currently being further improved and refined to speed the process up and to more clearly delineate responsibility for the end result.

26 雇用関係の特徴

●終身雇用制と忠誠心

ひとたび企業に採用されたら，上司の命令に従い，同僚たちとの協調を保ち，無難に仕事をしていれば，特に際だった業績を上げなくとも，その会社が倒産でもしないかぎり，解雇されない。また，さまざまな付加給付を受けることができるとともに，身分，生活とも保障される。いわば会社は，定年まで個人の生活を丸抱えするのである。それは，給与とそれに付随する諸手当にはじまり，社宅や独身寮といった住居の提供，また，さまざまの福利厚生施設を備えるなど，企業規模が大きくなればなるほどその恩恵も大きい。

就職してから定年まで，丸抱えで生活を保障してくれるということは，安心して働けるわけで，その意味では会社と従業員は運命共同体である。すなわち，企業が存続し，かつ発展成長することが，自らの生活基盤を安定させ，より豊かにさせることにほかならない。したがって，1つの企業に対する勤労者の定着率は高く，忠誠心が強いのも当然のことと言える。

●採用と人事

採用については，原則的に新卒者を対象にした年1回の定期採用である。採用人員については，業績により毎年変わるものの，組織としての年代構成のバランスなどを配慮し，計画的にある一定数は定期採用している。

採用に際しては，職務別に募集，採用するのではなく，会社として一括して採用し，採用基準としては，主として性格や出身学校などの学歴を重んじる。入社後は，会社の必要とする能力を身に付けさせるための教育訓練を定期的に行うとともに，数年ごとに配置転換をして，多面的な経験を積ませ，そうして蓄積された能力を定年までの長期にわたって，活用する。

結局，終身雇用によって生活は保障されているものの，また，教育や人事については本人の希望は考慮されるものの，最終的には会社の方針に従わざるをえない。

●女性の労働力と差別

一般的に女性の労働力は，男性と区別され，仕事も男性の補助的作業が主である。最近ではこれを差別として改善の動きも強まっているが，まだ現実には結婚その他の理由により，数年で離職するケースも多く，終身雇用を基礎とする日本の会社としては，男性と同じに扱うことはなかなか難しいというのが現状である。

Japanese Employment

● Lifetime Employment Security

Under Japan's employment system, an employee who does what he is told, gets along with his fellow workers, and makes no major blunders can reasonably expect to be employed with the same company guaranteeing his social standing and income for the rest of his working life even if he is not an especially outstanding performer—a commitment that holds under almost all conditions short of corporate bankruptcy. Among the many company benefits for which he is eligible in addition to his basic salary are special allowances, company-owned housing or dormitories for single employees, and various health and welfare benefits, their generosity directly proportional to the size of the company.

Because the Japanese company guarantees its workers' livelihoods until retirement, people can concentrate on their work in the realization that they and their company share a common fate. Knowing that the company's success will mean enhanced livelihood security and an improved standard of living for themselves, and working for the same company for all of their working lives, many Japanese identify strongly with their companies.

● Recruitment and Promotion

Most Japanese companies hire new employees in once-a-year recruitment drives during which prospective graduates are tested, interviewed, and finally hired. Each company decides beforehand how many new people it intends to hire given its own business outlook, the demographic balance within the company, and other considerations.

Job seekers are chosen not so much for their professional skills as for their character and academic background. Moreover, they are hired not by specific departments for specific jobs but by the company as a whole for a wide range of work. Once hired, new employees are trained in-house in the skills they will need and are reassigned every few years to give them broad generalist experience within the company and ensure their long-run competence.

Although the individual employee's abilities and aptitudes are taken into consideration in making these job-rotation assignments, it is the company's needs which ultimately take precedence.

● Female Employment

In most Japanese companies, women are hired under a separate system and assigned jobs as assistants to male employees. While pressure is building to end this discrimination, companies still find it difficult to justify extending equal employment opportunities and the underlying premise of lifetime employment to women when so many of them leave the job market after four or five years to get married or to pursue other non-business interests.

27 年功序列

年功序列制度は終身雇用制度とともに日本的経営の大きな特質と考えられているが，この年功序列と終身雇用は一体不可分の関係にあり，企業の個人丸抱えによる身分，生活保障上のセットとして考えられている。

●年齢給と職能給

日本の企業の賃金体系は年齢給が基本となっており，これに，役職手当や専門職などによる職能給，家族手当が加算される。こうした年功序列賃金は，終身雇用による従業員の生活を保障するという観点に立つ賃金体系として定着してきたものである。

しかし，高齢化社会の到来が急速に迫り，しかも高度経済成長期に大量に採用したため，今日の低成長時代にあって，人件費の支出が経営を圧迫するに至っている。そのため，ここ数年来，ほとんどの企業で賃金体系の見直しがなされている。

その主たる対策は，年齢給を抑え，職能給の割合を増やしていこうというものである。具体的には，年齢序列賃金制度に年齢の上限を定めて一定にし，その分は職能給で補おうというもので，職能についても細かく規定するとともに，資格制度を導入し，それぞれの給付水準を定めるなどの改訂が進められている。

●昇進制度の問題

戦後の日本経済の発展に大きく貢献したのは民間企業であり，とりわけ企業の推進力となったのは，当時の中堅社員以下の活力だった。そして，彼らの動機付けとなったのが出世志向，昇進志向の実現であった。高度経済成長期には，そういった志向に対して企業も充分に対応でき，年功による昇進も可能だったが，第1次石油危機以来の低成長期に入ると，とたんに対応しきれなくなり，ポスト不足が深刻な問題となった。

一方，今までの年功序列制度はいい意味での出世競争による活性化が図られていたが，今日のポスト不足による出世意欲の減退や企業に対する忠誠心の欠如などが懸念されるに及んで，そのために，企業によっては課制の廃止や職制の代わりに試験により上級資格を得るといった資格制度の導入を図るなど活性化に努めている。とはいえ，年功序列という制度そのものが徐々に破綻(はたん)しつつあることは否めない。その意味で，日本のサラリーマンにとって厳しい時代を迎えつつあると言えよう。

Seniority-based Rewards

Seniority-based rewards (both occupational title and wages) go hand in hand with lifetime employment as a distinguishing characteristic of Japanese management, and these two elements are often seen as the two sides of the single coin of the company's total embrace of the individual.

● Wages

In most Japanese companies, employees' receive basic salaries geared to their entry-level salaries and how long they have been with the company. These basic salaries are then supplemented by special allowances for managerial or technical expertise, family structure, or other special factors. This system of seniority-based wages was devised as a means of guaranteeing the livelihoods of all employees throughout their lifetime careers with the company.

However, with a working population skewed toward the older age groups and with the large numbers of workers hired during the rapid-growth 1960s, many Japanese companies, large and small, are finding their earnings squeezed by high personnel costs in today's slow-growth era. As a result, most companies have been forced to review their seniority-based wage systems.

Many have chosen to curtail the seniority-based share of wage determination (such as by putting a cap on age-indexed wage increases) while increasing the ability-based share. Companies are increasingly tying salary schedules to the individual's qualifications and abilities.

● Problems with Seniority-based Promotions

Japanese industry was the driving force behind the nation's amazing postwar recovery, and capable middle- and lower-rank workers were the main force behind industry. These people were motivated by the promise of promotion and improved social status as their companies grew. During the rapid-growth 1960s, corporate growth made it possible to accommodate these promotion needs with a steadily-expanding number of posts. However, with the slower growth in the aftermath of the 1973 oil crisis, there are fewer top posts being created and companies can no longer adequately reward all of their deserving employees.

Although this seniority-based system worked well by stimulating healthy competition for promotions, the shortage of higher-level openings has eroded employee expectations and even company loyalty. As a result, some companies are attempting to maintain employee morale by restructuring their organizations to allow wider involvement and by basing promotions more on ability to reward the better-qualified people. The entire system of seniority-based rewards is definitely under fire, and Japanese company employees today face a difficult and uncertain future.

28 労使関係

●企業別組合の体質

日本の労働組合の大多数は，その組織単位が企業または事業所別に編成され，組合員の資格も原則としてその企業の正式な従業員に限定されている。したがって，組合員の賃上げなどによる生活権の要求も，終身雇用制度，年功序列制度によって一応の水準は確保されているし，また，組合員といっても企業別組合では，企業の存続が前提であるため，経営者側とある程度の協調を図っていかざるを得ないしくみになっている。そのために，経営状態が悪い場合などには組合は強い要求を出さず，逆に経営者側に積極的に協力することすらある。こうした体質は会社側との癒着を生じやすく，御用組合化の危険性が常に付きまとう。

また，日本の企業内組合では，一般に下級管理職以下が組合員の資格を有し，それ以上の管理職は非組合員であり，経営者側となる。昨日まで組合員として組合の利益を代表していたのが，昇進によって今度は経営者側のテーブルに就くなどということもよくある光景である。

●団体交渉の方式

使用者と労働者個人との交渉に代わり，組合組織が組合員の利益を代表して使用者側と労働条件などに関して交渉を行い，協定を結ぶという方式は，戦後の日本では一般化している。

ただ，日本の場合，労使は運命共同体的関係にあり，組合側も経営状態を把握していることもあって，企業そのものの存立を危うくするような対立は避ける。労使ともにどこまで譲歩し，どこで妥協するかが交渉のポイントとなる。

●組合の経営参加

組合の経営参加は戦後の経営民主化に伴って進んできたが，形式としては労働協約で定める経営協議会方式が一般的である。これは，経営者側が経営に関する諸事項について労働組合に参加させる機関であって，討議事項としては，生産，福利厚生，人事に関する協議などが主要である。

かつては，「春闘」と称して大幅な（2けた台の）賃上げ率を勝ち取ってきた組合も，1976年以降の不況，石油危機後の低成長下では1けた賃上げに甘んじており，賃上げよりも雇用確保を重視して、経営者といっしょになって経営に協力しているのが現状である。

Industrial Relations

● Enterprise Unions

The vast majority of Japan's labor unions are organized not along craft or skill lines but as enterprise (or enterprise branch) unions with membership restricted principally to regular, fulltime employees at the specific company. Enterprise unions seek to maintain and improve their members' standard of living by bargaining for pay raises and defending employees' rights within the framework of lifetime employment and seniority-based rewards. Because it is an enterprise union, the union knows that its own survival depends on the company's survival. When times are tough, the union refrains from making aggressive demands and cooperates to help the company through the crisis. Inherent in this posture is the danger that the union will identify too strongly with the company and become a rubber-stamp "company union."

Membership in Japan's enterprise unions is limited to lower-level management people and below, meaning that a union member who is promoted to middle management is no longer eligible for union membership. Thus it is not unusual for someone who was on the union side of the negotiating table yesterday to find himself on the management side today.

● Collective Bargaining

The postwar Japanese pattern in industrial relations has been for management and union representatives to negotiate agreements regarding working conditions and other matters on behalf of all union members.

Realizing that their members' long-term prosperity is linked to the prosperity of the companies where they work, Japanese union leaders make an effort to be well versed in business conditions affecting the industry and to avoid doing anything that might jeopardize the company's survival. As a result, contract negotiations are always a delicate compromise between confrontation and cooperation.

● Worker Participation in Management

Unions gained a greater voice in management during the postwar democratization, and most companies now make provisions for labor-management consultative committees or other arrangements enabling the union to participate in a variety of management decisions, mainly in such areas as production, worker welfare, and personnel policy.

While past spring labor offensives (*shuntō*) have won significant (double-digit) percentage pay raises for union members, most unions have put their primary emphasis on job security since the mid-1970s and have been willing to settle for single-digit wage increases to help their companies through the recession and slower growth in the wake of the oil crises.

29 勤務時間・賃金

●労働時間

労働者1人当たりの1週間の労働時間は，平均41時間40分（1983年）。1975年以降，減少傾向にあるが，40時間を切っている欧米と比べると，まだ労働時間は長く，また大企業（従業員1000人以上）と小企業（同100人以下）との差が，5時間30分もあるなど，企業規模格差が依然として大きい。

これは，労働組合が企業別であり，労働協約も企業ごとに決められるからで，労働時間を労働協約で定めている企業は，いまだ25.6％と低いことによる。

●週休2日制と有給休暇

週休2日制を導入している企業は年々増え，1983年には50％を超えた。しかし，完全週休2日制を実施している企業は27％と，依然低い。またここでも大企業と小企業との格差は大きく，週休2日制を実施している大企業は97％なのに対して，従業員100人以下の小企業では43％であるなど，労働条件のさまざまな面でなお二重構造的様相が見られる。

有給休暇は1人平均14.8日認められているのに対して，実際の取得日数は8.8日と消化率は60％でしかない。理由は，一部は日本人の働き好きを反映し，一部は有給休暇を十分に享受できないほど，仕事に追われていることによる。

●賃金

給与所得者の賃金は，ふつう月給と年2回（夏季，年末）のボーナスによって支払われる。ボーナスは本来，会社の業績に応じて支給される報奨的，利益分配的性格のものであるが，日本では生活補給的色彩が濃く，年間の定期給与の一部として組み込まれている。

国税庁の調査によると，給与所得者の平均年収は356万8000円（1983年）。定期昇給は，各企業の賃金体系の中で，毎年1回行われるが，最近の低成長下で，実質所得の伸びが抑えられているのが現状である。

また，世帯別の収入で見ると，勤労者世帯の月平均の名目実収入は42万4000円となっているが（1984年「家計調査報告」），税金や社会保険料の上昇や，住宅ローンの負担など，勤労者の家計の余裕度は低下傾向にある。特に，税負担については給与から完全に天引徴収されるため，他の自営業者や農家などに比べて不公平だとの不満がある。

The Japanese Workweek and Wages

● The Workweek

In 1983, the average Japanese employee worked 41 hours and 40 minutes per week. Although the Japanese workweek has been shrinking since 1975, it is still longer than that in Western Europe and the United States where the average is under 40 hours. Domestically too, there is a differential of about $5\frac{1}{2}$ hours per week between the (shorter) workweek at Japan's large companies (1,000 or more employees) and that at small companies (100 or fewer employees).

Because most Japanese unions are enterprise unions, and because the workweek must be negotiated separately at each company, only 25.6% of all Japanese companies have formal agreements setting standard workweeks.

● Two-day Weekends and Paid Vacations

Every year, more and more Japanese companies are adopting the two-day weekend. While over 50% of all companies offered some form of two-day weekends in 1983, only 27% give two days off every week. Here too Japan's dual-structure economy presents a significant gap between large and small companies: 97% of the large firms and only 43% of the small firms have any two-day weekends.

As for paid vacations, the average Japanese worker is allowed 14.8 paid vacation days per year yet actually takes only 8.8 (60%). While this is partly because people enjoy their work, it is also in part because there is so much work to do that people cannot take all the paid vacation they have coming.

● Wages

Japanese salaried workers normally receive a monthly salary plus two bonuses annually, one in summer and one at year's end. Begun as a kind of supplementary profit-sharing similar to the dividends paid shareholders, bonuses are today an integral part of the Japanese salaried worker's earnings.

National Tax Administration Agency figures for 1983 showed the average employee earned ¥3,568,000. While wages are structured to include annual pay hikes, real income increases have been depressed during the slow-growth years.

The Prime Minister's Office's 1984 survey of household accounts found that households headed by salaried workers had an average monthly income of ¥424,000, but higher taxes and increased insurance and pension premiums combine with sizeable mortgages and other undeferrable expenses to leave little leeway in the household budget. Recently, Japan's salaried workers have begun voicing considerable dissatisfaction with the perceived inequity between the withholding of taxes on all salaried income and the self-declaration payments made by farmers and other self-employed people.

30 定年

●定年年齢

日本の企業の定年は，長い間55歳であった。55歳の定年で，人生50年と言われていた間はほぼ一生働くことができ，生活も保障されていた。しかし，戦後日本人の平均寿命が急速に伸び，1984年現在，男性74.5歳，女性80.2歳となり，定年以後約20年余も働く機会のないまま生活しなくてはならないという事態になってきた。高齢化社会の到来と合わせ，老後の生活という観点からも定年の年齢延長問題が，ここ数年議論されている。

政府は，企業に定年を60歳に引き上げるよう指導しており，現在ではほぼ半数の企業が60歳定年制を実施するに至っている。60歳というのは，公的年金の支給年齢が60歳であることから設定されたものだが，年金財政の問題から，公的年金の支給開始を65歳に引き上げることが検討されており，これに伴い，定年もさらに65歳にすることが議論されている。

●退職金制度

退職金制度は終身雇用・年功序列制度とともに，雇用慣行として定着している。これは，永年勤続に対する報奨と老後の生活を保障しようという性格のもので，一時金として支払われる。最近では，定年延長，あるいは従業員の高齢化とともに，退職金の見直しが図られている。その１つが退職金を年金として支払っていこうとするもので，公的年金を補完する制度として，また企業の資金の効率的運用という面から近年急速に普及している。

●老後の生活設計とカウンセリング

老後の生活保障問題は，日本では単に企業の問題としてではなく，社会全体の問題として政治，行政，労使ともに真剣に取り組んでいる。企業では，定年延長，企業年金制度の導入とともに，従業員の老後についての相談制度やカウンセリングを行っている。終身雇用という慣行から，退職後の生活設計の相談に乗り，適切なアドバイスをしようというもので，退職後の就職斡旋（あっせん）から老後に備えての財産形成の方法などを企業内制度として設置している。

老後の問題でいちばん切実なのは，雇用機会がないことであり，あるいはあっても，これまでの能力や技術を生かした再就職の道が閉ざされていることなどである。老後の生きがいの問題には，課題は多い。

Retirement

● Retirement Age

For a long time, the Japanese retirement age was 55. This standard, set at a time when people thought of the average life span in terms of two score and ten years, was premised upon providing workers guaranteed livelihoods for virtually their whole lives. Yet life expectancies have improved remarkably since the war, and the average in 1984 was 74.5 for men and 80.2 for women. Thus the average worker can expect to spend over 20 years as an unemployed retiree. Accordingly, there has been much debate in recent years over whether or not to raise the retirement age, especially since the population center is also growing older.

In response, the government is urging corporations to raise their official retirement age to 60 as of 1985, and nearly half of the nation's private companies have complied. Although this age-60 retirement was set in consideration of the fact that public retirement pensions begin at age 60, severe fiscal problems are forcing the government to consider postponing the start of such payments until age 65, which would suggest the retirement age may be raised again—this time to 65.

● Retirement Allowances

Along with lifelong employment and seniority-based wages, lump-sum retirement allowances are a traditional part of Japan's employment system. When most workers were working their entire lives, these rewards for long and loyal service were sufficient to see them through their post-retirement years. Today, however, there is increasing concern that, along with postponing retirement, pensions may also have to be revamped. One revision being considered is to shift away from lump-sum retirement allowances and toward pension supplements to the public pension payments, both to provide retirees with steady incomes and to enable companies to make more effective use of their pension-fund capital.

● Retirement Planning and Counseling

The problems plaguing Japan's senior citizens are of serious concern to all of Japanese society, and politicians, bureaucrats, and labor-management groups are all working hard to find solutions. Besides raising the retirement age and switching from lump-sum payments to annuities, companies are setting up in-house counseling services to help retired employees with everything from finding re-employment to financial planning.

Post-retirement work opportunities are few and far between, and those that do exist often fail to draw upon the skills learned in a lifetime of working. Nevertheless, many people believe that something is needed to make their lives fully meaningful, and this is another problem which must be solved as the Japanese population grows older.

31 ビジネスマンの付き合い

日本の企業は集団主義と言われるように，人間関係の和を重要視する。そのために，企業内ではフォーマルおよびインフォーマルなさまざまな催し物が行われる。

一般に人生の大半を１つの会社で過ごすために，おのずと付き合いは会社中心となり，こうした人間関係を円滑にすることは，ビジネスマンにとって重要な条件でもある。一方，商売上の付き合いも人間関係が重視され，上下関係に基づく儀礼的あいさつ，あるいは接待，贈り物など，独特の慣習がある。

●運動会，忘年会など

多くの会社では，定期的に組織全体，あるいは各セクションごとの行事が行われる。それは，従業員の家族も参加する運動会であったり，社員旅行，転勤者に対する送別会，あるいは歓迎会，年末の忘年会などさまざまである。

このような行事は，日本の会社の家族主義的慣習で，人間関係を緊密にするとともに，組織は運命共同体であるという意識を持たせ，組織の活性化を図るという効果もある。

会社内にはさまざまな同好会がある。スポーツから文学，囲碁，将棋といった趣味の分野に至るまであり，社内の厚生施設を利用し，活動している。こうした活動では労使の区別はなく，経営幹部も一般社員といっしょになって楽しむのが普通である。

●赤ちょうちん

日常的な付き合いで最もよく利用されるのが，赤ちょうちんと言われる大衆酒場である。就業時間が終わると同僚，もしくは上司たちと連れ立ち，飲みながら雑談するわけだが，インフォーマルな席として日ごろの不満などを言い合うなど，一種のストレス解消の場ともなっている。赤ちょうちんとともにマージャンも終業後の楽しみの１つで，マージャン屋はいつもビジネスマンでいっぱいである。

●ゴルフ

ビジネスマンの付き合いで，欠かせないのがゴルフである。商取引において，日本ではふだんの付き合いが重要とされ，しばしば接待と称して酒席に招待するが，この酒席とともに多いのがゴルフ接待である。そのためビジネスマンは，こぞってゴルフを始める。したがってゴルフは，必ずしも純粋に個人的趣味ではなく，仕事上の利益をも伴っている場合が多いのである。

Socializing

Japanese companies are very harmony-conscious, and this emphasis on people shows up most clearly in their emphasis on good interpersonal relations and the numerous formal and informal social events that most companies sponsor.

Since the Japanese worker spends the greater part of his life with the same company, his friendships tend to be primarily people he knows from work, and being able to get along well with the rest of the people at the office or the factory is an important prerequisite for business success. Socializing is an important aspect of business as the businessman works not only to stay on good terms with his superiors and his subordinates alike but also to woo customers with expense-account entertaining, receptions, and gifts.

● Athletic Competitions, Parties, and More

Most Japanese companies sponsor a number of regular company- or section-wide social events, including athletic competitions for employees and their families, employee excursions, farewell parties for people being transferred out and welcoming parties for newcomers, and year-end bashes.

All part of the family-like atmosphere that pervades many Japanese companies, these events are encouraged as a way of strengthening interpersonal relations, underscoring the group's shared destiny, and improving organizational morale.

Many Japanese companies also provide facilities for active in-house hobby groups, ranging from sports to literature and board games such as *go* and *shōgi*. Rather than having separate groups for managers and ordinary workers, employees from all organizational levels gather together in these groups to share in the enjoyment of their common interests.

● Stopping off at the Pub

The most common kind of socializing in many Japanese companies is outside the company and after hours—when a group of workers, with or without their boss, stops off at a local watering hole after work to relax over a cold one and talk off the stress of everyday work. Another favorite after-hours diversion is mahjong, a board game played in small parlors catering to the evening throng of businessmen.

● Golf

Golf is another indispensable part of the Japanese businessman's social life. With entertaining clients and potential clients alike such a very important part of the ordinary run of business, many clients are not only wined and dined but also taken out for a round of golf. As a result, businessmen often consider golf a business skill, and they see a trip to the local course not so much as a personal pleasure as a means to success in business.

32 ビジネスマンの1日

●通勤・会議

ビジネスマンの朝は早い。始業時間は8時半～9時というのが一般的であるが，通勤時間の平均が1時間以上もかかるため，7時ごろには家を出なくてはならない。おまけにこのラッシュアワーの通勤電車はかなり混雑を極め，ほとんど立ちっぱなしで，会社に着くまでにかなりの疲労を強いられる。そして，タイムカードを押し，仕事が始まる。

週に1度，あるいは月に1度といった定例会議から，販売会議，宣伝会議など各セクションごとの会議，また，部課長会議，支店長会議などの職制別の会議など，実にさまざまな社内会議が行われる。会議に参加する回数は職制が上がるほど多くなる傾向にあり，1日中会議などということも珍しいことではない。会議の時間は，一応決められてはいるものの結論がなかなか出ずに伸びてしまう，あるいは後日改めて会議を開くということもよくある。

●社員食堂・喫茶店

昼食時ともなると，オフィス街周辺のレストランなどは，ビジネスマンで満員となるが，会社には社内に社員用の食堂を常設しているところが少なくない。社員食堂は，会社が業者と契約して設置しており，財政的にも何割かを負担しているため，値段は市価よりも安い。いわば，社員食堂は福利厚生の一環であると同時に，社内にあることで業務効率を図る――例えば，社内コミュニケーションの促進，すぐ仕事に戻れるなど――意図をも含んでいる。

商談は社内で行われるのが普通である。商談の重要性や相手との関係にもよるが，一般的には，簡単な打ち合わせ程度の場合は喫茶店でお茶を飲みながら，あるいは雑談しながら行われることも少なくない。ビジネスマンにとっては，仕事であると同時に一種の息抜きにもなっている。もちろん経費は会社持ちである。

●退社後

所属するセクションにもよるが，退社時間がくると仕事をやめて，すぐ帰宅するという社員はほとんどいない。やりかけの仕事を終えるまで残業をするのが普通である。また，夜は取引先の接待も多く，帰宅が深夜に及ぶことも珍しいことではない。もっとも石油危機後は，接待費あるいは交際費を削減した会社が増え，いわゆる社用族は大幅に減ってきた。

A Day in the Life of a Japanese Businessman

● The Morning Commute and Meetings

The average Japanese businessman's day begins bright and early. Although not expected at work until 8:30 or 9: 00, most businessmen live at least an hour away and must leave the house soon after 7: 00. Invariably finding his rush-hour train packed with other commuters streaming into the city, he often has to stand most of the way and is worn out even before his workday begins. Once he gets to the office or factory, however, he punches in and gets right to work.

Aside from the regular weekly or monthly meetings, there are sales meetings, advertising meetings, and other meetings within each department, as well as interdepartmental management meetings at all levels. Generally, the higher you go on the corporate ladder, the more meetings there are to attend, and it is not uncommon for top executives to spend all day in meetings. Although meetings are scheduled well ahead of time, they often run over or have to be reconvened later when things take longer than expected.

● Company Cafeterias and Coffee Shops

Come lunchtime and the numerous restaurants in and around the business district are filled, even though many employees eat at in house cafeterias run by outside contractors offering food at subsidized prices. An extra benefit for employees, the company cafeteria also pays off for the company by promoting smoother intra-company communication, shorter lunch breaks, and better work efficiency.

While most business takes place in the office, a considerable portion is also transacted at nearby coffee shops where people can enjoy a cup of coffee and talk in a more relaxed setting. The decision on where to meet depends upon how important the meeting is and how relaxed an interpersonal business relationship there is. Generally, however, only relatively minor matters are worked out over coffee. Businessmen find coffee shops good places to combine business with pleasure by getting away from the office for a while. As you might expect, the company picks up the tab for this.

● Clock-out Time

It is the rare employee who manages to quit work and head home at the official quitting time every day. More often than not, people stay to see the job through to completion. Even when he does manage to get away from his desk, the businessman frequently has entertaining to do and often does not get home until the wee hours of the morning. Since the oil crises of the 1970s, however, there has been a considerable decline in the number of people living high on expense accounts as more and more companies have moved to rein in expense account entertaining.

33 ビジネスマンの一生

●学歴偏重社会

一流会社への就職には，学歴が大いに重要となる。つまり，東京大学を頂点とする国公立大学，および一流私立大学を卒業することがきわめて重要な条件となるとともに，入社以後の出世にも影響を与えるというのが実情である。そして，こうした一流大学に入るためには一流高校に入ること，というように学歴問題はエスカレートし，今では，小中学校の受験競争にまで及んでいる。

こうした受験競争は，つまりは一流企業に入り，一生安定した生活を獲得せんがためであるが，このような学歴社会に対して，教育のゆがみによる青少年の落ちこぼれ，非行化などが顕在化し，社会問題となっている。

●配転・転勤

入社後は，終身雇用，年功序列のもとで一応の生活は保障されるものの，その一方では，会社の命令に対しての拒否権，あるいは選択権はほとんどないと言ってよい。まず，どのセクションに配属されるかは会社が決める。転勤も辞令１つで，従わなければならない。特に，日本の企業では，ある一定の期間ごとに配置転換を行うので，勤めている間に何度かの配転，転勤を経験するのが一般的である。会社の命令に従わないと，社内においてきわめて不利な状況に追いやられる。

●家族との関係

ビジネスマンの生活が会社中心であるため，家庭は妻を中心に運営される。家計，子供のしつけ，教育などは妻に任せ，月給も全額妻に渡し，必要な小遣いを妻からもらうというのが一般的なビジネスマン家庭である。

●単身赴任

転勤はビジネスマンにとって避けられないことであるが，中年になっての転勤で多いのが単身赴任である。これは，マイホームを建てたためにその地を離れたくないという家族の希望とともに，子供の教育上の問題がその背景にある。それと，転勤の期間が数年であり，いずれ戻って来るという見込みもあるからで，我慢をするというのが実態である。しかし，任地が海外であったり，また，家族が離れて生活するというのは何かと問題があり，企業によっては制度的に見直しを図っているところもあるが，なかなか実効は上がっていない。

The Life of a Businessman

● Academic Credentials

Academic credentials are very important to getting a good job in Japan. Graduation from one of the nation's top national universities, particularly the preeminent University of Tokyo, or one of the more prestigious private colleges is an important consideration for anyone hoping to get hired by a big blue-chip company and to climb the corporate ladder. One of the surest ways of getting into one of these elite schools is to have been graduated from a first-rate high school. As the competition for admission to the leading high schools has escalated, intense competition has developed for admission to the better junior high schools and even the more academic-oriented elementary schools.

The goal of all of this fierce competition on entrance examinations is to attain the lifetime economic security that goes with working for a big company, but the extreme pressures this has generated have distorted the educational process and sparked such major social problems as school drop-outs and increased delinquency.

● Transfers

Once employed by a "good" company, the Japanese businessman enjoys lifetime employment and seniority-based wages, yet this lifelong economic security is balanced by the company's demand for unquestioning acquiescence. Ultimately, the company decides what kind of work he will do and where he will do it, and most employees are put through a long period of regular job rotation, often involving transfers to other cities. Trying though this is, to balk would be a blot on the employee's record, and few are so brave.

● Family Life

With the businessman devoting most of his attention to his work, it is usually up to his wife to run the home. It is she who takes care of the family budget and the children's socialization and education. Typically, the husband gives her his entire pay envelope and then she doles out his weekly or monthly allowance.

● Living away from Home

Relocations are a fact of life for many Japanese businessmen, and some middle-aged transferees reluctantly decide to leave their families behind. This decision is often based not only on the family's personal preference to remain in the community where they may own their own home but also on a desire to avoid the problems which relocations can pose for the children's education. Even though the assignment may last for several years, the businessman sticks it out alone in the knowledge that he will be able to return home eventually. Although companies are studying ways to alleviate the hardships of overseas postings and the various problems which arise from such split-family living, they have yet to find any effective institutional solutions.

34 日本的商談

●信用第一主義

欧米では，仕事を通じて付き合いが始まったとしても，ビジネスと個人的付き合いは区別するが，日本の商談ではそういった区別はあいまいで，たとえ，仕事の話が全くされない酒席や遊びの場でも，それは商談の１つのプロセスと考えられている場合が多い。つまり，商売上の信用は契約内容や契約条件を検討し，それに基づいて確実に実行することであるといった欧米の契約第一主義は，日本の商売では第二段階的な問題と考えられている。

日本の商売で第一に重要な点は，交渉相手が人間的に信用できるかどうかに懸かっている。したがって，外国人が日本の企業と商売をする場合は，電話や文書などによる交渉より，直接会って交渉することが肝要となる。日本人担当者は，何度か面接の機会を作るだろうが，それは，契約条件を詰めるという目的以外に，個人として信用がおける人間かどうかを観察しているのである。

●時間のかかる合意決定

日本では，商談の開始から契約成立までに非常に時間がかかる。交渉担当者の権限が欧米ほど明確でないということもあるが，意思決定までに，現場の人間の合意をも得るといった形が取られることが多いからである。

日本との交渉は気長に，誠意を持って当たることである。契約内容に対して性急にイエスかノーを迫ったところで交渉はスムーズにいかない。逆に関係を悪くすることすらある。日本の契約事項の検討というのは，単に契約書に書かれていることだけではなく，人間関係と同様に契約相手と長期的に取引していけるかということが重要なので，この点でも合意に時間がかかるのである。

●ビジネスの家族的志向

商売である以上，契約の履行は当然であるが，日本的商売においては最初から詳細な取引規定をせずに，大枠で合意することを好む。日本的合意というのは相手を信用したということである。いわば今後親戚（しんせき）としていっしょにやっていきましょうという意味であり，問題が起きたらそのつど話し合いで解決し，困ったときは助け合いましょうというわけである。したがって，いったん取引が始まると，その関係は長期的に継続される場合が多い。日本は商売の面においても家族的志向なのである。

Japanese Business Practices

● Mutual Trust

Western businessmen tend to make a clear distinction between business and pleasure, but this dividing line is a very fuzzy one in the Japanese business world. Socializing, for example, can be considered an integral part of the business relationship even if not a word of business is spoken, for such informal socializing contributes to establishing personal trust—and such personal trust is far more important in Japan than specific contractual relationships are. While the Western businessman builds trust in the negotiation and fulfillment of contractual obligations, the contract is a secondary problem to the Japanese businessman.

The most important thing in a Japanese business relationship is whether or not the people involved feel they can comfortably trust each other. Thus non-Japanese who establish business ties with Japanese companies soon learn that face-to-face contact is much more effective than phone calls or letters. Japanese businessmen meeting together repeatedly are not only working out the terms of the deal but are sizing each other up as human beings.

● Reaching an Agreement

This need to establish trust among the people concerned is part of the reason it often takes a long time to go from the start of negotiations to the signing of the contract in Japanese business. Other reasons are that the delegation of authority is not as explicit for Japanese negotiators as it would be in the West, and that the Japanese decision is made only with the consent of all of the people who will actually be involved in its implementation.

Japanese business decisions are made with an emphasis on sincerity and trust, and pressures for quick decisions are counterproductive in the Japanese context. In Japan, working out a business deal means more than simply hammering out the terms of a contract; it includes an effort to build mutual trust and long-term relations. Naturally, this cannot be done overnight.

● People-oriented Business

Fulfilling the contract is obviously an important part of any business deal, but in Japan the contract is not so much a detailed tome of specifics to cover every contingency as it is a general statement of the framework of the business relationship. Because business relationships are founded on mutual trust, they are somewhat like family ties. In the ideal situation, there is a deep and basic agreement to work together. If problems arise, they can be talked over and worked out, and if one side runs into trouble the other will often lend a helping hand. Once initiated, such business ties often last for many years, and even the world of business is characterized by a family-like closeness in Japan.

Notes

■1. Government

May 3 (5月3日) May 3 is a national holiday commemorating the Constitution. November 3, when the Constitution was first promulgated, is a national holiday designated Culture Day.

●National holidays

Jan. 1	Ganjitsu (元日) New Year's Day
Jan. 15	Seijin no Hi (成人の日) Adults' Day
Feb. 11	Kenkoku Kinen no Hi (建国記念の日) National Foundation Day
(Mar. 21)	Shunbun no Hi (春分の日) Vernal Equinox Day
Apr. 29	Tenno Tanjobi (天皇誕生日) Emperor's Birthday
May 3	Kenpo Kinenbi (憲法記念日) Constitution Memorial Day
May 5	Kodomo no Hi (子供の日) Children's Day
Sep. 15	Keiro no Hi (敬老の日) Respect-for-the-Aged Day
(Sep. 23)	Shubun no Hi (秋分の日) Autumnal Equinox Day
Oct. 10	Taiiku no Hi (体育の日) Sports Day
Nov. 3	Bunka no Hi (文化の日) Culture Day
Nov. 23	Kinro Kansha no Hi (勤労感謝の日) Labor Thanksgiving Day

■2. Postwar Politics

Tojo Hideki (東条英機) (1884-1948) Army general and Prime Minister between 1941 and 1944, Tojo was convicted at the Tokyo Military Tribunal for the Far East and executed in December 1948.

Yoshida Shigeru (吉田茂) (1878-1967) As head of the Liberal Party, Yoshida was Prime Minister between 1946 and 1954. He played an important role in Japan's postwar reconstruction.

■3. The Imperial Institution

named for the reigning emperor (元号) *Gengō*, also called *nengō*, are imperial reign names. Before the Meiji period, a single emperor often changed his reign name several times, but since then, only one *gengō* is used for each emperor's reign. Showa, the present Emperor's reign name, has been in use

●Some important *gengō*

Taika(大化)	645–650	Genroku(元禄)	1688–1704
Tenpyo(天平)	729–749	Kyoho(享保)	1716–1736
Engi(延喜)	901–923	Kansei(寛政)	1789–1801
Hogen(保元)	1156–1159	Tenpo(天保)	1830–1844
Heiji(平治)	1159–1160	Ansei(安政)	1854–1860
Bun'ei(文永)	1264–1275	Keio(慶応)	1865–1868
Tensho(天正)	1573–1592	Meiji(明治)	1868–1912
Keicho(慶長)	1596–1615	Taisho(大正)	1912–1926
Genna(元和)	1615–1624	Showa(昭和)	1926–
Kan'ei(寛永)	1624–1644		

since he ascended the throne in 1926.

■4. The Cabinet

●Postwar Prime Ministers

Higashikuni Naruhiko（東久邇稔彦）	Aug.	1945	～	Oct.	1945
Shidehara Kijuro（幣原喜重郎）	Oct.	1945	～	Apr.	1946
Yoshida Shigeru（吉田茂）	May	1946	～	May	1947
Katayama Tetsu（片山哲）	May	1947	～	Mar.	1948
Ashida Hitoshi（芦田均）	Mar.	1948	～	Oct.	1948
Yoshida Shigeru（吉田茂）	Oct.	1948	～	Dec.	1954
Hatoyama Ichiro（鳩山一郎）	Dec.	1954	～	Dec.	1956
Ishibashi Tanzan（石橋湛山）	Dec.	1956	～	Feb.	1957
Kishi Nobusuke（岸信介）	Feb.	1957	～	July	1960
Ikeda Hayato（池田勇人）	July	1960	～	Nov.	1964
Sato Eisaku（佐藤栄作）	Nov.	1964	～	July	1972
Tanaka Kakuei（田中角栄）	July	1972	～	Dec.	1974
Miki Takeo（三木武夫）	Dec.	1974	～	Dec.	1976
Fukuda Takeo（福田赳夫）	Dec.	1976	～	Dec.	1978
Ohira Masayoshi（大平正芳）	Dec.	1978	～	June	1980
Suzuki Zenko（鈴木善幸）	July	1980	～	Nov.	1982
Nakasone Yasuhiro（中曽根康弘）	Nov.	1982	～	Nov.	1987
Takeshita Noboru（竹下登）	Nov.	1987	～		

■5. Political Parties

Buddhist Nichiren sect（日蓮正宗） Nichiren Shoshu is a sect of Nichiren Buddhism which has its headquarters in Shizuoka prefecture. The Soka Gakkai is an independent lay organization of this sect.

■14. Japan's Postwar Economic Recovery

stilts（竹馬） See picture.

■17. Japan's Industrial Structure

vertical society（タテ型社会） A term coined by Nakane Chie of the University of Tokyo, the vertical society in Japan is reflected in the relationships between superior and subordinate in the office and between seniors and juniors in schools, clubs, and other organizations.

■21. Japan's Principal Manufacturing Industries

audio-visual age（AV時代） Audio-visual equipment was originally used in schools and other educational institutions, but with the advent of video discs and high-fidelity video recording equipment, there is a new focus on AV equipment for the home.

microcomputers（マイコン） *Maikon* is an abbreviation of ***maikurokonpyūtā***(microcomputer). Abbreviations of this kind are increasingly common. Some examples are:

ワー(ド)プロ(セッサー) *wā(do)puro(sessā)* <word processor

スト(ライキ) *suto(raiki)* <strike

△Stilts

タイプ(ライター)　*taipu*(*raitā*) <typewriter
デパート(メントストア) *depāto*(*mento-sutoa*) <department store
トイレ(ット)　*toire*(*tto*) <toilet
団(体)交(渉)　*dan*(*tai*) *kō*(*shō*) <collective bargaining

word processors (ワープロ)　The Japanese-language word processor has proved highly popular, and is fast replacing Japanese typewriters, which, because of the nature of the language, are cumbersome, difficult machines to operate.

Part-4
日本の文化
CULTURAL HERITAGE

1 建築

建築は，その土地の気候，風土，習慣に大きく制約される。日本は，湿潤で四季のある気候であることと，素材として木材が豊富であることなどから，建物は木造で，床下および室内の風通しをよくし，屋根には勾配をつけ，軒を出して気候に合わせている。座る生活に合わせて床上には畳を敷いている。

●仏教建築

寺院建築は中国の影響を強く受けているが，屋根の反りが少なく，軒が深い点，優美な曲線と直線のコントラストなど，日本化したものとなっている。*法隆寺，薬師寺など，7世紀の遺構が現在，奈良県下に数多く残されており，法隆寺は世界最古の木造建築である。

●神社建築

日本建築の最も古い様式を残しているのは神社で，高床式，彩色を施さない白木造り，かやぶき，地面に直接柱を立てる掘っ建て柱で，典型的なのは*伊勢神宮，出雲大社，住吉神社などである。上述の神社以外の神社は，神社建築の特徴のいくつかを残しながら，仏教建築の影響を受けた建築となっている。

●住宅建築

住宅建築は奈良時代までのものは遺構もないので明確ではないが，平安時代になると，寝殿造りが貴族の間では一般的になる。主人の起居する寝殿を中心に，対屋，池に臨む釣殿を造り，それぞれを廊下でつないだもので，家内は板敷きだった。室内に畳を敷きつめるようになったのは室町時代末期からで，さらに桃山時代になると書院造りが完成する。これは現代の日本建築に見られる*床の間，*違い棚，ふすまなどを備えた建築で，桂離宮，修学院離宮などがその代表的なものである。

●城郭建築

戦国時代から造られた城は，石組みと木骨に白壁で，3層～5層の高層建築を造り上げた。*姫路城がその典型である。

●西洋建築

明治維新後，*鹿鳴館などレンガ造りの西洋建築が新国家の威信を示すものとして建てられた。現存する明治の代表的建築の多くは，愛知県の犬山にある「明治村」に移築されている。昭和になると，造形学校のバウハウスや建築家ル・コルビュジエに学んだ建築家も現れたが，それが花開くのは戦後のことで，谷口吉郎，丹下健三らがコンクリートの素材を生かした仕事をし，さらにその後は白井晟一，黒川紀章らが，多様に発展させて世界的に活躍している。

Architecture

Architecture is shaped by circumstances of climate, geography, and customs. In Japan with its high humidity, seasonal change, and plentiful forests, wood has been the traditional building material. Traditional Japanese architecture has good foundation ventilation, airy rooms, slanted roofs, long overhangs, and *tatami*-covered floors.

● Buddhist Architecture

Buddhist temple architecture is heavily influenced by Chinese aesthetics, but some features are purely Japanese—the gentle curve of the roof, the deep eaves, and the general contrast between curved and straight lines. Typical is Horyuji* in Nara, the world's oldest wooden structure, and such 7th century temples as Yakushiji.

● Shinto Architecture

Shinto shrines represent the oldest Japanese architectural style. They are generally placed high above the ground, made of plain, uncolored wood, topped with thickly thatched roofs, and supported by pillars driven directly into the ground. Ise,* Izumo, and Sumiyoshi Shrines are typical, but other shrines show signs of Buddhist influence.

● Residences

There are very few private residences left from before the Nara period. By the Heian period a style called *shinden-zukuri* was popular with the nobility. Centered around the *shinden* (master's quarters), this style is characterized by an annex, open pavilion by a pond, and long connecting corridors. Floors were wooden, *tatami* not coming into common use until the end of the Muromachi period. In the Azuchi-Momoyama period a style called *shoin-zukuri* emerged incorporating many features now accepted as traditionally Japanese, including the *tokonoma** alcove, staggered shelves,* and *fusuma* paper sliding doors. Katsura* and Shugakuin Detached Palaces are superior examples.

● Castle Architecture

Castles were built throughout Japan during the tumultuous civil wars. Stone and wood with white plaster walls, castles were usually three to five stories high. Himeji Castle* is typical.

● Western-style Architecture

The earliest example of Western-style architecture was the Rokumeikan,* a brick structure built soon after the Meiji Restoration and epitomizing the new zeal for Westernization. Today, much of the architecture of that period is preserved in Meiji Village at Inuyama, Aichi prefecture. Japanese architects influenced by the Bauhaus and Le Corbusier appeared by the 1930s, but they were unable to show their full talents until after World War II. Taniguchi Yoshiro and Tange Kenzo, for example, are known for their work in concrete, and they have been joined by Shirai Seiichi, Kurokawa Kisho, and other internationally recognized architects in a multitude of styles.

2 庭園

欧米の庭園が，樹木や石材を幾何学的に整然と配置するのに対し，日本の伝統的庭園は，自然の一部を再現する風景式庭園である。水流，池，石組み，樹木，築山などの取り合わせで変化をつけ，自然のままの風情を出している。その考えが行きついたところが借景で，遠方の山や，そこから見える風景そのものを，庭の景色の一部として取り入れたものである。日本の伝統的庭園はこのように自然の景色の一部を織り込んだものであり，この日本庭園の様式が現代にも生きている。作庭の思想の上からは，日本の庭園は自然中心主義のものと，宗教性を帯びたものとの2つの流れに大別できる。

●自然中心主義の庭園

自然中心主義の庭園は飛鳥時代にさかのぼり，その日本庭園の様式を結晶させたのが寝殿造り庭園である。寝殿造り庭園は，築山，池，遣り水に樹木を配したものだが，現在，その完全な遺構は残っていない。自然中心主義の庭でもう1つ代表的なのは，江戸時代に造られた大名庭である。諸国の大名が，その国元や江戸の屋敷に造らせた大規模な庭園で，回遊式の庭に天下の名所を模した景観を造り，また名石，名木を豊富に使っている。日本三庭園と呼ばれる水戸の偕楽園，金沢の兼六園，岡山の後楽園などがそれであり，都市の中に大面積を持つ近代公園の性格を持ち，現代ではすべてが公園として一般公開されている。

●宗教性を帯びた庭園

宗教性を帯びたものとしては，平安時代後期から鎌倉時代にかけて造られた浄土庭園がある。当時流行した極楽浄土への信仰から生まれたもので，浄土曼荼羅などに描かれているように，池を掘り，その中に中島を造って橋で結び，その向こうに阿弥陀堂，金堂を設けたもので，京都宇治の平等院鳳凰堂庭園はその初期のもの，京都の金閣寺庭園は，浄土庭園と住宅庭園とが融合した末期のものである。

室町時代から禅宗寺院になって，「任運無作」という，ありのままにこだわらないことを本旨とし，山川草木すべてが仏の相を備えているという禅の精神にのっとり，抽象化，象徴化された庭が造られた。石組みを仏像になぞらえ，流れる水は白砂で表し，超自然的な深山幽谷の趣を表現した。それが石庭であり，枯山水である。京都の竜安寺の石庭，大徳寺・大仙院の庭園などがこれで，その抽象性は現代芸術における抽象性と相通ずるものが多い。

Gardens

In contrast to the geometric arrangement of trees and rocks in Western-style gardens, the traditional Japanese garden is a scenic composition mimicking nature. Elements of the Japanese garden include flowing water, ponds, groupings of stones, trees and shrubs, and artificial hills,* each in as natural-looking a state as possible to evoke the feeling of artlessness. The ultimate in Japanese garden philosophy is probably the concept of *shakkei* or "borrowed view"—a still-used ruse in which background elements such as mountains are incorporated into the garden's composition. Japanese gardens can be broadly divided into those which focus on naturalism and those with religious symbolism.

● Natural Gardens

Among the natural style gardens is the *shinden-zukuri* garden, a crystalization of extremely ancient Japanese garden motifs. The oldest recorded garden of this type—which includes artificial hills, ponds, and man-made streams among the foliage — dates back to the Asuka period. While no perfect examples of this type of garden exist today, the *kaiyū* gardens created for the feudal lords during the Edo period are also representative of this naturalist school. These *kaiyū* gardens, built both in their home fiefs and at their residences in Edo, often used exquisite stones and trees to create miniature reproductions of famous scenes. Kairakuen in Mito, Kenrokuen in Kanazawa, and Korakuen in Okayama—often called Japan's three best gardens—are of this type. Broad expanses of green in crowded cities, these three gardens are today popular public parks.

● Religious Gardens

Among gardens having religious significance are those in what is known as the Jodo style. Taking its name from the Jodo Buddhist sect, this garden style was developed in the late Heian and Kamakura periods and draws its symbolism from the belief in the Jodo paradise popular at the time. The focal point of this type of garden is the pond with a bridge arching to a central island, a major motif of the Jodo mandala. Behind the pond is the Amidado housing the figure of the Amida Buddha and the *kondō*.* The Hoodo garden at Byodoin, a temple in Uji south of Kyoto, is an early example of the Jodo style garden; and the Kinkakuji (Golden Pavilion) garden in Kyoto a later example combining the Jodo and the residential styles.

Beginning in the Muromachi period, garden-making was strongly influenced by Zen Buddhism and abstract symbolism became increasingly important. Groupings of rocks represented figures of Buddhas and white sand replaced flowing water in the sand and rock gardens of this period. Examples of this style include the rock garden at Kyoto's Ryoanji* and Daitokuji's Daisen'in garden also in Kyoto. The extreme abstraction of these gardens echoes abstract modern art.

3 音楽

外国のものを次々と貪欲なまでに吸収してきた日本人の特性は，音楽の分野にも発揮されている。クラシック，ポピュラー，ジャズ，ロック，シャンソン，歌謡曲，民謡，そして邦楽……。ありとあらゆる種類の音楽を，日本ではいながらにして聞くことができるし，外国からの音楽家の来日も盛んだ。一流ミュージシャンともなれば，切符が数万円するのも珍しくないが，それでもすぐ売り切れる。日本は外タレ天国という評判さえ海外にはあるほどである。

●歌謡曲とポピュラー

今日，一般大衆に最も愛されている音楽の双璧は歌謡曲とポピュラーだろう。歌謡曲は1914年の「カチューシャの唄」が日本では第1号と言われるが，その後，毎年多くのヒット曲を生んできた。「歌は世に連れ，世は歌に連れ」という言葉があるように，ヒット曲の変遷は時代の変遷でもあり，第2次世界大戦中の軍国歌謡などはそのほんの一例である。ポピュラーはクラシック音楽に対して通俗性，娯楽性を持った親しみやすい音楽一般を指し，いわゆるポピュラー・ソングからジャズ，シャンソン，ロック，映画音楽などまで含まれる。歌謡曲やポピュラーを歌う若い男女のタレント歌手たちはテレビ，ラジオの人気者で，歌番組は高視聴率を得ている。

毎年末には，その年に最もヒットした歌の歌手や作詞・作曲家を選ぶ「レコード大賞」などの賞の選考がある。また12月31日の夜ＮＨＫが放映する「紅白歌合戦」は，多数の人々がこれを見て年を越すため，国民的行事の名さえあり，ハワイなど海外にも衛星中継されている。

●そのほかの音楽

しかし，日本人は今や聞くばかりでなく，みずから歌うほうも盛んだ。特に，伴奏だけ入ったテープに合わせて歌うカラオケは，盛り場で，家庭で，宴会で，まさにブームだが，騒音公害や歌の著作権料などの問題も起きている。ちなみにカラオケとは，「歌の入っていない空のオーケストラ」という意味の略語である。

クラシックは歌謡曲，ポピュラーほど一般的でないが，ピアノやバイオリンは児童の稽古事として普及し，特にバイオリンの鈴木メソッドは国際的に知られている。世界の音楽コンクールでの入賞者も相次ぎ，海外で活躍するアーティストも増えており，クラシックの層は厚くなっている。また年末の「第九交響曲」の合唱コンサートの盛況は，世界にもあまり例を見ない現象と言われる。

Music

Music is one of the areas where Japanese have shown a particular aptitude for assimilating Western culture. Without ever leaving home, Japanese can hear everything from classical, top-forty, jazz, rock, chanson, *kayōkyoku* (Japanese popular music), *min'yō** (Japanese folk songs), and *hōgaku* (traditional Japanese music), and there is a constant stream by foreign musicians visiting Japan. It is not unusual for good seats at world-class concerts by foreign artists to cost hundreds of dollars—and even at those prices they often sell out quickly. Little wonder Japan is such a popular stop for touring foreign musicians.

● *Kayōkyoku* and Pops

The two best-loved types of music in Japan are *kayōkyoku* and pops. The first *kayōkyoku* hit was *Kachūsha no Uta* in 1914, and there have been numerous *kayōkyoku* hits every year since. Music both shapes and is shaped by popular attitudes, and changes in musical styles reflect changes in the times, as illustrated by the militarist songs that prevailed in Japan during the 1930s and early 1940s. In Japan, the term pops is used in contrast to classical music to describe lighter, entertainment-oriented music such as popular music, jazz, chanson, rock, and film sound tracks. Young *kayōkyoku* and pops stars appear regularly on radio and TV, drawing consistently high ratings.

Each December, music awards ceremonies are held to recognize the year's most popular songs, singers, lyricists, composers, and record albums; and on New Year's Eve NHK airs a song fest pitting male and female vocalists against each other in what has become a major cultural event ushering out the old year for a large portion of the nation's population. This program is also broadcast in Hawaii and elsewhere overseas.

● Other Favorites

Japanese also like to sing along, and the most recent craze has been *karaoke*—taped accompaniments for amateur singers—and *karaoke* now pours forth from entertainment districts, homes, and banquet halls everywhere. However, this *karaoke* boom has in turn sparked disputes over excessive noise levels and copyright infringement. The word *karaoke* is an abbreviation of *kara-ōkesutora* (empty orchestra) meaning the sound track minus the lead vocal.

Western classical music may not be as popular as *kayōkyoku* and pops, but many Japanese children take piano and violin lessons, and the Suzuki method* of violin practice is famous both in Japan and abroad. The growing number of Japanese walking off with honors at international musical contests and performing overseas, especially in the classical field, is one indication of how much Western music has become a part of Japanese culture. As another indication, there are lavish choral performances of Beethoven's Ninth every year-end throughout Japan.

4 邦楽

●邦楽の種類

邦楽は，一般的には，日本の音楽の総称であるが，普通には洋楽の対語として用いられ，洋楽以外の日本の伝統音楽すべてを指す。用いる楽器の種類によって次のように分類することができる。

• **雅楽**　宮廷の行事の際に演奏される儀式音楽。古代に中国・朝鮮から入った音楽で，日本音楽の最も古い姿を残しているものと言える。

• **声明**（しょうみょう）　仏教の典礼音楽で，声楽。仏教伝来とともに輸入され，その後の日本音楽に大きな影響を与えた。

• **琵琶**（びわ）**楽**　戦国時代以降，戦記物などを琵琶（*）の伴奏で語る音楽として発達した。弾き語りで演奏される声楽曲である。

• **能楽**　現在の「能」の形式が大成したのは，室町時代初期である。能は，音楽と舞踊と劇の総合芸術であり，能の音楽は，「謡（うたい）」という声楽と「囃子（はやし）」という器楽から成り立っている。

• **箏**（そうきょく）**曲**　箏曲とは，琴（*）の曲のほか，琴・三味線（しゃみせん）（*）・尺八（*）の合奏曲も指す。琴は13弦の撥弦（はつげん）楽器。江戸時代に三味線音楽と結び付いたことによって発達した。大正から昭和初期にかけて数多くの名曲を残した宮城道雄は，箏曲界に大きな影響を与えた。

• **尺八楽**　尺八は鎌倉時代から虚無僧（*）が読経の代わりに吹いた立笛。長さが1尺8寸(約55cm)であることから，尺八と呼ばれた。

• **三味線音楽**　三味線は，3弦で，猫か犬の皮を張った胴を持つ日本の代表的な楽器。江戸時代に広く使われるようになった三味線は，歌舞伎・人形（*）浄瑠璃（じょうるり）などの劇場音楽として，また数多くの歌い物音楽の伴奏として現在も使われている。

• **民謡**　各地で歌い継がれてきたもの。労働歌が多い。

●邦楽の特色

洋楽の音階が7音音階であるのに対し，近世邦楽は5音音階である。リズムは，2拍子，4拍子の偶数拍子が大部分で，3拍子はほとんどない。歌が多く，純器楽曲は少ない。楽器は，ふつう声楽の伴奏楽器として用いられるが，声楽の進行と微妙に一致しない複雑なズレがある。また，三味線・琴・尺八など，楽器の構造に由来する雑音的要素も邦楽の複雑な音色として好まれる。

明治に洋楽が入って以降，洋楽が日本の音楽の主流で，邦楽は洋楽に圧倒されてきた。しかし，近年，邦楽が見直され，愛好者も増えている。外国人の愛好者も多くなった。

Traditional Japanese Music

● Types

Hōgaku, traditional Japanese music, is classified by the type of instruments used. Ceremonial court music introduced from China and Korea, *gagaku* is the oldest type of traditional Japanese music. Buddhist liturgical chants are called *shōmyō*. Introduced into Japan at the same time as Buddhism, *shōmyō* had a profound impact on the development of native Japanese music. A type of short lute, the *biwa** was a favored instrument of accompaniment for long chanted ballads about great battles and heroic deeds, and this music is called *biwa-gaku*. Noh as it is performed today gelled in the Muromachi period. An art combining song, dance, and drama, noh is characterized by its *utai* chorus and *hayashi* flute and percussion instrument accompaniment, all of which combine to form *noh-gaku*. *Sōkyoku* is music performed on the *koto** (a 13-string zither) or by an ensemble of *koto*, *shamisen** (three-stringed long lute), and *shakuhachi** (vertical flute) players. *Koto* music flowered in the Edo period along with *shamisen* music. Miyagi Michio, a composer of *sōkyoku* active in the early years of the 20th century had a major influence on this type of traditional music. *Shakuhachi-gaku* is all of that music played on the *shakuhachi*, a type of vertical bamboo flute formerly played by wandering Buddhist monks.* The name for this instrument derives from the fact that it is one *shaku* and eight (*hachi*) *sun* (approximately 55cm) long. Made of cat or dog hide and having only three strings, the *shamisen* is a uniquely Japanese instrument and its music the uniquely Japanese *shamisen-ongaku*. An extremely popular instrument in the Edo period, the *shamisen* is an important accompaniment to kabuki and puppet theater drama,* and it continues to be used today as accompaniment for many Japanese songs. Folk songs are called *min'yō*. Found throughout Japan, many *min'yō* are work songs.

● Characteristics

In contrast to the seven-note scale of Western music, traditional Japanese music is based on a five-note scale and has primarily two- and four-beat rhythms as opposed to a three-beat time. Most traditional music consists of songs with instrumental accompaniment, and there are very few purely instrumental compositions. The instrumental accompaniment seldom progresses exactly in step with the song. The "noise" that is an inevitable part of the sound of the *shamisen*, *koto*, *shakuhachi*, and other traditional instruments is appreciated for the unique tone it gives to the music.

Since it was first introduced into Japan full-force in the late 19th century, Western music has become very popular, overshadowing traditional music. Still, interest in traditional music has been reviving in recent years, and many audiences include appreciative non-Japanese.

5 能*

能は歌にあたる「謡」と，それに伴う演技(型と言う)と舞いから成る仮面劇である。能の美しさは様式的な美しさで，劇的な演技はなるべく抑えて緊縮された動きの中に幽玄な趣を出そうとするところにある。能は台本に相当する謡本によって上演され，演者のほかに謡の合唱の部分を受け持つ「地謡」があり，演奏は笛・大鼓・小鼓*によって行われ，演ずる曲によっては太鼓が加わることがある。

役はシテ方・ワキ方・狂言方・囃子方がそれぞれ分担し，ほかの役を演ずることはしない決まりになっている。シテ方は主役の登場人物とそのツレを受け持つほかに地謡を担当する。ワキ方はワキとそのツレ，狂言方は間狂言と言って1曲の能の前場と後場をつなぐ役を演ずるほか，能の間に番組を挟んでユーモラスに演じて見せる。囃子方はそれぞれ上記の楽器を受け持つ。これらの役で仮面をつけるのはシテ方(能面)と狂言方(狂言面)だけで，ワキ方はつけないことになっている。

●能の歴史

能は先行芸能の散楽や田楽能から発展し，室町時代に観阿弥・世阿弥父子によって大成を見た伝統芸能で，社寺や時の将軍足利義満などの庇護のもとにしだいに完成した。特に豊臣秀吉がこれを好み，自ら演じたのは有名な話である。能は江戸時代にも大名たちの保護を受け，武家の式楽として栄えた。そのため，明治になって武家社会が廃れると能も衰微の運命を甘受することになる。しかし，関係者の努力でなんとか生命を保ちながら今日に及び，最近は古典芸能見直しの気運もあって，若い人々の間に愛好者が増えている。

●舞台と能組み

能の舞台は普通の劇場のように額縁舞台ではなく，正面と脇正面が観客席(見所と言う)にはり出していて，演者が登場してくる橋懸という通路(歌舞伎の花道に当たる)を持って楽屋と通じている。特に舞台装置はなく，必要があれば簡素な形をした家屋や岩屋の作り物が運び出される程度で，舞台背景には1本の老松が描かれている。

能の現行曲はほぼ250番あるが，大きく「神・男・女・狂・鬼」の5つに分けられ，プログラム(能組みと言う)を作成するときはこの順序に従う。「神」は祝言性の勝ったもの，「男」は武人の修羅の悲劇を描き，「女」は能の美の中心的なもの，「狂」は異常な情況に置かれた心理葛藤を，切能の「鬼」は文字通り鬼畜が登場する。

Noh*

Noh is a type of masked dance-drama in which extreme stylization of the actors' movements and the narrative music evoke a beautiful, mysterious atmosphere. The only script for a noh play is a song book called an *utai-bon* with narrative chants and songs sung by a chorus to the accompaniment of flutes, large and small hand drums,* and, at times, a large drum.

The performers are defined by their roles. These are the *shite* principal actor, the *waki* subordinate actor, the *kyōgen* comic actor, and the chorus and musicians, none of which are interchangeable. The principal actor directs not only his own performance in the leading role, but also that of his companion, the *tsure*, and the singing of the chorus. In the same way the *waki* or subordinate actor oversees his own role and that of his *tsure*. The *kyōgen* actor will sometimes provide a brief explanation of events between acts, and he performs in humorous sketches, also called *kyōgen*, which provide comic relief between plays. Music plays an important role throughout, for the musicians and chorus are as vital to a noh performance as the actors. Masks may sometimes be worn by the *shite* and the *kyōgen* actors, but never by the *waki*.

● History

Originating in dramatic performances at religious festivals in the middle of the 14th century, noh as it is known today was developed in the Muromachi period by Kan'ami and his son, Zeami, and flourished under the patronage of Shinto shrines and Buddhist temples and such authoritative figures as the Ashikaga shogun Yoshimitsu. Toyotomi Hideyoshi was an enthusiastic supporter of noh who delighted in playing leading roles himself. Noh continued to flourish in the Edo period under the patronage of the daimyo and became a favored entertainment of the military class. Because of this close association with the samurai, however, noh declined rapidly in the Meiji period when the samurai lost their position of supremacy. Still, devotees have managed to keep the noh theater alive, and it is enjoying renewed popularity as the Japanese people today evidence a growing interest in their traditional arts.

● Stage

Unlike the conventional stage, the noh stage has an extension on one side that acts as a side stage and a bridge connecting it to hidden dressing rooms and providing an entrance for actors similar to kabuki's *hana-michi*. Very few stage props or settings are used, although there is always a single pine tree painted on the back wall of the stage.

The 250 or so noh plays which continue to be performed today are divided into five groups: plays about gods, warriors, women, the deranged, and demons.

6 歌舞伎

東京・銀座にある歌舞伎座，京都・四条通にある南座などは，いつも観客でにぎわっている。数百年からの歴史を持つ日本の代表的伝統芸能は，今なお脈々とその生命力を保っている。

●歌舞伎の歴史

起源は出雲大社の巫女，阿国が江戸時代初期，京都で歌舞伎踊りをしたのに始まる。「かぶき」とは「傾く」のことで，異様な容姿・所作を意味した。今日の総合演劇としての歌舞伎の原型は，それまでの，容色をもって観客の人気を得ていた女歌舞伎，若衆歌舞伎から脱皮し，技芸をもって俳優の本分とした野郎歌舞伎からである。特に元禄・享保年間には専門の脚本作家が登場，俳優も京阪には坂田藤十郎，芳沢あやめ，江戸には市川団十郎という名優が輩出し，1つの頂点に達した。その後一時人形浄瑠璃劇に人気を譲るが，18世紀後半には再び盛り返した。また，回り舞台やせり上げなど，舞台装置も工夫開拓された。一方，活動の中心は上方から江戸に移った。

代表的作者には近松門左衛門，鶴屋南北，河竹黙阿弥らがいる。中でも江戸時代から明治にかけて活躍した河竹黙阿弥は，それまでの歌舞伎劇を集大成した第一人者である。明治以降は大きな変化を見ることなく今日に至っている。近世の名優としては明治に尾上菊五郎(5代)，市川団十郎(9代)，市川左団次(初代)が，大正に尾上菊五郎(6代)，中村吉右衛門(初代)がいる。

●歌舞伎の特色

歌舞伎は役者中心の演劇であり，役者の持っている魅力に支えられている。特に女形の持つ独特の雰囲気は多くの外国人をも引き付ける。女歌舞伎が禁止され，やむをえず男が演じたわけだが，長い歴史の中で独自の世界を作り上げるに至った。今日，若手女形として人気のある坂東玉三郎は海外公演でも大成功を収めた。歌舞伎役者はほとんど世襲で，幼児から厳しい稽古を積み，伝統を守っている。

舞台の役者は屋号で声援される。主な屋号には，市川団十郎＝成田屋，松本幸四郎＝高麗屋，中村歌右衛門＝成駒屋，尾上菊五郎＝音羽屋などがある。舞台下手(客席から向かって左)に観客席を貫いて作られた花道(役者の通り道)を入退場しながら役者と観客はいっそうの一体感を味わう。

脚本の種類は大きく分けて貴族や武士の世界を描いた時代物と，庶民の生活を描いた世話物とがある。

Kabuki*

Tokyo's Kabuki-za* and Kyoto's Minami-za consistently play to full houses as kabuki continues to draw upon its centuries-old tradition to remain a vital force in Japanese theater today.

● History

Kabuki's roots go back to an Izumo shrine maiden* named Okuni* who performed "kabuki" (the name taken from the word *kabuki* meaning to act in an unusual manner) dances in Kyoto during the early Edo period. On the way to today's mature genre, kabuki passed through a number of stages, including *onna* kabuki with women dancing provocatively, *wakashū* kabuki in which young men replaced the women, and *yarō* kabuki performed by older men for its artistic merits. By the late 17th century, authors were writing especially for the kabuki stage and great actors were emerging, among them Sakata Tojuro and Yoshizawa Ayame in the Osaka-Kyoto district and Ichikawa Danjuro in Edo. After later losing audience to puppet plays, kabuki came back stronger than ever in the late 18th century. As staging became more elaborate with revolving stages and hoists, the center of action shifted from the Osaka-Kyoto area to Edo.

Among the best-known kabuki playwrights are Chikamatsu Monzaemon, Tsuruya Nanboku, and Kawatake Mokuami. Kawatake especially is remembered for having collected much of the earlier repertoire. Despite Japan's modernization after 1868, kabuki has not undergone any fundamental changes. Some of the best-known greats of the modern kabuki stage are Onoe Kikugoro V, Ichikawa Danjuro IX, Ichikawa Sadanji I, Onoe Kikugoro VI, and Nakamura Kichiemon I.

● Characteristics

Kabuki is an actor's theater, and the actor's skill is all. Many foreign observers have been drawn to kabuki for its women's roles gracefully performed by male *onna-gata* in conformity with kabuki's long-standing tradition of banning women from the stage. Bando Tamasaburo, for example, the most popular *onna-gata* in kabuki today, has also been lionized overseas. Kabuki names are generally hereditary, and actors' children undergo rigorous training from a very early age.

Every kabuki actor has a *yagō*,* called out by appreciative members of the audience when he cuts an especially striking figure. Some of the most famous *yagō* are Naritaya (Ichikawa Danjuro), Koraiya (Matsumoto Koshiro), Narikomaya (Nakamura Utaemon), and Otowaya (Onoe Kikugoro). Another unique feature of kabuki is the *hanamichi*, a long passageway running directly through the audience at the left of center stage, and having principal actors make their entrances and exits along the *hana-michi* helps to draw the audience into the performance itself.

Kabuki's main themes include both tales of war and court life and everyday psychological conflicts that the townspeople could identify with.

7 文楽・日本舞踊

●文楽

歌舞伎とともに近世演劇を代表する文楽は，文楽座から発祥した操り人形芝居の名称で，別に人形浄瑠璃とも呼ばれる。歌舞伎ほどポピュラーではないが，生身の演者によるよりも人形の演じる芝居にいっそうの魅力を見いだす通的外国人も増えている。

文楽の起源は室町時代で，江戸時代になり，京阪を中心に発展し，完成した。太夫・三味線弾きが義太夫浄瑠璃を演奏するのに合わせて人形を遣う。しかも1つの人形を3人がかりで遣う。人形は首・肩板・胴・手から成り，足は原則として男にしかない。1mから1.5mの大きさで，重いものは10kgにもなる。主遣いが首・胴・右手，左遣いが左手，足遣いが足を受け持つ。女の人形には足がないのが普通だが，着物のすそをつまんでさばくことによってそれらしく見せる。本来表情のない人形は，黒い頭巾，黒い衣服をまとった人形遣いによって魂を吹き込まれたかのように，嘆き，笑い，怒る。

代表的作家近松門左衛門は江戸時代に，『国性爺合戦』『曽根崎心中』『心中天網島』など不朽の名作を残し，それは今も観客の胸を打つ。武家社会を題材にした時代物にしろ，庶民を主人公にした世話物にしろ，人間や人間関係の本質を詩情豊かに追究したところに，時代を越えて人々の心を動かさずにはおかないものがあるのだろう。文楽は現在，重要無形文化財となり，人間国宝に数人が指定されている。

●日本舞踊

発生は古代までさかのぼり，『古事記』にアメノウズメが舞ったという「天岩屋伝説」が記されている。現在の日本舞踊の代表と言えば，歌舞伎とともに歩み，古くからの各種の舞踊の要素が集大成されている歌舞伎踊りを挙げることができる。一方，19世紀に京阪の宴席を中心に，能の影響を受けて発達した，上方舞いも忘れることができない。共に三味線を主体の伴奏音楽によって演じられる。前者は当然劇的要素が濃く，動きも活発。後者の動きは極端に少なく，1畳の畳の中で舞うとさえ言う。

日本舞踊が，西洋の舞踊，すなわちバレエと最も異なる点は，バレエがトウシューズでつま先立ち，跳躍するのに対し，日本舞踊はすり足で，むしろ腰を入れて足拍子を踏むところにある。家元制度の下に西川，藤間，花柳，井上など多数の流派があるが，現在，最大の流派は花柳流。生け花，茶道同様に習い手の大半は女性である。

Bunraku and *Buyō*

● *Bunraku**

The traditional Japanese puppet theater is known as *bunraku*, a name derived from Osaka's Bunraku-za theater. While not as popular as kabuki, *bunraku* with its all-puppet cast appeals to a discriminating audience that includes a growing number of foreigners.

Although the earliest forms of *bunraku* appeared in the Muromachi period, it was in the Edo period that it became popular in Kyoto and Osaka. *Bunraku* demands close cooperation among the ballad-reciting chanter,* the *shamisen* accompanist, and the three operators required for each puppet. *Bunraku* puppets measure 1-1.5 meters high and can weigh up to 10 kg. Each of the three operators has responsibility for different parts—the principal operator for the head, torso, and right hand, the first assistant for the left hand, and the second assistant for the feet—and all have devoted many years to their art of bringing the puppets to life. While dolls for female characters do not usually have feet, the hems of the kimono are moved to give the illusion of feet. Even though the puppets have little facial expression, the operators manage to make them weep, laugh, and get angry very realistically. Onstage, the operators are inconspicuously clothed in black.

The greatest *bunraku* playwright was Chikamatsu Monzaemon, who wrote such classics as *Kokusenya Kassen* (Battles of Coxinga), *Sonezaki Shinjū* (Love Suicides at Sonezaki), and *Shinjū Ten no Amijima* (Love Suicides at Amijima). Modern audiences find that many of these plays still possess dramatic power and themes—romantic love, the star-crossed lovers' suicide, and war—that transcend time. *Bunraku* has been designated an Important Intangible Cultural Asset,* and several *bunraku* artists have been named Living Cultural Treasures.*

● *Buyō*

Buyō is a generic word used to refer to traditional Japanese dance forms. The earliest mention of Japanese dance is in the *Kojiki*. Best-known are the kabuki dances which use elements from the kabuki stage, although the *kamigata* dance which developed in the 19th century Kyoto-Osaka area and is patterned after noh dance is also an important tradition. Both are performed to *shamisen*-centered accompaniment, the kabuki dancing retaining the stage's vigorous movements and the *kamigata* dance showing powerful restraint and taking place in a small area.

Buyō differs conspicuously from ballet and other Western dance forms in that while ballet dancers wear toeshoes to dance on their toes and perform leaps, *buyō* performers tend to move in shuffling motions. Among the many *buyō* schools existing today under the traditional *iemoto* system of master-led schools are the Nishikawa, Fujima, Inoue, and (most popular) Hanayagi schools. As with flower arrangement and the tea ceremony, most *buyō* students are women.

8 大衆芸能

大衆芸能は寄席を舞台に，庶民の娯楽として栄えてきた。テレビ・ラジオの台頭とともに娯楽の王座は奪われたが，今日では寄席ばかりでなく，テレビ・ラジオにも進出し，再び現代の娯楽として大きな位置を占めている。以下，主な大衆芸能を挙げると——

●落語

江戸時代初期に起こり，江戸，大坂を中心に栄え，多くの流派を生む。世相人情を風刺しながら，こっけいな話の展開と話術で聴衆を笑わせ，話の最後には巧みに「落」をつけるのが定型である。まだ駆け出しの落語家は「前座」と呼ばれ，高座では初めのほうに出演する。また，一座の主たる格の芸人は「真打ち」と呼ばれ，最後に出演する。真打ちとは，それだけの値打ちがある落語家を言う意味でついたが，今日では一人前になり，披露を済ませた芸人は「真打ち」と呼ばれている。最近は真打ち昇格試験も行われるようになった。

●講談

落語と並ぶ日本特有の話術芸能で，江戸・元禄時代に『太平記』を講じた名和清左衛門が祖とされる。政談や武勇伝，御家騒動，あだ討ち，侠客伝，人情物語などを語り聞かせる。当初は「講釈」と言い，明治に入って「講談」と呼ばれるようになった。全盛期は大正までで，宝井馬琴，一龍斎貞山，神田伯山などを輩出するが，第2次世界大戦後は衰退した。

●漫才

古くは13，14世紀ごろ，初春などに太夫と才蔵の2人が連れ立ち，おもしろおかしく掛け合いを演じ，悪魔を払い，年の繁栄を祝った「万歳」に端を発している。漫才はその現代化であり，明治末期に関西で始まり，発展してきた。出し物は作者が別にいる場合もあるが，自作自演も多い。また最近は2人にこだわらず，多数で演ずるものや，楽器などバンド入りのものもある。時代の進展とともに漫才も影響を受け，若手コンビによるテンポの速い漫才が人気を得ている。

●浪花節

講釈，物語，演劇，文芸作品などを材料とし，三味線を伴奏に，独特の節回しで歌い，語るもので，独演である。江戸中期大坂に出た浪花伊助からこの名で呼ばれ，明治に入り桃中軒雲右衛門が盛り上げた。義理人情，勧善懲悪を内容としたものが多く，「浪花節的」と言えば，義理人情に傾きがちなことの代名詞である。「浪曲」とも言う。

Popular Entertainment

Popular entertainment was once the specialty of the *yose* theater. Though the *yose* has been supplanted by television and radio, *yose* entertainment continues to survive as staple fare in the new media.

● ***Rakugo****

This comic monologue originated in the early Edo period in the stories of human foibles told with vivid expression and ending with skillfully delivered punch lines called *ochi* (the character *ochi* is also read *raku* to give *rakugo* its name). *Rakugo* flourished in Edo and Osaka, and many schools of storytelling evolved. Novice performers are called *zenza*, since they open the bill in the typical *yose* program, and experienced storytellers of exceptional skill are called *shin-uchi* and perform last. *Shin-uchi* was formerly a title reserved for only the best *rakugo* artists, but today it is accorded any *rakugo* storyteller who has finished his apprenticeship. Recently, a *shin-uchi* examination has been instituted to rank storytellers.

● ***Kōdan***

This form of storytelling is said to have begun with the recitation of tales from the 14th-century *Taiheiki* military ballad in the Edo period as perfected by Nawa Seizaemon. *Kōdan* stories are of historical events, military exploits, succession disputes in daimyo households, vendettas, heroic figures and sentimental tales of human nature. Originally called *kōshaku*, this type of storytelling or recitation has been known as *kōdan* since the Meiji period. At its height in the early 20th century when such artists as Takarai Bakin and Ichiryusai Teizan were in their prime, *kōdan* has declined since the war.

● ***Manzai***

Comic banter usually performed by two artists, *manzai* goes back to the 13th and 14th centuries when such performances were a common entertainment for ushering in the new year and exorcising devils, and the name is said to come from the "manzai" at the end. Modern *manzai* developed in the late 19th century in the Kansai region. Though some *manzai* acts are scripted by professional writers, most are thought up by the performers. Recent *manzai* acts have sometimes included more than two people and have even musical accompaniment. *Manzai* has changed considerably with the times. Today rapid-paced dialogues by young performers are especially popular.

● ***Naniwa-bushi***

Japanese narrative ballads, *naniwa-bushi* (also called *rōkyoku*) are recited by a solo chanter to the accompaniment of a single *shamisen*. Stories are derived from *kōshaku*, drama, and literature. Originated by Naniwa Isuke in the Osaka area in the mid-Edo period, *naniwa-bushi* was popularized by Tochuken Kumoemon at the turn of the century. Most *naniwa-bushi* tales are of sacrifice, sentiment, and morality, and the term is often used to mean tear-jerking self-sacrifice.

9 生け花(華道)

茶の湯と同様，生け花も室町時代，将軍足利義政の下，東山文化の中で華道として成立した。四季に恵まれた日本には四季の花々があり，野にあるそれらの素材を単に切り取って飾るだけでなく，そこに1つの芸術的理念を展開させたもの，それが生け花である。つまり自然の容姿風体を生かし，あるいは生ける際の花材の構成に天地人の形式を取り入れて華道の理念としている流派が多い。

生け花は，時代に応じてさまざまな様式を生んできた。そして今日なお生き続けているものに，立華(りっか)，生花(せいか)，投入(なげいれ)，盛花(もりばな)がある。流派は2000～3000あるが，最大のものは池坊で，弟子の数100万人と言われる。これに次ぐのは小原流，草月流などである。

• **立華** 書院の床の間の飾り花として，池坊専慶が室町時代に創造した。松・桃・竹・柳・紅葉(もみじ)・ヒノキなどが使われ，後述の生花のように，必ずしも瓶口に直接挿して水を揚げる形を取らない。立華と称するのは，草木の立ち伸びる姿から，立てる形を取ったためで，花や木を素材に針金などを用いて容姿を整え，1つの風景の再現を意図している。

• **生花** 花を生けるという表現は，もともとは生花に対して使われていた。江戸時代中期，客をもてなす生け花として生まれ，主として床の間に置かれた。投入や盛花と異なり，花を挿す器は大地を象徴し，草花の部分的な美しさよりも，草木が伸びゆく生命力を表そうとする。品格の高さ，流麗，端正さが生花の特徴である。

• **投入** 深い花器に花枝を自然の姿のまま，無造作に投げ入れたように挿したところからこの名が生まれた。床の間につるす場合と，柱にかける場合，床の間に置く場合の3通りの形式がある。生花同様江戸時代から。

• **盛花** 水盤やかごを用い，器に花を盛るような形で生けるところからこの名がついた。明治末期，洋花の栽培や洋風建築の増加により，床の間の装飾に限らないものとして考案された。小原流，草月流，安達式など，盛花は現代の生け花の主流と言える。

戦後の住宅環境の変化――洋風建築や小さな間取り――は，生け花にも影響を及ぼした。伝統にとらわれない新しい様式の創造は，前衛生け花として市民権を得，華道から造形芸術へと変貌しつつある。また，流派にこだわらずフラワーデザインを楽しむ人も増えている。

Flower Arrangement

Together with the tea ceremony, ikebana (also known as *kadō* or way of the flower) was established in the Muromachi period as a central part of the Higashiyama culture under the shogun Ashikaga Yoshimasa. Because Japan is blessed with changing seasons and plentiful flora, it was not enough simply to go out and pick flowers from the field. They had to be displayed artistically, and this is the heart of ikebana. At times this artistic arrangement entails making them look as close to their ideal natural state as possible, and at times the elements of the arrangements are used to represent the heavens, earth, and man; both of these being important principles in many schools.

Ikebana has developed numerous styles over the years. Some of the most common today are explained below. All told, there are 2-3,000 different schools of ikebana. The largest of these is Ikenobo, with over a million students. Other important schools include Ohara and Sogetsu.

· ***Rikka**** This style was developed by Ikenobo Senkei in the Muromachi period for decorating the *tokonoma* with flowers. Using pine, peach, bamboo, willow, maple, cypress, and other plants, this style is not as concerned as, say, *seika*, with putting the stems in contact with the vase or even the water. Because *rikka* is a standing or vertical style, and indeed the name derives from the use of protruding branches, it uses supporting materials in an attempt to recreate an entire landscape.

· ***Seika**** This style of using flowers as they appear in real life developed in the mid-Edo period as a *tokonoma* arrangement for the delight of guests. Unlike *nageire* or *moribana*, *seika* uses the vase to represent the earth and attempts to portray not beauty but rather the power of flowers in the field. *Seika* is characterized by its elegance, flow, and breadth.

· ***Nageire**** This style derives its name from the fact that flowers are simply "thrown into" a tall vase and allowed to fall naturally. These tall vases can be hung from the ceiling, hung on a pillar, or placed in the *tokonoma*. Like *seika*, it developed in the Edo period.

· ***Moribana**** This style uses water trays* or even basket-clad containers and derives its name from the fact that flowers are piled up for show. It was conceived in the late Meiji period as a modern reaction to the traditional *seika* and to make use of Western flora and forms outside of the *tokonoma*. Favored by the Ohara, Sogetsu, Adachi, and other schools, *moribana* is perhaps the preeminent modern form.

The postwar shift to Western-type housing with smaller rooms has also affected ikebana. New forms have been created ignoring traditional rules and avant-garde ikebana has come to be a recognized form as some styles even use artificial flowers. At the same time, increasing numbers of people are enjoying flower design unfettered by tradition.

10 茶の湯(茶道)

日本人の書いた英文書として，今なお名著と言われる『茶の本』の中で，著者岡倉天心は，「茶道とは，日常生活のむさくるしい諸事実の中にある美を崇拝することを根底とする儀式である」(桶谷秀昭訳)と簡にして要を得て書いている。奈良時代に中国から伝えられた茶が，異国・日本で茶道として独自の文化を開花させたのはなぜか。茶の湯にこそ，日本文化の特質が内包されているのかもしれない。

●茶の湯の歴史

日本に初めて茶が渡来したのは，奈良時代，遣唐使たちによってである。一時廃れたが，鎌倉時代には再び広まり，室町時代，将軍足利義政の下で，村田珠光が四畳半の侘茶方式を始めるに及び，茶は芸術性を高め，茶道となった。そしてこれを大成したのが，安土・桃山時代の千利休である。利休は豊臣秀吉の庇護を受けたがやがて対立，1591年，秀吉の命により切腹した。茶道は子孫に受け継がれ，表千家，裏千家，武者小路千家の，いわゆる三千家を生んだ。流派としてはこの三千家を中心に，藪内家，遠州流，宗徧流など多くの流派を生み，今日に至っている。中でも淡交会を組織する裏千家は，戦後いち早く海外へ進出し，茶道の国際化に大きな役割を果たした。

●作法と心得

庭園や寺社の境内などに臨時の席を設けて行う野点の形式もあるが，茶道に茶室は欠かせない。そしてこの茶室という狭い空間こそが茶文化をはぐくんだ。茶を点てることは点前と言い，その手順は，茶碗に抹茶を入れて釜の湯を注ぎ，茶筅でかき回し泡立てる。飲み方は右手で茶碗を取り，左の手のひらに乗せ，茶碗を向こうから手前に回す。飲んだ後は指先でぬぐい，指は懐紙(懐中の紙)でふく。しかし，茶道とは単に茶を飲むのではなく，茶碗をはじめとする茶道具，茶室の調度，露地(茶庭)などの鑑賞，そして主人と客との心の交流にこそ本質がある。

千利休は茶の湯の心得を，「四規七則」と説いた。「四規」とは和敬清寂で，和敬は茶会での亭主と客相互の心得。清寂は茶室，茶庭の清らかで閑寂な雰囲気を言う。「七則」は他人に接するときの心構えで，「茶は服(飲みかげん)のよきように点て，炭は湯の沸くように置き，冬は暖かく夏は涼しく，花は野にあるように入れ，刻限は早めに，降らずとも雨具の用意，相客に心せよ，の7つが秘事」と言う。

The Tea Ceremony

One of the best English-language books by a Japanese author is Okakura Tenshin's* *The Book of Tea* (1906), in which Okakura characterizes teaism as "a cult founded on the adoration of the beautiful among the sordid facts of everyday existence."

● History of the Tea Ceremony

The tea ceremony was introduced into Japan from China during the Nara period. After initially fading into obscurity, it was revived in the Kamakura period and spread during the Muromachi period thanks to the enthusiasm of the shogun Ashikaga Yoshimasa and his tea master Murata Juko, who originated the *wabicha* style of using a $4\frac{1}{2}$-mat room and enhanced the artistic and spiritual aspects to develop a discipline known as *sadō* (the way of tea). In the Azuchi-Momoyama period, *sadō* was further refined by Sen no Rikyu. Rikyu gained the patronage of Toyotomi Hideyoshi, but the two later had a falling-out and in 1591 Hideyoshi ordered Rikyu to commit ritual suicide. His teachings were carried on by his descendants, three of whom established the three Senke schools of tea: Ura Senke, Omote Senke, and Mushakoji Senke. In addition to these three main schools, other influential schools include the Yabunouchi, Enshu, and Sohen schools, all of which are active today. Ura Senke began being taught overseas immediately after the war, and it has played a major role in *sadō*'s internationalization.

● Etiquette

Traditionally, the tea ceremony is held outside or in a small room set apart from other buildings, and it is this simplicity of setting more than anything else which epitomizes the spirit of tea. In the serving of the tea, the *temae*,* the host spoons some powdered green *matcha** tea into a ceramic teabowl,* adds hot water from the kettle,* and stirs briskly with a small whisk.* In receiving the tea, the guest takes it with his right hand and, steadying it on his left palm, turns it once or twice before drinking. After drinking, the guest wipes the rim with his finger and then his finger with a small napkin. In addition to the tea, appreciation of the utensils, the room decor, and the garden, as well as the chemistry between host and guests, are all essential elements of *sadō*.

Sen no Rikyu established four rules for the rapport between host and guests and the simple beauty and tranquility of the tea room and garden and seven guidelines for the host's attitude: "Serve the tea with insight into the guest's soul, prepare the charcoal to heat the water best, make your guest feel warm in winter and cool in summer, arrange the flowers so they look like wild flowers, be quick and efficient, be prepared for rain even on a clear day, and be attentive toward all guests. These are the seven keys."

11 書道

書道は*毛筆と*墨を使い，漢字や仮名文字を書く一種の造形芸術である。西洋でも，文字を象形化したり装飾化するカリグラフィーの伝統はあるが，書道の持つ芸術的奥深さには及ばない。アルファベットと比べ，文字それ自体が持つ意味や毛筆の多様性などが，書道を芸術へと高めた。昨今は外国人にも関心が高まっている。

正月２日，新年に初めて文字を書く書き初めの儀式は今日も残っており，吉方に向かってめでたい言葉や詩歌を書く。小中学生の大がかりな書き初め大会も，例年催されている。

●書道の歴史

日本の書道はもともと中国の王羲之が祖と言われ，中国の書が日本に入ったのは奈良時代である。平安時代前期には空海，嵯峨天皇，橘逸勢の３人が特に三筆と言われ，中国風の雄勁な書風を代表した。さらに中期には小野道風，藤原佐理，藤原行成が現れ，三蹟と言われた。彼らはそれまでの中国風に対し，優美典雅な日本風の和様書道（上代様とも言う）の創造に功績があった。藤原行成は世尊寺流を興し，また，小野道風は青蓮院流（後の御家流）など後代の書道に大きな影響を与えた。南北朝時代に興った御家流は，江戸時代には一切の公文書に採用され，また寺子屋でも習字にもっぱら使われた。

このように，書は時代を象徴する雰囲気を有し，今日，書道ブームと言われるほどの隆盛の中で，バラエティーに富んだ自由な書が愛好され，また，女性書家の進出が目だっている。

●書体の種類

文字の書体には，*楷書，*行書，*草書，それに仮名がある。楷書は字形が方正で，動きが少なく，安定した書体のため，真書とも言われる。行書は楷書と草書の中間的存在で，楷書では固すぎ，草書では難解であるために考え出された書体。草書は行書をさらに崩し，点画を略したものを言い，最も早く書くことができる。と同時に，造形上の自由が大きいために，芸術性も高いところから，書家に好まれている。

この草書体の究極に生まれたのが仮名で，平安時代，主に女性によって使われたので，女手とも呼ばれ，和歌の流行とともに発展した。漢字の雄渾に対して，優美，流麗である。書は表現美（線，形，流れ，余白，墨色など）と内容美（風格，意味），さらに書家の人となりがあいまって成立，鑑賞される。

Calligraphy

Japanese calligraphy, *shodō*, is a highly developed art form using brush* and black ink* to write Japanese and Chinese characters. While similar to the decorative calligraphy of the West, *shodō* is more deeply rooted as a fine art form, in part because every character has meaning in and of itself and because of the great diversity of character shapes. *Shodō* is increasingly admired by Japanese and foreigners alike.

The *kakizome* held on January 2 marks the first writing of the new year and is still regularly performed today. Facing an auspicious direction, participants write out felicitous words and phrases. *Kakizome* competitions are annual elementary and junior high school events.

● History

Shodō traces its origins to China, where the master calligrapher Wang Xizhi is traditionally credited as the father of the art. It was introduced into Japan in the 8th century. The early Heian contemporaries Kukai, Emperor Saga, and courtier Tachibana no Hayanari are respectfully referred to as the Sanpitsu or Three Great Brushes, and their calligraphy is considered representative of Chinese calligraphy's classic beauty. In the 10th and 11th centuries these three were succeeded by the Sanseki (the Three Traces): Ono no Tofu, Fujiwara no Sukemasa, and Fujiwara no Yukinari. These three masters developed the first uniquely Japanese calligraphy style, known as *wayō* (also *jōdaiyō*). Fujiwara no Yukinari's style led to the formation of the Sesonji school and Ono no Tofu served as a model for the Shoren'in school which later evolved into the Oie style of calligraphy. The Oie style was used for official documents in the Edo period and was the predominant style taught in the *terakoya* schools of that period.

Just as calligraphy has changed over the ages, the revived interest in calligraphy today is characterized by its broad latitude for creativity and the increasing number of women masters.

● Calligraphy Styles

There are three basic styles: *kaisho*,* *gyōsho*,* and *sōsho*.* *Kana* might be added as a fourth style. *Kaisho*, a block style with little movement, is also called *shinsho*. *Gyōsho* is an intermediate style neither as stiff as *kaisho* nor as flowing as *sōsho*. *Sōsho* is a highly cursive style written with swift strokes. Its freedom and aesthetic appeal has made *sōsho* a very popular style.

Kana originated in the more extreme forms of *sōsho*. Because it was the primary script for Heian women, *kana* was at one time referred to as *onnade* (women's writing). *Kana* developed with the growing popularity of *waka* poetry. Compared to the boldness of Chinese characters, *kana* is elegant and refined. Japanese calligraphy is judged not only by its surface beauty and meaning but also by the calligrapher's character.

12 絵画

日本画は緑青(ろくしょう)，辰砂(しんしゃ)などの岩絵具や墨を，*にかわ水で溶いて，毛筆で紙，絹布，などに描くものである。西洋絵画の油絵は，顔料を油で溶くことによって色を自由に混ぜ合わせ，好みの色彩が得られるが，日本画ではそれはできず，また，重ね塗りもできない。

日本画には単色画と彩色画がある。単色画には，墨の線だけによる「白描(はくびょう)」と，墨の濃淡によって物体の量感や空間を表す「水墨画」がある。いずれも中国から伝わった技法であり，白描は平安時代末の「鳥獣戯画」絵巻が代表的なもので，水墨画は室町時代の雪舟によって日本的な水墨画が生み出されたとされている。

彩色画は当初は仏画として移入された。この技法が根付くのは平安時代になってからで，四季の草花や自然，風俗などが柔らかい線と穏やかな色彩で描かれた。これを「大和絵(やまとえ)」と言う。

●絵巻物

中でも，平安時代末，鎌倉時代初めから盛んになった日本独自な型式が絵巻物である。絵画と，その説明を何枚も並べて，長い巻物にしたもので，寺の縁起や人物の歴史が，時間を追って展開され，全体で1つの物語を作っている。「源氏物語絵巻」などが代表作。

●障屏画(しょうへいが)

室町時代末期から安土・桃山時代にかけて，中国・宋の絵画と大和絵とを融合させた*狩野派の絵画が寺や城の装飾に用いられた。これらは「障屏画」と呼ばれ，障子(しょうじ)や*屏風(びょうぶ)などの大画面に，花鳥や人々の風俗などを豪華けんらんに描いた。狩野永徳，長谷川等伯らが代表的画家。さらに江戸時代初期には，俵屋宗達，尾形光琳(こうりん)などが現れ，それまでのさまざまな伝統的な画風を自由な立場で独自に発展させた。

●洋画

日本に洋画がもたらされたのは江戸時代末期で，オランダから写実的画法が入ってきた。明治維新後，黒田清輝，浅井忠らがフランスへ留学し，当時最新の印象派の影響を受けて帰り，藤島武二，青木繁，坂本繁二郎らに伝えた。

他方日本画も，岡倉天心に率いられた菱田(ひしだ)春草，横山大観らが，写実を加えて近代化を図った。だが，今日も日本の絵画は版画，抽象画を除き，日本的な感性と市場性ゆえに，国際舞台に出る画家は少ない。

Painting

Traditional-style Japanese paintings are executed by brush on paper and silk with such pigments as verdigris (green copper rust), cinnabar, and *sumi* ink diluted with liquid glue.* Unlike Western oil painting in which colors can be mixed and applied in thick layers, *nihon-ga* is limited in its colors and their application.

Nihon-ga can be broadly divided into mono- and polychrome works. Monochrome paintings include simple line sketches and *suiboku-ga* washes with subtle differentiations of tone. Both are techniques introduced from China, and are represented, respectively, by the late Heian-period *Chōjū Giga* (Scrolls of Frolicking Animals and Humans) and the purely Japanese-style of Sesshu, a Muromachi-period painter.

The earliest polychrome paintings in Japan were of Buddhist subjects, and it was not until the Heian period that a truly Japanese style of polychrome painting known as *yamato-e* evolved. In addition to its subtle lines and soft colors, *yamato-e* is distinguished by its depicting the changing seasons and people involved in various activities.

● *E-makimono*

Many of the best-known *yamato-e* are *e-makimono*, horizontal scrolls which first appeared in the late Heian period and early Kamakura period. They consist of long scrolls with alternating text and pictures telling a story in chronological order. The *Genji Monogatari Emaki* (Tale of Genji Scrolls) are among the most famous *e-makimono*.

● *Shōhei-ga*

From the end of the Muromachi period well into the Azuchi-Momoyama period, the Kano School,* which combined Chinese and *yamato-e* styles, supplied the primary decorative painting for temples and castles. Known as *shōhei-ga*, this decorative painting was executed on sliding doors and folding screens.* Subjects included birds and flowers and people painted in a sumptuous style. Major artists of the period include Kano Eitoku and Hasegawa Tohaku. Later, in the early Edo period, such artists as Tawaraya Sotatsu and Ogata Korin imbued this kind of decorative art work with freedom and vitality.

● Western-style Painting

At the end of the Edo period, realistic Western-style painting was introduced by the Dutch. Following the Meiji Restoration, Japanese artists such as Kuroda Seiki and Asai Chu traveled to France and were influenced by the impressionist painters. The new art concepts these men brought back to Japan were avidly pursued by such people as Fujishima Takeji, Aoki Shigeru, and Sakamoto Hanjiro.

Influenced by Western techniques, artists such as Hishida Shunso and Yokoyama Taikan created modern *nihon-ga* under the patronage of Okakura Tenshin. Except for those working in woodblock printing and abstract painting, few Japanese artists are active internationally today, in part because of the uniquely Japanese sense of their work.

13 浮世絵*

江戸時代に，江戸を中心に風景や庶民の風俗などを描いた，主として多色刷りの版画を浮世絵と呼ぶ。当時「浮世」と呼ばれていた歌舞伎や遊里の風俗を描いたためにこの名がある。こうした風俗画が現れるのは江戸時代初期の1670年代で，菱川師宣が墨一色摺りによる木版画を売り出し，師宣は浮世絵の創始者と呼ばれている。

●春信，歌麿，写楽

18世紀半ば，歌舞伎の繁盛，出版の隆盛などから浮世絵の人気が高まり，また木版技術の進歩もあって，多色刷りの浮世絵である錦絵が鈴木春信によって作られた。春信は美人画を描き，また，多色刷りゆえ，背景も描けるようになった。この美人画の様式を独自に発展させたのが喜多川歌麿で，雲母摺という，背景に雲母を入れて輝きを出した美人の上半身像で(これを大首絵と言う)，女性の肉体美を優美に描き出した。大首絵で女性美を表した歌麿に対し，歌舞伎の役者の表情の変化から内面の性格までを，芸術性高く描き出したのが東洲斎写楽である。1794年5月から翌年2月までの10か月間に，江戸で上演された歌舞伎の役者の絵ばかり約150種を描いて，すい星のように消えて行った写楽が，どんな人であったのかわかっていない。

●北斎，広重

19世紀に入ると，美人画・役者絵は多数描かれるが，芸術性の高いものは失われていく。この時代に浮世絵に新風を送り込んだのが葛飾北斎と安藤広重で，新しいテーマとして風景画を創出した。北斎は西洋銅版画の影響を受けて風景画を志したと言われており，「富嶽三十六景」で，大胆な構図と色彩を見せて人気を得，以後各地の名所などのシリーズを描いた。90歳まで生きて，木版画ばかりでなく，肉筆画も多く残している。広重は「東海道五十三次」のシリーズで，日本の自然と旅行く人々を叙情豊かに描いて北斎をしのぐ人気があった。後に「木曽街道六十九次」など，日本各地に題材を取ったシリーズものを作った。

浮世絵は，19世紀末のヨーロッパにもたらされ，その大胆な構図や色彩のコントラストだけで陰をつけない画法などが，ドガ，マネ，ゴッホらの印象派の画家に衝撃を与えた。近代美術への影響の大きさは，日本国内よりも欧米で高く評価されている。

Ukiyo-e*

This term is used to describe the pictures, many of them color prints, depicting Edo-period scenes and customs. The name comes from the fact that many showed the *ukiyo* (floating world) of the theater and pleasure quarters. The first such pictures appeared in the 1670s when Hishikawa Moronobu discovered a way to make monochromic woodblock prints.

● Harunobu, Utamaro, and Sharaku

Ukiyo-e became very popular in the mid-18th century with the flowering of kabuki and the spread of publishing. As printing technology evolved, it became possible to print full-color art, and Suzuki Harunobu created the full-color *nishiki-e* prints. Harunobu drew pictures of beautiful women in full color and with great background detail. Yet it was for Kitagawa Utamaro to bring these pictures of beautiful women to their full glory. Utamaro was particularly skilled at the *ō-kubi-e* showing beautiful women from the waist up, and these superb portraits often used backgrounds sparkling with mica. In contrast to Utamaro's sensual pictures of beauties, Toshusai Sharaku turned his skills to powerfully depicting the expressive character of the kabuki theater. In a meteoric career, he produced about 150 different pictures from the leading kabuki plays in Edo between May 1794 and February 1795, but little is known about his person.

● Hokusai and Hiroshige

Going into the 19th century, there were vast numbers of inferior prints of beautiful women and kabuki actors, and the genre seemed beset with imitation and exaggeration until Katsushika Hokusai and Ando Hiroshige breathed new life into it by turning their talents to the virgin field of landscapes. Hokusai is thought to have started doing landscapes under the influence of Western copper plates. He later became famous for his *36 Views of Mt Fuji* for their dynamic compositions and gorgeous colors, and he followed this success up with other series of pictures of famous tourist sites. Hokusai lived to be 90 and has left behind many woodblock prints and even paintings. Hiroshige's *53 Stations on the Tokaido* won him a place as Hokusai's main rival, for their rich depiction of Japanese scenery and the sights of travelers, and he also went on to do other series of other famous spots, including *69 Stations on the Kiso Kaido*.

Many ukiyo-e pictures were taken to Europe in the late 19th century, where their sweeping compostion and striking colors, plus the fact that they did not use shadows, attracted the interest of Degas, Manet, van Gogh, and the other impressionists. A major influence on modern art, ukiyo-e are more appreciated in the West than in Japan.

14 陶磁器

日本では約1万年前から土器が作られ，その時代・様式によって縄文土器，弥生土器の名が付けられているが，陶磁器が作られるのはずっと後になる。日本では木工が盛んであるうえ，漆の技術が早くから発達していて，日常雑器にはこれらを用いていたからである。

●陶器

日本最初の陶器は，奈良時代に中国の唐三彩を模して作られたと思われる，奈良三彩と呼ぶ白・緑・茶の釉薬を用いたものである。その多くが正倉院に伝わっているものであるため，正倉院三彩とも呼ばれている。奈良三彩の後，日本では約500年近く陶器は作られず，この間は須恵器と呼ぶ灰黒色の硬く焼き締めた土器が日本全国で作られたが，それも平安時代末期にはほとんど姿を消してしまった。

本格的な陶器が焼かれるのは鎌倉時代で，瀬戸の藤四郎という人が，中国から技術を移入したもので，壺や水差し，香炉，仏具などが作られた。この後室町時代に至るまでの間に瀬戸のほか，信楽，常滑，丹波，備前，越前で陶器が作られるようになり，これらを日本の六古窯と呼んでいる。

戦国時代を経て豊臣秀吉により天下統一が成され，茶の湯が盛んになるに従い，瀬戸の陶工が移った美濃で志野，黄瀬戸，織部など，日本独特の味わいを持つ茶陶が作られ，ほかに信楽，伊賀，備前，京都などでも茶器が盛んに焼かれた。加えて，秀吉による朝鮮進攻の際，大名たちが朝鮮の陶工たちを連れ帰って各地に窯を作り，陶磁器作りはたいへん盛んになった。

●磁器

朝鮮の李参平が，1616年に肥前有田で磁器の焼成に成功，日本の磁器作りが始まる。さらに酒井田柿右衛門が色絵を始めたことにより，有田の磁器は大変有名になり，その後オランダとの貿易を通じて，ヨーロッパにも伝えられるようになった。その積み出し港が伊万里であったため，「伊万里焼き」とも呼ばれ，ヨーロッパでももてはやされた。特にドイツのザクセン王アウグスト2世は，ドレスデン城内に陶磁器研究所を作り，多くの伊万里焼きのコレクションを研究し，後にマイセン窯を作って，ヨーロッパでも磁器を作るようになった。

日本の陶磁器作りは時代を下るに従い盛んになり，全国各地に窯が築かれ，江戸末期には日常雑器もすべて陶磁器を用いるようになった。ことに瀬戸では有田から磁器製法を学び，日常雑器を盛んに作ったため，陶磁器一般を「せともの」と呼ぶようになり，現代に至っている。

Ceramics

Earthenware was made in Japan some 10,000 years ago. Despite the centuries of earthenware production, glazed pottery and porcelain were not made until much later, partly because it was possible to meet daily needs with advanced woodworking techniques and lacquer ware.

● Pottery

The first Japanese glazed pottery was a white, green, and brown ware imitation of Tang three-colored ware. Called Nara three-colored ware, this is also known as Shosoin three-color ware because many representative pieces are in the Shosoin* depository. The next glazed ware to appear, nearly 500 years later, was a hard, gray, ash-glazed ware known as Sue ware and made nationwide. Sue disappeared in the late 12th century.

True mass production of glazed ware began in the Kamakura period when a potter named Toshiro used Chinese techniques to make urns, pitchers, incense burners, and Buddhist liturgical instruments in the Seto district. By the Muromachi period, potting had spread beyond Seto to kilns in the Shigaraki, Tokoname, Tanba, Bizen, and Echizen regions. Today these are known as the Six Ancient Kilns.

Potting took on new sophistication with the unification of the country under Toyotomi Hideyoshi and the spread of the tea ceremony. Seto potters moved to new clay deposits at Mino where they produced Shino, Ki-Seto, Oribe, and other distinctly Japanese tea implements. Tea utensils were also made in Shigaraki, Iga, Bizen, and Kyoto. Although their efforts to invade Korea ended in failure, Hideyoshi's generals brought back many skilled prisoners, among them potters who breathed new life into Japanese ceramic manufacture, building new and better kilns and producing high-quality wares.

● Porcelain

One of these Korean potters, Ri Sampei, discovered porcelain clay in Arita and succeeded in firing porcelain ware in 1616. This was the first Japanese porcelain production. Another Arita potter, Sakaida Kakiemon, painted his porcelains with brilliant colors, and soon Arita and Kakiemon porcelains were famous nationwide. Arita ware was exported by Dutch traders in the Edo period, becoming known in Europe as Imari* ware because it was shipped out of Imari port. Augustus II of Saxony collected Imari ware and commissioned the experts at his Meissen kiln near Dresden to study it and find out how it was made. The result was the first true porcelain produced in Europe.

Pottery and porcelain production spread throughout Japan in the 18th and 19th centuries, and ceramics were in common daily use by the late Edo period. Using porcelain production technology from the Arita kilns, the Seto kilns turned out such a volume of dishes and utensils of all kinds that the term *seto-mono* is today synonymous with ceramics.

15 漆器*

漆器は木・竹・布などの製品の上に，漆の木から取った天然のラッカー(塗料)を塗り付けたもので，日本，中国をはじめ東南アジア一帯で2千数百年も昔から用いられてきた生活工芸品である。英語で陶磁器がchinaと呼ばれるのに対し，漆器はjapanと呼ばれる。それは，陶磁器が中国で高度に発達し，元時代から世界に輸出されていたのに対し，漆器は日本で家具・武器・食器・生活雑器などに幅広く使われ，さらに美術工芸品としても発達し，15，16世紀にポルトガル・オランダとの貿易によってヨーロッパに広く紹介されたからである。

●漆器の歴史

漆の木の原産地は中国またはチベットと言われ，これがアジア各地に広まったものである。漆器は，日本では約2000年前の縄文(じょうもん)時代のものが出土しているが，漆器作りの技法が中国から伝わったものか，日本で独自に発展したものかは意見が分かれている。ただ，技術が飛躍的に進歩したのは，6世紀に入って大陸との交流が活発になり，中国の優秀な技術が輸入されたためである。このころになると，実用品ばかりでなく，美術工芸品としての価値を持つものも作られるようになった。

しかし，それまで漆器の用途として最も多かった食器は，江戸時代末ごろから陶磁器が広く使われるようになり，また明治以後は金属器も使用され，塗料も化学塗料が作られたため，漆器は伝統工芸品や，美術工芸品としてのみ生き残るようになった。現在も輪島塗，会津(あいず)塗，春慶塗などが作られている。

●漆器の利点

古来，漆が使われてきたのは，接着剤としての機能，塗料として木・竹・布などを保護する機能，そして色素を混ぜることによって装飾の機能を持つからである。出土品の例から見ると，古代には主に武器の接着・保護剤として弓，刀のつかなどに用いられ，次いで，木製の食器類などの保護塗料として，後に装飾性も加わり，家具などにも広く用いられるようになったようである。

乾燥後の漆は非常な強度を持っており，奈良時代には，木芯(しん)の上に麻の布で成型し，漆を何度も塗り，さらに麻布を重ねるという技法で，仏像を作ったほどである。これらは乾漆仏と呼ばれているが，奈良・興福寺の国宝・八部衆立像，十大弟子立像など，等身大の像が1200年後の現在も細部に至るまで完全な形を保っている。

Lacquer ware*

Lacquer ware is made of wood, bamboo, cloth, or other material coated with layers of lacquer extracted from the lacquer tree. Lacquer ware was being produced in China, Japan, and throughout Southeast Asia more than two millenniums ago. In Japan, lacquer-making was developed to such a degree of sophistication that the term japan has become the generic term for lacquer ware just as china is used for porcelain ware. By the time Yuan-period China (1271-1368) was exporting sophisticated porcelains and celadons, Japan was using lacquer for furniture, weapons, dishes, and other daily utensils and producing exquisite works of lacquer art. In the 15th and 16th centuries japan was exported to Europe by Portuguese and Dutch traders.

● History

Indigenous to China and Tibet, the lacquer tree has been widely cultivated throughout Asia. Japanese lacquer ware dating back more than 2,000 years to the Jomon period has been discovered in archaeological digs, but opinion is divided on whether lacquer-making techniques were introduced from China or developed spontaneously in Japan. In either case, rapid advances in lacquer-making technology were made when active trading with the continent was initiated in the 6th century and superior technology was introduced from China. It is from about this time that lacquer ware acquired an aesthetic as well as a practical value.

Near the end of the Edo period utilitarian lacquer ware was widely replaced by ceramic ware. From the Meiji period lacquer ware was further supplanted by metal ware and artificial varnishes. Today the best Japanese lacquer ware (dishes and eating utensils) is preserved primarily as an art form. Well-known types of contemporary lacquer ware include Wajima, Aizu, and Shunkei ware.

● Characteristics

Lacquer has been used since ancient times as an adhesive and as a varnish to protect wooden, bamboo, and cloth objects. It has also been mixed with color pigments for decorative effect. The earliest known use of lacquer in Japan is as an adhesive and protective varnish for bows and sword hilts. It was later applied as a protective coating to wooden utensils, this use gradually developing into an elaborate decorative technique for many other objects such as furniture.

Dried lacquer is extremely strong and durable, and in the Nara period was used to make dry-lacquer sculptures. The basic form, shaped with hemp fabric covering a wooden core, was coated with repeated layers of lacquer and cloth. Well-preserved specimens of this type of Buddhist sculpture over 1,200 years old include the Hachibushu, a National Treasure, at Kofukuji in Nara and the Judai Deshi (ten disciples of Buddha).

16 日本刀*

●日本刀の特徴

西洋の刀が「突き，刺す」を目的とする両刃の剣であるのに対し，日本刀は「切る」を目的とする片刃の刀である。日本刀は，刀剣の必要条件である「折れず，曲がらず，よく切れる」という機能を備えていることと，美術工芸品としても十分に鑑賞にたえるできばえを見せているところに特徴がある。

日本刀は，2種または3種の地金を何度も何度も打ち延ばして鍛錬し，焼き入れによって硬度を増し，最後に研磨するという日本独自の製法でできあがっている。これは諸外国に例を見ない優れた技術で，ぴんとはった曲線，均整のとれた形，地肌・刃文の変化などに美しい魅力を持っている。

●日本刀の歴史

片刃で反りを持つ日本刀の基本形式は平安時代に完成し，鎌倉時代には優れた刀工が輩出した。16世紀半ばに鉄砲が伝来するまでは，日本刀は主要な武器であった。鉄砲に武器としての主役の座を譲って後，江戸時代300年の太平の世の中で，実際の戦闘に使われることはなかった。そして明治維新後の近代社会では，刀を帯びることは禁止され，現在では，美術工芸品として鑑賞されることが主となっている。

●武士の魂

江戸時代，儒教思想に裏付けされた武士の道徳律である武士道が大成されると，日本刀は，その象徴とされた。刀を帯びることは武士だけに許された特権であり，一般の商人，農民には許されなかった。それはすなわち，国民の1割弱の武士が9割を占める農民や商人を支配する体制を維持するためにも必要なシンボルであり，またそのための小道具でもあったのである。

武士たちは刀を神聖なものとし，家の名誉と誇りを示すものとして，代々の宝とした。曇りやすくさびやすい刀をいつも光らせ，武士の魂としてたいせつに扱った。

日本の時代劇映画や，1970年の三島由紀夫の割腹自殺から，日本刀に切腹の道具としてのイメージを持つ人がいるかもしれない。この切腹も江戸時代には刀を持つ武士にだけ許された刑で，名誉な死に方であった。

The Japanese Sword*

● Characteristics

Whereas the Western sword is a two-edged weapon for penetrating and stabbing, the Japanese sword is a single-edged weapon for slashing and cutting. In addition, the Japanese sword must fulfill the three functional requirements of not breaking, not bending, and cutting well—as well as being an aesthetically pleasing work of craftsmanship.

Japanese swords are made by repeatedly heating, flattening, folding, and tempering two or three different metals to produce a strong blade which is then honed to a razor-sharp edge. The technology used in making these ancient blades surpassed anything available in the West at the time, and the Japanese sword's graceful curve, symmetrical shape, and the changes in the *jihada* (blade) and *hamon* (temper patterns) make it a work of art.

● History

The Japanese sword achieved its basic single-edged curved shape in the Heian period and reached new heights of excellence with many outstanding swordsmiths in the Kamakura period. For centuries, the sword remained the primary weapon for fighting. Yet once firearms proliferated in the mid-16th century, swords came to be used more and more for ceremonial purposes and less and less for combat. Finally, swords were relegated to museums and private collections in the modern period when the Meiji government banned their wearing after the Restoration of 1868.

● Soul of the Swordsman

Although peace prevailed in the Edo period, the sword remained a symbol of *bushi-dō* (the way of the warrior) and its Confucian-based ethic. The wearing of swords was a class privilege restricted to the samurai class and forbidden to merchants and farmers. In effect, the sword served as both symbol and instrument of the samurai 10% of the population's domination over the 90% of the people engaged in commerce and agriculture.

The true samurai revered a good sword, and superior blades were passed down from generation to generation as treasured heirlooms. Yet this elegantly powerful work of art has a propensity to tarnish and rust, and it was a mark of pride for the samurai to spend the time and care needed to keep his sword ever-gleaming.

Despite this many-faceted history, there are still some people who think of the sword solely as an instrument for disembowelment, both because of the cut-em-up samurai movies and because of author Mishima Yukio's dramatic *seppuku* in 1970. However, it should be noted that such ritual *seppuku* was limited to the samurai in the Edo period, since they were the only ones permitted to carry swords, and was perceived as an honorable and atoning death.

17 *日本人形

日本人にとって人形は，大昔から縁の深いものであった。古墳時代の埴輪はその好例だし，文楽は，人形が芸術にまで高められたケースである。子供たちが人形相手に遊ぶのも，平安時代にすでに始まっているし，魔よけや呪術的意味合いからも，人形は用いられてきた。

●ひな人形と武者人形

年中行事の中にも，人形は組み込まれている。中でも女の子の祭りである3月3日のひな祭りにはひな人形を家庭に飾り，子供たちの幸福を願って白酒などを飲む。

また5月5日は男の子の節句で，雄々しく育つようにと武者人形を飾る。ひな人形も武者人形も，いずれもその期間に限って飾られ，後はまた翌年までしまわれる。中には代々何百年も伝えられた，家宝のような人形もある。今日では多分に儀式化し，またデパートなどの商業主義に利用されがちだが，人形に託しての夢や幸せへの願いは，依然生きていると言えよう。

●博多人形とこけし

郷土玩具にも，人形は多数見られる。中でも今日，最もポピュラーなものは，博多人形とこけしである。博多人形は九州・博多の特産で，粘土で型を作り，素焼きにしてから彩色を施したもの。写実的で彩色も繊細，題材は子供から老人，歌舞伎役者，力士などきわめて幅広く，観賞用に愛好されている。こけしは東北地方の木製人形で，ろくろでひいた円筒状の胴に丸い頭を付け，女の子の顔を描き，胴体には赤や紺，黄などの2，3色で花や線の模様を描く。同じ東北でも場所によって形と模様が異なり，8～10の系統に分かれ，こけしを見れば産地がわかる。こけしは子消しに由来するという説もあるが，今日ではもっぱら観賞用に製造販売されている。

●木目込人形・嵯峨人形・御所人形

今日もなお日本人形として広く愛されているものに，木目込人形，嵯峨人形，御所人形などがある。木目込人形は，木彫の人形原型に各種のきれ地をはって，端を溝に埋め込む手法で作り，これをきめ込むと言うところからこの名がある。嵯峨人形は，木彫に金箔や絵具で色彩を施した小人形。御所人形は，江戸時代に京都の公卿たちが大名に対する贈答の返礼として与えていたもので，肌の白い，頭の大きな幼い男児の裸人形である。さらに現代はこうした伝統的な日本人形ばかりでなく，新しい人形の創作活動も盛んに行われている。

Japanese Dolls*

Japanese history contains many references to dolls. One ancient example is the *haniwa** of the Kofun period. Dolls have even been used as an artistic medium, as in the *bunraku* puppet theater. In the Heian period, some dolls were used as children's toys and others as talismans to dispel demons or work voodoo.

● Festival Dolls

Dolls are also featured in traditional Japanese festive events. One of these is the *Hina Matsuri* (Doll Festival) on March 3 when girls place *hina* dolls on step-like tiers in the family living room, offer prayers for good fortune, and drink a sweet sake-based drink called *shiro-zake*.

Boys have their turn on May 5, when they ornament their homes with warrior dolls inspiring them to be strong and brave. On both of these days, the dolls are put away the following day until next year. Some of these traditional dolls are heirlooms handed down for several centuries. Even though these festivals have become highly ritualized and commercialized, the dolls continue to represent parents' hopes for their children.

● Regional Dolls

Dolls are an important part of the toy-craft traditions associated with various regions of Japan. The most popular regional dolls today are the *hakata* and *kokeshi* dolls. *Hakata* dolls, named after the city in northern Kyushu where they are produced, are painted figures made of bisque-fired clay. Painted realistically and in fine detail, *hakata* doll motifs range from children to old people, kabuki actors and sumo wrestlers, and they are collected as ornaments. *Kokeshi* dolls, products of the northeastern Honshu region, are made of wood and include a cylindrical torso decorated with multicolor floral and linear patterns and a spherical head on which a young child's features are painted. *Kokeshi* shapes and patterns vary depending on exactly where they come from, and each of the eight to ten different types of *kokeshi* is distinctive to its place of origin. Although some people have theorized that the name *kokeshi* may have originally symbolized infanticide, *kokeshi* dolls are today manufactured and sold merely as decorative ornaments.

● Collector's Items

Other dolls popular with collectors include *kimekomi*, *saga*, and *gosho* dolls. *Kimekomi* dolls are carved from wood and clothed with real fabric wedged into narrow grooves. *Saga* dolls are wooden figures gilt in gold or painted. *Gosho* dolls, usually chubby baby boys with white skin and oversized heads, were favored by Edo-period court nobles in Kyoto. Today, the traditional-doll industry is still alive and flourishing alongside manufacturers of new doll designs.

18 日本の文学(1)—古代

●最古の歴史書

日本には仮名文字と「真名」と呼ばれる漢字があり，これらの文字を組み合わせて文章がつづられている。その中の漢字は5世紀ごろ中国大陸より朝鮮半島などを経て日本に伝えられ，今日も活用されている。漢字が伝来する以前は日本には文字はなく，したがって文献的なものも見られず，民族の伝承は人から人へ語り伝えられていた。また，漢字が伝えられて以後仮名文字が草案されるまで，しばらくは漢字による日本語の表記が行われた。日本の古い歴史書と言われる『天皇記』や『帝紀』などは残念ながら残っていないが，古代皇室の皇位継承を中心とした記録であったらしい。

●『古事記』と『日本書紀』

現存する最古の歴史書『古事記』は全3巻より成り、上巻は神の系譜と神話、中巻は神武天皇から応神天皇，下巻は仁徳天皇から推古天皇までの叙述である。天武天皇の命により稗田阿礼・太安万侶が712年に完成した。続いて舎人親王・太安万侶らにより720年、『日本書紀』全30巻が成立した。神代から持統天皇の代までを漢文の編年体でつづったもので，前書同様，皇室の系譜や民族の古い伝承を明らかにする政治的目的のもとに完成した。以後『続日本紀』(797年)，『古語拾遺』(807年ごろ)，『日本後紀』(840年)，『続日本後紀』(869年)というように編纂されている。

●初の地誌『風土記』

元明天皇の713年，各地に地方のありさまを編述させた『風土記』は，日本では初めての地誌で，今日完全な姿で残っているのは『出雲国風土記』(今の島根県)だけ。常陸(茨城県)，播磨(兵庫県)，肥前(長崎県)，豊後(大分県)は一部欠落して伝わっている。内容は地名起源の説話，伝説，生活習慣，信仰と行事，産業と産物など多岐にわたり，民俗学的にも貴重な史料となっている。

●『万葉集』と『懐風藻』

現存する最古の歌集『万葉集』は全20巻あり，大伴家持が中心となって編纂した。8世紀中ごろから約150年間の，上は天皇から下は無名の民衆まで，長歌・短歌含めて約4500首が集められ，万葉仮名と呼ばれる表記法が用いられている。また，『懐風藻』は当時の公式表記に漢文が用いられていたことを反映して，盛んに詠まれた漢詩を集めた日本最古のもので，751年の採録である。撰者も諸説あり，詩文も大陸詩の模倣の域を出ないものが多い。

Japanese Literature (1) (Formative Years)

● Oldest Recorded

Japan has both what are called *mana* characters (*kanji*, from Chinese characters which came to Japan from China via the Korean peninsula in the 5th century or so) and *kana* phonetic simplifications combined in the written language. Because Japan had no written language prior to *kanji*'s introduction, there are no records remaining from before the 5th century. Even after *kanji* was introduced, it still took a while to devise *kana*, and early Japanese literature was all written in *kanji*. Among the oldest works are the *Tennōki* and the *Teiki*, thought to have been geneological records of the imperial clan. Though there are no known copies existent of these works, they are mentioned in later writings.

● *Kojiki* and *Nihon Shoki*

The oldest historical work which still exists is *Kojiki*, a three-volume text with volume one recounting the Japanese mythology, volume two depicting the reigns of Emperors Jinmu* through Ojin, and volume three describing the reigns of Emperors Nintoku through Suiko. It was compiled by Hieda no Are* and O no Yasumaro* in 712 for the Emperor Tenmu. Soon afterward, in 720, Toneri Shinno* and O no Yasumaro completed the thirty-volume *Nihon Shoki*. This was a chronology of the emperors from earliest times and was clearly intended to legitimize the emperor as a political authority. It was later reedited and reissued as *Shoku Nihongi* (797), *Kogo Shūi* (c. 807), *Nihon Kōki* (840), and *Shoku Nihon Kōki* (869).

● *Fudoki*

In 713, the Emperor Genmei ordered local regions to record conditions there, and these records became Japan's first comprehensive local records, *fudoki*. Today, the only volume which remains intact is the one on Izumo no Kuni (now Shimane pref), and parts are missing from the records from Hitachi (Ibaraki pref), Harima (Hyogo pref), Hizen (Nagasaki pref), and Bungo (Oita pref). Explaining the area's name, recounting local legends, depicting lifestyles, outlining religious beliefs and rites, and detailing local industry and products, the *fudoki* are invaluable reference sources for cultural anthropologists.

● *Man'yōshū* and *Kaifūsō*

The *Man'yōshū*, the oldest extant anthology of poems, is a 20-volume work compiled by Otomo no Yakamochi* and others. Compiled over approximately 150 years starting in the mid-8th century, *Man'yōsyū* includes about 4,500 poems* from poets in all walks of life, from exalted emperor to anonymous peasant. It is written mostly in what is called *Man'yō-gana*. By contrast, *Kaifūsō* is a 751 anthology of poems in *kanji*, most of which, perhaps because they are written in the more formal *kanji* script, tend to follow the continental form rather closely.

19 日本の文学(2)──王朝

●王朝文学の先駆け

8世紀の終わり近く，都が平城(奈良)から平安(京都)に移され，以後12世紀後半の武家政治の台頭まで，政治はこの地を中心に行われ，皇室をめぐる貴族社会は全盛を極めた。この時代は公式文書に用いられた漢文に対し，生活に即した仮名文字の発達もあって，和歌や物語文学がけんらんたる花を開く。その先駆けとなったのが，美しい天女かぐや姫を主人公とする『竹取物語』(9世紀)である。

●王朝文学の傑作『源氏物語』

『竹取物語』と同じころ書かれ，『源氏物語』に影響を与えたと言われる『伊勢物語』は，在原業平(ありわらのなりひら)ではないかと思われる人物を主人公とする歌物語である。和歌を物語の軸に据えたものとしては『大和(やまと)物語』『平中物語』などがその後に続く。王朝文学の傑作と言われる『源氏物語』は，日本文学の代表作としても定評がある。作者は紫式部がほぼ定説になっており，1010年ごろ成立した，全54帖(じょう)という大長編小説である。天皇の子でありながら母が身分の低い女性であったため臣籍に降(くだ)った光源氏(ひかるげんじ)という貴公子を主人公とする正編44帖と，その子の薫(かおる)君(きみ)を主人公とする10帖から成る，宮廷生活を中心とする女性遍歴の恋物語である。

●女流の日記文学

『源氏物語』の作者が著したものに『紫式部日記』がある。当時の宮廷サロンに仕えて暮らしていた女性には和歌をよくし，そのころ盛んに編まれた勅撰(ちょくせん)の和歌集に入集するものもたいへん多かったが，日記や随筆が書かれたのも王朝文学の特色である。このほか，代表的なものに『蜻蛉(かげろう)日記』(藤原道綱母(ふじわらのみちつなのはは)作)，『和泉式部日記』，『更級(さらしな)日記』(菅原孝標女(すがわらのたかすえのむすめ)作)などが知られ，随筆文学では清少納言(せいしょうなごん)の『枕草子(まくらのそうし)』(11世紀初め)がある。こうして見ると王朝文学は女流の花盛りの観を呈するが，これも男性文字と言われた漢字に対する仮名文字の発達があったからである。男性による最初の仮名書きの作品に『土佐日記』(紀貫之(きのつらゆき)作・10世紀)という旅日記がある。

●説話文学『今昔物語』ほか

けれども王朝文学の花盛りの陰には，庶民生活の不安を反映する物語も生まれている。『日本霊異記(りょういき)』(9世紀)，『今昔物語』(12世紀)，『宇治拾遺物語(うじしゅうい)』『古今著聞集(ちょもんじゅう)』(ともに13世紀)などで，これらの説話文学は仏教の教えを説く因果応報をはじめ，動物と人間の婚姻譚(たんよう)，妖怪(かい)譚などで埋められている。

Japanese Literature ② (Court Literature)

● Prelude

In the late 8th century, the capital moved from Heijokyo (Nara) to Heiankyo (Kyoto), and Kyoto became both the home of the imperial court and the center of political power until the rise of the military governments in the late 12th century. During this period, *kanji* writing was used for official documents and *kana* script for private communications. *Waka* and narrative literature flourished. Harbinger of this new age was *Taketori Monogatari* (Tale of the Bamboo Cutter) written in the 9th century about the beautiful Kaguyahime (Princess Kaguya) from the stars.

● *Tale of Genji*

Ise Monogatari (Tales of Ise), written about the same time and thought to have influenced *Genji Monogatari* (Tale of Genji), is a collection of poems featuring a hero probably patterned after Ariwara no Narihira.* Subsequent works such as *Yamato Monogatari* and *Heichū Monogatari* continued this pattern of building novels around a core of *waka*. Yet the real flowering of Heian court literature is *Genji Monogatari*, acclaimed as a Japanese literary classic. Most scholars accept that this was written by Murasaki Shikibu* around 1010 in an epic 54 volumes. With 44 volumes on Hikaru Genji, an imperial son relegated to low rank because of his mother's lowly status, and 10 volumes on his son Kaorunokimi, it is a rich depiction of the life of men and women at court.

● Women's Diaries

Another work by the same author is *Murasaki Shikibu Nikki*. While many court women wrote *waka*, as collected in the *Chokusen* anthology, this era in Japanese literature is typified more by the many essays and diaries which they wrote. Among the best-known of the diaries are *Kagerō Nikki* (The Gossamer Years) by Fujiwara no Michitsuna's mother and *Izumi Shikibu Nikki* and *Sarashina Nikki* by Sugawara no Takasue's daughter. Sei Shonagon's* carly-11th-century *Makura no Sōshi* (Pillow Book) is representative of the essays. Much of this rich literature written by women was written in the *kana* script while *kanji* was left to men for use in official writings, and the first book written by a man in *kana* was the 10th-century *Tosa Nikki* travel diary by Ki no Tsurayuki.

● *Konjaku Monogatari* and Other Epics

Along with this flowering of court literature, there was also a literature being born telling of the common man's plight. These include the 9th-century *Nihon Ryōiki*, the 12th-century *Konjaku Monogatari* (Tales of a Time That is Now Past), and the 13th-century *Ujishūi Monogatari* and *Kokon Chomonjū*. These bizarre tales of fantasy included stories with morals illustrating Buddhist teachings, fables of marriages between animals and people, and accounts of strange, fantastic beasts.

20 日本の文学(3)──武家もの

●軍記物語の誕生

12世紀半ばに起こった保元の乱を契機として，武士階級による中央政権への進出が始まり，やがて源氏や平家による武家政治の実現を見る。もちろんそこには源平両軍の流血の政権交替劇が行われたわけで，その中から起こってきたのがいわゆる軍記物語である。保元の乱を扱った『保元物語』，平治の乱の『平治物語』，源平合戦と平家の滅亡を描いた『平家物語』などがあるが，これらの3書は初めから筆で書かれたものではなく，いずれも琵琶法師によって街頭で語られたものを原型として成立を見たユニークなものである。もともと「語り物」として発生したものなので，音読しても快い語感の響きを持っている。特に『平家物語』は軍記物語の最高傑作と言われ，盛衰と興亡を一身に担った平家一門の滅びゆく姿は，美しくもまた哀れ深い。

●その他の軍記物語

平家を滅ぼした源氏は現在の鎌倉市に幕府を開き，以後北条氏が執権として政治を掌握し，次の足利氏が京都・室町に幕府を樹立するという，武家政治にもそれなりの変遷がある。そうした世相を反映して軍記物語が世に歓迎され，13世紀半ばに成立を見た『源平盛衰記』，14世紀の『曽我物語』『太平記』，15世紀初めの『義経記』などが代表的作品である。特に『太平記』は江戸時代には「太平記講釈」と言って太平記読みが流行し，庶民の間にまで親しまれた。

そのほか，歴史物語としては『大鏡』『今鏡』『水鏡』(いずれも12世紀)があり，異色の書としては僧慈円が仏教の理念に立ってまとめた『愚管抄』(13世紀)がある。また，鎌倉幕府の公的記録と言われる『吾妻鏡』も武家社会を知る上で，重要な史料となっている。

●隠者の文学『方丈記』『徒然草』

武士の身分を捨て，遁世の道に生きた西行の歌集『山家集』(12世紀)や，大火，辻風，遷都，飢饉，大地震などを体験したことから，これを末世の世相として市井の暮らしに無常を感じ，山家に隠棲した鴨長明の随筆集『方丈記』(13世紀)，神官の家に生まれながら出家し，自由な生活に身を置いた吉田兼好の，為政者の徳や宗教家のあり方，人の進むべき道などを説いた随筆集『徒然草』(14世紀)は，今日もなお人生の思索の書として，広く読まれている。

Japanese Literature (3) (Medieval)

● Tales of Battle

With the Hogen uprisings* of the mid-12th century, the warrior class seized power and military governments were installed first under the Genji* and then the Heike* clans, each transfer accomplished by bloody fighting between the opposing camps. The literature that emerged from this were the tales of battle, including *Hōgen Monogatari*, *Heiji Monogatari* about the Heiji rebellion,* and *Heike Monogatari* (Tale of the Heike) about the rise and fall of the Taira clan. These three tales are distinctive in that they originated not as written literature but as ballads sung by traveling *biwa-hōshi** minstrels—and they are still stirring when read aloud. Of the three, *Heike Monogatari* is acclaimed as an epic tale of battle par excellence, and it impresses readers even today with its elegantly compassionate tales of how the Tairas fell into decline and ruin.

● Other Tales of Battle

Having vanquished the Tairas, the Minamoto established their military government in what is now Kamakura. This was soon followed by a string of military rulers including the Hojo regents and then the Ashikaga who set up their government in Kyoto. Military epics were favored in these turbulent times, among them the 13th-century *Genpei Seisuiki* (Rise and Fall of the Genji and Heike),14th-century *Soga Monogatari* (Tale of the Soga Brothers) and *Taiheiki*, and 15th-century *Gikeiki* (Yoshitsune). *Taiheiki* was especially well received, and *Taiheiki* readings were popular among the townsfolk as late as the Tokugawa shogunate.

Other historical works include the 12th-century mirror books: *Ō Kagami* (Great Mirror), *Ima Kagami* (Mirror of the Present), and *Mizu Kagami* and the 13th-century *Gukanshō* (Notes on Foolish Views), which is somewhat different in expounding Buddhist teachings. *Azuma Kagami*, said to be the official record of the Kamakura government, is invaluable for historians seeking to learn more about that period's warrior society.

● Tales of Seclusion

At the same time, this period also saw *Sanka-shū* (The Mountain Hermitage), a 12th-century anthology of poems by Saigyo, a warrior who became dissatisfied with the way things were and withdrew from the secular world; *Hōjōki* (13th century) in which Kamo no Chomei recounts the fires, storms, famines, earthquakes, and other disasters which convinced him of the futility of man's constant struggle for aggrandizement; and the 14th-century *Tsurezuregusa* (Essays in Idleness) by Yoshida Kenko, a hermit who was raised in a shrine but left to seek his freedom and ended discussing the principles that should govern the way we live. All of these are read and studied by people even today for their insights into human nature.

21 日本の文学(4)──町人もの

●町人文学の起こり

徳川氏が政治の実権を握っていた江戸時代は，江戸(今の東京)や大坂を中心に栄えた町人文化の時代でもあった。それというのも，太平に慣れた武士に代わって経済の基盤に根を据え，主導権を握っていたのは商人たちのほうであったからである。特に印刷技術が開発され，木版刷りの技術が普及すると出版業者・職業作家が現れ，いきおい町人ものの文学，読み物が出版されるようになった。十返舎一九の滑稽本『東海道中膝栗毛』や式亭三馬の『浮世風呂』，滝沢馬琴の伝奇小説『南総里見八犬伝』(ともに19世紀)などは空前のベストセラーになっている。

●井原西鶴の文学

江戸時代町人文学の代表的作者と言ったら，井原西鶴を真っ先に挙げなくてはなるまい。愛欲小説『好色一代男』『好色一代女』，町人の経済生活を描いた『日本永代蔵』『世間胸算用』などは彼の代表作で，特に『好色一代男』は現実主義的な近代小説に先駆けた作品とも言われ，主人公・世之介の，7歳から60歳までの女性遍歴を描いた物語で，『源氏物語』を下敷きにしてストーリーが展開する。

●日本のシェークスピア・近松門左衛門

西鶴と同じころ活躍した浄瑠璃・歌舞伎狂言作者の近松門左衛門も忘れてはならない人である。当時市井に頻発した心中事件にヒントを得て書いた『曽根崎心中』『心中天網島』，飛脚問屋の忠兵衛と遊女梅川の悲恋を描いた『冥途の飛脚』，中国・明朝の遺臣と日本女性の間に生まれた男子がやがて明朝を復興しようとする『国性爺合戦』などは今日もよく上演され，大向こうをうならせている。そのほか江戸時代の劇作家では近松半二，鶴屋南北，河竹黙阿弥などが知られている。

●怪談集『伽婢子』と『雨月物語』

浅井了意の『伽婢子』(1666年)は怪異談集で，この中には三遊亭円朝が高座に乗せて評判をとった『怪談牡丹灯籠』の原話も入っている。これは18世紀の中ごろ成立した上田秋成の『雨月物語』にも多大の影響を与えている。秋成には，このほか『春雨物語』という怪異談集がある。ところで，歌舞伎の『東海道四谷怪談』(鶴屋南北作)もそうであるが，このように怪異談が好まれた世相の背景には，庶民の不安感があったことも見逃がせない。

Japanese Literature (4) (Town Pleasures)

● Prelude

The Edo period of Tokugawa rule was a time of renaissance centered on the townsfolk of Edo (now Tokyo) and Osaka. When peace returned to the land, actual control passed from the warriors to the merchants who held the economic reins. At the same time, the development of printing technologies and the appearance of publishers made it possible for people to make a living by writing, and this in turn spurred the emergence of literature for the masses. Among these 19th-century best sellers were Jippensha Ikku's *Tōkaidōchū Hizakurige* (Shank's Mare), Shikitei Sanba's *Ukiyoburo* (Bathhouse of the Floating World), and Takizawa Bakin's *Nansō Satomi Hakken-den* (Satomi and the Eight Dogs).

● Ihara Saikaku

Ihara Saikaku is perhaps the single most important popular writer of the Edo period. Among his works are *Kōshoku Ichidai Otoko* (Life of an Amorous Man) and *Kōshoku Ichidai Onna* (Life of an Amorous Woman), depicting the floating world of people who live for sexual gratification, and *Nihon Eitaigura* (The Japanese Family Storehouse) and *Seken Munezanyō* (Worldly Mental Calculations) on the lifestyle of the merchant class. *Kōshoku Ichidai Otoko*, for example, is almost modern in its realism as it details the hero Yonosuke's 54-year quest for pleasure much in the manner of the *Genji Monogatari*.

● Japan's Shakespeare

Another figure who deserves recognition is Chikamatsu Monzaemon, who wrote for both the puppet and kabuki theaters. Even today, his *Sonezaki Shinjū* (Love Suicides at Sonezaki) and *Shinjū Ten no Amijima* (Love Suicides at Amijima) drawing upon the many love suicides of the time, *Meido no Hikyaku* telling of the tragic love between the shopowner* Chubei and the courtisan Umegawa, and *Kokusenya Kassen* (Battles of Coxinga) of the attempt by the Chinese-Japanese son of a Ming descendant to reestablish the Ming dynasty are popular. Among the other well-known playwrights of the Edo period are Chikamatsu Hanji, Tsuruya Nanboku, and Kawatake Mokuami.

● Tales of the Supernatural

Published in 1666, Asai Ryoi's *Otogibōko* is a collection of horror tales including the original *Botan-dōrō* as popularized by the raconteur San'yutei Encho.* This work also had a major influence on the 18th-century *Ugetsu Monogatari* by Ueda Akinari (who also wrote the *Harusame Monogatari* (Tales of the Spring Rain) collection of hair-raisers). Also in this same genre is Tsuruya Nanboku's *Tōkaidō Yotsuya Kaidan* (Ghost Story of Tokaido Yotsuya), and the popularity of horror stories seems to reflect the anxiety of the city people concerning their livelihoods and status.

22 日本の文学(5)—近代

●近代文学への歩み

江戸時代の鎖国政策から脱し明治に入ると，日本の近代化への歩みは着実に進められ，文学もまた二葉亭四迷のツルゲーネフに関する翻訳紹介や上田敏の訳詩集『海潮音』などに見られるように，海外の文芸思潮を取り入れ，新しいあり方を探ってきた。そうした運動推進の代表的な人に坪内逍遙がいる。逍遙は小説・戯曲・評論・翻訳に幅広く活動した人であるが，1885年に『当世書生気質』という小説を発表するとともに，従来の勧善懲悪主義を排し，写実主義を提唱した文学論『小説神髄』を世に問い，一躍注目を浴びた。そのほか逍遙には戯曲『桐一葉』『役の行者』などがあり，また『シェークスピア全集』の翻訳は高く評価されている。

●森鷗外と夏目漱石

明治も中ごろになると，二葉亭四迷の『浮雲』，幸田露伴の『五重塔』，樋口一葉の『たけくらべ』『にごりえ』，徳富蘆花の『不如帰』などの小説が評判になった。そうした中でも森鷗外，夏目漱石の創作活動は際だっている。鷗外は陸軍軍医としてドイツに留学した体験を生かし，処女作『舞姫』を1890年に発表，2年後にはアンデルセンの『即興詩人』を翻訳している。また，その後に書かれた『雁』は現代小説のサンプルとして不動の評価を得ている。一方漱石はロンドンに留学し，帰国後代表作『吾輩は猫である』『坊ちゃん』『草枕』などを次々に発表，近代文学のひとつの頂点を極め，その門下から多くの有力作家が輩出した。

●自然主義の作家

日露戦争前後，島崎藤村や田山花袋などの自然主義を唱える作家が台頭し，藤村の『破戒』，花袋の『蒲団』などが代表的役割を果たした。自然主義は，その後も近代文学の最も大きな運動として，広く影響を及ぼしていく。

●明治の詩歌

1882年に訳詩・創作詩で編んだ『新体詩抄』が出版され，以後新体詩と呼ばれる新しい詩の領域が開かれる。代表的詩人としては島崎藤村・土井晩翠などがいる。19世紀も終わりに近いころ，与謝野鉄幹が短歌革新運動を起こし『明星』を創刊するや，鉄幹夫人となった晶子や石川啄木・北原白秋・高村光太郎などの俊秀が結集した。同じころ正岡子規も空想や偶像を排して写実を尊ぶ短歌・俳句運動を展開している。

Japanese Literature (5) (Post-restoration)

● Toward a Modern Literature

With the opening of the country shortly after the Meiji Restoration, Japan began a process of modernization that involved a receptiveness to imported ideas and a search for new modes, as epitomized by Futabatei Shimei's translated introduction to the life and work of Turgenev and Ueda Bin's *Kaichōon* (Sound of the Tide) anthology of translated poems. Foremost among the experimenters is Tsubouchi Shoyo. While he was active as a novelist, playwright, critic, and translator, he is best known for the 1885 novel *Tōsei Shosei Katagi* (The Character of Modern Students) and for *Shōsetsu Shinzui* (Essence of the Novel) in which he rejected the hoary traditions and called out for a more realistic fiction. In addition, he is also known for his plays such as *Kiri Hitoha* and *En no Gyōja* and his translation of the complete works of Shakespeare.

● Ogai and Soseki

The popular novels near the turn of the century were Futabatei Shimei's *Ukigumo* (Drifting Clouds), Koda Rohan's *Gojū no Tō* (Five-storied Pagoda), Higuchi Ichiyo's *Takekurabe* (Growing Up) and *Nigorie* (Muddy Bay), and Tokutomi Roka's *Hototogisu* (Namiko). Yet the two luminaries of the period were Mori Ogai and Natsume Soseki. Drawing upon his years as an army physician in Germany for study, Ogai published his first novel *Maihime* (Dancing Girl) in 1890 and followed that two years later with a translation of Andersen's *Improvisators*. His later *Gan* (Wild Geese) still stands as an exemplary modern novel. Soseki, returning home from his studies in London, marked new heights in modern literature with his outpouring of *Wagahai wa Neko de Aru* (I am a Cat), *Botchan*, *Kusamakura*, and more. He was a prolific writer who had a profound influence upon many later writers.

● Naturalism

Around the time of the Russo-Japanese War, there was a spate of naturalist writers including Shimazaki Toson, prominent for his *Hakai* (Broken Commandment), and Tayama Katai (known for *Futon*). This naturalist school has since been a major component and influence in modern Japanese literature.

● Poetry

The 1882 *Shintaishi Shō* (Collection of New Style Poetry) of translated and original poetry opened up new vistas for poetry. Shimazaki Toson and Tsuchii Bansui were among the best-known poets. In the late 19th century, Yosano Tekkan urged radical reforms in the *tanka* and founded *Myōjō* magazine in Tokyo as a vehicle for such brilliant poets as his wife Akiko, Ishikawa Takuboku, Kitahara Hakushu, Takamura Kotaro, and others. About the same time, Masaoka Shiki was campaigning for *tanka* and haiku able to deal with the fantastic and grotesque in realistic terms.

23 日本の文学(6)―現代

●大正期の『白樺』

1910年創刊された同人雑誌『白樺』で活躍した作家に武者小路実篤・志賀直哉・里見弴・有島武郎・有島生馬らがいる。『白樺』は関東大震災後に廃刊するまで，文芸・美術雑誌として大正期の文壇や画壇に大きな影響を与えた。中でも志賀直哉の長編小説『暗夜行路』は現代文学の金字塔とも言われ，高い評価を得ている。

●芥川龍之介と永井荷風

虚構の世界での自己表出に生きた作家としては芥川龍之介がいるが，彼は長編には全く手を染めず，終始短編作家で通した異色の存在である。代表作に『今昔物語』や『宇治拾遺物語』に材を仰いだ『羅生門』『地獄変』『鼻』などがある。永井荷風の長編小説『腕くらべ』や『墨東綺譚』は遊廓や私娼窟に材をとった作。

●谷崎潤一郎と佐藤春夫

永井荷風の推称を受けて世に出た作家に谷崎潤一郎がおり，谷崎と親交があった作家に佐藤春夫がいる。春夫と谷崎夫人の恋愛は2人の友情を裂く不幸な出来事となったが，ともに大正から昭和の戦後まで活躍した代表的作家である。

●川端康成と横光利一

1924年創刊された『文芸時代』により，新感覚派運動を起こした作家に川端康成・横光利一らがいる。彼らは既存の現実主義にあきたらず，官能や神経に病的な敏感さを見せ，意匠や装飾に新しいものをねらった。川端の代表作『伊豆の踊子』『雪国』，横光の『日輪』『旅愁』などは今日も広く読まれている。川端は日本人では初めてのノーベル文学賞を受賞(1968年)している。

●現代の詩人

明治に起こった新体詩は大正に入るとしだいに影をひそめ，代わって日常使用されている言葉で音律を踏まずに書く自由律口語詩が普及する。萩原朔太郎の『月に吠える』『青猫』『氷島』，高村光太郎の『道程』『智恵子抄』，宮沢賢治の『春と修羅』などの詩集は，その代表的なものである。また，この時期にフランスの詩人アンドレ・ブルトンの提唱する超現実主義，ベルレーヌ，バレリーやマラルメを指導者とする象徴主義が日本詩壇を真っ向から揺さぶった。

そのほか大正から昭和の戦前にかけては，外国文学の翻訳紹介が次々に行われ，カフカ，フォークナー，マルロー，ドストエフスキー，トルストイなどがよく読まれている。

Japanese Literature (6) (Early Twentieth Century)

● ***Shirakaba***

Founded in 1910, the literary magazine *Shirakaba* was home to Mushanokoji Saneatsu, Shiga Naoya, Satomi Ton, Arishima Takeo, Arishima Ikuma, and many others; and it was both lectern and showplace for the artists of the era until it ceased publication after the Great Kanto Earthquake* of 1923. Especially notable was Shiga Naoya, whose long novel *An'ya Kōro* (Dark Night's Passing) is acclaimed as the masterpiece of early-20th-century literature.

● **Akutagawa and Nagai**

Perhaps the writer who best expressed himself in fiction was Akutagawa Ryunosuke, who is also unusual for having written only short stories. He is famous for *Rashōmon*, *Jigokuhen* (Hell Screen), *Hana* (Nose), all patterned after *Konjaku Monogatari* and *Ujishūi Monogatari*, and others. Nagai Kafu is known for his long novels such as *Udekurabe* (Geisha in Rivalry) and *Bokutō Kidan* (Strange Tale from the East of the River) set in Japan's red-light districts.

● **Tanizaki and Sato**

Among the writers drawn to literature by Nagai Kafu is Tanizaki Jun'ichiro, and among those encouraged by Tanizaki is Sato Haruo. While the two men's friendship was poisoned by Sato's affair with Tanizaki's wife, they were major literary figures even as late as the postwar period.

● **Kawabata and Yokomitsu**

Two of the novelists who took part in the neo-sensationalist literary movement launched by the magazine *Bungei Jidai* in 1924 were Kawabata Yasunari and Yokomitsu Riichi. Rebelling at the prevailing realism, they invented new styles and forms in an effort to stimulate both mind and spirit. Even today, Kawabata is widely read for *Izu no Odoriko* (Izu Dancer) and *Yukiguni* (Snow Country) and Yokomitsu for *Nichirin* (The Sun) and *Ryoshū* (Traveler's Sadness). In 1968, Kawabata became the first Japanese to win the Nobel Prize in Literature.

● **Modern Poets**

After an early popularity, the new-style poetry movement began to fade, and its place was taken by a free poetry using everyday language in unmetered lines. Typical are Hagiwara Sakutaro's *Tsuki ni Hoeru* (Howling at the Moon), *Aoneko* (Blue Cat), *Hyōtō* (Frozen Island); Takamura Kotaro's *Dōtei* and *Chieko Shō* (Chieko's Sky); and Miyazawa Kenji's *Haru to Shura* (Spring and Asura). At the same time, Japanese poetry was shaken by the surrealism of the French poet André Breton and the symbolism of Stéphane Mallarmé, Paul Verlaine, and Paul Valéry.

Translations of foreign works were also very much in vogue, and Kafka, Faulkner, Malraux, Dostoevski, Tolstoi, and many others were widely read in Japan.

24 日本の文学(7)──戦後

●敗戦国日本の文学の担い手

第2次世界大戦が終わったとき，敗戦の虚脱から最も早く立ち上がったのが文学ではなかろうか。言論の自由，出版の自由がそれに拍車をかけた。作品の内容も戦争の悲惨さ，残虐さに材を求めたものが多い。第1次戦後派と呼ばれるそれらの人々を挙げると梅崎春生・大岡昇平・武田泰淳・椎名麟三・中村真一郎・三島由紀夫などがおり，それに続く第2次戦後派として安部公房・堀田善衛などがいる。特にフィリピンにおける戦争体験をつづった大岡昇平の『俘虜記』や『野火』などは，戦後文学の一時期を画するものである。典雅な文体の中に，不倫・背徳といった時代に先行する観念によって出発を見せた三島由紀夫は『仮面の告白』『金閣寺』など，次々に問題作を発表するかたわら，劇作家としても『鹿鳴館』『十日の菊』といった評判作を書いた。現代における人間行動の意味を追求する作品で戦後文学の花形となった井上靖は，日本文学の伝統をひく私小説のほかに歴史小説・社会派小説・詩・エッセーなど幅広く題材を手がけている。

●太陽族の流行

特需景気をあおった朝鮮戦争を境として，敗戦の様相がしだいに薄れてくると，文学にもそれなりの動きが現れ，既成の道徳や価値観を否定し，あるいは打破しようとする若者を描く小説が登場してくる。石原慎太郎の『太陽の季節』がそれで，「太陽族」や「慎太郎刈り」などの流行語やヘアスタイルまで生んだ。これよりやや遅れて『死者の奢り』『飼育』などの作品で登場した大江健三郎は，戦後青春の疎外感などを特異な文体で定着させた作家と言われている。

●民主主義文学の動き

しかし，また一方では社会主義的民主化運動を反映した作家も登場した。『播州平野』『風知草』などの作品を戦後いち早く発表した宮本百合子は，すでに戦前に『貧しき人々の群』『伸子』などの長編で知られたプロレタリア文学の旗手でもあった。佐多稲子や徳永直もプロレタリア文学の戦前戦後を支えた代表的作家である。

●戦後文学の広がり

戦後の混乱期を経てしだいに世相が落ち着いてくると，読者の要求もさまざまな広がりを見せ，純文学と大衆文学の距離が縮まり，中間小説と呼ばれる作品の流行を見るに至った。推理小説なども昨今は全盛期を迎えた感がある。

Japanese Literature (7) (Postwar)

● Bearers of the Torch

Literature was one of the first fields to recover from Japan's defeat in World War II. Encouraged by freedom of the press and freedom of expression, literature flourished, much of it depicting the suffering and misery of war. The first wave of postwar authors included such people as Umezaki Haruo, Ooka Shohei, Takeda Taijun, Shiina Rinzo, Nakamura Shin'ichiro, and Mishima Yukio; and this was soon followed by a second wave including Abe Kobo, Hotta Yoshie, and others. Among the landmark works of the first wave were Ooka Shohei's *Furyoki* (Prisoner of War) and *Nobi* (Fires on the Plain) based upon his wartime experiences in the Philippines. Employing an elegant sytle to depict vice and depravity, Mishima Yukio caught the temper of the time with *Kamen no Kokuhaku* (Confessions of a Mask), *Kinkakuji* (Temple of the Golden Pavilion), and other sensationalist works. At the same time he was also active as a playwright of such highly acclaimed works as *Rokumeikan* (Deer Cry Pavilion) and *Tōka no Kiku*. Inoue Yasushi was another star of postwar literature as he questioned human values and behavior with consistently good writing in the traditional I novels, historical novels, socially conscious novels, poems, essays, and the broad spectrum of genres.

● *Taiyō-zoku*

As the prosperity induced by the Korean War took hold and people forgot the despair of defeat, literature also took a new turn with novels depicting a new breed of Japanese who rejected the old values and moral standards. With Ishihara Shintaro's *Taiyō no Kisetsu* (Season of Violence), the term *taiyō-zoku* (sun tribe) was born and Shintaro haircuts became all the rage. Just slightly later, Oe Kenzaburo appeared as one of the most perceptive observers of this postwar alienation as depicted in *Shisha no Ogori* (Lavish are the Dead) and *Shiiku* (The Catch).

● Democratic Literature

Yet there were also other authors who wrote to propagate their ideals of socialist democratization. Miyamoto Yuriko, who came out with *Banshū Heiya* (Banshu Plain), *Fūchisō*, and other works soon after the war, had established her reputation as a proletariat writer before the war with such novels as *Mazushiki Hitobito no Mure* (A Flock of Poor People) and *Nobuko*. Other proletariat writers active in both the wartime and postwar eras were Sata Ineko and Tokunaga Sunao.

● Spread of Postwar Literature

As things settled down after the war and more people started reading again for more diverse purposes, a wider rift developed between pure literature and popular literature, and a very popular form developed called in-between novels. Mysteries and other mass-appeal literature entered a golden age.

25 和歌

●和歌の形式

日本で最も古く，しかも中世・近世・現代を問わず多くの歌人たちに強い影響を与えているのは，何と言っても8世紀に編纂(へんさん)された『万葉集』である。その中には長歌・短歌が含まれていて，今日なおその形式が重視されている短歌は「あかねさす(5音)，紫野行(むらさきの)き(7音)，標(しめ)野行き(5音)，野守(のもり)は見ずや(7音)，君が袖(そで)振る(7音)」(額田王(ぬかだのおおきみ)の歌)のように31音で構成されている。今日では長歌は全く影をひそめ，短歌が主流となっている。短歌の形式がいつどのような経過をたどって古代歌謡の世界に愛用され，定着したのかは，いまだにはっきりとは解明されていない。

●勅撰(ちょくせん)和歌集の意味

天皇の命により公的に編纂された歌集を「勅撰和歌集」と呼んでいるが，その中に撰(えら)ばれ，入集するということはたいへん名誉とされた。勅撰の最初のものは10世紀初めに編まれた『古今和歌集』で，以後『後撰和歌集』『拾遺(しゅうい)和歌集』というように続き，16世紀の室町時代まで21集に及ぶ。内容はどの集もほぼ春・夏・秋・冬・賀歌・別れの歌・旅の歌・恋の歌などで構成され，きわめて広範囲にわたっている。

●宮廷のサロン化

これらのことからもうかがわれるように，特に平安(今の京都)に都があった8世紀から12世紀までは，皇室を中心に貴族の間で和歌がもてはやされた。判者(審判者)を設けて歌合わせの座で作の優劣を競ったり，意中の女房(にょうぼう)へ手紙に代えて恋歌を贈ったり，歌を詠むことはさながら日常茶飯事のように扱われ，宮廷そのものが歌の一大サロン化するほど盛んだった。

しかし，それも空想や想像の産物としてしだいにあきたりなく思う者も現れ，12世紀に活躍した歌僧西行(さいぎょう)の『山家(さんか)集』のように，実際に自然の中に身を置いて詠んだ歌が尊ばれるようになってくる。

●現代の短歌

今日も短歌は衰えを見せず，同人誌や会報を中心とする会員の練成が行われており，手軽にだれでもできる文芸として愛されている。その中には，一部現代語を用語とし，必ずしも音律の形式にこだわらない自由律短歌の運動もないではないが，やはり主流を成しているものは依然古語の幽玄性を尊ぶ31文字の形式であり，その伝統の根強さと，色あせぬ短歌の魅力には，不思議な感銘さえ覚えさせられる。

● Form

The *Man'yōshū* compiled in the 8th century is the oldest and most influential collection of Japanese poetry. In it are two types of poetry: *chōka* and *tanka*. While the *chōka* has nearly disappeared as an art form, the shorter 31-syllable *tanka* has been popular throughout Japanese history and today characterizes the mainstream of Japanese poetry, although it remains unclear exactly how the ancient poets developed the *tanka*. The following *tanka* by Princess Nukada (7th century) is a classical example of the *tanka* verse form.

A-ka-ne-sa-su	In the purple field
Mu-ra-sa-ki-no yu-ki	Of blooming madder,
Shi-me-no yu-ki	In the forbidden meadow you run.
No-mo-ri wa mi-zu ya	Won't the guard see
Ki-mi ga so-de fu-ru	You waving to me?

● Imperial Anthologies

Imperial anthologies were frequently compiled over the centuries and it was considered a great honor to have one's poems included. The earliest imperial anthology is the *Kokin Wakashū* (Collection of Ancient and Modern Times) compiled in the early 10th century. It was followed by the *Gosen Wakashū* (Later Collection) and by the *Shūi Wakashū* (Collection of Gleanings). By the Muromachi period, 21 such anthologies had been compiled of poems treating a wide range of subjects and themes; verses on the four seasons, celebratory lines, songs of parting and of travel, love poems, and so forth.

● Court Poetry

Writing and reciting poetry was a favorite pastime of the ancient Japanese nobility, particularly between the 8th and 12th centuries when the capital was located in Kyoto. Formally judged poetry contests were held frequently, court lords and ladies* communicated in poetry, and poetry was an integral part of court life in every way.

Not everyone was satisfied with the rarified poetry of the court, however. The 12th-century poet-priest Saigyo preferred to walk the countryside, immersing himself in nature. *Sanka-shū* (The Mountain Hermitage) is one product of his wanderings.

● Contemporary *Tanka*

Tanka remain a fresh and vital form of poetic expression. As a literary art in which anyone can participate, *tanka* have attracted numerous would-be poets who gather in groups to polish their composition skills and publish *tanka* magazines and journals. There is a movement of sorts in experimental *tanka* using modern language and unfettered by restrictions of rhythm, but for the most part the classical 31-syllable form with its clearly defined word devices and ethereal quality remains the most popular. There is much to be admired in the durability and timeless appeal of the ancient *tanka* poetry.

26 俳句

●連歌の発生

平安時代のころから盛んに行われた歌合わせは，それぞれが詠んだ歌の優劣を競うものであったが，14世紀ごろから1つの歌の上の句（5・7・5音）と，下の句（7・7音）を別の人が詠む，いわゆる「付け句」のゲームがもてはやされるようになった。その上の句を「発句」，下の句を「挙げ句」と呼ぶ。しかしそれだけでは単純なので，次々に歌をつないで行く形式も行われ，こうした座の文学を「連歌」と呼び，取り持つ役を「連歌師」と言った。連歌師は「宗匠」「連歌会所奉行」などと言われ，これを職業とする人さえ現れた。特に15世紀，室町時代に活躍した宗祇やその門人の宗長などはよく知られている。また連歌作者の二条良基が著わした歌論書『近来風体抄』(1387)，これも良基の撰に成る連歌集『菟玖波集』(1356)，宗祇など3人の連歌を集めた『水無瀬三吟百韻』(1488)などは，今日でもよく読まれている。

●俳句の発生

伴吟者を必要とする不便さからか，今日では連歌を詠み興ずることはほとんど行われなくなったが，俳句のほうは単独でもできる文芸としてたいへん盛んである。俳句は，連歌の上の句，つまり「発句」を詠む形式が独立したもので，「荒海や（5音），佐渡に横たふ（7音），天の河（5音）」（松尾芭蕉の句）のように，世界にも例を見ない17音で構成する短詩型文学である。

短い形式だけに，詠まれる内容はむだのない，それでいて豊かなイメージであることが要求される。そのために春夏秋冬いずれかの季節を表す用語，「季語」を詠み込むことが原則として考えられている。また，それらの「季語」を分類整理した「歳時記」が広く用いられている。

俳句は当初「俳諧」と呼ばれ，滑稽の意味を持っていたが，いつしかそうした要素はもっぱら「川柳」という分野に引き継がれ，俳句はしだいに芸術性を高めるべく練磨される。17世紀に活躍した松尾芭蕉とその門人たち，18世紀の与謝蕪村・小林一茶などは特記すべき俳人たちである。特に西行の足跡を慕って各地を旅した芭蕉の『奥の細道』や多くの紀行俳文集は今日もよく読まれている。現代の俳句はさまざまな改革運動が進められたりしたが，大きな変化は望めないというのが現状である。

Haiku

● *Renga*

In the poetry contests of the Heian period poets vied to compose the best poem. In the 14th century, however, a new form of entertainment evolved of linked verse in which one poet would compose the first three lines (5-7-5 syllables) of a poem and another would complete it with two more lines (7-7 syllables). The first three lines are called *hokku* and the remaining two the *ageku*. To include more people and make it more interesting, this pattern was repeated in long *renga* or linked-verse compositions. Poets who excelled in this kind of work were called *renga-shi* and given such titles as *sōshō* or *renga-kaisho-bugyō*. There even emerged a professional class of *renga-shi*. Particularly famous *renga* masters include the 15th-century Sogi and his disciple Socho. Nijo Yoshimoto's authoritative work *Kinrai Fūtai Shō* (Notes on Poetic Styles of the Recent Past) written in 1387, his *Tsukuba-shū* collection of *renga* compiled in 1356, and the 1488 *Minase Sangin Hyakuin* sequence by the *renga* master Sogi and two other poets are still widely read.

● Haiku

Because they require several participants, *renga* are seldom composed today. Haiku, originally the *hokku* of a *renga*, however, remain popular as an independent form. Only 17 syllables, the haiku is one of the most succinct poetic verse types in the world. A good example is Matsuo Basho's verse:

A-ra-u-mi ya	How rough a sea
Sa-do ni yo-ko-ta-u	and, stretching over Sado Isle,
A-ma-no-ga-wa	the Galaxy

(Tr. Harold B. Henderson)

Its concise form mandates that the haiku convey a rich imagery with no superfluous words. Seasons are pictured with *kigo* words typical of the season, and these seasonal indicators are such a common device in haiku that several glossaries known as *saijiki* have been compiled solely for the convenience of the haiku poet.

Derived from *haikai*, the haiku was originally an introductory comic verse. Satirical verse evolved as an independent genre known as *senryū*, however, and haiku were refined into a highly sophisticated form of serious poetry. Some of the most famous haiku poets are the 17th-century Matsuo Basho and his disciples and Yosa Buson and Kobayashi Issa in the 18th century. Many of these poets wrote haiku travelogues still enjoyed today, the most well-known probably being Basho's *Oku no Hosomichi* (The Narrow Road to the Deep North) written to commemorate his retracing of the northern route traveled by the *waka* poet-priest Saigyo. Still a popular medium, haiku continue to be written today, but, although experiments in new haiku forms have been made, there is little prospect for any drastic changes in the genre.

27 日本のコミック

●新聞漫画

日本の新聞には必ず漫画(多くは4コマ)が載っている。時に世相を風刺し，時に庶民の哀歓を描き，一服の清涼剤として，多数の読者の共感を得ている。

新聞漫画の代表としては，まず長谷川町子の「サザエさん」がある。戦後間もなく始まり，ほぼ4半世紀にわたり，1974年まで『朝日新聞』に長期連載された。主婦であるサザエさんを中心に，一家7人を巡る，明るくユーモラスな生活描写は，そのまま日本人の庶民の暮らしの反映でもあった。登場人物たちが皆，海にちなむ名前なのは，著者が海岸を散策中にこの漫画の想を得たからという。何と言っても主人公サザエさんの，明るく，お人好しで，少々慌てん坊のパーソナリティーが人気の秘密で，新聞連載が終わった後も，テレビのアニメで放映されている。また「サザエさん」には時々の世相，流行も巧みに取り入れられ，世相史的役割も果たした。

これを例えば，アメリカの長寿新聞漫画「ブロンディー」と比べると，「ブロンディー」はブロンディーと夫ダグウッドが中心で，話題も夫婦の間柄に重点が置かれているのに対し，「サザエさん」は，夫よりもむしろ弟，妹，母親といった家族に多く題材を求めており，日米社会の違いがおのずと反映している。現実には「サザエさん」とは逆に，日本の社会は核家族化が進んでおり，一面，大家族への憧憬(どうけい)の裏返しであったかもしれない。

現在，人気の新聞漫画にはサトウサンペイの「*フジ三太郎」(『朝日新聞』)がある。1965年開始のロングランで，万年ヒラ社員のフジ三太郎の喜怒哀楽は，世の大半のサラリーマンのそれでもあろう。1980年代に入り，女性部長，女性係長が新たに登場したのは，まさに漫画は世相の鑑(かがみ)である。

●劇画

今日，出版界を席捲(せっけん)しているのは，上に述べた4コマ漫画ではなく，より物語性のある漫画，すなわち，劇画と呼ばれるものである。従来は漫画と言えば(新聞漫画を除き)子供の読み物であったが，1970年前後から始まった劇画ブームの主体はむしろ青年層で，漫画週刊誌は何誌にも及び，膨大な発行部数を誇っている。一般に，笑いよりストーリー性が強く，時代物，闘魂物，人情物，評伝等々バラエティーに富む。しかし売らんかなのあまり，エロ，グロ，ナンセンスも横溢(おういつ)し，問題も抱えている。

Manga

● Newspaper Strips

Just about all of Japan's many daily newspapers carry comic strips, mostly of the four-frame format. These comic strips, with themes ranging from pointed social satire to poignant renderings of everyday joys and sorrows, provide light interludes of relaxation for millions of Japanese readers.

The classic newspaper comic is Hasegawa Machiko's *Sazae-san*. This comic strip started in the *Asahi* soon after the war and did not end until 1974. Centered on the fictional housewife Sazae-san, it depicts the problems of the typical Japanese three-generational household. Author Hasegawa decided to name all the characters after things found in the sea because the inspiration for the strip came while she was walking by the shore. The key to *Sazae-san*'s success has been the cheerful, good-natured, and slightly befuddled personalities of its main characters. Even after the *Sazae-san* newspaper strip had ended, the series was continued on television. At times *Sazae-san* has included social commentary and current fads, making it a chronicle of its times.

Compared to the *Blondie* comic strip in the United States, which centers on the relationship between Blondie and her husband Dagwood, *Sazae-san* embraces the whole family and is, if anything, more concerned with Sazae's relations with her brother, sister, and mother, and this difference may be indicative of the differences between Japanese and American societies. In fact, however, postwar Japanese society has been shifting toward the nuclear family, and in this sense *Sazae-san* may actually represent the extended family of the past.

Today, the most popular newspaper comic strip is Sato Sanpei's *Fuji Santarō*,* also in the *Asahi*. Begun in 1965, this series featuring the daily ups and downs of the perennial corporate minion Fuji Santaro depicts the lives of many young Japanese men. A remarkably accurate mirror on contemporary Japanese culture, *Fuji Santarō* has included some female executives among its characters since 1980.

● Comic Books

Yet the most successful comics in print today are not the four-frame strips but the longer comic-book stories called *geki-ga*. With the exception of newspaper comics, virtually all comics up until the late 1960s were for children, but since then there has been a phenomenal boom in *geki-ga* for teenagers and young adult readers, and all manner of comic-filled weeklies have won huge followings. Generally, they are more serious than comical, and the rich variety of themes includes historical drama, warfare, melodrama, and biography. However, many include an alarming amount of erotic, brutal, and bizarre material.

28 仏教

●仏教の歴史

仏教が日本に公式に伝えられたのは538年，朝鮮の百済からとされているが，すでに5世紀には大陸からの渡来人によって持ち込まれ，信仰されていたと言われている。インドから中国という中央集権国家を経て日本に伝わったことと，そのとき，日本が中央集権国家確立の時期であったことから，鎮護国家の色彩の濃い仏教となった。

6世紀末から奈良時代を通じ，仏教は天皇家をはじめ，有力氏族に支持され，国教的存在となり，聖徳太子の建立した法隆寺をはじめ，興福寺，東大寺，薬師寺，唐招提寺など当時の遺構は世界最古の木造建築として1200～300年後の今日にまで伝わっている。

仏教は，日本に初めて持ち込まれた系統的な思想体系であったため，それ以後の日本に計り知れない影響を与えた。思想，文化ばかりでなく，仏教は建築，金属工芸，さらに医学，農業技術に至るまでの文明の代名詞でもあった。中国からもたらされる仏教文化・文明は，これ以後，平安時代，室町時代，さらに江戸時代に至るまで，日本にとっては常に学ぶべき新文化，新技術であった。

平安時代中期に起こった，一種の終末思想である末法思想は，政治や社会の乱れ，その後の，武士の台頭による戦乱に裏付けられて急速に広まり，鎌倉時代の新仏教を生む下地を作った。鎌倉仏教と呼ばれる日蓮宗，浄土宗，浄土真宗，禅宗など，今日の日本の仏教の主流を成す宗派は皆この時代に生まれたものである。いずれも，奈良時代以来の仏教の貴族的，学問的な色彩とは異なり，一心に「南無妙法蓮華経」の題目や「南無阿弥陀仏」の念仏を唱えたり，座禅に打ち込むことだけで救われるという個人的，庶民的なものであり，それゆえに爆発的に信徒を増やしていった。江戸時代にはキリスト教禁圧のため，すべての人々に地域の寺への登録を強制し，檀家制度が作られ，寺は幕府の末端管理機構として檀家の冠婚葬祭をつかさどるようになった。

●現代の仏教

現代では仏教信徒は約8100万人(1983年末)とされており，伝統仏教が地方で根強い力を持っているのに対し，大都会では日蓮宗系の創価学会(1700万)，立正佼成会(580万人)，霊友会(310万人)など，第二次世界大戦の少し前に作られた在家仏教団体が大きな力を持っている。近年では伝統仏教も新仏教も，互いに宗教協力によって共存共栄し，平和や難民救済などに協力している。

Buddhism

● History

Buddhism is generally said to have been introduced into Japan in 538 from the (Korean) Paekche kingdom. Visitors had actually introduced it much earlier, however, and there were Japanese adherents as early as the 5th century. Buddhism made its way to Japan from India through centralized China just when Japan was itself consolidating into a centralized state, and the newly unified Japanese nation quickly adapted Buddhism's teachings to its own mores and needs.

From the end of the 6th century, Buddhism was the main faith of the imperial and other ruling clans—virtually a national religion, at least as far as the nobility was concerned. Prince Shotoku (574-622), one of Buddhism's strongest adherents, commissioned the building of the Horyuji, today the oldest wooden building in the world, and this was followed by the construction of other temples which exist to this day: Kofukuji, Todaiji, Yakushiji, and Toshodaiji.

The first systematic religious philosophy to be introduced into Japan, Buddhism had a profound cultural and philosophical impact. Architecture, metallurgy, medicine, and even agricultural techniques, were strongly affected by Buddhist concepts. Further waves of new Buddhist teachings from China continued to add to Japanese culture in succeeding periods, from the Heian period all the way through the Edo period.

Political and social unrest and the rise of the warrior class in the mid-Heian period gave credence to an apocalyptic Buddhism* that laid the foundation for a new Buddhism in the Kamakura period. This new Buddhism emerged as the Nichiren,* Jodo, Jodo Shinshu,* and Zen sects—still the leading Buddhist sects—teaching a salvation through grace that was quite different from the intellectual Buddhist philosophy of the Nara-period nobility. These sects taught that simple repetition of "*Namu myō hōren gekyō*" (I place my faith in the Lotus Sutra of the God Law) or "*Namu amida butsu*" (I place my faith in Amida Buddha), or meditation in the case of Zen, were sufficient to save one's soul. With its much broader popular appeal, the new Buddhism spread rapidly, and this was reinforced in the Edo period by the shogunate's *danka* system requiring all families to be registered with one of the country's many Buddhist temples. Instituted as an instrument for repressing Christianity, this system also helped the government keep tabs on the people.

● Buddhism Today

As of 1983, there were 81 million registered Buddhists. The traditional sects are still strong in the rural areas, but new Nichiren-based sects founded just before World War II have won many urban adherents—including Soka Gakkai (17 million), Rissho Koseikai (5.8 million), and Reiyukai (3.1 million). Old and new Buddhist sects coexist today in ecumenical harmony, actively promoting peace and aiding refugees.

29 禅

禅の根本目標は，菩提(悟り)を求めて参禅生活に励み，すべての衆生(人類と全生物)が救われるのを待って，自分もまた救われようと願うことである。

●禅の歴史

仏教では悟りを得る方法の1つとして古くから座禅を行ってきたが，中国に起こった禅宗では座禅に徹することを要求し，日常生活すべてを座禅の修行の一環であるとしている。

日本には12世紀末に栄西によって臨済宗が，鎌倉時代初めに道元によって曹洞宗がもたらされた。臨済宗は座禅をしながら，師匠から次々に出される「公案」と呼ぶ問題を考え，それを解決することによって悟りを開こうという派。主に貴族や上級武士に支持された。京都の大徳寺，南禅寺，鎌倉の建長寺，円覚寺などがこの派に属する。

曹洞宗の特徴は道元が言っているように「只管打坐」である。つまり，ひたすら座禅をすることによって悟りを開こうとするもの。権力と虚栄を嫌った道元は福井県の山中に永平寺を開いて，だれでもが悟りを開けるのだと，下級武士や一般の人々に座禅を勧めた。

江戸時代初期には，中国から来朝した隠元によって新たに黄檗宗が開かれた。経文や動作，飾りなどすべて中国風そのままであることを特徴とした。

●禅と日本文化

禅が日本文化に与えた影響は大きい。特に室町時代，中国との交流が盛んで，その先端に立った臨済宗の僧侶が，貴族や上級武士の間に中国文化を紹介した。文学では，禅僧を中心にした漢文学が「五山文学」の名で呼ばれた。五山とは，最も格式の高い5つの禅寺のことである。絵画では水墨画が中国からもたらされると同時に，雪舟ら多くの禅僧が山水画や頂相と呼ばれる肖像画を描いている。また庭園では禅の精神にのっとった飾り気のない石庭，枯山水の庭などが作られた。さらに茶も，栄西により抹茶による喫茶法が伝えられ，安土・桃山時代には千利休をはじめとする多数の茶の宗匠が禅を学び，その精神を生かしたわび茶を生み出した。

現代，禅宗は信徒は約900万人で，仏教の1割強であるが，仏教寺院約7万5000のうち2万1000が禅宗系で，特に曹洞宗は約1万5000と，全寺院の2割を占めている。これらの寺院では一般の信徒を含めた参禅会などを開いている。海外へは鈴木大拙が積極的に紹介し，曹洞宗では弟子丸泰仙がヨーロッパへの布教に力を入れた。

Zen

The Zen practitioner seeks enlightenment through discipline and meditation and awaits salvation for himself and for all sentient beings.

● History

The *zazen* meditative posture has long been a Buddhist technique for attaining enlightenment. It was the Zen sect, originating in China, however, which first taught that all of life, every act of eating, sleeping, walking, and sitting, could be applied to meditative purposes.

The monk Eisai introduced the Rinzai sect of Buddhism from China in the late 12th century and the monk Dogen introduced what is now the Soto school of Buddhism soon afterward in the early Kamakura period. Stressing the combination of *zazen* with *kōan*, paradoxical riddles put by a master to provide the substance for meditation, the Rinzai sect was especially popular among upper-class samurai and nobility. Daitokuji and Nanzenji in Kyoto and Kenchoji and Enkakuji in Kamakura are Rinzai temples.

The Soto sect stresses meditation, claiming that single-minded devotion to *zazen* is sufficient to attain enlightenment. Dogen had little interest in power or fame and established his monastery in the mountains of Fukui prefecture far from the capital. Teaching that anyone can attain enlightenment, he drew many followers from the lower samurai classes and the common people.

Another Zen sect, the Obaku school, was introduced from China by Ingen in the early Edo period. Its sutras are read in Chinese, and its rituals and decor retain a strong Chinese flavor.

● Culture

Zen has had a profound influence on Japanese culture. Rinzai monks were important in introducing Chinese culture to the Muromachi establishment. Gozan literature, the writings of monks at the five major Zen temples, contributed much to literature. The Zen influence was strong in painting as well, and Sesshu and others produced outstanding ink paintings and portraits.* The rock and sand gardens considered so typical of Japan are also Zen creations. Likewise, the tea ceremony traces its origins back to the first powdered tea brought back from China by Eisai, and a number of tea masters, including Sen no Rikyu, learned about Zen and suffused the tea ceremony with the Zen spirit.

Today, there are about nine million registered Zen followers, or about 10% of all Japanese Buddhists. Of the roughly 75,000 Buddhist temples in the country, 21,000 are Zen temples (15,000 of them Soto sect). These temples sponsor a variety of activities to propagate their teachings including short Zen "training camps" for their followers. Suzuki Daisetz* introduced Zen to the West, and Deshimaru Taisen* of the Soto sect did much to popularize it in Europe.

30 神道

神道が果たして宗教であるのか否か，これまでも論議が絶えなかった。神道には，宗教の要件である教義，聖典，宗団，布教などの明確なものがないからだ。一般に「神道」と言った場合，「日本民族に固有の神，神霊に基づいて発生し，展開してきた宗教の総称」であるとされているが，神や神霊についての信念や伝統的な祭祀(さいし)ばかりでなく，広く生活習俗や伝承されている考え方などもその中に含まれる。

現代の日本人は，日常は全く神道と無関係だと言えるが，正月の初もうで，神社の祭り，受験のときの合格祈願，七五三などのときには神社に参拝し，結婚式は神式でやることが多い。

古来の神社神道は，日本の原始信仰である農耕神・土地神・祖先神崇拝に基づくものであり，氏神などとも呼ばれ，氏族集団によって祭られたものである。祭神は八百萬(やおよろず)の神と言われるように多種多様である。原始神道においては，3，4世紀に至るまで神殿も作らなかった。4世紀に大和(やまと)政権がほぼ日本を統一し，古代国家が成立すると，原始神道は天つ神と国つ神(天神地祇(ちぎ))を祭る古代神道に発展した。天つ神は大和政権の神で，天皇が最高の祭司となり，地方神の国つ神の上に置かれた。また大和政権系神話に各地の氏族神話を取り入れ，記紀神話を作り上げた。最初の神道の教義が現れるのは平安時代中期になってからで，仏教の天台宗，真言宗の教理と結び付いた本地垂迹説(ほんじすいじゃく)がそれである。これはインドの仏・菩薩(ぼさつ)が日本でさまざまな神となって現れるという奈良時代からある神仏習合を主仏従神として理論化したものである。中世，近世に至り，伊勢神道，吉田神道，復古神道など，神道の独自性を説く理論が作られ，明治になると，皇室の祭祀を基準に，神社の祭祀・教義を統一して，神職は祭祀だけを行い，国民すべてを氏子とする国家神道を作り上げた。

戦後は，神社個々が宗教法人となり，文化庁の統計には神社の申告によって信徒1億人(1983年)となっているが，NHKの調査(1981年)では，「神道を信仰している」という人は3％にすぎない。

教派神道には金光教(こんこう)，大本教(おおもと)，禊教(みそぎ)など数百の教団があるが，国家神道中心の戦前にはしばしば迫害を受けた。信徒数は約1000万人。

民俗神道は田の神，かまど神，道祖神などを家庭や個人で祭るもので，生活習慣と結び付き，今も地方に残っている。

Shinto

Because it lacks the usual trappings of religion, there is still some question whether Shinto should be classified as a religion. Basically, Shinto is the name generally given to Japan's indigenous beliefs, rituals to native spirits, daily practices, and traditional ways of thinking.

Though Japanese are not consciously Shinto, many Shinto customs are still practiced, including visiting a shrine during the New Year's holidays, taking part in local Shinto shrine festivals, praying to the Shinto gods for success in school exams, and taking children to be blessed by shrine deities at *Shichi-go-san*. Most weddings are Shinto.

Shinto originated in the Japanese worship of agrarian, earthly, and ancestral gods. Every *uji* or clan had a tutelary god known as an *uji-gami*, and the Shinto gods are collectively known as *yaoyorozu no kami* (lit. the eight million deities). Ancient Shinto did not bother to erect shrines until the 3rd or 4th century. Not until the country was unified under the Yamato in the 4th century did Shinto begin to acquire a clear hierarchical structure with the Yamato gods and high-priest emperor at top and local gods at bottom. The first known Japanese histories were efforts to legitimize the imperial line by merging myths and legends concerning local *uji-gami* with the Yamato mythology. No Shinto doctrine as such, however, was postulated until the mid-Heian *Honjisuijaku* doctrine stipulating that the Shinto gods were really manifestations of Buddhist deities,* thereby linking indigenous beliefs to Buddhist teachings.* In the feudal and early-modern periods, a number of sects emerged professing an independent and pure Shintoism. These included Ise, Yoshida, and Fukko Shinto. In the Meiji era the government made a determined effort to promote emperor worship and all the trappings of Shinto. Local shrine teachings and festivals were brought into line with the national doctrine, and local priests lost the authority to do much but conduct ceremonies.

After the war, state and religion were separated and Shinto became just one more of the many Japanese religions. While 1983 statistics volunteered by Shinto shrines show 100 million Shinto followers, a 1981 NHK survey showed only 3% of the people identifying as Shinto.

There are numerous Shinto sects, including Konkokyo, Omotokyo, and Misogikyo, though many of them were prosecuted in the zeal to establish State Shinto prior to World War II. Today these more-than-500 sects claim 10 million believers.

Folk Shinto is closely tied to local and family religious practices. Its worship of the gods of the fields, the hearth, and all things close to home remains an integral part of local customs in many regions today.

31 キリスト教

●伝来から現在まで

日本にキリスト教が最初に伝来したのは，1549年，カトリック・イエズス会の宣教師フランシスコ・ザビエルの来日によってであった。宣教師たちとともにもたらされる南蛮貿易の利益に大いに関心のあった大名たちが布教を歓迎したため，たちまち多数の信徒を獲得した。1590年前後で信徒20万人は，当時の人口から言えばたいへんな比率である。しかし，密月時代は短く，豊臣秀吉の禁教令(1587年)で突如終わる。江戸幕府はさらに弾圧を強化して，多くの殉教者を生み，悲劇は1637年の島原(しまばら)の乱で頂点に達する。こうして日本が再びキリスト教の信仰の自由を認めるのは1873年，明治新政府になってからであった。その間，一部の信者は“隠れキリシタン”として細々と信仰の火を守った。

現在，キリスト教信者は約140万人。カトリック，プロテスタントはもとより既存のあらゆる宗派が入っている。ザビエルに始まる初期布教時代と比べ，この数字はあまりにも少ない。しかも，ほぼ横ばいである。結婚式は神式で，葬式は仏式でと，宗教に対してよく言えば寛容，悪く言えば無頓着(とんちゃく)な日本人にとって，キリスト教はしょせん根付かぬものなのだろうか。元来，多神教的であった神道の影響が根底にあるのだろうか。同じアジアにある隣国・韓国では，仏教と比べてもキリスト教が大きな影響力を有しているのを考えると，これはきわめて興味深い現象である。

●日本文化の中のキリスト教

とはいえ，日本のキリスト教の問題は単に量に還元できないのも事実である。信者の数こそ少ないが，明治以降の日本の近代化に，キリスト教およびその文化が及ぼした影響は測り知れない。それは時にライフスタイルとして，道徳として，倫理として，日本人の生活に入り込んでいる。

教育，特に女子教育や中等教育に果たした役割も大きい。今日でもミッションスクールは約800校(中高校)を数え，他のどの宗教学校よりも多い。新島襄(にいじまじょう)，内村鑑三，植村正久など，優れた思想家を輩出し，また，社会事業の分野でもキリスト教は大きな力を果たした。その人道主義は社会主義運動にも関連し，いわゆる，キリスト教社会主義の流れを作った。今日，キリスト教信者には作家の遠藤周作，曽野綾子，評論家の犬養道子(いぬかい)，故大平正芳元首相など著名人も少なくない。

Christianity

● Historical Development

Christianity was brought to Japan by a group of Jesuit missionaries led by Francis Xavier in 1549. Christianity spread rapidly, thanks to the open-arms policy of feudal lords who appreciated that the missionaries brought not only a new religion but also new trade opportunities. By around 1590, there were about 200,000 Japanese Christians—a significant portion of the population at that time. However, this proved to be a brief honeymoon for Christianity in Japan, for in 1587 Toyotomi Hideyoshi suddenly banned the new religion. Suppression of Christianity became stricter under the Tokugawa regime, coming to a tragic climax in 1637 when a Christian rebellion in Shimabara* was crushed. Japan continued to ban Christianity until 1873, when freedom of religion was reinstated by the Meiji government, yet throughout this period the flame of Christian belief was surreptitiously maintained by small groups of "closet Christians."

Including Catholics, Protestants, and all the other denominations, Japanese Christians now number about 1.4 million. As a percentage of the total population, this is fewer than there were in the 16th century. With Shintoist weddings and Buddhist funerals, Japanese may be termed tolerant or even indifferent to religion, and they are not very receptive to Christian conversion. Perhaps this is because of Japan's polytheistic Shinto roots, but Japan presents a striking contrast to the situation in such neighboring Asian countries as South Korea where Christianity ranks right alongside Buddhism in popularity.

● Christianity in Japanese Culture

However, Christianity's impact on Japanese culture cannot be measured by numbers alone. Although only a small percentage of Japanese are Christians, Christian thought has had an major impact on Japan during its modernization beginning in the late 19th century. Christian lifestyles, moral codes, and ethics have become interwoven into Japanese life.

Christianity has also come to play a major role in education, especially for girls' schools and secondary schools. There are currently some 800 mission schools at the secondary level, far more than there are non-Christian religious schools. Many of Japan's great modern thinkers have been Christian, including Niijima Jo, Uchimura Kanzo, and Uemura Masahisa, and Christians have also figured prominently in social work. Along the way, many of these humanists developed ties with socialism, resulting in a Christian current that forms part of Japan's socialist movement. Among the famous Japanese Christians of recent years are the novelists Endo Shusaku and Sono Ayako, social commentator Inukai Michiko, and the late former Prime Minister Ohira Masayoshi.

32 神話

日本の神話は，『古事記』(712年)と『日本書紀』(720年)の最初の部分に出ている神々の物語を指すのが普通である。

記紀の神話は，その舞台によって，高天原(たかまがはら)，出雲(いずも)，日向(ひゅうが)の3つに分けられる。天皇の祖神で，神々の王者である太陽神アマテラス(※)が支配するのが高天原つまり天上の国であり，まずそこで天地開びゃく，イザナギ・イザナミの国生み・神生みや，天岩屋(あめのいわや)などの物語が展開する。次いで出雲神話では出雲地方(今の島根県東部)を主要な舞台として，スサノオとオオクニヌシが主神として活躍する。天孫降臨の前提として，オオクニヌシが高天原から派遣された神々に，国土を献上するいわゆる国譲りをする。日向神話は日向地方(今の宮崎県)が舞台で，アマテラスの命により，その孫ニニギが日向の高千穂の峰に降りる天孫降臨によって，日本を創始する。

各神話は，天地の開びゃくから国生みへ，国生みから国譲りへ，国譲りから天孫降臨へと，互いに因果関係を持って時間的に結び付けられ，究極的には，神の子孫である天皇の国土統治を合理化する物語になっている。このように高度な国家的・政治的配慮を持ってつくられている点が，他民族に見られない日本神話の特色である。

『古事記』によって，よく知られた神話を3つ紹介する。

• 国生み　イザナギ，イザナミの男女2神は天神から矛(ほこ)を与えられ，海上を流れ動く大地を固めるよう命じられる。そこで2神は矛を海に入れてかき回し，それを引き上げると，そのしずくが固まって島になった。そこに降りて柱を立て，2神は柱を右と左から回り，出会った所で結婚し，次々と島を生んでいった。

• 天岩屋　弟スサノオの暴状を怒ったアマテラスが天岩屋に隠れたため，天下が暗やみになった。神々が相談して，物を飾り，祝詞(のりと)をあげ，アメノウズメに半裸で踊らせた。外の笑い声につられてアマテラスが岩戸を少し開いたので，タヂカラオが手をとって引き出し，世が再び明るくなった。同種の話は広く太平洋周辺民族にも見られる。

• 八岐大蛇(やまたのおろち)　出雲国簸川(ひのかわ)の上流に，頭と尾がそれぞれ8つに分かれた大蛇がすみ，娘を次々に食べるので，スサノオが酒を飲ませて退治し，助けた娘と結婚する。三種の神器の1つである剣を大蛇の尾から得た。

Mythology

Japanese mythology is based on stories in the 712 *Kojiki* (Record of Ancient Matters) and the 720 *Nihon Shoki* (Chronicle of Japan). Broadly divided according to its three principal scenes of action—Takamagahara (the High Plain of Heaven), Izumo, and Hyuga—Japanese mythology tells of Japan's creation and the adventures of its numerous gods.

Takamagahara, is eventually ruled by the sun goddess Amaterasu,* ancestor of the emperor. The earliest Takamagahara myths deal with the separation of heaven and earth, the creation of land by the gods Izanami and Izanagi, the many other gods to which they give birth (including Amaterasu), and Amaterasu's flight to a heavenly cave.

The Izumo myths center in the Izumo district (eastern Shimane prefecture) and deal primarily with the adventures of Amaterasu's brother, Susanoo, and his descendant, Okuninushi.

Taking place in what is now Miyazaki prefecture, the Hyuga tales deal primarily with the god Ninigi who descends to Mt. Takachiho under orders from Amaterasu to subdue and rule the land, in the process establishing the imperial line and the Japanese nation.

From the separation of heaven and earth to the establishment of the imperial line, this mythology marshals divine descent to buttress imperial authority in a blatantly nationalistic and political mythology.

● ***Kojiki* Myths**

Three myths from the *Kojiki* are especially well known. The first tells of Izanagi and Izanami, male and female deities, who are given a spear and told to solidify the drifting land. They thrust the spear into the sea and stir the churning brine. When they lift the spear, drops of brine harden to form an island. Izanagi and Izanami descend to the island and erect a pillar around which they walk from opposite directions. They unite upon meeting, giving birth to the Japanese islands.

The Amenoiwaya myth concerns Amaterasu and Susanoo. Angered by his violent behavior, she sulks in the heavenly cave and, deprived of her light, all is plunged into darkness. The other gods try to entice her out. Finally, the goddess Amenouzume dances half naked, much to the delight of all, and Amaterasu, lured by the unexpected sound of laughter, moves the great rock blocking the cave entrance to see what is going on. The god Tajikarao pulls her out and the world is once again blessed with her light. Similar myths are found throughout the Pacific.

One of the best-known Susanoo myths is about the great eight-headed, eight-tailed serpent of the Hino River in Izumo. Susanoo tricks the dreaded devourer of sacrificial maidens into drinking sake and kills it while it lies in stupor. In one of the serpent's eight tails, Susanoo discovers a sword which later becomes one of the three imperial regalia, along with a mirror and a curved jewel.

33 昔話

昔話は，語り初めが「昔，昔」，語り納めが「…であったとさ」のような一定の形式を持ったものを言う。出てくる時代・場所・人物を特定せず，空想的である点が伝説と異なる。

日本の昔話の研究は，まだ数十年にしかならないが，昔話への関心は強く，すでに何万という昔話が収集され，民俗学，文学など各分野からの研究が進められている。最近では，ユング派分析家の河合隼雄(かわいはやお)が，日本の昔話の深層を分析して，西洋人の自我は「男性の意識」であるのに対し，日本人の自我は「女性の意識」とする説を発表して注目された。

●五大昔話

室町時代末期ごろに成立し，江戸時代から明治にかけて有名昔話として定着した五大昔話が日本人によく知られている。

・かちかち山(※)　爺(じじい)は畑からいたずらタヌキを捕らえて帰る。タヌキは爺の留守に婆(ばば)をだまして殺し，婆に化けて爺に婆汁を飲ませる。悲しむ爺のために，ウサギがタヌキに大やけどをさせ，とうがらしを塗り付ける。最後にタヌキをどろの舟に乗せて沈め，殺す。

・猿かに合戦　ずるい猿は自分の拾ったカキの種をカニの拾った握り飯と交換する。カニがまいたカキの種が大きな木になり，実を結ぶと，猿はカニをだまして熟した実を食べ，青い実をカニに投げつけて殺す。カニの子は，うす・きね・ハチ・クリの助けで親のあだを討つ。

・舌切りすずめ　のりをなめたスズメを意地悪な婆は舌を切って追い出す。優しい爺がスズメの宿を訪ね，つづら(※)をもらう。小さいつづらを選ぶと，中に大判(※)・小判や宝が入っていた。婆はそれをまねてスズメの宿を訪ね，大きいつづらをもらうと，中から蛇・ムカデや化け物が出てくる。決まり文句→「舌切りすずめ，お宿はどこだ」

・花さか爺　正直者の爺がかわいがっていた犬に教えられて木の下から宝を掘り出す。死んだ犬を埋めた場所に大きな木が生え，爺がそれでうすを作ってもちをつくと，大判・小判が出てくる。うすの灰で枯れ木に花を咲かせて爺は殿様に褒められる。それをまねた隣の爺はことごとく失敗する。決まり文句→「ここ掘れワンワン」

・桃太郎(※)　川で洗濯をしていた婆が拾った桃から子供が生まれる。桃太郎と名づけられたその子は，大きくなって日本一のきび(※)だんごを持って，犬・猿・キジを連れて鬼が島へ鬼退治に行き，宝物を持って帰る。決まり文句→「大きな桃がどんぶらこどんぶらこと流れてきた」

Folk Tales

Japanese folk tales, like folk tales everywhere, have set patterns starting with "Once upon a time" and ending with "and that's the way it was." Unlike legends, all the elements of the folk tale are imaginary.

It is only in the last few decades that scholars have begun to study Japanese folk tales, but interest is strong and specialists have already collected tens of thousands of stories. The Jungian analyst Kawai Hayao did a celebrated psychological study of Japanese folk tales that found that, in comparison to the masculine ego revealed by Western folk tales, Japanese folk tales suggest a feminine ego.

Five Muromachi folk tales have remained especially popular.

• ***Kachikachi-yama****(Kachikachi Mountain) An old man captures a *tanuki*, a kind of badger, and takes it home. While the old man is out, the *tanuki* tricks his wife and kills her. He then transforms himself into the old woman and when her husband returns serves him soup containing her flesh. To avenge the old man, a rabbit burns the *tanuki*, rubs hot peppers into its charred skin, and sets it adrift on a boat of mud, finally drowning it.

• ***Saru Kani Gassen***(Battle Between the Monkey and the Crab) A bad monkey tricks a crab into trading his rice ball for the monkey's persimmon seed. Yet the crab plants the seed and it sprouts into a tree laden with fruit. The monkey tricks the crab again and eats the fruit, throwing unripe fruit at the crab and killing it. The crab's children eventually get revenge with the help of a mortar and pestle, bee, and chestnut.

• ***Shitakiri Suzume***(Tongue-cut Sparrow) Finding a sparrow eating her laundry starch, a mean old woman cuts its tongue out. Her gentle husband visits the sparrow's home and is given a choice of gifts. He takes the smaller box,* only to find it full of money* and treasure. Hearing this, the old man's greedy wife also visits the sparrow and takes the bigger box home, only to find it full of snakes, centipedes, and goblins.

• ***Hanasaka Jijii***(Ash Scatterer) An honest old man's dog leads him to buried treasure. When the dog dies, a great tree sprouts from its grave. The old man cuts down the tree and makes a mortar in which he pounds rice. To his astonishment, gold coins come out of the mortar. After his jealous neighbor burns the mortar, the old man scatters its ashes onto a withered tree, making it bloom and pleasing the local lord. Each time, the neighbor's attempts to mimic his feats end in disaster.

• ***Momotarō****(Peach Boy) A child is born from a great peach an old woman discovers floating down a stream. Named the Peach Boy, he grows into a sturdy youth and sets out on a journey to Devil Island carrying the best millet dumplings* in Japan and accompanied by a dog, a monkey, and a pheasant. He and his companions defeat the devils in battle and return home laden with treasure.

34 伝説

伝説は，具体的な事物と結び付いていて，真実と信じられている言い伝えである。昔話のように，決まった形式や空想性・娯楽性を持たない。日本には，昔話と同じく，伝説も豊富である。出てくる主役によって，ふつう次のように分類する。

自然伝説……動植物，鉱物，天体，気象，地形，火，水など
歴史伝説……神仏，聖地，長者，偉業，事件，地名など
信仰伝説……各種の神(田の神・山の神ほか)，各種の霊（樹・岩石ほか)，幽霊，妖怪(ようかい)など

●有名伝説

• 浦島伝説　若い漁夫の浦島太郎は，釣ったカメを助けたお礼に竜宮城に招かれ，乙姫(おとひめ)と3年間楽しく暮らす。故郷に帰るとすでに700年たっている。心細さのあまり乙姫との約束を破って，みやげの玉手箱を開くと紫の煙が上がり，たちまち老人となる。これは丹後国（今の京都府北部）水の江の「浦島の子」という漁夫の伝説に基づく，「浦島太郎」の物語で，伝説は『万葉集』『日本書紀』『丹後国風土記(ふどき)』その他に見え，室町時代には『御伽草子(おとぎぞうし)』や能の「浦島」になった。世界に広がる仙郷滞留譚(たん)，竜宮伝説の1つである。

• 羽衣伝説　駿河国(するがのくに)(今の静岡県)三保の松原で天女が水浴びをしているところへ漁夫が通りかかり，天女の羽衣をとってしまう。天に帰れなくなった天女は男の妻になり，子供が生まれる。天女は後に羽衣を取り戻して天に帰る。原形は『駿河国風土記』『近江国(おうみのくに)風土記』『丹後国風土記』に出ており，能に「羽衣」がある。異類婚姻譚の1つ。

• 弘法(こうぼう)伝説　弘法大師(空海)が諸国を遍歴した際に生まれた伝説。弘法大師がサトイモを所望したのを断ると，サトイモが石になったというたぐいの話が各地にたくさん残っている。このほか実在の人物に関する伝説は，小野小町，源義経(よしつね)，弁慶，徳川光圀(みつくに)(水戸黄門)など数多い。

• 金太郎　金太郎は相模国(さがみのくに)(今の神奈川県)の足柄山(あしがらやま)で，山うばに育てられ，クマ・シカ・猿などを友とした。怪力で全身赤く，まさかりを持ち，腹掛けをした子供の姿で描かれる。成人して源頼光(よりみつ)に仕えて坂田金時と名乗り，大江山の酒呑童子(しゅてんどうじ)を退治して四天王の1人となった。今でも金太郎にあやかって強くなるようにと，5月5日の端午(たんご)の節句には，金太郎の像を飾る風習がある。

Legends

Legends are stories linked to historical persons and events believed to have once existed or happened. Not purely imaginary amusement, they lack folk tales' set formula. Japan's numerous legends are usually classified into nature legends of animals, plants, metals and minerals, heavenly bodies, weather, geography, fire, water, and so on; historical legends of gods, sacred sites, wealthy merchants, heroic deeds, events, and place names, etc.; and religious legends of gods (e.g. fields and mountains), spirits (of trees and rocks), ghosts, and goblins.

• ***Urashima Tarō*** A young fisherman, Urashima Taro, saves a turtle, and the grateful turtle takes him to Ryugujo, the Palace of the Dragon King, where he spends three happy years with the king's daughter, Otohime. He gets homesick, however, and returns home only to find that 700 years have passed. Alone and at a loss what to do, he breaks open the magic box which Otohime had given him with strict instructions to keep it closed. In that very instant he ages. This story is based on a legend of Mizunoe in the ancient province of Tango (now part of Kyoto prefecture) about a fisherman named Urashima no Ko. The legend appears in several ancient compilations including the *Man'yōshū*, *Nihon Shoki*, and the Tango *Fudoki*. In the Muromachi period it was retold in *otogi-zōshi** short stories and made into the noh play *Urashima*. Such tales about visits to enchanted lands are common worldwide.

• ***Hagoromo*** (Feathered Robe) In Miho no Matsubara in Suruga province (now Shizuoka prefecture), a fisherman comes upon an angel bathing in a lake. He takes away her beautiful feathered robe and, unable to return to heaven without the robe, the angel marries the fisherman and has his child. Finally she retrieves her robe and flies off to heaven. A tale of marriage between a celestial being and a human, *Hagoromo* appears in the Suruga, Omi, and Tango *Fudoki*. It is also the basis for a well-known noh play.

• ***Kobō* Legends** Legends about the monk Kobo Daishi (a.k.a. Kukai) and his travels abound. In one story Kobo Daishi is refused some sweet potatoes and turns them to stone. There are many other legends concerning historical figures such as Ono no Komachi,* Minamoto no Yoshitsune, Benkei,* and Tokugawa Mitsukuni (a.k.a. Mito Komon).

• ***Kintarō*** Raised on Mt. Ashigara in Sagami province (Kanagawa prefecture) by a mountain ogress, Kintaro is a child of superhuman strength. Friends with the mountain animals, he is commonly depicted as bright red, wearing a bib, and carrying a hatchet. As an adult Kintaro becomes Sakata no Kintoki, a trusted follower of Minamoto no Yorimitsu.* After capturing Shutendoji,* who had been terrorizing the Mt. Oe area, Kintaro becomes one of the four trusted followers* of Minamoto no Yorimitsu. It is customary to display a Kintaro doll on May 5, Boy's Day, to symbolize the hope that sons will be as strong and brave as Kintaro.

Notes

△Horyuji

△Ise Shrine

△Katsura Detached Palace

△Himeji Castle

△*Tokonoma*

△Ryoanji

△*Komusō* with *shakuhachi*

■1. Architecture

Horyuji (法隆寺) Said to have been built in 607. The current structure is probably a relatively recent reconstruction.

Ise Shrine (伊勢神宮) Located in the city of Ise in Mie prefecture, the Ise Shrine is dedicated to Amaterasu, sun goddess and legendary ancestor of the imperial house.

tokonoma (床の間) An alcove, usually in a traditional-style Japanese guest room, with a slightly raised floor, the *tokonoma* is used to hang scrolls and as a setting for ornaments and flower arrangements.

Katsura Detached Palace (桂離宮) Located in the southwestern section of Kyoto.

Himeji Castle (姫路城) Also known as Shirasagi-jo, Himeji Castle was completed in 1610 and is located in the city of Himeji in Hyogo prefecture.

Rokumeikan (鹿鳴館) Built in 1883 in Hibiya, Tokyo, this was a social club for the elite and state guests. The Rokumeikan came to symbolize cultural achievement at a time when it was deemed important to adopt all things Western.

■2. Gardens

artificial hills (築山) Mounds of dirt or sand made to look like mountains.

kondō (金堂) Building enshrining an image of a temple's principal object of worship. Called the *kondō* or golden hall, because either the image or the interior of the building, or both, were gilded with gold.

■3. Music

min'yō (民謡) In a broad sense, folk songs are also a part of traditional Japanese music. Songs which were once very much a part of daily life, *min'yō* are today primarily sung only for parties, *bon-odori* dances, and on other special occasions. Every region has its own unique folk songs.

Suzuki method (鈴木メソッド) Suzuki Shin'ichi began his Talent Education Movement in the city of Matsumoto in Nagano prefecture. His method is based on the theory that "anyone's talent can be developed through education."

■4. Traditional Japanese Music

wandering Buddhist monks (虚無僧) The *komusō* did not wear monk's robes or shave their heads, but instead wore cylindrical straw hats, that completely hid their faces, and

△*Biwa*

△*Shamisen*

△*Koto*

played the *shakuhachi*. In the Edo period, this was a favorite disguise of warriors who had committed crimes and who hoped to escape punishment.

puppet theater drama (人形浄瑠璃) *Ningyō-jōruri* are puppet plays performed to the accompaniment of *jōruri* narration. Today, *ningyō-jōruri* is most commonly referred to as *bunraku*, the name of the only surviving puppet theater troupe.

■5. Noh

See picture.

■6. Kabuki

shrine maiden (巫女) A *miko* is unmarried woman at a Shinto shrine who performs dances and recites incantations to the gods.

Okuni (阿国) (?-1607?) The supposed founder of kabuki, also known as Izumo no Okuni.

yagō (屋号) A kabuki actor's stage name.

■7. *Bunraku* and *Buyō*

ballad-reciting chanter (太夫) *Tayū* is an informal title bestowed upon performers of the highest rank in several traditional performing arts. A *jōruri* singer is very often called a *tayū*, as is the case in *gidayū-jōruri*, a type of *jōruri* ballad chanting first developed by Takemoto Gidayu I, and marked by its powerful delivery and accompaniment by a large, deep-toned *shamisen*.

Important Intangible Cultural Asset (重要無形文化財) Men and women who have been designated Bearers of Important Intangible Cultural Assets because they preserve important techniques in traditional crafts and arts and the performing

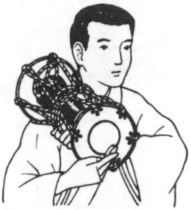
△small hand drum

△Kabuki-za

△Noh

△Kabuki

△*Bunraku*

△*Rakugo*

arts.

Living Cultural Treasures (人間国宝) A more popular name for Bearers of Important Intangible Cultural Assets.

■8. Popular Entertainment

rakugo (落語) See picture.

■9. Flower Arrangement

water trays (水盤) A shallow, ceramic or metal dish with a flat bottom used in flower arranging.

△*Rikka*

△*Seika*

△*Moribana*

△*Nageire*

■10. The Tea Ceremony

Okakura Tenshin (岡倉天心) (1862-1913) More popularly known by his pen name, Tenshin, Okakura Kakuzo was a prominent art critic and philosopher. He studied under Earnest Fenollosa and was an ardent promoter of Japanese arts.

matcha (抹茶) A high-quality tea ground into a fine powder. *Matcha* is dissolved in hot water and whipped to a froth with a bamboo whisk.

whisk (茶筅) A bamboo whisk used in preparing *matcha*.

△Tools for the tea ceremony

△*Temae*

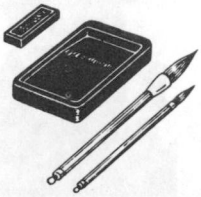
△Brushes and black ink

■11. Calligraphy

brush (毛筆) A brush made of sheep, *tanuki*, rabbit, or other animal hair inserted into a thin bamboo tube or wooden handle.

black ink (墨) A block of ink rubbed on a wet stone to produce the ink used in calligraphy and painting. Made of the oily ash residue of burned vegetable oil and pine roots mixed with various fragrances, combined with natural glue, and formed into solid blocks.

■12. Painting

liquid glue (にかわ水) A liquid glue made from boiled animal and fish skins, tendons, and bones. *Nikawa-mizu* is used to treat paper and silk in *nihon-ga* because it facilitates the application of the chalk-like white undercoating.

Kano School (狩野派) The Kano School dominated Japanese painting from the end of the Muromachi period through the Edo period. Founded by Kano Masanobu, this school flourished under the patronage of successive shoguns and produced many masters such as Motonobu, Eitoku, Sanraku, and Tan'yu.

folding screens (屏風) Folding screens used as room dividers and protective screens, *byōbu* also served a decorative purpose. Made of paper or cloth stretched on wooden frames, *byōbu* consist of two, four, six, or more panels that fold together accordion-fashion.

△*Kaisho*

△*Gyōsho*

△*Sōsho*

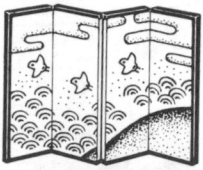

△*Byōbu*

■13. Ukiyo-e

△Harunobu

△Utamaro

△Sharaku

△Hokusai

△Hiroshige

■14. Ceramics

Shosoin (正倉院) A Nara-period repository of imperial treasures located in the Todaiji compound in Nara. Famous for its collection of Tang China and Nara-period art objects.

△Imari

Imari (伊万里) A port city in northern Saga prefecture in Kyushu.

■15. Lacquer Ware

■16. The Japanese Sword

△Lacquer ware

△Japanese sword

■17. Japanese Dolls

haniwa (埴輪) Low-fired earthenware figures found in and around Kofun period tombs.

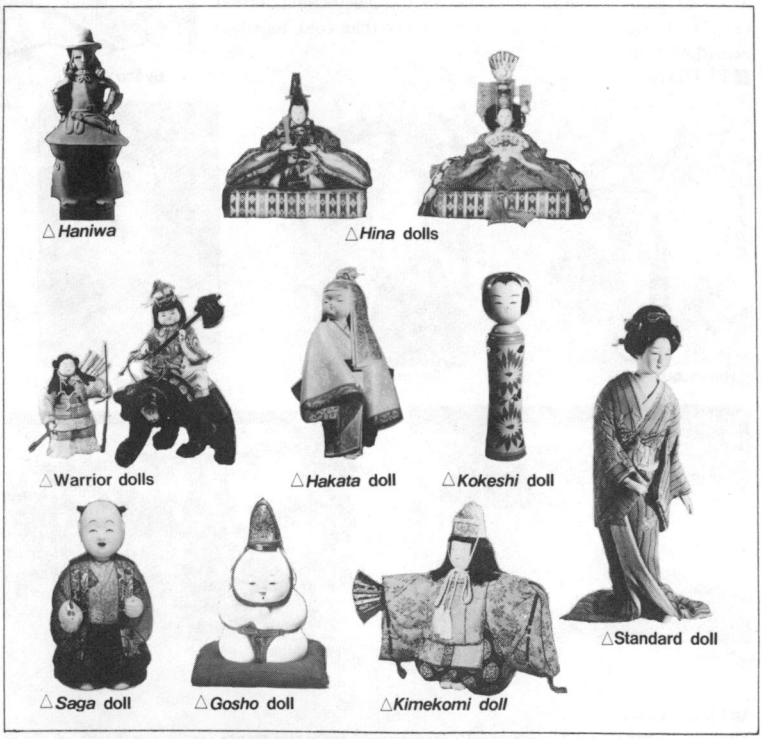

△*Haniwa*

△*Hina* dolls

△Warrior dolls

△*Hakata* doll

△*Kokeshi* doll

△Standard doll

△*Saga* doll

△*Gosho* doll

△*Kimekomi doll*

■18. Japanese Literature (1) (Formative Years)

Emperor Jinmu (神武天皇) Legendary first emperor to appear in the earliest records of ancient Japan.

Hieda no Are (稗田阿礼) (?-?) A person of prodigious memory, Hieda no Are is said to have memorized the contents of the *Teiki* and *Kyūji*. O no Yasumaro recorded Hieda no Are's account of these records in the *Kojiki*.

O no Yasumaro (太安万侶) (?-723) A court noble and man of letters.

Toneri Shinno (舎人親王) (676-735) The fifth son of Emperor Tenmu.

Otomo no Yakamochi (大伴家持) (718?-785) Court official and poet.

4,500 poems Though the *Man'yōshu* contains two types of *waka* poetry, *chōka* and *tanka*, the *tanka* are by far the most numerous. The *chōka* has three or more alternating lines of five and seven syllables and always ends with a seven-syllable line. The *tanka* has 31 syllables arranged in a 5-7-5-7-7-syllable pattern.

■19. Japanese Literature (2)(Court Literature)

Ariwara no Narihira (在原業平) (825-880) Poet.

Murasaki Shikibu (紫式部) (?-?) A mid-Heian period court lady, poet, and writer who wrote the world's first novel, the *Tale of Genji*.

Sei Shonagon (清少納言) (?-?) A mid-Heian period court lady, poet, and writer. Though her real name and dates of birth and death are not known, she was a sensitive and eloquent writer noted for her essays compiled in *Makura no Sōshi* (Pillow Book).

■20. Japanese Literature (3)(Medieval)

Hogen uprisings (保元の乱) A military disturbance in Kyoto in 1156 sparked by rivalries within the imperial household.

Genji (源氏) Another name for the Minamoto clan.

Heike (平家) Another name for the Taira clan.

Heiji rebellion (平治の乱) A clash between Minamoto and Taira forces in 1159 which forced the Minamoto out of the court and placed the Taira in a position of power.

biwa-hōshi (琵琶法師) Blind, minstrel monks who played the *biwa*. The term *hōshi* is another name for monk.

△*Biwa-hōshi*

■21. Japanese Literature (4)(Town Pleasures)

shopowner (飛脚問屋) The *hikyaku* were swift-footed couriers supplied by a *hikyaku-donya*, a business establishment specializing in courier services.

San'yutei Encho (三遊亭円朝) (1839-1900) A highly talented *rakugo* storyteller. His many original stories contributed to the great popularity of *rakugo* in the Meiji era.

■23. Japanese Literature (6)(Early Twentieth Century)

Great Kanto Earthquake (関東大震災) This massive earthquake on September 1, 1923, extended from the Kanto region out to Shizuoka and Yamanashi prefectures. The earthquake and the fires that followed left 140,000 dead or missing.

■25. *Waka*

court ladies (女房) *Nyōbō* were originally ladies in-waiting of high rank within the imperial palace and in the homes of the nobility.

■27. *Manga*

△*Fuji Santarō*

(*Asahi Shinbun*; March 31, 1984)

It's hay fever.

■28. **Buddhism**

apocalyptic Buddhism (末法思想) *Mappō* is a concept of the end of the world expressed in Buddhist terms. After the attainment of *nirvana* by Sakya (the historical Buddha), according to this concept, there are three periods. The *shōbō*, a thousand years of "true law," the *zōbō*, a thousand years of "imitative law," and finally the *mappō*, the "latter day of the law" when people fail to live by Buddhist law and are unable to attain enlightenment. This last stage was believed to have begun in 1052 in the mid-Heian period when the military's rise to ascendency plunged Japan into internal turmoil. The people of this period were very much concerned with the after-world and many sought the saving grace of the Amida Buddha.

Nichiren sect (日蓮宗) A Buddhist sect founded by the priest Nichiren. See p. 17.

Jodo Shinshu (浄土真宗) A Buddhist sect established by Shinran. See p. 17.

■29. **Zen**

portraits (頂相) *Chinzō* (or *chinsō*) are full- or half-size portraits of eminent Zen monks. Their extreme realism is unusual in Japan given the lack of a portraiture tradition.

Suzuki Daisetz (鈴木大拙) (1870-1966) A prominent Buddhist scholar who introduced Zen to the West.

Deshimaru Taisen (弟子丸泰仙) (1914-82) Deshimaru became a Zen monk in 1965 after turning fifty and traveled extensively overseas, establishing 60 Zen meditation halls in Europe and northern Africa.

△*Zazen*

■30. **Shinto**

Buddhist deities (菩薩) *Bosatsu* or bodhisattvas are holy beings on the threshold of enlightenment who vow not to become Buddhas until they have helped all other beings to attain the same state.

Buddhist teachings Two Buddhist sects that Shinto developed close ties with were the Tendai and Shingon sects. Tendai is a Buddhist sect introduced from China in the Heian period by the priest Saicho who established the sect's headquarters at Enryakuji on Mt Hiei near Kyoto. The founders of the Jodo, Nichiren, and Zen sects in the later Kamakura period were all Tendai monks. Shingon was a purely Japanese Buddhist sect based on the esoteric Buddhist teachings introduced from

China in the early Heian period by the priest Kobo Daishi (a.k.a. Kukai).

■31. Christianity

Christian rebellion in Shimabara (島原の乱) A 1637 rebellion by Catholic Christians of Kyushu against the suppression of their faith. Instigated by the farmers and merchants of the Amakusa Islands off the Shimabara peninsula, the rebellion only served to make the shogunate step up its suppression of Christianity and close Japan to the rest of the world.

■32. Mythology

Amaterasu (アマテラス) Amaterasu O-mikami, child of the gods Izanagi and Izanami and ancestral god of the imperial family. Ise Shrine in Mie prefecture is dedicated to Amaterasu. An important deity for an agricultural society, the sun goddess was probably gradually incorporated into the imperial lineage as the imperial power grew.

■33. Folk Tales

Kachikachi-yama (かちかち山) In this tale the rabbit burns the *tanuki* by creeping up behind it and setting fire to the straw it is carrying on its back. The word *kachikachi* is an onomatopoeia for the clicking sound of the flint the rabbit uses.

box (つづら) The *tuzura* box woven of strong *tsuzura* vines was used to store clothes.

money (大判, 小判) *Ō-ban, ko-ban* were oval gold and silver pieces used as currency in the Edo period.

Momotarō (桃太郎) The peach is a symbol of long life and the tale of Momotaro probably originated in the story of an old couple who were rejuvenated by eating peaches and then had a child. The peach was also believed to be effective in warding off devils and other evil creatures.

millet dumplings (きびだんご) Dumplings made of millet were thought to bestow great strength upon a person. Hence, the ability of Momotaro and his companions, a dog, monkey, and pheasant, to vanquish the devils.

■34. Legends

otogi-zōshi (御伽草子) Anonymously written fiction, moralistic stories, and legends.

Ono no Komachi (小野小町) An early Heian period poet. Though little is actually known about Ono no Komachi, she is believed to have been a great beauty, and there are many legends about her which have been employed as themes in noh chants and *jōruri* narration.

Benkei (弁慶) (?-1189) A monk, Benkei died protecting his master Minamoto no Yoshitsune, younger brother and rival of Minamoto no Yoritomo. Benkei is a popular hero figuring prominently in *otogi-zōshi* and kabuki and noh dramas.

Minamoto no Yorimitsu (源頼光) (948-1021) A warrior of the mid-Heian period renowned for his courage.

Shutendoji (酒呑童子) A legendary bandit said to have preyed on women and children. He appears in *otogi-zōshi* and

△Momotaro

△*Tsuzura*

△Benkei

△Kintaro

kabuki and noh plays.

four trusted followers (四天王) Originally the four Buddhist guardian deities, *shitennō* is also used in reference to particularly faithful retainers and followers of historical and legendary heroes. The term is still used today.

Part-5
超自然・動植物のイメージ
AFFINITIES WITH NATURE

1 犬・猫

●犬

［イメージ］ 英語の表現と同じように，日本語の表現でも犬のイメージはよくない。「犬死にする」は「むだに死ぬ」の意味だし，単に「イヌ」と言えば，「スパイ，回し者」のことで侮辱語である。

［昔話］ 犬は縄文時代から家畜として飼われていた。昔話の「桃太郎」や「花さか爺」にも，犬は重要な役割で出てくる。白い犬は霊犬とされていたので，昔話の犬はしばしば白い犬として語られる。

［故事］ 江戸幕府の5代将軍徳川綱吉は，仏教を信じるあまり生類憐れみの令を出して犬や鳥獣の保護を命じ，それを厳しく励行したため，庶民の反感を買い，「犬公房」と言われた。

現代では，昭和初期の「忠犬ハチ公」の話が有名である。ハチは毎日，主人を東京・渋谷駅に見送り，出迎える習慣があったが，主人の死んだ後10年間も駅で主人の帰りを待ったという。ハチは当時の小学校の教科書に取り上げられ，日本中の人気者になった。死後はく製にされて博物館に保存され，渋谷駅前には銅像がある。

最近では，自動車事故に遭った主人をかばって，左前足を切断した盲導犬に，人間並みの保険金が下りて話題をまいた。

［風習］ 日本では，欧米のようにしつけを厳しくしない。また愛犬は死ぬまでかわいがるが，不要な犬は簡単に捨てる風習がある。

日本では犬に「太郎」「ジョン」といった人名や，「クロ」「ポチ」といった犬専用の愛称をつける。犬の鳴き声は「ワン，ワン」。

●猫

［イメージ］ 猫のイメージは悪く，「猫を殺せば七代たたる」とか「化け猫」などと言う。日本には魔女の手先という迷信はない。

日本で猫と言えば，夏目漱石の猫を主人公にした小説『吾輩は猫である』を思い出す人が多い。

［風習］ 昔から猫が飼われたのは，ネズミを退治してもらうため。

飲食店など客商売の家で「招き猫」という置き物を飾る。後足で身を立て，一方の前足を挙げて人を招いている猫の像で，顧客，財宝を招く縁起物とされている。

［表現］ 仲が悪いのは，欧米では猫と犬だが，日本では猿と犬で，「犬猿の仲」と言う。猫の好物は，英米ではミルク，日本ではかつおぶしである。そこから「猫にかつおぶし」という表現が生まれた。猫の鳴き声は「ニャン，ニャン」「ニャー，ニャー」。

Dogs and Cats

● Dogs

Derogatory phrases referring to dogs are common in Japan as they are in the West. Thus to die like a dog is to die meaninglessly and to call someone a dog is to accuse him of being a spy or dupe.

Dogs are believed to have been domesticated in Japan as early as the Jomon period. White dogs, thought to be especially auspicious, often appear in such folk tales as *Momotarō* and *Hanasaka Jijii.*

Tokugawa Tsunayoshi, the fifth Tokugawa shogun and an ardent Buddhist, ordered the protection of all animals, especially dogs. So extreme were his regulations concerning dogs that he was ridiculed by the common people as the Dog Shogun. A more recent story is the 1920's tale of the faithful dog, Hachiko* who met his master at Tokyo's Shibuya station at the end of every workday. Even after his master died one day at work, Hachiko continued to wait at the station for 10 years. Hachiko's story was in elementary school texts and he became a popular symbol of devotion. After his death, Hachiko's body was put in a museum, and there is a bronze statue of him in front of Shibuya station. Most recently, the story of a seeing-eye dog who protected his master in a car accident caused quite a stir, both for the dog's bravery and because the dog was covered by as much insurance as a human.

Dogs are not usually trained as rigorously in Japan as they are in the West. While pets are generally well taken care of, unwanted dogs are often abandoned. Dogs may be given such human names as Taro and Jon or such strictly dog names as Kuro and Pochi. The onomatopoeia for a dog's bark is *wan-wan.*

● Cats

Cats do not have a very savory reputation in Japan, as evidenced by the saying "Kill a cat and you will be cursed for seven generations" and the many tales about *bake-neko* or monster cats, but there are no superstitions such as those of the West which portray the cat as the minion of witches. Perhaps the most famous cat in Japan is the hero of Natsume Soseki's* *I Am a Cat.*

Traditionally, cats were kept to kill rats. In restaurants and other forms of businesses in which customer turnover is important, it is customary to display a figure of a *maneki-neko** or beckoning cat. Sitting upright with one paw raised in a beckoning motion, the *maneki-neko* is thought to invite customers and riches.

In the West, animosity between cats and dogs is assumed, but in Japan this animosity is thought to exist between dogs and monkeys, such that two people who cannot get along are said have a dog-and-monkey relationship, *ken'en no naka.* In Japan a cat's favorite dish is *katsuo-bushi* (dried bonito flakes) rather than cream or milk, and the expression *neko ni katsuo-bushi* is a warning not to put temptation in people's way. A cat's meow in Japanese is *nyan-nyan* or *nyā-nyā.*

2 馬・牛

●馬

[イメージ]　昔，馬は神霊の乗り物として神聖視された。「神馬（しんめ）」として神社に奉納されたり，白馬，葦毛（あしげ）馬は神の召すものとして，常人が乗ることを禁じられたりしたこともある。

その一方で，馬は「馬鹿（ばか）」と書くように，頭が悪いと考えられていたらしい。「馬の耳に念仏」とか「馬耳東風」という表現は，いくら言ってもなんの反応もないことだし，「どこの馬の骨かわからない」と言えば，素性のわからない人を軽べつした言い方である。

馬を精力的と見るのは欧米と同じである。「馬力」と言えば，英語のhorsepowerのほかに，活力，体力を意味する。

[伝説]　神が馬に乗って来臨した跡とか，英雄が乗っていた愛馬の足跡と称する「馬蹄石（ばていせき）」が各地に残っている。武将や貴人が馬をつないだという「駒（こま）つなぎ松」「駒つなぎ桜」も多い。

[表現]　日本人は馬から長い顔を想像し，「馬面（うまづら）」というのは長い顔のたとえ。「馬が合う」は気が合うこと。馬の鳴き声は「ヒヒン」。

[利用]　馬は昔から農耕・軍事・輸送用などに広く使われてきた。東日本に馬の産地が多い。

日本でも競馬は人気があるが，欧米のように上流階級から下層階級までが熱狂するというようなことはない。

一部で馬肉を食べる習慣があり，肉が桜色なので「さくら肉」または「さくら」と言う。

●牛

[イメージ]　牛には遅鈍，忍耐のイメージがある。しかし，イギリスのジョン・ブルが持つ，男性的力強さと忍耐力のイメージとは異なる。

のろいものの代表とされ，遅いことを「牛の歩み」と言う。国会では「牛歩戦術」という投票の引き延ばし作戦がよく採られる。

[表現]　牛がごろっと横になっているようすからの連想で，食後横になることを「牛になる」と言って嫌う。大いに飲んで食べるのは「牛飲馬食」である。牛の鳴き声は「モー」。

[利用]　牛も昔から農耕・輸送用に使われてきた。日本人が牛乳を飲み，牛肉を食べるようになったのは明治中期以降で，牛肉を使った独特の料理にすきやき，※しゃぶしゃぶ，※牛丼（ぎゅうどん）がある。

Horses and Cows

● Horses

The horse has traditionally been treated as a sacred creature and *shinme* or divine horses were once commonly kept at Shinto shrines. Also in the past, commoners were forbidden to ride white or dappled horses considered to be servants of the gods. Still, the horse is thought of as a rather stupid creature as epitomized in the word *baka*, written with the characters for horse and deer, and such expressions as *uma no mimi ni nenbutsu* (prayers to a horse's ears) and *baji tōfū* (the east wind in a horse's ear) referring to someone who never listens. Another expression, *doko no uma no hone ka wakaranai*, is used to describe a person of questionable character, someone whose antecedents are completely unknown. The horse is a symbol of power in Japan as in the West. *Bariki* is like its literal translation "horsepower" but also has connotations of vitality and stamina.

There are many legends of gods descending to earth on horses and of heroes and their steeds. Rocks called *batei-seki*, thought to be the hoofprints of these horses, are to be found throughout Japan. Pine trees and cherry trees to which famous warriors and nobility are believed to have tied their horses also abound.

A person with a long face is described as *uma-zura* or horsefaced. To get along well with someone is expressed as *uma ga au*. A horse's neigh in Japanese is *hihin*.

Horses have traditionally been employed in agriculture and transport and as military steeds. Horse breeding and raising is most prevalent in eastern Japan today, but racing, although popular, does not have the wide appeal it does in the United Sates and Europe. Some Japanese eat horse meat, and it is often referred to by the euphemism *sakura-niku* or simply *sakura* because of its pink, cherry blossom color.

● Cows

The cow has a plodding persevering image and, unlike John Bull's masculinity and fortitude, is often used to represent dullards and slowpokes. To walk like a cow, *ushi no ayumi*, is to be extremely slow. In the Diet, opposition legislators sometimes try to delay passage of controversial legislation by walking to the ballot box at a snail's pace in what is called *gyūho-senjutsu* or "cow-walk tactics."

A person who lies down immediately after eating is warned that he will turn into a cow—a reference to the ungainly sight of a reclining cow. To eat and drink in excess is called *gyūin bashoku* (drinking like a cow and eating like a horse). A cow's mooing sound in Japanese is *mō*.

As with horses, cows have been traditional beasts of burden for transport and agriculture. Japanese did not drink milk or eat beef in appreciable amounts until the 20th century, but today there are many popular beef dishes including sukiyaki, *shabu-shabu*,* and *gyūdon*.*

3 タヌキ・キツネ

●タヌキ

[イメージ]　日本人はタヌキに俳味と禅味と，特有の飄逸さを与えた。大きな腹を張り出し，小笠を首にかけ，酒どくりと通帳を下げた信楽焼の像にそれがよく出ている。昔話の「かちかち山」では，タヌキは悪役だが，どこか間が抜け，憎めないところがある。

昔からタヌキは化けて人をだますとされる。いろいろなものに化けるほか，音をまねるのが得意で，走る汽車やひづめの音などを出す。

[昔話・伝説]　昔話や伝説には欠かせない動物。「文福茶がま」は命を助けられたタヌキが，恩返しに茶がまに化けて福をもたらす話である。「証城寺のたぬきばやし」は伝説に基づくよく知られた童謡。

[表現]　「たぬきそば」は，天ぷらの揚げかすを入れたそば。「たぬきおやじ」は，ずるい，年取った男の人を言う。「たぬき寝入り」は，眠っているふりをすることで，タヌキを急に驚かすと仮死状態になることからきている。「たぬきばやし」は，タヌキの腹鼓による囃子のこと。夜どこからともなく聞こえてくる祭ばやしを，タヌキが腹鼓を打っていると考えたことから。

●キツネ

[イメージ]　キツネもタヌキ同様，化けて人をだますと考えられてきた。タヌキが「大入道」や「高僧」など男に化けるのに対し，キツネは「女」に化ける。火と関係が深く，夜，山野に見える怪火を「きつね火」と言う。きつね火が連なって嫁入り行列のちょうちんのように見えるのが「きつねの嫁入り」である。「きつねの嫁入り」はまた，日が照っているのに雨が降ることも指す。

性質は陰性でずる賢いとされる。この点は欧米と同じである。

[俗信]　キツネは稲荷神社の神の使いとされ，一般に「いなり」と言うと，稲荷神社，キツネ，いなりずしなどを指す。

ある種の精神異常の症状を「きつねつき」とする俗信がある。ついたキツネは，専門の祈禱師に頼んで落としてもらう。

[昔話・伝説]　女に化けて人間の男と結婚する「きつね女房」をはじめ，キツネも昔話・伝説によく登場する。

[表現]　「きつねうどん」は，キツネの好物である油揚げを入れたうどん。「いなりずし」は，甘く煮た油揚げに酢飯を詰めたもの。

Tanuki and *Kitsune*

● *Tanuki*

The *tanuki*, sometimes translated into English as racoon dog, holds a special place in Japanese folklore. Both loved and feared, the *tanuki* is often depicted in ceramic statues* with a large protruding stomach, a small straw hat around its neck, a flagon of sake in one hand, and its account book strapped to its waist. In the folk tale *Kachikachi-yama* (Kachikachi Mountain), the *tanuki* is cast as the villain, but he is still a playful villain with a certain innocence about him that makes him impossible to hate.

From ancient times, *tanuki* have been thought to have the power to trick people by changing their appearances. Not only could they change their appearance, they were also supposed to be very good at imitating sounds such as of a locomotive or hoofbeats.

The *tanuki* figures prominently in many legends and folk tales. *Bunbuku Chagama* (The Miraculous Tea Kettle) is the story of a *tanuki* who turned into a tea kettle and brought good fortune to someone who had saved its life. There is also a well-known children's song based upon the legend of *Shojoji no Tanuki Bayashi* *(The Song of the Tanuki of Shojoji).

Tanuki-soba is noodles with tempura crumbs in the broth. A *tanuki oyaji* is a crafty old man. *Tanuki-neiri* is playing possum and comes from the *tanuki*'s habit, when surprised, of pretending to be dead or asleep. *Tanuki-bayashi* is the sound of drums heard distantly in the night and comes from the fact that the *tanuki* is supposed to enjoy beating his drum-like belly.

● *Kitsune*

Like the *tanuki*, the *kitsune* or fox is thought to be able to change its appearance. While the *tanuki* usually changes into a man, be it a huge monster* or a great priest, the fox usually changes into a woman. This pattern of changing into a woman also shows up, for example, in *Kitsune Nyōbō* (Fox Wife), a tale of a fox who changed into a woman and married a man.

Foxes are also associated with fire, and the distant fires sometimes seen at night are referred to as foxfire. Because it looks like a line of foxfire, having a long line of lanterns in a bridal procession is referred to as *kitsune no yomeiri* or the fox's bridal procession. The same term also refers to when it rains even though the sun is shining.

In both East and West, the fox is a crafty animal with a sociable personality. In Japan, it is also the guardian deity of the Inari shrines, and hence *inari* can be used to refer to *inari-zushi*—rice stuffed deep-fried *tōfu* (*abura-age*). The fox's fondness for *abura-age* also explains its use as a main ingredient in *kitsune-udon*.

People who are slightly deranged are thought to be possessed by a fox, and special priests might be employed to exorcise the fox.

4 タイ・コイ

●タイ

［イメージ］　タイは「めでたい」に通じるところから，縁起物とされ，結婚式をはじめとする祝儀の席に欠かせないものである。「腐ってもタイ」という表現は，もともと優れた価値のあるものは落ちぶれてもそれなりの価値があるという意味で，日本人のタイへの愛着ぶりをよく表している。

［伝説］　日本は古代からタイを食べてきたので，いろいろ伝説が残っている。タイの産地瀬戸内海には，その昔，*神功皇后の船にタイが寄ってきたので，祝いの酒樽を投げ入れたところ，たくさんのタイが酒に酔って浮き上がってきたという伝説がある。今でもその場所では，毎年，春先にタイが浮くが，これは実は強い潮流でタイが浮袋の調節機能を失うためである。

［利用］　タイは数種類がよく知られているが，その中で最も珍重され，味がよいのはマダイである。瀬戸内海では，4～6月ごろ産卵のために外海から入ってきたマダイを桜ダイと言って賞味する。これは性ホルモンの関係で，体色が濃い赤色，つまり婚姻色を帯びるところから名づけられたものである。ただ，味は，産卵期よりも，冬から早春にかけての旬のほうが勝る。刺し身，塩焼きその他，マダイの料理法は多い。タイの眼球はビタミンB_1に富むことで知られている。

●コイ

［イメージ］　欧米では薄汚い魚，大食いで貪欲，ばか者といった，あまりよくないイメージを持たれているが，日本と中国では，勇気・忍耐・努力の象徴であり，男子の意気を表す。コイは滝を上って竜になるという中国の伝説に由来する，「こいの滝登り」という表現は，立身出世を意味する。古くは中国の伝説に従って，魚の王とされたが，江戸時代以降はタイがコイに取って代わった。

［行事］　男の子がコイにあやかって立身出世するようにという願いから，5月5日の端午の節句に，戸外に「こいのぼり」(紙または布でコイの形に作った吹き流し)を立てる風習がある。

［表現］　「まないたのこい」は，運命を他人に握られ，逃げ場のない状態を言う。

［利用］　日本のニシキゴイは，観賞用として世界的に有名。

Sea Bream and Carp

● Sea Bream

Because the Japanese name for sea bream, *tai*, suggests the word *medetai* (auspicious), it is considered a celebratory food often gracing the table at weddings and other happy occasions. "Even a rotten *tai* is worthwhile," a saying to indicate that something of great value always retains some of its worth no matter how low it falls, expresses the high esteem the Japanese people have for the sea bream.

Sea bream figures prominently in Japanese legends. A tale from the Inland Sea area where sea bream abound tells how the legendary Empress Jingu* ordered a barrel of sake thrown overboard when a school of sea bream appeared by her ship. Made drunk by the sake, the sea bream floated to the surface ready for the taking. This tale is actually based on a natural phenomenon in which strong seasonal currents deprive the sea bream of its ability to regulate its depth with its swimming bladder, forcing it to the surface.

While the name of *tai* is given to a wide range of fish, the *madai* or sea bream is the most highly valued. In the Inland Sea, sea bream come in from the outer ocean to breed in the spring between April and June. These fish are called *sakura-dai* and are especially prized for their deep pink color resembling the color of cherry blossoms.

The sea bream is considered to be most delicious in the cold winter months and the early spring. It is eaten in many ways, the most popular being as *sashimi* and salted and grilled. The eyes of the sea bream are especially rich in vitamin B_1.

● Carp

The carp tends to be considered a dirty, foolish glutton in the West. In Japan and China, however, the carp is a masculine symbol of valor, endurance, and tenacity. The carp's annual upstream fight to get to its spawning grounds—in Chinese legends its climb up waterfalls to turn into a dragon—symbolizes a male child's healthy and vigorous growth and acceptance into society. In keeping with Chinese tradition, the carp was long considered the king of fish in Japan, until it was usurped by the sea bream in the Edo period.

The *koi-nobori*, flying carp made of paper or cloth and attached to a tall flagpole, which are part of the May 5 Children's Day's ornamentation, symbolize every parent's wish that sons will grow to be strong and brave like the carp.

A carp on the chopping board, *manaita no koi*, refers to someone whose fate is in the hands of another and who has no way of escape.

The colorful *nishiki-goi* are ornamental carp bred over centuries, and Japanese *nishiki-goi* are today known the world over.

5 ツル・カラス

●ツル

[イメージ]　「ツルは千年，カメは万年」と言われ，ツルは長寿でめでたい鳥とされている。そのため，「折(メ)りづる」を糸でたくさんつないだ「千羽づる」を病気見舞いに持っていったりする。ＪＡＬのマークはツルである。祝儀用の風呂敷(ふろしき)などにもよくツルの文様が描かれている。

白い美しい姿から，ツルには清純なイメージもある。昔話の「鶴(つる)女房」には，清純な魂を持つツルの化身とそれを取り巻く醜い人間の世界とが対照的に描かれている。また，権威者，優れた者のイメージもあり，「つるの一声」は，権威者，有力者などが多くの人の意見や議論を押さえつける一声を指す。「はきだめにつる」は，つまらない所に不似合いに優れたものが入ってくることのたとえである。

[伝説]　ツルは小枝や羽をくわえて運ぶ習性があるので，ツルが稲穂を運んできて稲作が始まったとする，「穂落とし伝説」がある。豊臣秀吉が糸の間にツルの羽を織り込んで，「つる毛の陣羽織」を作ったという話もある。

[種類]　日本ではタンチョウ・ナベヅル・マナヅルが見られる。山口県ではナベヅルが県の鳥，北海道ではタンチョウが道の鳥になっている。

●カラス

[イメージ]　カラスのイメージは悪い。黒い姿，雑食性，耳ざわりな鳴き声などから，昔から不吉なことの象徴とされている。この点は，洋の東西を問わず同じである。

[俗信・信仰]　カラスの異常な鳴き方を死の前兆としたり，ふんがかかるのを凶兆とする人は，今でもいる。

カラスを神のお使いとする神社は全国各地にあり，「からす祭り」が行われる。カラスに食物を与え，その食べ方で神意を占ったり，農作の豊凶を占ったりもする。

[表現]　黒いもののたとえに用い，「髪はからすの濡(ぬ)れ羽色」のように言う。「からすの行水」は，カラスが水浴びするときのように，入浴時間の短いことのたとえ。「からすの雌雄」は，カラスは雌，雄ともに黒くて区別しにくいので，２つのものがよく似ていて区別しにくいことを言う。カラスの鳴き声は「カーカー」。

[種類]　ハシボソガラスとハシブトガラスの２種が普通。

Cranes and Crows

● Cranes

As in the old saying that a crane lives for 1,000 years and a tortoise 10,000, the crane is a symbol of longevity. Drawing upon this, origami paper cranes* are often strung in strings of 1,000 and presented to patients recovering from an accident or illness. Japan Airlines also uses the crane in its logo, and the crane is a common motif on *furoshiki* used at weddings and other auspicious occasions.

Because of its beautiful white form, the crane is also symbolic of purity. The folk tale of *Tsuru Nyōbō* (Crane Wife), for example, is a story of the conflict between the pure-hearted crane and the despicable world of man. The crane also carries connotations of authority and excellence, and the term *tsuru no hitokoe* refers to the way a word from a man of authority or learning can overcome the objections of the masses. *Hakidame ni tsuru* (lit. crane in the trash) refers to a person of quality who is unaccountably in a lowly state.

Because the crane often flies with a twig or feather in its beak, legend has it that the crane brought the first ear of rice to begin Japan's tradition of rice cultivation. Another story tells how Toyotomi Hideyoshi wove crane feathers into a fabric to create a surcoat.

The three most common cranes found in Japan are the Japanese crane (Hokkaido's prefectural bird), hooded crane (Yamaguchi's prefectural bird), and white-naped crane.

● Crows

Crows have an unsavory reputation. Garbed in black, these scavengers with their ear-grating caw have traditionally been seen as harbingers of ill fortune in Japan as in the West.

An abnormal cawing of crows is said to portend a death, and many people believe even today that getting hit with crow droppings brands a person marked for disaster.

Yet there are also numerous shrines which celebrate the crow as messenger of the gods and hold Crow Festivals. Fortune-tellers in some areas claim to be able to tell if the harvest will be good or poor by the way a crow eats its prey.

The crow is symbolic of blackness, as in the expression that someone's hair is as black as crow's feathers slick with water. *Karasu no gyōzui* (a crow's dip) refers to a very quick bath. Finally, since both male and female crows are black and it is very difficult for non-crows to tell them apart, *karasu no shi-yū* is equivalent to the English six of one, half a dozen of the other to describe two things that are virtually indistinguishable. A crow's caw is *kā-kā* in Japanese.

The two most common species of crow in Japan are the carrion crow and the jungle crow.

6 松

［イメージ］ 松は常緑樹で，樹齢が長く，巨木となるところから，長寿や節操を表すめでたい木とされる。正月や祝いの席に松の生け花や盆栽を飾るのはこのためである。めでたく縁起のよいものなので，松は家紋にも選ばれ，その種類が100以上もある。

［由来］ 「神が天降るのを待つ」とする語源説があるように，松は古くから神木とされてきた。正月に立てる門松も神を招き寄せるというのが起源である。

［故事・伝説］ 全国各地に，文学作品，伝説，神社仏閣の縁起，有名な武将・高僧の故事や伝説と結びついた老樹・名木が1500以上もあり，天然記念物に指定されているものもある。『万葉集』には松に関する歌が約80種，能にも「高砂」「老松」など松にちなんだ名作がある。「高砂」は祝いの席で今でも謡われる。

［表現］ 「松の内」は，正月の松飾りのある間のことを言い，現在は1月7日までである。

［利用］ 松は日本の山野のいたるところに自生し，観賞・実用の両面で日本人の生活と切っても切れないものとなっている。岩手・群馬・福井・岡山・山口・島根・愛媛・沖縄の各県が県の木に指定しているのを見てもそれはわかる。日本に自生するのは，クロマツ・アカマツ・ゴヨウマツなど7種。植林・庭園樹・盆栽のほか，材は土木・建築・器具・パルプ用として広く用いられる。

日本の風景に松は欠かせない。白砂青松の舞子の浜（兵庫県），羽衣伝説の三保の松原（静岡県），虹の松原（佐賀県）の三大松原をはじめ，松の名所・歌枕は多い。ただ最近は開発や松食い虫の被害によって，昔の面影をとどめている所が少なくなった。

「松竹梅」はめでたいものとして，正月や慶事に生け花や盆栽として飾る。起源は中国で，中国では寒さに耐えて美しい姿を見せるところから画題とされていたのが，日本へ来てめでたいものとなった。飲食店などで料理の品質，価格を示すとき，上・中・下としないで松・竹・梅とする習慣がある。露骨さを避けるためであろう。

［マツタケ］ マツタケは，秋にアカマツ林に自生する。日本人は昔からこの芳香を持ったキノコを好み，マツタケ狩りなどをして楽しんできたが，最近はあまりとれなくなり，きわめて高価なものとなった。

Pine Trees

Because pines are majestic evergreens that grow into towering trees, they are taken as symbolic of longevity and steadfastness. Pine decorations or bonsai* are set out at New Year's and on other auspicious occasions. Thought to portend good things, the pine has been incorporated in over 100 family heraldic designs.*

As seen in the theory that says the pine stand "pining" for the day the gods descend to earth, the pine has long been accorded a certain reverence. Even the *kado-matsu* set out at New Year's are there to invite the gods in.

Pine trees abound throughout Japan as venerated figures in literature, historical legends, founding fables for shrines and temples, and other folklore, and there are over 1,500 famous old trees throughout Japan, some of which have been designated for protection as natural monuments.* There are about 80 poems about pine trees in the *Man'yōshu*, and many of the famous noh plays have pine themes, including *Takasago* (performed even today on festive occasions) and *Oimatsu* (Ancient Pine).

The term *matsu-no-uchi* refers to the time the New Year's *kado-matsu* are left out, today until January 7.

Indigenous to Japan's hills and plains, pine trees have long been valued for both scenic and practical purposes. The pine has been designated the official prefectural tree by Iwate, Gunma, Fukui, Okayama, Yamaguchi, Shimane, Ehime, and Okinawa. There are seven species native to Japan, including the *kuro-matsu* black pine, *aka-matsu* red pine, and *goyō-matsu* five-needled pine. In addition to being used for decorative purposes, in gardens, and in bonsai, pine are favored for construction material, furniture, pulp, and other industrial uses.

Pine is an essential part of any Japanese landscape, and there are many famous trees including those along white-sanded Maiko Beach (Hyogo pref), *Hagoromo*'s pined plain at Miho (Shizuoka pref), and *Niji no Matsubara* (Saga pref). However, even these scenic sites are losing their splendor to the encroachments of development and the pine weevil.

The *shō-chiku-bai* (pine, bamboo, and plum) combination signifies good fortune and is used in flower arrangements or bonsai on festive occasions. Originating in China as a trio able to withstand the cold and still appear beautiful, this combination took on connotations of good fortune when transplanted to Japan. Very often this same threesome is used in restaurants as names for the three levels of quality (and price) of its dishes.

Matsutake is a mushroom that grows naturally near red pine in the fall and is savored for its fragrant odor. People used to go *matsutake*-gathering, but it has become scarce in recent years and turned into an expensive gourmet item.

7 竹

［イメージ］　竹は強い萌芽力，まっすぐにすくすく伸びる生長力，常緑のすがすがしい姿，地下茎の豊かな広がり，などから繁栄の象徴とされる。竹はまた神霊を招くとされ，正月の門松に添える。

中国では竹を，梅・ラン・菊とともに四君子と言い，君子のように節操の正しい植物とみなしている。さっぱりした性格を「竹を割ったような」と言うように，竹は淡白さ，純粋さをも表す。

［伝説・昔話］　竹にちなむ伝説は中国，日本ともに多い。「竹林の七賢」は，中国の西晋時代に，世俗を避けて竹林にこもり清談に時を費やした7人を言う。昔話では日本の『竹取物語』（9世紀）が有名。竹から生まれたかぐや姫が，5人の貴族と帝の求婚を退け，8月15日の満月の夜に月の世界に帰っていくという物語。最古の仮名による物語文学である。

［行事］　年中行事にも魔よけとして竹，笹が取り入れられている。関西では1月10日の初えびすに，商売の神恵比寿さまに参って商売繁盛を祈り，笹に札・大判・小判・俵・槌などを結び付けた縁起物の「福笹」を買う。6月20日，京都の北郊鞍馬寺では，大蛇を退治した故事にちなみ，雄蛇になぞらえた青竹を切る竹切式を行う。7月7日の七夕には，笹竹に5色の短冊に願いごとなどを書いて飾る。

［表現］　「竹に木を接ぐ」は不調和なことをするたとえ。「破竹の勢い」は，竹を割るときのように，とどまることを知らない猛烈な勢いのこと。「やぶ医者」は下手な医者のこと。竹やぶの葉は少しの風でもザワザワするところから，ちょっとした風邪でも大騒ぎをする医者という意味だが，真偽のほどはわからない。「やぶ蛇」は，やぶをつついて蛇を出す，つまりしなくてもよいことをして，自分の不利を招くたとえ。

［利用］　日本の温暖多湿の気候が適しているため，日本の竹は美しく，日本画の重要な題材となっている。「竹にすずめ」，「竹にとら」は図柄の組み合せの妙を言う。

竹は日常生活の中でも重要で，植栽用のほか，建築や生活調度品の材料になる。尺八，能管も竹が材料である。地震のとき竹やぶへ逃げると安全と言う。竹やぶは地下茎が網のように広がり，ちょうどハンモックに乗ったような状態になるからである。

Bamboo

Bamboo is a very strong plant that grows very straight, very tall, and very quickly. With a sturdy root structure, it is symbolic of prosperity. Bamboo is also used in the New Year's *kado-matsu* decorations for its attraction to the gods.

In China, bamboo is grouped with *ume*, orchid, and chrysanthemum as one of the four gentlemanly plants because it is supposed to be as straight-arrow as a true gentleman. Simple and unadorned, the bamboo is symbolic of purity and innocence, as in the adjectival phrase "*take o watta yō na*" (like fresh-split bamboo).

Bamboo figures in many ancient tales from both China and Japan. *Chikurin no Shichi-ken* (Seven Sages of the Bamboo Grove), for instance, is a Chinese tale of seven scholars who fled the vulgar life of the Western Chin dynasty and lived pure lives in a bamboo grove. Among the best-known Japanese tales is the 9th-century *Taketori Monogatari* about a beautiful maiden who was born of bamboo and, rejecting numerous suitors, ascended to the heavens on a moon-lit night in mid-August. This is, in fact, the oldest known narrative literature in *kana* script.

Bamboo and bamboo-like *sasa* are used in many festivals to ward off evil. In the Kansai area, for example, merchants pray to the god of commerce (Ebisu) and purchase lucky *sasa* branches decorated with replicas of coins, straw rice bundles,* and mallets* at Hatsu Ebisu* on January 10. On June 20, the festival at Kyoto's Kuramadera Temple celebrating the death of the great serpent features the cutting of green bamboo symbolizing the serpent. Tanabata, on July 7, includes writing one's aspirations on five-color paper streamers and hanging them on bamboo branches for the gods to see.

Putting bamboo and wood together is synonymous with disharmony. *Hachiku no ikioi* indicates the powerful momentum needed to break bamboo. A *yabu-isha*, though its etymology is not clear, refers to a quack doctor, perhaps because just as bamboo leaves rustle in the slightest breeze, an incompetent doctor makes a great to-do about even the slightest ailment. Finally, *yabu-hebi* comes from the likelihood that poking a clump of bamboo may well flush a snake. It is reaping ill fortune from an unnecessary act, a little like not letting sleeping dogs lie.

Because Japan's warm, humid climate is well-suited to bamboo cultivation, bamboo is very pretty and is a popular motif in traditional Japanese paintings of sparrows or tigers in bamboo groves. Bamboo is also an integral part of Japanese life, as a decorative plant, building material, and numerous kinds of utensils for daily use. Many wind instruments* are also made of bamboo. For years, people were told to run into the bamboo groves in the event of an earthquake because the bamboo's strong root structure would hold the earth together.

8 桜

［イメージ］ 桜は日本の国花である。日本人にとって，桜は花の中の花であり，「花」と言えば桜を考える。欧米人のように，桜からサクランボのなる桜の木を思い浮かべるようなことはない。

一般に桜はめでたいものとされる。桜の咲く4月に入学し，入社する習慣のある日本では，希望に満ちた第一歩，明るい未来といったイメージが桜と強く結び付いている。また花びらの塩漬けに熱湯を注いだ桜湯は，めでたいものとして結婚式など祝いの席に出される。

めでたさとは逆に，日本人は桜の花に滅亡，死も見る。昔の武士や第2次世界大戦以前の軍人は，戦場で桜のように潔く散るのを本領としたし，歌舞伎で桜の花の出る場面は怪異が跳梁（ちょうりょう）し，悲運が起こることが多い。「桜は七日」という言い方があるように，花の盛りがきわめて短く，一夜の風に誘われて散ってしまうから，桜に潔さ，はかなさを感じたためであろう。

［名歌］ 梅の奈良時代を経て，国風文化の隆盛とともに，平安時代には桜が最も愛好されるようになる。『古今和歌集』にも桜の歌が断然多い。以来1000年有余，その伝統は続き，桜を取り入れた文学作品や故事・伝説は枚挙にいとまがない。

日本人の心情をよくとらえた名歌2首を挙げる。

▷願はくは花の下にて春死なむそのきさらぎのもちづきのころ

平安時代末期から鎌倉時代初期に活躍し，桜の詩人と言われた西行（さいぎょう）の歌の1つ。彼は歌のとおり2月に死に，希望に従って桜のある塚に眠っている。西行の歌で構成した夢幻能「西行桜」がある。

▷敷島の大和（やまと）心を人問はば朝日ににほふ山桜花

江戸時代中期の国学者本居宣長の作。清楚な山桜を大和心の表象と見た名歌である。

［表現］ 「花より団子」は，風流より実利を取ること。「さくら」は売り手となれ合いで買ってみせ，他の客の購買心をあおる者を言う。元は芝居の無料の見物人を言い，桜の花見が無料でできることからきている。「花にあらし」は，好事には障害の多いことのたとえ。

［種類］ 現在多く見られるのは明治初年から広まったソメイヨシノである。それ以前はヤマザクラが普通であった。日本では，花見の時期になると，天気予報といっしょに桜前線（ソメイヨシノの開花前線）の北上予想が発表される。

Sakura

The cherry blossom is Japan's national flower—the flower of flowers, and synonymous with the word flower. Japanese love the cherry tree not for its juicy red fruit but for its fluffy pink blossoms.

The cherry blossom is a felicitous symbol. For children just starting school and graduates starting in new jobs alike, April's cherry blossoms suggest a bright future. *Sakura-yu*, a tea-like drink of salted cherry petals, is served at weddings and other auspicious times.

Yet there is also a dark side. To old-time samurai, there was no greater glory than to die on the battlefield like scattered cherry blossoms. In kabuki dramas, cherry blossoms often portend a villain's rampage or imminent disaster. Resplendent in full bloom, cherry blossoms seldom last more than a week, and they are easily swept away with one strong wind, a fleeting beauty that suggests purity and transience.

Plum (*ume*) blossoms were favored in the Nara period, but gave way to the cherry with the emergence of Heian culture. *Kokin Wakashū* (Collection of Ancient and Modern Poetry) has numerous poems on cherry blossoms, a tradition which has continued for over 1,000 years. There seems no end to cherry blossom literature and legends.

Two poems tell the Japanese fondness for the cherry blossom.

Ne-ga-wa-ku wa	I would die in the spring,
ha-na no shi-ta ni te	under the blossoms,
ha-ru shi-na-mu	in the second month
so-no ki-sa-ra-gi no	at the time of
mo-chi-zu-ki no ko-ro	the full moon.

Written by Saigyo, a poet of the late Heian and early Kamakura period noted for his verses on cherry blossoms, these lines proved prophetic, for Saigyo did indeed die in the second month of the lunar calendar and cherry trees shade his grave. *Saigyō Zakura* is a noh performance based on Saigyo's poetry.

The second is by Motoori Norinaga, a mid-Edo *Kokugaku* scholar.

Shi-ki-shi-ma no	If one should ask,
Ya-ma-to-go-ko-ro o	what is the spirit of Japan—
hi-to to-wa ba	Shining in the morning sun,
a-sa-hi ni ni-o-u	these blossoms of the
ya-ma-za-ku-ra-ba-na	mountain cherry.

The phrase *hana yori dango* (dumplings over flowers) refers to a preference for tangible goods rather than elegance. A *sakura* is a shill who raves about his mock purchase. Originally referring to people who were admitted to plays free, the term arose because cherry blossoms are free for the viewing. *Hana ni arashi* (flowers before the storm) suggests the bad likely to follow good fortune.

Most cherry trees today are *somei-yoshino*, which supplanted the mountain cherry in the early Meiji period. Spring weather forecasts include reports on the "*sakura* front" as the blossoms sweep north.

9 梅・桃

●梅

［イメージ］ 梅は清楚，清雅，気品，忍耐などのイメージを持つ。早春，百花にさきがけ，高い香気を放って咲く梅の花の愛好者は多い。

［故事・伝説］ 梅は奈良時代に中国から渡来した。当時は万事が中国風であったから，中国に倣って梅が好まれ，『万葉集』では萩に次いで118首が詠まれている（桜は第5位で40首）。

平安時代，菅原道真が九州の大宰府に流されるとき，「東風吹かば匂ひおこせよ梅の花あるじなしとて春な忘れそ」と自邸の庭で梅の木に詠みかけた別離の歌は有名。これがもとで，その梅の枝が大宰府まで飛んで行って根づいたという飛び梅伝説が生まれた。

［表現］ 「梅にウグイス」は取り合わせのよいこと。「梅に桜」は美しい物やよい物が並んでいることのたとえ。

［利用］ 花は白色，淡紅色，紅色など。花木用は庭木，盆栽として観賞する。各地に名木があり，天然記念物に指定されたものもある。果樹用は6月ごろ熟した果実を梅干し・梅酒・梅酢などにする。

水戸の偕楽園，九州の太宰府天満宮など梅の名所が各地にある。茨城・福岡・大分県では郷土の花，茨城・大分では県の木になっている。

●桃

［イメージ］ 『古事記』に，桃を投げて神の窮地を救ったという神話があるように，悪魔を払う魔よけの木とされる。桃は中国原産で，中国でも，古来，邪気を払う仙果とされ，桃源郷を彩る花であった。

［故事］ 平安時代，清少納言は紅梅を花木の第一としたのに対し，紫式部は近くで眺める桃が勝るとした。

［風習］ 3月3日のひな祭りは桃の節句と呼ばれ，ひな人形といっしょに桃の花を飾る。

［昔話］ 桃は五大昔話の1つ「桃太郎」を連想させる。

［表現］ 「桃栗3年柿8年」は芽ばえてから実がなるまでの年数を言う。桃は成長も早いが寿命も短い。

［利用］ 桃は梅の後，桜の前に，淡紅色または白色の豪華な花をつける。観賞用のハナモモは採果用とは別品種。

Plum and Peach

● Plum

The plum, *ume*, is neatness, purity, dignity, and patience. Blossoming in early spring, its sweet fragrance has won it many admirers.

Introduced from China in the Nara period when everything Chinese was in vogue, the plum figures in 118 *Man'yōshū* poems, second only to the Japanese bush clover (*hagi*) in popularity as a motif. (The cherry ranks fifth with only 40 poems.)

One of the most famous poems the Heian scholar-statesman Sugawara no Michizane* wrote before being exiled to Dazaifu* in Kyushu is a poignant ode to the plum in his Kyoto garden. Legend has it that Michizane's plum tree flew to Dazaifu and took root there in response to this poem:

Ko-chi fu-ka ba	When the east wind blows
ni-o-i o-ko-se-yo	release your fragrance,
u-me no ha-na	flower of the plum.
a-ru-ji na-shi to-te	Even without your master there
ha-ru na wa-su-re so	forget not the spring.

Ume ni uguisu (warbler in a plum) refers to a perfect match, and *ume ni sakura* (plum plus cherry) means a pairing of beautiful objects.

Blossoming white, pink, or red, plums are planted as ornamental trees and make exquisite bonsai. There are famous plum trees throughout Japan, some protected under the Cultural Properties Law. The plum is picked in June to be salted* or used for plum wine or vinegar.

Mito's Kairakuen Park and Dazaifu's Tenmangu Shrine are noted for their plum blossoms. The plum is the Ibaraki and Oita prefectural flower and tree and the Fukuoka prefectural flower.

● Peach

The peach is considered good for warding off evil. It is mentioned in the *Kojiki* (Record of Ancient Matters) as an instrument of salvation used to rescue a god from predicament. In China, where it originated, the peach tree was believed to keep away ills of all kinds while its flowers were symbols of the earthly paradise of Shangri-La.

In the Heian period, Sei Shonagon declared the red plum supreme among all flowers while Murasaki Shikibu claimed the peach was best.

The *momo no sekku* on March 3 is also celebrated as the Doll Festival, and sprigs of peach blossoms are commonly displayed with the ornamental *hina-ningyō* dolls. *Momotarō*, one of the best-known Japanese folk stories, is about a heroic youth born from a peach.

The peach grows quickly but has a short life span. Peach and chestnut trees are said to take three years to mature, and the persimmon eight.

White or pale pink, the peach blossoms after the plum and before the cherry. The ornamental peach is a different variety from the trees cultivated for their fruit.

10 幽霊

［イメージ］　幽霊は，うっとうしい雨の夜，草木も眠る丑三つ時（午前2時～2時半）に，川端や井戸の柳の下で，生前のままの姿で現れる。幽霊は怨恨によって出るのであるから，まず「恨めしや」と言う。それから，こまごまと恨みを述べていく。これが中世から近世にかけて，文学的，演劇的に手が加えられてでき上がった幽霊の型である。幽霊はふつう死霊（死者の霊）で，亡霊と言うこともある。

幽霊には足がないとされ，幽霊が出るとまず足の有無を見るというのが日本の常識（ただし，歌舞伎や能には足のある幽霊が出る）。また，幽霊の話は夏のものと考えられていて，夏になると歌舞伎・落語・テレビなどがいっせいに怪談の特集を組む。この風習はすでに江戸時代からあって，当時は明かりを1つずつ消しながら怪談を次々に話し合い，真っ暗になったとき幽霊が出るとした百物語の会が開かれた。

［妖怪との違い］　幽霊が妖怪・お化けと異なる点は，現れる時と場所が一定しない，縁故のある人の前に生前の姿のままで出る，関係のある特定個人にしか認められない，など。

［怪談］　『日本霊異記』（9世紀）や『今昔物語』（12世紀）のころから日本に怪談は多い。中でも知られるのは，怪異短編小説集の『雨月物語』（18世紀）である。これをもとにした映画「雨月物語」は，1953年のベニス映画祭でグランプリを受賞した。

「耳なし芳一」は，芳一という琵琶法師が滅亡した平氏一門の亡霊の前で琵琶を弾唱し，それを他言したため両耳をもぎとられる話。小泉八雲が『怪談』（1904年）に書いて広く知られるようになった。

1825年に初演された歌舞伎『東海道四谷怪談』は通称『四谷怪談』として知られる。浪人民谷伊右衛門が，女房のお岩を殺し後妻の縁で出世しようとするが，お岩の亡霊に悩まされるという筋。実説・風説を取り混ぜて四世鶴屋南北が作った，怪談物・生世話物の傑作である。

落語の『怪談牡丹灯籠』は，1861～64年に成立した人情話。艶麗な怪談話として有名である。中国の怪奇小説や実話を参考にして，落語家三遊亭円朝が作った。お露という娘が浪人萩原新三郎を恋い慕って亡くなり，盆の13日の夜，女中お米が下げる牡丹灯籠を持って，足のないとされている幽霊がカランコロンとげたの音を響かせて新三郎を訪れるという設定で，複雑な話がからみ合い，結局悪人が滅び，善人が栄える話になっている。

Ghosts*

Japanese ghosts are said to appear on dreary, drizzly nights in the third hour of the cow (2:00-2:30 a.m.) when even the trees and grasses sleep. Most often materializing under willow trees beside rivers or wells, they are nearly always the spirits of people who have died unhappy deaths and bear grudges. A ghost's first words are "*urameshiya*" (a curse upon you) followed by a long recital of its grievances. This is the ghost depicted in the literature and drama of the middle ages and early modern Japanese history. Such specters are also called *shiryō* or *bōrei*.

The Japanese ghost is distinguished by its lack of feet, something that is always checked for in confrontations with such spirits. (As exceptions, kabuki and noh ghosts are expected to have feet.) Ghosts are assumed to be summer creatures, and ghost stories are standard fare on summer kabuki drama, *rakugo* stories, and television programs. A popular pastime in the Edo period was to take turns telling ghost stories, blowing out a lamp with the end of each story until everything was plunged into darkness and all was right for the ghosts to appear.

Unlike *yōkai* apparitions and *bakemono* goblins, ghosts can appear anywhere anytime, generally taking the same form as they had before dying, and can often be seen only by the people they are appearing to.

Ghosts stories are to be found in such ancient compilations as the *Nihon Ryōiki* (9th century) and the *Konjaku Monogatari* (12th century). An especially well known compilation of short ghosts stories is the *Ugetsu Monogatari* (18th century), and a film based on this work won the Grand Prix at the 1953 Venice Film Festival.

Miminashi Hoichi (Earless Hoichi) was popularized by Lafcadio Hearn* in his 1904 book *Kwaidan*. In it, an itinerant *biwa* player, Hoichi, chances upon the spirits of the Taira* clan which had been wiped out by the rival Minamoto clan. He plays his *biwa* for them, but the spirits tear his ears off when he recounts his strange experience to others.

First performed in 1825, *Tōkaidō Yotsuya Kaidan* (often called simply *Yotsuya Kaidan*) is the most famous kabuki ghost play. A masterless samurai kills his wife so that he may make a more advantageous match with another woman, but she comes back as a revengeful ghost to haunt him. A mixture of real and imaginary events, this play written by Tsuruya Nanboku IV is a good example of the realistic ghost story genre of kabuki drama.

*Botan-dōrō** is a popular *rakugo* ghost story combining elements of Chinese ghost stories and true incidents written by the *rakugo* master Sanyutei Encho. About a young maiden named Otsuyu and a masterless samurai named Hagiwara Shinzaburo, it has all of the trappings of the traditional story, including love, death, the clip-clopping of wooden *geta*,* and justice triumphant in the end.

11 妖怪(1)──鬼・天狗

●鬼

[イメージ]　人に似て，牛の角とトラのきばがあり，口は耳まで裂け，裸でトラの皮のふんどしを締めている。人を捕らえて食うと言われる。非情，怪力，勇猛の象徴である。風神・雷神など荒々しい神を鬼の姿で表す。

[行事]　節分(立春の前日)の夕暮れ，悪鬼を払い，疫病を除くために，ヒイラギの枝にイワシの頭を刺したものを戸口に立て，いった大豆を，「福は内，鬼は外」と言いながらまく風習がある。

[伝説]　平安時代，平城京の羅生門に住む鬼は，毛深くて爪が長く，刀のような歯を持っていて，人を捕まえた。渡辺綱がその鬼の片腕を切り落としたという。また，丹波国大江山に住む酒呑童子という鬼(盗賊)は，財をかすめ，婦女子を略奪するので，源頼光やその四天王の渡辺綱・坂田金時たちによって退治された。この話は絵巻・御伽草子・草双紙・浄瑠璃・歌舞伎などの題材となっている。

[昔話]　昔話の「桃太郎」や「一寸法師」などに，鬼は重要な敵役として登場する。

[表現]　「鬼に金棒」は，ますます強さが増すたとえ。「鬼のいぬ間に洗濯」は，怖い人の留守中に楽をすること。「鬼の首をとったよう」は，大成功を喜ぶようすの表現。

●天狗

[イメージ]　天狗は深山に住み，神通力があって空中を自由に飛行できる。大天狗は赤顔で鼻が高く，羽うちわを持つ。その部下に烏天狗，木葉天狗がいるとされる。

天狗は山伏が祭った山の神の像なので，山伏の姿をしている。

[世間話]　天狗の思想は中国伝来。平安時代，天狗は流星やトビとみられ，人についたり，未来を予言した。鎌倉時代には天狗による「神隠し」(人が突然行方不明になること)が，しばしばあったという。

天狗のしわざとされる話は多い。「天狗倒し」は理由がないのに突然暴風のような激しい音がして物が倒れること。「天狗笑い」は深山で高笑いする声や多数の人の声が聞こえること。

[表現]　「天狗になる」は，天狗のように鼻を高くすること，つまり自分について自慢することを言う。

Monsters and Apparitions (1)

● *Oni**

Resembling humans, but having the horns of a cow and the fangs of a tiger, the *oni* has a mouth running from ear to ear and wears a tigerskin loincloth. *Oni* are said to eat people, and they represent ruthlessness, prodigious strength, and daring. Strong and virile gods such as the gods of wind and thunder are depicted as *oni*.

At *setsubun* (the day before the first day of spring on the lunar calendar), it is customary to tack a sardine head pierced with a holly branch over the door and scatter roasted soybeans from the entrance, chanting, "*Fuku wa uchi, oni wa soto!*" ("In with good luck, out with demons!") to drive away evil spirits and disease.

There is an ancient tale from the Heian period about a hairy *oni* with long claws and saber-like teeth who lived in the capital city's Rashomon* gate and captured people passing through. The warrior Watanabe no Tsuna is said to have cut off one of this creature's arms. Another *oni*, a thief named Shutendoji who lived on Mt. Oe in the Tamba district, preyed upon women and young girls until he was captured by Minamoto no Yorimitsu and his warriors Watanabe no Tsuna, and Sakata no Kintoki. This tale of daring has inspired many of the *otogi-zōshi* stories of feudal Japan, the popular literature of the Edo period, the *jōruri* puppet theater, and kabuki. Folk tales in which *oni* appear include *Momotarō* (Peach Boy) and *Issun-bōshi** (One Inch Boy).

Oni ni kanabō refers to making one invincible (by giving an *oni* an iron pike), while *oni no inu ma ni sentaku* expresses the relief one feels when someone one fears is away. To achieve a major success is likened to beheading an *oni* as in *oni no kubi o totta yō*.

● *Tengu**

A mythical mountain creature, the *tengu* has supernatural powers that allow him to fly about. The *Ō-tengu* or Great Tengu has a red face and immensely long nose, and carries a feathered fan. Under him are *karasu tengu* (crow *tengu*) and *konoha tengu* (leaf *tengu*). The *tengu* are worshipped by *yamabushi*,* mountain ascetics, and are usually depicted wearing the *yamabushi*'s distinctive clothing.

The *tengu* idea is of Chinese origin, and in the Heian period falling stars and kites were thought to be *tengu* capable of possessing people's spirits and predicting the future. In the Kamakura period, sudden disappearances were attributed to kidnapping by *tengu*.

Many natural phenomena were thought to have been the doings of *tengu*. When an object falls over with a crash for no apparent reason, a *tengu* is said to have pushed it over. *Tengu warai* refers to distant sounds heard in the mountains of shrill laughter or of many people speaking. To become a *tengu* is to grow a long nose, in other words to become conceited.

12 妖怪(2)—河童(かっぱ)・1つ目小僧

●河童(*)

[イメージ] 河童は川や池，沼など淡水に生息する水陸両生の動物である。身長は1m内外，4，5歳の子供のようで，目が丸く，口がとがり，手足に水かきを持つ。肌は赤黒または青黒，全体がぬめぬめし，鱗甲(りんこう)がある。頭髪が少なく，中に皿が隠れ，その皿に水があれば活動力があると言われる。相撲が好きで人によく挑戦する。また，人や牛馬を水に引き込んで，肛門(こうもん)から肝をとる。

河童は人に害を与えるけれども，人に捕らえられてわび証文を書いた，秘伝の妙薬をくれた，田植えを手伝ってくれた，田の水を引いてくれた，といった話が各地に残されているように，どこか憎めない，愛敬のある一面がある。よく漫画の題材にされるのはそのせいである。

[由来] 妖怪は，神が落ちぶれたものと言われ，河童も水底に住む小童神が変化したものとされてきたが，最近では，妖怪と神とは別で，人々によって祭られる超自然が神，祭られない超自然が妖怪という説が出されている。

[伝説] 河童の伝説は，北海道を除く全国に分布する。地方によって形態・習性が異なり，川太郎，ガタロなど異名も多い。

[表現] すし屋でキュウリを「かっぱ」と言うのは，キュウリが河童の好物とされているから。キュウリを食べながら川を渡ると，河童に川に引き入れられると言われる。「おかっぱ」という髪型は，河童の髪型からきた。「河童の川流れ」は，達人でも時には失敗することのたとえ。「河童の屁(へ)」または「屁の河童」は，全く容易でなんでもないこと。

●一つ目小僧(*)

[イメージ] 一つ目小僧は，その名のとおり目が1つの妖怪である。ふつう，口が耳まで裂け，人を脅かすとき舌を出す。一本足で飛び飛びに歩くとか，小僧でなく大入道であるとか，地方によって形態はさまざまである。

[由来] 昔，神の名代(みょうだい)である神主を普通の人と区別するため，片目を傷つけた。その神主の霊が妖怪に落ちぶれたというのが従来の見方である。

[風習] 関東地方では，旧暦の2月8日(事初め)，12月8日(事納め)の夜に，一つ目が来るとされ，門口に目かごを掲げ，ヒイラギの枝を挿して，静かに家に引きこもる風習があった。長野県や奈良県でも，一つ目が出て人を食うとされている日があり，その日は山に入らなかった。

Monsters and Apparitions (2)

● *Kappa**

The *kappa* is a supernatural amphibious creature residing in rivers, lakes, and swamps. Around a meter tall, about the size of a four-or-five-year old child, the *kappa* has large round eyes, a protruding mouth, and webbed hands and feet. Its skin is either dark red or green, slimy, and covered with scales. The *kappa* has very little hair on the top of its head which is shaped like a saucer. As long as this saucer is full of water, the *kappa* retains its supernatural powers. A great sumo lover, the *kappa* will often challenge people to wrestle with it. Another, more gruesome, favorite pastime is dragging people, horses, and cows into the water and pulling out their livers through the anus.

Although the *kappa* does harm people sometimes, there are many tales of contrite *kappa* asking forgiveness for their mischief, giving people magical potions, or helping with farm chores. Cartoons have contributed to the *kappa*'s lovable but mischievous image. These spirits are said to be fallen water gods, but the trend recently has been to distinguish between gods (supernatural forces that are worshipped) and spirits (supernatural forces that are not worshipped).

Tales of *kappa* are to be found throughout Japan, except Hokkaido. The *kappa*'s appearance and characteristics vary somewhat by region, and it has many other names such as *kawatarō* and *gataro*.

Cucumber are called *kappa* in sushi shops because they are thought to be a *kappa* favorite. To cross a river while eating cucumbers is to tempt a *kappa* to pull you into the water. Bobbed hairstyles are called *okappa* because they resemble the *kappa*'s coiffure. The unexpected failure of someone who is expected to excel is said to be *kappa no kawa nagare* (a drowning *kappa*). *Kappa no he* and *he no kappa* (a *kappa*'s breaking wind) refers to something that is very easy to do—a breeze.

● *Hitotsume-kozō**

Characterized by a single eye, the *hitotsume-kozō* has a mouth that goes from ear to ear and sticks out its tongue to scare people. Some stories depict it hopping about on a single leg, while in others it takes the form of a giant ogre rather than a young boy.

The *hitotsume-kozō* are said to come from the ancient messengers of the gods, who were half-blinded to distinguish them from mere mortals.

In the Kanto region *hitotsume* were thought to appear on the nights of the eighth days of the second and twelfth lunar months, the days marking the beginning and the end of the year. It was customary to remain indoors on these nights and to place openwork baskets pierced with holly branches against the entrance of the home to ward away the evil apparition. In Nagano and Nara prefectures there were certain days on which *hitotsume* were thought to eat people, and people did not venture into the mountains on these days.

Notes

■1. Dogs and Cats

Natsume Soseki (夏目漱石) (1867-1916) Novelist and English literature scholar. With Mori Ogai (1862-1922), one of Japan's most important modern writers. *Wagahai wa Neko de Aru* (I Am a Cat) was his first novel.

■2. Horses and Cows

shabu-shabu (しゃぶしゃぶ) A dish of thinly sliced meat dipped in boiling water and eaten with a sauce and various condiments.

gyū-don (牛丼) Slices of cooked beef and vegetables atop a bowl of rice.

△Hachiko

△*Maneki-neko*

△*Gyūdon*

△ *Ceramic tanuki*

△*Ō-nyūdō* (huge monster)

■3. *Tanuki* and *Kitsune*

ceramic statues (信楽焼の像) The most popular ceramic *tanuki* are those made in the town of Shigaraki in southern Shiga prefecture.

Shojoji no Tanuki Bayashi (証城寺のたぬきばやし) A legend about many large and small *tanuki* who sing and beat their round bellies, frolicking in a *bon-odori*. These *tanuki* were alleged to appear in the yard of a temple in Kisarazu in Chiba prefecture on the night of the harvest moon.

■4. Sea Bream and Carp

Empress Jingu (神功皇后) A legendary figure who appears in the *Kojiki* and the *Nihon Shoki*, consort of the Emperor Chuai. She is said to have mustered an army and sailed to conquer the kingdom of Silla on the Korean peninsula.

■5. Cranes and Crows

origami paper cranes (折りづる) See picture.

■6. Pine Trees

natural monuments (天然記念物) Animals, plants, natural formations, and the regions in which they exist that have been

△ *Origami paper cranes*

△Bonsai

designated as important natural monuments by the Minister of Education.

●Some heraldic designs

■7. Bamboo

mallets (槌) By shaking one of these magical mallets and repeating the name of whatever one desires, one will be granted every wish.

Hatsu Ebisu (初えびす) Festivals honoring the god Ebisu are held on January 10 and 20 and October 20 in many regions as well as on the twentieth day of the eleventh month by the lunar calendar. The first, held on January 10, is called Hatsu Ebisu.

wind instruments (尺八, 能管) The five-hole *shakuhachi* is the more commonly played flute. The *nōkan* has seven holes and is used in noh accompaniment.

△Straw rice bundle

△Mallet

■9. Plum and Peach

Sugawara no Michizane (菅原道真) (845-903) A court official exiled to Dazaifu in Kyushu. A scholar and master calligrapher, Sugawara is celebrated today as Tenjin-sama, god of letters.

Dazaifu (大宰府) A regional administrative post during the era of the *ritsuryō* government located in what is now Fukuoka prefecture.

salted (梅干し) *Ume-boshi* are plums pickled in salt and purple perilla leaves and dried in the sun.

■10. Ghosts

Lafcadio Hearn (小泉八雲) (1850-1904) Author and translator, Lafcadio Hearn was born in Greece, raised in Dublin, and arrived in Japan in 1890. He wrote many works introducing Japan to the world, among them *Glimpses of Unfamiliar Japan* (1894) and *Kokoro* (1896).He is known in Japan by his Japanese name, Koizumi Yakumo.

Taira (平) Beginning with Taira no Kiyomori, the Taira clan dominated court politics near the end of the Heian period. The

△*Ghost* (by Maruyama Okyo, 18th century)

clan was annihilated in the Battle of Dannoura, fought against their arch-rival the Minamoto clan, only 20 years after they had first risen to power. The *Heike Monogatari* telling of the rise and fall of the Taira clan is colored by the Buddhist concept of transiency.

botan-dōrō (牡丹灯籠) A lantern made of silk crepe with a *botan* (peony) motif.

■11. Monsters and Apparitions (1)

Issun-bōshi (一寸法師) The story of a boy only one *sun* (approximately three centimeters) tall. With a needle as a sword and a bowl and chopstick as boat and oar, Issun-boshi makes his way to Kyoto where he becomes a retainer to a princess. On his way to make an offering to Kannon for the princess, Issun-boshi is accosted by two *oni* whom he quickly defeats. He uses the *oni's* magical mallet, called *uchide-no-kozuchi*, to make himself tall and becomes a brave warrior.

△*Botan-dōrō*

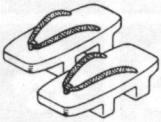

△*Geta*

△Rashomon

△*Yamabushi*

●Monsters and apparitions

Appendix and Indices

Chronology of Japanese History……342
日本史年表

Japanese Index ……348
日本語索引

English Index……359
英語索引

Chronology of Japanese History
日本史年表

◇Cultural events
◆Political events

Period	Year	Events
Diluvial (洪積世)	BC 30,000	◇First human occupation of central Japan (exact date uncertain) ◇Old Stone Age; chipped stone tools; no pottery
Jomon (縄文時代)	10,000	◇New Stone Age; Jomon pottery; chipped and polished stone and bone tools 〈縄文文化時代〉
Yayoi (弥生時代)	c.300	◇Rice cultivation, bronze, and iron introduced from the continent 〈弥生文化時代〉 ◇Yayoi pottery is produced and metal and stone tools used 〈弥生土器〉
	c.184	◆The Chinese history *Wei Zhi* mentions a nation called Yamatai with a woman ruler named Himiko whose power extended to more than 30 other polities 〈卑弥呼王となる〉
Kofun (古墳時代)	AD c.300	◇Large tomb mounds built marking advent of the Tomb Culture 〈古墳文化の発生〉 ◆Most of Japan united under the Yamato court 〈大和朝廷全国統一〉 ◇Korean immigrants from the Paekche kingdom introduce continental culture to Japan. 〈大陸文化伝来〉
	c.538	◇Buddhism introduced into Japan when the king of Paekche sends envoys with Buddhist images and sutras (one theory dates this 552) 〈仏教伝来〉
	593	◆Prince Shotoku becomes regent for Empress Suiko 〈聖徳太子摂政〉
	603	◆12-cap rank system established within Yamato court 〈冠位十二階制定〉
	604	◆Seventeen-Article Constitution is drafted legitimizing centralized Yamato state and emperor's supreme authority 〈憲法十七条制定〉
	607	◆Ono no Imoko sent as court emissary to Sui China 〈遣隋使派遣〉 ◇Horyuji constructed and Asuka culture flourishes 〈法隆寺建立・飛鳥文化〉
	630	◆Inugami no Mitasuki sent as imperial emissary to Tang court in China 〈遣唐使派遣〉
	645	◆Taika Reforms instituted after Soga family's dominance of imperial court ends with assassination of Soga no Iruka by Prince Naka no Oe and others. Emperor Tenmu ascends the throne using the reign name of Taika 〈大化の改新〉
	680	◇Emperor Tenmu constructs Yakushiji 〈薬師寺創建〉
	701	◆Taiho Code of laws completed establishing a single code for the whole nation 〈大宝律令完成〉
	708	◇Wado Kaiho, first Japanese coins, minted. 〈和銅開珎〉
	710	◆Capital moved to Heijokyo(now Nara), city modeled on the Chinese capital of Chang-an 〈平城京遷都〉

Period	Year	Events
Nara (奈良時代)	712	◇*Kojiki*, Japan's first official history, compiled by O no Yasumaro and Hieda no Are 〈『古事記』〉
	713	◇Provincial governments ordered to compile regional records known as *fudoki* 〈『風土記』〉
	720	◇*Nihon Shoki*, first of Six National Histories, compiled by Prince Toneri and O no Yasumaro 〈『日本書紀』〉
	751	◇*Kaifūsō*, first anthology of Chinese poetry written by Japanese, is compiled 〈『懐風藻』〉
	752	◇Ceremonies held at Todaiji to commemorate completion of Great Buddha 〈東大寺大仏開眼供養〉
	754	◇Chinese monk Ganjin introduces Ritsu Buddhism 〈律宗伝わる〉
	?	◇*Man'yōshū*, first anthology of *waka* poetry and written with *man'yō-gana*, compiled 〈『万葉集』〉
Heian (平安時代)	794	◆Capital moved to Heiankyo (now Kyoto) to escape the dominance of Nara's Buddhist temples and to right corruption in imperial court 〈平安京遷都〉
	805	◇Saicho establishes Tendai sect of Buddhism 〈天台宗の開宗〉
	806	◇Kukai establishes Shingon sect of Buddhism〈真言宗の開宗〉
	807	◇Inbe no Hironari compiles the *Kogo Shūi*, a collection of myths and legends not found in the *Kojiki* or *Nihon Shoki* 〈『古語拾遺』〉
	c.822	◇Buddhist monk Kyokai writes *Nihon Ryōiki* (Miraculous Stories of Japan), the earliest Japanese example of Buddhist fables 〈『日本霊異記』〉
	887	◆Fujiwara no Mototsune appointed *kampaku*, thereby cementing Fujiwara control over imperial court 〈藤原基経関白〉
	894	◆Sugawara no Michizane orders halt to missions to Tang China 〈遣唐使中止〉
	901	◆Sugawara no Michizane exiled to Dazaifu in Kyushu 〈菅原道真大宰府に左遷〉
	905	◇*Kokin Wakashū*, first imperial anthology of *waka* poetry, compiled by Ki no Tsurayuki, Ki no Tomonori, and others 〈『古今和歌集』〉
	c.935	◇Ki no Tsurayuki writes *Tosa Nikki*, first diary written in *kana* 〈『土佐日記』〉
		◇Kuya promulgates Buddhist teachings of Amida Buddha and Pure Land paradise and recitation of *nenbutsu*, Amida's name 〈空也念仏を広める〉
	c.974	◇Fujiwara no Michitsuna's mother writes *Kagerō Nikki* (The Gossamer Years), the first diary of literary consequence written by a woman 〈『蜻蛉日記』〉
	985	◇Genshin (a.k.a. Eshin Sozu) writes *Ōjōyōshū* (Essentials of Pure Land Rebirth), a major influence on development of Pure Land Buddhism 〈『往生要集』〉
	c.1001	◇Sei Shonagon's *Makura no Sōshi* (Pillow Book) written 〈『枕草子』〉
	c.1007	◇Izumi Shikibu's *Izumi Shikibu Nikki* written 〈『和泉式部日記』〉
	c.1010	◇Murasaki Shikibu's *Murasaki Shikibu Nikki* and *Genji Monogatari* (Tale of Genji) written 〈『紫式部日記』『源氏物語』〉

Period	Year	Events
Heian (平安時代)	1053	◇Byodoin's Phoenix Hall constructed 〈平等院鳳凰堂建立〉
	c.1058	◇Sugawara no Takasue's daughter writes *Sarashina Nikki* 〈更級日記〉
	1086	◆Emperor Shirakawa retires to become first of the cloistered emperors 〈白河上皇院政開始〉
	c.1101	◇Historical narrative *Eiga Monogatari* (A tale of flowering Fortunes) written 〈『栄華物語』〉
	c.1107	◇*Konjaku Monogatari* written 〈『今昔物語』〉
	c.1131	◇*Ō Kagami* (The Great Mirror), first critical history, appears, followed by three more *kagami* texts, *Ima Kagami* (1170), *Mizu Kagami* (late 12th c), and *Masu Kagami* (c. 1376) 〈『大鏡』『今鏡』『増鏡』〉
	1156	◆Hogen Disturbance marks ascendency of warrior class 〈保元の乱〉
	1159	◆Heiji Disturbance leads to rise of Taira clan 〈平治の乱〉
	1175	◇Honen founds Jodo sect of Buddhism, inaugurating new era in Japanese Buddhism centered in Kamakura 〈浄土宗の開宗〉
	1185	◆Taira clan annihilated by Minamoto clan in Battle of Dan no Ura 〈平氏滅亡〉
	1191	◇Eisai (a.k.a. Yosai) returns from China and promulgates Rinzai sect of Zen Buddhism 〈臨済宗広まる〉
Kamakura (鎌倉時代)	1192	◆Minamoto no Yoritomo acquires the title of shogun, marking establishment of Kamakura *bakufu* government 〈源頼朝征夷大将軍〉
	1203	◆Hojo Tokimasa becomes first regent of Kamakura shogunate, establishing Hojo clan's authority 〈北条時政執権〉
		◇Buddhist sculptors Unkei and Kaikei complete statue of Kongo Rikishi for Todaiji's south gate 〈東大寺南大門の金剛力士像〉
	1205	◇*Shin Kokin Wakashū* anthology of poetry compiled by Fujiwara no Sadaie and others 〈『新古今和歌集』〉
	1212	◇Kamo no Chomei writes *Hōjōki* (Ten-foot Square Hut) 〈『方丈記』〉
	1213	◇Shogun Minamoto no Sanetomo compiles *Kinkai Wakashū* poetry anthology 〈『金槐和歌集』〉
	c.1220	◇Monk Jien writes his critical history *Gukanshō*, revising it after the Jokyu Disturbance 〈『愚管抄』〉
	1224	◇Shinran founds Jodo Shinshu sect of Buddhism 〈浄土真宗の開宗〉
	1227	◇Dogen returns from China and establishes Soto sect of Buddhist teachings 〈曹洞宗の開宗〉
	?	◇*Heike Monogatari* becomes one of most popular war tales 〈『平家物語』〉
	1253	◇Nichiren promulgates Nichiren sect of Buddhism 〈日蓮宗広まる〉
	1274	◆Force of 40,000 Mongols attempts to invade northern Kyushu (Bun'ei no Eki) 〈文永の役〉
	1281	◆Mongols attempt second invasion with force of 140,000 but fail (Koan no Eki) 〈弘安の役〉
	c.1300	◇*Azuma Kagami* written 〈『吾妻鏡』〉
	c.1330	◇Yoshida Kenko writes *Tsurezuregusa* 〈『徒然草』〉
	1333	◆Fall of Kamakura *bakufu* 〈鎌倉幕府滅亡〉

Period	Year	Events
Muromachi (室町時代)	1338	◆Ashikaga Takauji acquires the title of shogun, marking beginning of Muromachi *bakufu* 〈足利尊氏征夷大将軍〉
	1356	◇Nijo Yoshimoto compiles *Tsukuba-shū*, first collection of *renga* poetry 〈『菟玖波集』〉
	c.1370	◇*Taiheiki* chronicle of northern and southern courts written 〈『太平記』〉
	1397	◇Ashikaga Yoshimitsu builds Kinkakuji at Kitayama in Kyoto, marking flowering of Kitayama culture 〈金閣，北山文化〉
	c.1400	◇Zeami writes *Fūshi Kaden* (The Transmission of the Flower of Acting Style) 〈『花伝書』〉
	1401	◆Ashikaga Yoshimitsu sends Japan's first emissary to Ming China 〈第1回遣明船派遣〉
	1467	◆Onin Disturbances 〈応仁の乱〉
	1489	◇Ashikaga Yoshimasa builds Ginkakuji at Higashiyama in Kyoto, marking flowering of Higashiyama culture 〈銀閣，東山文化〉
	1543	◇Portuguese traders land at Tanegashima, introducing guns to Japan 〈鉄砲伝来〉
	1549	◇Francisco Xavier arrives in Kagoshima as Christian missionary 〈キリスト教伝来〉
	1573	◆Oda Nobunaga exiles Ashikaga Yoshiaki, 15th Ashikaga shogun, ending Muromachi period 〈室町幕府滅亡〉
Azuchi-Momoyama (安土・桃山時代)	1583	◇Toyotomi Hideyoshi builds Osaka Castle, symbolic of Azuchi-Momoyama culture 〈大坂城築城〉
	1590	◆Toyotomi Hideyoshi succeeds in uniting country 〈豊臣秀吉全国統一〉
	1592	◆Hideyoshi launches four-year attempt to invade Korean peninsula (Bunroku no Eki) 〈文禄の役〉
	1597	◆Hideyoshi launches second attempt to invade Korean peninsula (Keicho no Eki) 〈慶長の役〉
	1600	◆Tokugawa Ieyasu emerges victorious at Sekigahara 〈関ケ原の戦い〉
Edo (江戸時代)	1603	◆Tokugawa Ieyasu acquires title of shogun, officially establishing Edo *bakufu* government 〈徳川家康征夷大将軍〉
	1612	◇Tokugawa Ieyasu issues edict prohibiting Christianity 〈キリスト教禁止令〉
	1624	◇Katsura Detached Palace, famous for its *shoin* style architecture and *kaiyū* gardens, completed 〈桂離宮建立〉
	1635	◆Codes of conduct are issued by Tokugawa shogunate to control daimyo, including *sankin-kōtai* system requiring daimyo to spend alternate years in Edo and leave families as hostages when returning to their fiefs 〈参勤交代の法制化〉
	1637	◆Shimabara Uprising 〈島原の乱〉
	1639	◆Japan closed to foreign commerce 〈鎖国の完成〉
	1654	◇Chinese monk Ingen promulgates Obaku sect of Zen Buddhism 〈黄檗宗伝わる〉
	1682	◇Ihara Saikaku writes *Kōshoku Ichidai Otoko* (The Life of an Amorous Man) 〈『好色一代男』〉
	c.1694	◇Haiku poet Matsuo Basho writes *Oku no Hosomichi* (The

Period	Year	Events
Edo (江戸時代)		Narrow Road to the Deep North) 〈『奥の細道』〉
	1703	◇Chikamatsu Monzaemon's drama *Sonezaki Shinjū* (The Love Suicides at Sonezaki) performed at Takemoto-za *jōruri* puppet theater 〈『曽根崎心中』〉
	1776	◇Ueda Akinari publishes *Ugetsu Monogatari* (Tales of Moonlight and Rain) series 〈『雨月物語』〉
	1798	◇*Kokugaku* scholar Motoori Norinaga completes *Kojiki Den* study of *Kojiki* 〈『古事記伝』〉
	1802	◇Jippensha Ikku published first book in *Tōkaidōchū Hizakurige* (Shank's Mare) series 〈『東海道中膝栗毛』〉
	1814	◇Takizawa Bakin began to publish 98 volumes of *Nansō Satomi Hakken-den* (Satomi and the Eight Dogs), and completed them in 1842 〈『南総里見八犬伝』〉
	1829	◇Katsushika Hokusai creates "Thirty-six Views of Mt Fuji" 〈『冨嶽三十六景』〉
	1833	◇Ando (Utagawa) Hiroshige publishes "Fifty-three Stations on the Tokaido" 〈『東海道五十三次』〉
	1858	◆Unequal commercial treaty with United States signed, followed by similar treaties with the Netherlands, Russia, Britain, and France 〈日米修好通商条約調印〉
Meiji (明治)	1868	◆Meiji Restoration 〈明治維新〉
	1877	◆Satsuma Rebellion, last major rebellion against Meiji government reforms 〈西南の役〉
	1885	◇Tsubouchi Shoyo publishes *Shōsetsu Shinzui* (The Essence of the Novel) and fictional work, *Tōsei Shosei Katagi* 〈『小説神髄』『当世書生気質』〉
	1889	◆The Constitution of the Empire of Japan is promulgated 〈大日本帝国憲法発布〉
	1890	◆First session of Imperial Diet is held 〈帝国議会開設〉
		◇Mori Ogai writes *Maihime* (The Dancing Girl) 〈『舞姫』〉
	1894	◆Anglo-Japanese Commercial Treaty providing for abolishment of extraterritoriality signed, the first revision of unequal treaties 〈第1次条約改正〉
		◆Outbreak of Sino-Japanese War 〈日清戦争〉
	1904	◆Outbreak of Russo-Japanese War 〈日露戦争〉
	1905	◇Natsume Soseki writes *Wagahai wa Neko de Aru* (I am a Cat) 〈『吾輩は猫である』〉
	1910	◇Mushanokoji Saneatsu, Shiga Naoya, and others establish *Shirakaba* (White Birch) school of writing 〈『白樺』創刊〉
	1911	◆Second revision of unequal treaties, recognizing Japan's right to set own tariffs 〈第2次条約改正〉
Taisho (大正)	1914	◆First World War 〈第一次世界大戦〉
	1915	◇Akutagawa Ryunosuke writes *Rashōmon* 〈『羅生門』〉
	1923	◆Great Kanto Earthquake leaves 140,000 dead or missing 〈関東大震災〉
	1925	◆Peace Preservation Law enacted to quell communists and anarchists prior to enactment of universal (manhood) suffrage 〈治安維持法発布〉
	1931	◆Manchurian Incident 〈満州事変〉

Period	Year	Events
Showa (昭和)	1937	◇Kawabata Yasunari writes *Yukiguni* (Snow Country) 〈『雪国』〉
	1939	◆Start of Second World War (Germany invades Poland) 〈第二次世界大戦〉
	1941	◆Japanese bombing of Pearl Harbor triggers Pacific War 〈太平洋戦争〉
	1945	◆Atomic bombs dropped on Hiroshima and Nagasaki 〈原爆投下〉
		◆Japan accepts terms of Potsdam Declaration and surrenders unconditionally 〈ポツダム宣言受諾〉
		◆*Zaibatsu* business combines broken up in effort to democratize economy 〈財閥解体〉
	1946	◆Agrarian land reforms instituted 〈農地改革〉
		◆Tokyo Tribunal convened 〈極東国際軍事裁判〉
		◆Postwar Constitution promulgated 〈日本国憲法公布〉
	1950	◆Outbreak of Korean War 〈朝鮮戦争〉
	1951	◆San Francisco Peace Treaty signed with 48 nations. Prime Minister Yoshida Shigeru signs Mutual Security Treaty with United States 〈平和条約・日米安保条約調印〉
	1953	◇NHK begins television broadcasting 〈NHKテレビ放送開始〉
	1954	◆Police Law and Self-Defense Forces Law enacted and Defense Agency established 〈自衛隊発足〉
	1960	◆U.S.-Japan Security Treaty revised 〈日米新安保条約調印〉
	1964	◇Tokaido shinkansen goes into operation 〈東海道新幹線開通〉
		◇20th Olympics held in Tokyo 〈東京オリンピック開催〉
	1970	◇Expo '70 in Osaka held 〈大阪万国博〉
	1972	◆Joint communique issued by Prime Minister Tanaka Kakuei and Chinese Premier Zhou Enlai marks normalization of Japan's relations with People's Republic of China 〈日中国交回復〉

Japanese Index
日本語索引

太字数字は、説明あるいはイラスト・写真のあるページを示しています。

あ，ア

合気道・**146**
あいさつ・**50**, **52**, 224
あいづち・**50**
葵祭り・104, **160**
赤ちょうちん・**224**
あか抜け・34
握手・52
芥川龍之介・**280**
あぐら・**52**
浅井了意・276
『朝日新聞』・110, 112
足利義政・252, 254
足利義満・16, 244
飛鳥文化・14, **65**
遊び・**154**
あだ・34
あだ討ち・250, 300
安土・桃山時代・**18**, **68**
油揚げ・90, **157**, 318
安部公房・282
安倍晋太郎・176
アマチュア野球・**138**
アマテラス・298, **311**
天の岩戸伝説・天岩屋 22, 248, 298
アメノウズメ・248, **298**
あやとり・154, **162**
有島生馬・280
有島武郎・280
在原業平・272, **309**
安定成長時代・32, 190, **192**
安藤広重・**260**, **307**
『暗夜行路』・280

い，イ

いき・**34**
池坊専慶・252
生け花・**252**, 324 →華道
囲碁・**150**, 224
イザナギ，イザナミ・298
イザヤ・ベンダサン・60
石川啄木・278
意思決定・**212**
石原慎太郎・148, 282
『伊豆の踊子』・280
出雲神話・**298**
出雲大社・236, 246
伊勢講・132, **161**
伊勢神宮・236, **304**
イタイイタイ病・122
1月1日・**98**
(日本人の)1日・**76**
(日本人の)1年・**46**
(日本人の)一生・**48**
「一寸法師」・334, **340**
稲荷神社(いなり)・**70**, 318
いなりずし・157, 318
犬・242, 300, **314**
井上靖・282
井原西鶴・18, **276**
伊万里焼き・262, **308**
医療保険・**124**
入れ墨・36, 71
イワシ・28, 334
隠元・292
隠者の文学・**274**
院政・14, **66**
インフレ・**190**, 208

う，ウ

ウィルキンソン，E.・60
上田秋成・276
上田敏・278
ヴォーゲル，E.F.・60
『ウォール・ストリート・ジャーナル』・110
鵜飼い・22, **69**
浮世絵・18, **260**
「雨月物語」(映画)・332
『雨月物語』(小説)・**276**, 332
ウサギ小屋(に住む働き蜂) 32, 82
牛・**316**
氏神・294
『宇治拾遺物語』・272, 280
うす・22, 300
歌合わせ・284, 286
謡・242, 244
ウチとソト(人間関係)・**62**
うどん・88, **157**
うなずき・**50**
馬・**316**
梅・326, 328, **330**
梅干し・330, **339**
浦島(太郎)伝説・**302**
裏千家・254
漆・22, **69**, **264**
うるち米・90, **157**
運動会・128, **224**
運命共同体・214, 218, 224

え，エ

映画・**148**
栄西・292
ＡＶ時代・204, **233**
英雄・**58**
栄久庵憲司・34, **71**
エコノミック・アニマル 30, 38, 48
江戸・18, 104
江戸時代・**18**
ＮＨＫ・46, 76, **112**, **156**, 240
ＮＨＫ教育テレビ・112
ＦＡ機器・204, 206
絵巻物・**258**, 334
エレクトロニクス産業 **206**
演歌・40, **71**
縁起物・314, 326
婉曲表現・**50**, 62
遠足・**128**
『役の行者』・278

お，オ

お稲荷さん・28, **70**

オイルショック(石油危機) 148, 166, 182, 190, 192, 206, 208, 216, 218, 226
王義之・256
大坂・18, **68**, 250, 276
王貞治・138, **161**
王朝文学・272
黄檗宗・292
ＯＡ機器・30, 204, 206
大江健三郎・282
大岡昇平・282
大首絵・260
大伴家持・270, **309**
オートレース・**152**
大入道・318, **338**
太安万侶・270, **309**
大判・300, **311**, 326
大晦日・98
岡倉天心・254, 258, **306**
尾形光琳・258
阿国・246, **305**
『奥の細道』・286
押し入れ・84, **156**
おじぎ・**52**
おせち料理・**92**, 98, 158
汚染・122
織田信長・18, 58, **68**
お茶・86　→茶の湯
小津安二郎・148
お手玉・154, **162**
『御伽草子』・302, **311**, 334
『伽婢子』・276
お年玉・98
おとそ・46, **71**
鬼・300, **334**, **340**
鬼ごっこ・154
小野小町・302, **311**
小野道風・256
お花・86　→生け花
帯・86, 100, 144, **156**
おひたし・90, **157**
表千家・254
親方・142, **162**
折りヅル・102, 322, **338**
音楽・**240**, 242
音楽脳・42
温泉・134, **161**
女形・246

か，カ

絵画・**258**
海外旅行・32, 106, **132**
会議・**226**
外交・**184**
楷書・**256**, **307**
懐石・92, 158
会席料理・**92**, 158
外タレ天国・240
怪談・**332**
『怪談』・332
怪談集・**276**
『怪談牡丹灯籠』・276, **332**
『海潮音』・278
『懐風藻』・14, **270**
戒名・96, **158**
偕楽園(水戸)・238, 330
雅楽・**242**
書き初め・256
核・186, 210
家具・**84**
核家族・44, **78**, 288
学閥・**176**
閣僚・170, 176
学歴偏重社会(高学歴社会) 48, 80, **228**
家計・**78**, **80**, 108, 130, 188, 228
『蜻蛉日記』・272
「かごめかごめ」・154
かしわもち・100, **159**
数の数え方・**54**
河川・10, **64**, **122**
数え年・100, **159**
刀→日本刀
「かちかち山」・**300**, **311**, 318
かつおぶし・314
学校生活・**128**
葛飾北斎・136, **260**, **307**
かっぱ(すし)・336
河童・**336**, **340**
桂離宮・236, **304**
家庭・**78**, **228**
家庭裁判所・**180**
華道・16, 26, **252**　→生け花
加藤清正・104, **160**
門松・98, 159, 324, 326
仮名・14, 24, 56, **256**, 270, 272, 326
狩野永徳・258
嘉納治五郎・144
狩野派・258, **307**
歌舞伎・18, 36, 142, 242, 244, **246**, 248, 260, **305**, 328, 332, 334
歌舞伎踊り・246, 248
歌舞伎座・246, **305**
かぶと・100
鎌倉時代・16
鎌倉時代の彫刻・16, **67**
鎌倉仏教・16, 24, 290
神・168, 294, 302, 316, 334
上方舞い・248
カメ・302
『仮面の告白』・282
賀茂の競馬・304, 152, **160**
鴨長明・274
家紋・324, **339**
歌謡曲・240
カラーテレビ・84, 200, 204,
カラオケ・32, 70, 136, **240**
カラス・**322**
空手・26, 144, **146**
枯山水・238, 292
河竹黙阿弥・246, 276
川端康成・**280**
瓦屋根・82, **156**
観阿弥・244
簡易裁判所・180
観光・102, 104, **132**
漢字・12, 24, 56, 256, 270
人間主義・**62**
関東大震災・280, **309**
官僚・官僚制度・**178**

き，キ

議院内閣制・164, 170
祇園祭り・**104**, **160**
記紀神話・294, 298
企業集団・**196**
企業別組合・**218**
『菊と刀』・**60**
『義経記』・**274**
(日本人の)起源・**20**

季語・26, **69**, 286
気候・**10**
起床時間・76
「木曽街道六十九次」 260
喜多川歌麿・**260**, **307**
北原白秋・278
北山文化・16, **67**
喫茶店・**226**
キツネ・**318**
きね・22, 300
紀貫之・272
きびだんご・300, **311**
基本的人権・**164**
義務教育・48, 126
木目込人形・**268**, **308**
着物・86, 98, **157**
ギャンブル・152
旧憲法・164
弓道・144, **146**
牛丼・316, **338**
給与・給料・182, 214
教育・48, 228, 296
教育改革・**126**
教育制度・**126**
教育費・48, **80**
狂言方・244
共産党・**172**, 184
行書・**256**, 307
行政府・164
行政テクノクラート・178
共通1次(試験)・126
競艇・**152**
極東国際軍事裁判・**166**
キリスト教・16, 96, 102, **296**
義理人情・**40**, 250
『桐一葉』・278
金閣・16, **67**
銀閣・16
『金閣寺』(小説)・282
金閣寺庭園・238
近世・**18**
近代・**18**
「金太郎」・**302**, **311**
金太郎あめ・24, **69**
勤務時間・220
金曜会・196
『近来風体抄』・286
勤労意識・**30**

く，ク

空海・256, 302
『愚管抄』・274
国生み・**298**
熊野講・132, **161**
組合・**218**
暮らし・**74**
クラシック音楽・240
クリスマス・28, **102**
車社会・**116**
黒川紀章・236
黒沢明・148
軍記物語・16, **274**

け，ケ

経済・**190**
経済協力・**188**
警察・120
傾斜生産方式・190, 198
競馬・**152**, 316
競輪・**152**
ゲームウォッチ・154
劇画・**288**
げた・332, **340**
月給・**220**, 228
結婚・48, **94**, 214
結婚式・94, **158**, 294, 296, 320, 328
月曜会・196
検挙率・120
元号・168, **232**
健康保険・**124**
言語行動・**50**
言語脳・42
源氏・274, **309**
原始時代・**12**
『源氏物語』・14, 24, 34, **272**, 276
「源氏物語絵巻」・258
原子力の平和利用・**210**
原子力発電・**210**
遣隋使・12
現代・**18**
現代日本人・**20**
建築・**236**
剣道・26, 144, **146**
遣唐使・12, 14, 150, 254
原日本人・**20**
『源平盛衰記』・274
憲法改正・166
兼六園(金沢)・238
元禄時代・250
元禄文化・18

こ，コ

碁・**150**, **162**
コイ・**320**
小泉八雲・332, **339**
こいのぼり・100, **159**, 320
講・**132**
公案・292
公営ギャンブル・**152**
公害・**122**
公害反対運動・**122**
光化学スモッグ・122
高校野球・**138**
甲子園大会・**138**
皇室・136, **168**, 270, 272, 284, 294
講釈・250
『好色一代男』・**276**
『好色一代女』・276
公正取引委員会・198
厚生年金・124
高速道路・116
拘束名簿式比例代表制 174
幸田露伴・278
講談・**250**
公地公民制・14, **65**
膠着語・56, **72**
高等学校・48, 126, 128, 146
講堂館・144
高等裁判所・**180**
高度経済成長・32, 38, 48, 88, 116, 122, 148, 166, 178, 190, **192**, 194, 202, 216
弘仁・貞観文化・14
「紅白歌合戦」・46, 240
交番・**120**, **160**
興福寺・264, 290
弘法大師・256, 302
公明党・**172**
河本敏夫・176
後楽園(岡山)・238
小売店・208
高齢化社会・30, **44**, 124, 216, 222

5月5日　48, **100**, 268, 302, 320
五月人形・100, **159**
5月3日・164, **232**
『古今和歌集』・14, 284, 328
国技館・142
国際協力・188
『国性爺合戦』・248, **276**
国鉄・118
国土・**10**
国風文化・14, **66**, 328
告別式・**96**
国民健康保険・124
国民所得・124, 188
国民総生産・188, 190
国民年金・124
国民の祝日・**232**
極楽浄土・36, 71, 238
こけし・268, **308**
『古語拾遺』・270
『古今著聞集』・272
ござ・136, **161**
五山文学・292
『古事記』・14, 22, 142, 248, **270**, 298, 330
『五重塔』・278
御所人形・**268**, **308**
『後撰和歌集』・284
古代・**12**
古代文学・**270**
五大昔話・**300**
こたつ・44, **84**, 156
こだま(新幹線)・118
国会・164, 170, 316
国会議員・164, 170
小鼓・244, **305**
琴・242, **305**
子供の遊び・**154**, **162**
子供の日・**100**
ことわざ・28, 38, 144
小林一茶・286
小判・300, **311**, 326
古墳・12, 20
古墳時代・12, **64**
五味五色五法の料理 **92**
コミック・**288**
虚無僧・242, **304**
米・**90**, 134
雇用関係・**214**
娯楽観・**32**
ゴルフ・32, 134, **140**, **224**
『今昔物語』・**272**, 280, 332
金堂・238, **304**
こんにゃく・22, **69**
コンピューター・206

さ，サ

西行・274, 284, 286, 328
最高裁判所・164, **180**
才蔵・250
財閥解体・**190**
裁判官・164, 180
裁判所・164, 180
裁判制度・**180**
採用・**214**
酒井田柿右衛門・262
坂田藤十郎・**246**
坂田金時・302, 334
嵯峨天皇・256
嵯峨人形・**268**, **308**
坂本龍馬・58, **72**
さくら(肉)・316
桜・**136**, **328**
鎮国・18, 278
笹・102, **326**
「サザエさん」・**288**
『ザ・サン』・110
さしみ・**90**
『ザ・ジャパニーズ』 38, **60**
座禅・290, 292, **310**
佐多稲子・282
雑誌・114
殺人発生率・74
茶道・16, 26, 34, 248, **254**
茶道具・254, **306**
サトウサンペイ・288
佐藤春夫・**280**
里帰り・46, **71**
里見弴・**280**
さび・26, **34**, **70**
ザビエル，フランシスコ 296
『更級日記』・272
「猿かに合戦」・**300**
『山家集』・274, 284
3月3日・48, **100**, 268, 330
参議院・164, **174**
参議院議員・170, **174**
産業構造・**194**
産業政策・**198**
産業組織・**196**
三金会・196
『サンケイ新聞』・110, 112
三権分立・**164**, 180
『三国志』・104, **160**
3C・84,
三社祭り・**104**, **160**
三種の神器・298
三審制・180
山水画・26, **69**, 292
三水会・196
三蹟・256
三千家・254
三大松原・324
三筆・256
サンフランシスコ講和条約 **166**, 184, 190
三遊亭円朝・276, **309**, 332
山陽新幹線・118
三和グループ・196

し，シ

詩・278, 280
GHQ・148, **166**
GNP・192, 208
GNP1%・186
(明治の)詩歌・**278**
自衛隊・**186**
ジェスチャー・**52**, **54**
慈円・274
志賀直哉・280
信楽焼・262, 318, **338**
只管打坐・292
磁器・**262**
四規七則・**254**
式亭三馬・276
(農産物の)自給率・202
しぐさ・**52**
仕事納め・46, **71**
自殺・**36**
死生観・**36**
自然観・**26**, 28
自然環境・**10**
自然主義の作家・**278**
シソ・22, **69**
「舌切りすずめ」・**300**

7月7日・**102**, 326
七五三・28, 48, **100**, 108, 294
「七人の侍」・148
視聴率・**112**
漆器・**264**, **308**
十返舎一九・276
シテ方・244
私鉄・**118**
四天王・302, **312**
自動車・28, 116, **200**, **204**
自動車産業・**204**
死の儀式・**96**
地バン, 看バン, カバン 174
自分(ジェスチャー)・**54**
司法府・164
司法組織・**180**
島崎藤村・278
島原の乱・296, **311**
社員食堂・**226**
釈迦・98
社会党・166, **172**, 184
社会福祉・124
社会保険・124, 220
社会保障・74, **124**
社会民主連合・**172**
尺八・242, 326, **304**, **339**
尺八楽・**242**
借景・238
『ジャパン・アズ・No.1』・**60**
しゃぶしゃぶ・316, **338**
三味線・242, 248, **250**, **305**
三味線音楽・**242**
しゃもじ・104, **160**
11月15日・48, 100
『拾遺和歌集』・284
修学院離宮・236
就学率・126
修学旅行・**128**
衆議院・164, **174**
衆議院議員・170, 174
週休2日制・**220**
宗教・16, 24, 26, 30, 96, 102, 168, 238, 294
宗教心・**28**
十五年戦争・18, **69**
習字・102, 130, **159**, 256
柔術・144
終身雇用制度・**214**, 216, 218, 222, 228
就寝時間・76
重層文化・**24**
住宅建築・**236**
住宅問題・74, 76, 80, **82**
集団主義・**38**, 128, 212, 224
自由党・166, 172
柔道・**144**
重箱・92, 158
自由民権運動・110
自由民主党・**166**, 170, **172**, 174, 176
重要無形文化財・248, **305**
儒学・18, 24
儒教・12, 38, **65**
塾・**130**
主権在民・**164**
受験戦争・48, 128, **130**, 228, 294
守護大名・16 →大名
首相・**170**, **233** →総理大臣
主食・90
出版・60, **114**
出版社・114
酒呑童子・302, **311**, 334
書院造り・236
上越新幹線・118
荘園・14, **65**
城郭建築・**236**
正月・28, 46, 86, 92, **98**, 154, 324, 326
小学校(小学生)・48, 126, 128, 130, 256
正月休み・46, 128
将棋・**150**, **162**
将軍・18, **67**
焼香・96, 158
障子・82, **156**, 258
「証城寺のたぬきばやし」 318, **338**
昇進制度・**216**
精進料理・**92**, 158
『小説神髄』・278
正倉院・262, **307**
浄土教・14, **66**
聖徳太子・12, **65**, 290
浄土宗・36, 290, **310**
浄土真宗・290, **310**
浄土庭園・**238**
消費・**106**
消費者物価(指数)・208
障屏画・**258**
『正法眼蔵』・36
声明・**242**
縄文時代・**12**, **64**,
縄文土器・262, **64**
縄文文化・22
しょうゆ・**90**, 134
照葉樹林文化・10, **22**, 56
生類憐れみの令・314
浄瑠璃・36, **71**, 334
昭和・**18**, **68**
諸行無常・34, **70**
食事・76, 90
食生活・**88**, 106
『続日本紀』・270
『続日本後紀』・270
食料費・**80**
女性の労働力・**214**
書体・256
書道・**256**
女流日記文学・**272**
白井晟一・236
『白樺』・280
城・**236**
真打ち・250
進学問題・128
進学率・48, 126
新幹線・**118**
神功皇后・320, **338**
新憲法・**164**, **168**
人口・**10**
人口密度・10
『新古今和歌集』・16
真言宗・294, **310**
新婚旅行・132
人事・214
神社建築・**236**
心中・**36**, 40, **71**
新自由クラブ・170
『心中天網島』・248, 276
新書判・114, **160**
『新体詩抄』・278
新素材産業・**206**
寝殿造り・236
寝殿造り庭園・**238**
神道・28, 168, **294**
新聞・**110**, 122, 288
新聞漫画・**288**
『人民日報』・110
神武天皇・270, **308**
信用第一主義・**230**
新鷽・16, 24, **67**

神話・22, 270, **298**

す，ス

水産業・**202**
水盤・252, **306**
水墨画・258, 292
睡眠時間・76
スーパー(マーケット) 106, 208
菅原孝標女・272
菅原道真・330, **339**
すき焼・92, 316
スサノオ・298
すし・88, 92, **157**
鈴木大拙・292, **310**
鈴木春信・**260**, **307**
鈴木メソッド・240, **304**
スポーツ・**140**
住まい観・**82**
墨・256, 258, **306**
住友グループ・196
住吉神社・236
相撲・**142**, **161**, 336
『駿河国風土記』・302
座る(ジェスチャー)・52

せ，セ

世阿弥・136, 244
生花・**252**, **306**
生活時間・**76**
政権政党・**172**
正座(ジェスチャー)・**52**
政治・166
清少納言・134, 272, **309**, 330
成人式・48, 86, 108
税制・**182**
税制改正・182
(主要)製造業・**204**
政党・**172**
歳暮・40, **108**
西洋建築・**236**
石庭・238, 292
石油危機 →オイルショック
『世間胸算用』・276
節句・**48**, **100**, **159**, **268**, **330**
雪舟・258, 292
切腹・36, 266
節分・334
説話文学・**272**
瀬戸の藤四郎・262
せともの・**262**
禅・34, 238, **292**
選挙・**174**
戦後・78
全国高等学校野球大会・**138**
戦国時代・**16**
戦国大名・16 →大名
前座・250
禅宗・16, 26, 36, 92, 238, 290, **292**
専守防衛・186
戦前・78
戦争放棄・164
先端技術製品・**206**
千利休・34, **70**, 254, 292
選抜大会(高校野球)・138
前方後円墳・12, **64**
川柳・286
占領下・占領軍・126, 164, 172, 190

そ，ソ

創価学会・**172**, 290
箏曲・**242**
葬式・28, **96**, 296
草書・**256**, 307
宗匠・34, **71**, 286
宗長・286
贈答・**108**
曹洞宗・36, **292**
雑煮・98, **158**
総理大臣・136, 164, 176, 178, **233** →首相
組閣・**170**
『曽我物語』・274
『曽根崎心中』・248, 276
そば・88, 98, 108, **157**
そろばん・130

た，タ

タイ・**320**
第一勧銀グループ・196
第1次産業・194
大学・48, **126**
大学生活・**128**
大学入試・126
大学野球・**138**
大化の改新・12, **65**
耐久消費材・**84**, 106, 192
太鼓・98, 244
第5世代コンピューター 206
醍醐の花見・136
代参講・132
第3次産業・194
大衆芸能・**250**
大正・**18**, **68**, 86, 242
大正デモクラシー・18, **69**
退職金制度・**222**
大豆加工食品・90, 92
大徳寺・292 (大仙院の庭園)・238
第2次産業・194
第2次世界大戦・38, 124, 164, 168, 240, 250, 282, 290
大日本帝国憲法・164
『太平記』・250, 274
太平記講釈・274
太平洋戦争・18, 26
大鵬・142
太陽族・148, **282**
「太陽の季節」(映画)・148
『太陽の季節』・282
平・332, **339** →平家・平氏
「高砂」・324
高見山・142
高村光太郎・278, 280
宝くじ・**152**
滝沢馬琴・276
竹・**326**
竹馬・190, **233**
竹下登・176
武田信玄・58, **72**
『竹取物語』・**272**, 326
大宰府・330, **339**
畳・52, **84**, 144, 236, 248
タヂカラオ・298
タテ型社会・196, **233**
タテマエ・**62**
七夕・**102**, 326
谷口吉郎・236
谷崎潤一郎・**280**
タヌキ・300, **318**
旅・**134**
玉造の湯・134, **161**
田山花袋・278
太夫・248, 250, **305**
俵・326

俵屋宗達・258
短歌・270, **284**, **309**
檀家制度・290
丹下健三・236
端午の節句・48, **100**, 302, 320
短冊・102, **159**, 326
単身赴任・**228**
団体交渉・**218**

ち，チ

治安・**120**
違い棚・236, **304**
地下鉄・**118**, 120
近松半二・276
『近松物語』・148
近松門左衛門・18, 40, 246, 248, **276**
「竹林の七賢」・326
地誌・**270**
地方議員・174
地方裁判所・**180**
地方選挙・**174**
茶・22, **69**
茶懐石・92
茶釜・254, **306**
茶筅・254, **306**
『茶の本』・**254**
茶の湯・86, 92, 252, **254**, 262, 292　→茶道
茶碗・254, **306**
中学校・48, 126, 128, 146, 256
中元・40, **108**
忠犬ハチ公・**314**, **338**
駐在所・120
中世・**16**
中選挙区制・174, 176
長歌・270, **284**
彫刻(鎌倉時代)・16, **67**
『鳥獣戯画』・258
朝鮮戦争・166, 190, 282
町人文学・**276**
調味料・**90**
勅撰和歌集・14, 272, **284**
貯蓄率・80
賃金・**216**, **220**
頂相・292, **310**

つ，ツ

通学・**76**
通勤・**76**, 82, **226**
通勤電車・38, 114, 226
通勤ラッシュ・38, 62, 76, 226
通産省・178, 198, 206
築山・238, **304**
『菟玖波集』・286
漬物・34, 88
槌・326, **339**
土井晩翠・278
つづら・300, **311**
角田忠信・42
坪内逍遥・278
釣り・**140**
釣り書・94
ツル・**322**
「鶴女房」・322
鶴屋南北・246, 276, 332
ツレ・244
『徒然草』・16, 274

て，テ

庭園・26, **238**, 254, 292
定期採用・**214**
定期昇給・220
低成長時代・30, 32, 216, 218, 220
定年・48, **222**
弟子丸泰仙・292, **310**
鉄鋼業・**204**
鉄道網・**118**
鉄砲伝来・16, 266
テニス・32, **140**
手ぬぐい・108, **160**
デフレ・190
点前・254, **306**
手招き(ジェスチャー)・**54**
寺子屋・18, **68**, 102, 256
テレビ・32, 110, **112**, 138, 142, 154, 206, 240, 250, 288, 332
テレビ局・112
転勤・**228**
天狗・**334**, **340**
電子機器産業・204
伝説・58, 102, 300, **302**, 316, 318, 320, 322, 324, 326, 330, 334, 336
天台宗・294, **310**
伝統的日本食・**92**, **158**
天然記念物・324, **338**
天皇・**164**, **168**
天引き・182, 220
天平文化・14, **65**
てんぷら・88, 92, **157**
天武天皇・270
電話普及率・74

と，ト

土居健郎・60
「東海道五十三次」・260
東海道新幹線・118
『東海道中膝栗毛』・276
『東海道四谷怪談』・276, **332**
陶器・**262**
東京オリンピック・144
東京大学・126, 144, **160**, 176, 178, 228, **232**
「東京物語」・148
東京六大学・138, **161**
道元・36, **292**
同好会(社内)・**224**
湯治・**134**
陶磁器・**262**, 264
統治のしくみ・**164**
東州斎写楽・**260**, **307**
唐招提寺・290
東条英機・166, **232**
『当世書生気質』・278
道祖神・28, **70**, 294
東大寺・290
東大閥・176
桃中軒雲右衛門・250
豆腐・90
東北新幹線・118
道路網・**116**
道路整備・**116**
徳川家光・18
徳川家康・18, **58**, **68**
徳川綱吉・314
徳川光圀・**58**, 302
独占禁止政策・**198**
徳富蘆花・278
徳永直・282
床の間・236, 252, **304**
『土佐日記』・272
年越しそば・46, **71**

都市対抗野球大会・138
都市の暮らし・**74**
栃錦・142
ドッジ, J.・190
舎人親王・270, **309**
土俵・142, **161**
トラ・104, 334
「寅さんシリーズ」・**148**
ドラビダ語・56, **72**
豊臣秀吉・18, **58**, **68**, 136, 244, 254, 296, 322

な, ナ

内閣・164, **170**
永井荷風・**280**
長島茂雄・138, **161**
中曽根康弘・176, 184
中根千枝・60
中野浩一・152
投入・**252**, **306**
仲人・94
納豆・22, 90
夏目漱石・**278**, 314, **338**
夏休み・**46**, 128
ななくりの湯・134, **161**
浪花伊助・250
浪花節・**250**
南無阿弥陀仏・290
南無妙法蓮華経・290
奈良三彩・262
奈良時代・**14**
成田講・132, **161**
名和清左衛門・250
『南総里見八犬伝』・276
南北朝時代・256

に, ニ

にかわ水・258, **307**
錦絵・260
二条良基・286
日米安全保障条約・**166**,184, 186
日米関係・**184**
日米貿易摩擦・200
日蓮・16, **67**
日蓮宗・290, **310**
日蓮正宗・172, **233**
日露戦争・18, **69**, 278
日記文学・**272**
日清戦争・18, **69**
日ソ関係・**184**
日本画・**258**
日本株式会社・178, 198
日本髪・98, **159**
『日本経済新聞』・110, 112
日本語・12, 24, **42**, **56**, 270
日本語使用人口・56
『日本後紀』・270
(日本国)憲法・**164**, **168**, 186
日本三庭園・238
『日本書紀』・14, 22, 142, **270**, 298, 302
日本食・88, **92**
日本人と付き合う法・**62**
『日本人とユダヤ人』・60
日本人論・**60**
日本庭園・**238** →庭園
日本的家具・**84**
日本的経営・30, 216
日本的産業政策・**198**
日本的商談 **230**
日本刀・**266**, **308**
日本人形・**268**, **308**
日本の位置・**10**, **64**
日本舞踊・**248**
日本民主党・172
『日本霊異記』・272, 332
日本料理・92
入学試験・126
『ニューヨーク・タイムズ』 110
『ニューヨーク・デイリー・ニュース』・110
女房・284, **309**
人形浄瑠璃・18, 242, 246, 248, →文楽
人間国宝・248, **306**
人情・**40**, 250

ぬ, ヌ

額田王・284

ね, ネ

猫・242, **314**
ねぶた祭り・**104**, **160**
根回し・62
年賀状・98, **158**
年金制度・**124**
年功序列制度・**216**, 218, 222, 228
年始回り・46, 98
年中行事・28, 98, **100**, 128, 268, 326
年齢給・**216**

の, ノ

脳・**42**
能・16, 242, **244**, 248, 302, **305**, 324, 332
能楽・**242**
能管・326, **339**
農業・**202**
農村の暮らし・**74**
農地改革・**190**
農地解放・166
野点・254
祝詞・298
ノンプロ(野球)・**138**

は, ハ

俳諧・286
俳句・26, 34, **286**
配転・**228**
馬鹿・316
『破戒』・278
『葉隠』・36, **71**
博多どんたく・104, 160
博多人形・**268**, **308**
袴・86, 100, **157**
墓参り・28, **96**
白水会・196
幕藩体制・18, 24, **68**
幕府・16, 150
白鳳文化・14, **65**
「羽衣」(能)・302
羽衣伝説・**302**, 324
派出所・**120**
長谷川等伯・258
長谷川町子・288
パソコン・206
パチンコ・32, **70**, **152**
バツ(×)・**54**
初もうで・28, **70**, 98, 294
「花さか爺」・**300**, 314
花見・**136**, **161**
花道・244, 246
埴輪・268, **308**

羽根つき・98，**154**，**162**
ハネムーン・94，132
派閥・170，**176**
刃文・266
囃子・**242**
囃子方・**244**
春休み・128
バレンタインデー・102
藩校・18
犯罪・120
万歳・**54**
坂東玉三郎・246

ひ，ヒ

美意識・**34**
ビー玉遊び・154
ヒイラギ・334，336
稗田阿礼・270，**309**
非核三原則・**186**
東山文化・16，**67**，252
ひかり（新幹線）・118
彼岸・28，**70**，96
飛脚・276，**309**
樋口一葉・278
菱川師宣・260
菱田春草・258
ビジネス・230
ビジネスマン・62，224，226，228
左脳・42
引っ越しそば・**108**
一つ目小僧・**336**，**340**
ひな人形・100，**159**，**268**，**308**，330
ひな祭り・48，**100**，268，330
ビニール風呂敷・136，**161**
姫路城・236，**304**
被用者保険・124
屏風・258，**307**
琵琶・242，**305**，332
琵琶楽・**242**
琵琶法師・274，**309**，332
びんざさら・104，**160**

ふ，フ

ＶＨＦ局・112
笛・98，244
「冨嶽三十六景」・136，260
武家文学・274
武士・16，36，38，146，168，178，246，274，290，328
富士講・132，**161**
「フジ三太郎」・**288**，**310**
フジテレビ・112
武士道・**36**，266
武士の魂・266
藤原氏・14，**66**
藤原道綱母・272
ふすま・82，**156**，236
二葉亭四迷・278
双葉山・142，**162**
普茶料理・92
物価・**208**
仏教・12，14，24，26，28，30，34，36，92，272，**290**，294，296，314
仏教建築・**236**
仏式の葬儀・**96**
『風土記』・**270**
布団・**84**，134，**156**
芙蓉グループ・芙蓉会 196
ブライダル産業・94
『ブラウダ』・110
振袖・86，**157**
風呂・84
風呂敷・136，**161**，322
プロ野球・**138**
プロレタリア文学・282
「ブロンディー」・288
文化・**22**，**24**
文学・**270**，**272**，**274**，**276**，**278**，**280**，**282**
文庫本・114，**160**
ふんどし・334
「文福茶がま」・318
文楽・**248**，268，**305**
→人形浄瑠璃
文楽座・248
文人画・18，**68**

へ，ヘ

平安京・14
平安時代・**14**
平均寿命・**44**，124，222
平均年収・74，220
平家・274，**309**　→平氏
『平家物語』・16，**274**
平氏・332　→平家
平治の乱・274，**309**
『平治物語』・274
平城京・**14**，334
『平中物語』・272
平和主義・164
ベネディクト，Ｒ．Ｆ．60
弁慶・302，**311**

ほ，ホ

防衛・184，**186**
防衛力・**186**
貿易構造・**200**
貿易摩擦・184，**200**，204
邦楽・240，**242**
『方丈記』・16，**274**
法然・16，24，**66**
忘年会・**224**
法隆寺・236，290，**304**
ボーナス・46，**220**
木鐸・110，**160**
保険・**124**
保元の乱・274，309
『保元物語』・274
菩薩・294，**310**
牡丹灯籠・332，**340**
『坊ちゃん』・278
北方領土返還問題・184
『不如婦』・278
ポピュラー・240
ボトム・アップ方式・**212**
本・**114**
盆・96，**98**，104
盆踊り・98，**159**
盆栽・324，330，**338**
本膳料理・**92**，158
本地垂迹説・294
ホンネ・**62**

ま，マ

マージャン・32，**150**，**162**，224
マイコン・154，204，206，**233**
マイコンゲーム・154
『毎日新聞』・110，112
マイホーム・74，78，80，

228
マイホーム志向・**82**
幕の内弁当・**34**
『枕草子』・14, 134, 272
正岡子規・278
松・244, **324**
松尾芭蕉・18, 34, 286
マッカーサー元帥・166
マツタケ・**324**
抹茶・254, 292, **306**
松の内・98, **158**, 324
末法思想・290, **310**
祭り・**104**
真名・270
招き猫・314, **338**
まわし・142, **161**
漫画・**288**
万歳・250
漫才・**250**
マンション・82, **156**
万葉仮名・270
万葉集・**14**, **270**, **284**, 302, 324, 330

み，ミ

見合い(結婚)・**94**
右脳・42
巫女・246, **305**
みこし・104, **160**
三島由紀夫・266, 282
みそ・90, 134
溝口健二・148
みそ汁・88, 90, **157**
三井グループ・196
密教・14, **66**
三菱グループ・196
水戸黄門・**58**, 302
南座・246
源義経・**58**, 302
源頼朝・16, **58**, **66**
源頼光・302, **311**, 334
身延講・132, **161**
身ぶり・**52**
三保の松原・302, 324
「耳なし芳一」・**332**
宮城道雄・242
三宅一生・86
宮沢喜一・176
宮沢賢治・280
宮参り・100
宮本百合子・282
民社党・**172**
民主主義文学・**282**
民謡・240, **242**, **304**

む，ム

昔話・**300**, 302, 318, 322, 326
武者小路千家・254
武者小路実篤・280
武者人形・100, **268**, **308**
紫式部・272, **309**, 330
村田珠光・254
村八分・38, **71**
室町時代・**16**
室町幕府・16

め，メ

明治・18, **68**
明治維新・58, 72, 168, 236, 258, 266
名湯・**134**
『冥途の飛脚』・**276**
メンコ遊び・154, **162**

も，モ

毛筆・256, 258, **306**
もち・22, **69**, 98, 300
本居宣長・328
もののあわれ・**34**
紅葉狩り・**136**
桃・**330**
桃太郎・**300**, **311**, 314, 330, 334
桃の節句・48, **100**, 330
桃山文化・18
森鷗外・**278**
盛花・**252**, **306**
森英恵・86
モンゴロイド・20

や，ヤ

野球・**138**, 140
ヤクザ・148, **162**
薬師寺・236, 290
屋号・246, **305**
八岐大蛇・**298**
山田洋次・148
大和絵・258
大和朝廷・12, 178, 294
山伏・334, **340**
山本寛斎・86
山本七平・30, **70**
弥生時代・12, **64**
弥生土器・64, 262
野郎歌舞伎・246

ゆ，ユ

ＵＨＦ局・112
有給休暇・**220**
幽玄・26, **69**
遊女・40, **71**
幽霊・302, **332**, **339**
浴衣・104, **160**
湯川秀樹・42, **71**

よ，ヨ

洋画・**258**
妖怪・**334**, **336**, **340**
『用心棒』・148
洋服・**86**
横座り・**52**, **53**
横綱・**142**, **161**
横光利一・**280**
与謝野晶子・278
与謝野鉄幹・278
与謝蕪村・**286**
芳沢あやめ・246
吉田兼好・274
吉田茂・166, **232**
(内閣)・**166**, 170, 184
寄席・250
『四谷怪談』・332
予備校・48, 126
読売ジャイアンツ・138
『読売新聞』・110, 112
よろい・**100**, **159**

ら，ラ

ライシャワー, E.O. 38, 60
ライフサイエンス産業・**206**
落語・**250**, **306**, 332
ラジオ・**112**, 142, 240, 250
ラジオ局・112

羅生門・334, **340**
「羅生門」(映画)・148
『羅生門』(小説)・280
ラッシュ・アワー
→通勤ラッシュ
蘭学・18, **68**
乱塾時代・**130**

り，リ

力士・86, 142, **156**, **161**, 268
離婚・**94**, 180
李参平・262
立華・**252**, **306**
立法府・164
律令・12, 14, **64**, 178
流通産業・**208**
竜安寺の石庭・238, **304**
料理・**92**
旅行・**132**
禀議制・**212**
林業・**202**
臨済宗・**292**
臨時教育審議会・126

れ，レ

レコード大賞・240
レジャー・32, 132, 152
連歌・16, **286**

ろ，ロ

浪曲・**250**
労使関係・**218**
老人医療・124
老人福祉・80
老人問題・**44**
労働運動・190
労働改革・190
労働観・**30**
労働協約・218, 220
労働組合・**218**, 220
労働三法・190
労働時間・**220**
浪人・126, **161**, 332
老齢年金・124
6・5・3・3制・126
六古窯・262
6・3・3・4制・48, 126
鹿鳴館(建築)・236, **304**
『鹿鳴館』・282
ロッキード汚職事件・172
ロボット・28, 30, 188, 206
ロマンポルノ・148, **162**

わ，ワ

和・26, 38, 224
ワープロ・204, 206, **234**
和歌・26, 256, 272, **284**
『吾輩は猫である』・278, 314
ワキ方・**244**
渡辺綱・334
わび・26, **34**, **69**
わび茶・254, 292

ことわざ・表現

犬死にする・314
いわしの頭も信心から・28
牛になる・316
牛の歩み・316
歌は世に連れ世は歌に連れ 240
馬が合う・316
馬面・316
馬の耳に念仏・316
梅にウグイス・330
梅に桜・330
恨めしや・332
鬼に金棒・334
鬼のいぬ間に洗濯・334
鬼の首をとったよう・334
河童の川流れ・336
河童の屁・336
髪はからすの濡れ羽色 322
からすの行水・322
からすの雌雄・322
きつねの嫁入り・318
牛歩戦術・316
腐ってもタイ・320
苦しいときの神頼み・28
犬猿の仲・314
こいの滝登り・320
さくら・328
桜は七日・328
柔よく剛を制す・144
戦後，強くなったのは女性と靴下・78
竹に木を接ぐ・326
竹にすずめ・326
竹にとら・326
竹を割ったような・326
たぬきおやじ・318
たぬき寝入り・318
男子厨房に入るべからず 88
つるの一声・322
ツルは千年，カメは万年 322
出る釘は打たれる・38
天狗になる・334
どこの馬の骨かわからない 316
ともに白髪の生えるまで 94
長いものには巻かれろ・26
にわかやもめ・46
猫にかつおぶし・314
猫を殺せば七代たたる 314
はきだめにつる・322
馬耳東風・316
破竹の勢い・326
花にあらし・328
花より団子・328
福は内，鬼は外・334
屁の河童・336
松の内・**324**
まないたのこい・320
村八分・38, **71**
桃栗3年柿8年・330
やぶ医者・326
やぶ蛇・326
礼に始まり礼に終わる・144

English Index
英語索引

Bold-faced page numbers are for further explanations and/or illustrations.

A, a

Abe Kobo • *283*
Abe Shintaro • *177*
abura-age • *91*, ***157***, *319*
academic credentials • ***229***
agglutinative language • *57*, ***72***
agrarian land reform • *191*
aikidō • ***147***
aizuchi • *51*
Akutagawa Ryunosuke • ***281***
Amaterasu • *299*, ***311***
amateur baseball • ***139***
ancient history • ***13***
Ando Hiroshige • ***261***, *307*
anti monopoly act • ***199***
Aoi Matsuri • *105*, ***160***
apocalyptic Buddhism • *291*, ***309***
apparitions • ***335***, ***337***
architecture • ***237***
Arishima Ikuma • *281*
Arishima Takeo • *281*
Ariwara no Narihira • *273*, ***309***
armor • *101*, ***159***
arrests • ***121***
artificial hills • *239*, ***304***
Asai Ryoi • *277*
Ashikaga Yoshimasa • *253*, *255*
Ashikaga Yoshimitsu • *17*, *245*
Asuka culture • *15*, ***65***
athletic competitions • ***225***
audio-visual age • *205*, ***233***
automobiles • *117*, *201*, ***205***, *207*
automobile racing • *153*
automotive Japan • ***117***
ayatori • *155*, ***162***
Azuchi-Momoyama period • ***19***, ***68***

B, b

bakemono • *333*
bakuhan • *19*, ***68***
ballad-reciting chanter • *249*, ***305***
bamboo • ***327***
Bando Tamasaburo • *247*
banzai • ***55***
baseball • ***139***
Battles of Coxinga • *249*, *277*
beckoning • ***55***
Benkei • *303*, ***311***
bicycle racing • ***153***
binzasara • *105*, ***160***
biwa • *243*, ***305***, *333*
biwa-gaku • ***243***
biwa-hōshi • *275*, ***309***
black ink • *257*, ***306***
bon • *97*, ***99***, *105*
bon-odori • *99*, ***159***
bonsai • *325*, *331*, ***338***
Book of Tea • *255*
book-loving people • ***115***
Botan-dōrō • *277*, *333*, ***340***
bottom-up approach • *213*
bowing • ***53***
Boy's Day • *303*
broading interests • ***33***
brush • *257*, ***306***
Buddhism • ***291***
Buddhist architecture • ***237***
Buddhist deities • *295*, ***310***
Buddhist feeling • *35*, ***70***
Buddhist Nichiren sect • *173*, ***233***
Buddhist teachings • *295*, ***310***
Buddhist wakes and funerals • ***97***
Bunbuku Chagama • *319*
bunjin-ga • *19*, ***68***
bunko-bon • *115*, ***160***
bunraku • ***249***, *269*, ***305***
Bunraku-za • *249*
bureaucracy • ***179***
bushi-dō • ***37***, *267*
businessman • *63*, ***225***, ***227***, ***229***
buyō • ***249***

C, c

Cabinet • *165*, ***171***, *177*
calligraphy • ***257***
calligraphy styles • ***257***
carp • ***321***
castle architecture • ***237***
cats • ***315***
ceramics • ***263***
ceramic statues • *319*, ***338***
cha-kaiseki • *93*, ***158***

changes in employment patterns • ***195***
changes in the industrial structure • ***195***
changing consumer trends • ***107***
characteristics of Japanese culture • ***25***
cherry blossom (viewing) • ***137, 329***
chic • ***35***
Chikamatsu Hanji • *277*
Chikamatsu Monogatari • *149*
Chikamatsu Monzaemon • *19*, ***41***, *247, 249, 277*
Children's Day • *49, 101, 321*
children's festivals • ***101***
children's games • ***155***
Chōjū Giga • *259*
Christianity • *17*, ***297***
Christian rebellion in Shimabara • *297*, ***310***
Christmas • *29*, ***103***
chūgen • *41*, ***109***
chūzaisho • ***121***
climate • ***11***
closet • *85*, ***156***
closet Christians • *297*
clothing • ***87***
coffee shops • ***227***
collective bargaining • ***219***
college life • ***129***
comic books • ***289***
commuting • *77, 83, 227*
company cafeterias • ***227***
compulsory education • *127*
concepts of nature • ***27***
condominiums • *83*, ***156***
conflict between *giri* and *ninjō* • ***41***
Confucian teachings • *13*, ***65***
Constitution • ***165***, *169, 187*
consumer durables • ***85***
conversational counterpoint • ***51***
cormorant fishing • *23*, ***69***
counting • ***55***
courtesan • *41*, ***71***
court ladies • *285*, ***309***
court poetry • *285*
cows • ***317***
cram schools • ***49, 127, 131***
cranes • ***323***
crime • ***121***
crows • ***323***
cultural characteristics • ***23***

D, d

danka system • *291*
Dazaifu • *331*, ***339***
decision-making process • ***213***
defense policy • ***187***
democratic literature • ***283***
Deshimaru Taisen • *293*, ***310***
Diet • *165, 171*
division of powers • ***165***
Dogen • *37, 293*
dogs • ***315***
dohyō • *143*
Doi Takeo • *61*
Doll Festival • *49, 101, 269, 331*
dōsojin • *29*, ***70***
drafting alternatives • ***213***
Dravidian languages • *57*, ***72***

E, e

early modern era • ***19***
economic animals • *31, 39, 49*
economic cooperation • ***189***
economic democratization • ***191***
Edo period • *19*
educational reform • ***127***
education system • ***127***
Eisai • *293*
Ekuan Kenji • *35*, ***71***
elections • ***175***
electronics (industry) • ***205, 207***
e-makimono • ***259***
Emperor • *165, 169*
Emperor Jinmu • *271*, ***308***
Emperor Saga • *257*
emphasis on the group • ***63***
employment • ***215***
employment patterns • ***195***
Empress Jingu • *321*, ***338***
enka • *41*, ***71***
enterprise unions • ***219***, *221*
esoteric Buddhist sects • *15*, ***66***

F, f

family • ***79***
family life • ***229***
farming • ***203***
female employment • ***215***
festival dolls • ***269***
festivals • ***105***
feudal era • ***17***
feudal lords • *19*, ***67***
15 years of war • *19*, ***69***
53 Stations on the Tokaido • *261*
films • ***149***
fisheries • *195*, ***203***
fishing • ***141***
flower arrangement • ***253***
folding screens • *259*, ***307***
folk tales • ***301***

food • ***91***
foreign policy • ***185***
foreign works on Japan • ***61***
forestry • ***195, 203***
formations of factions • ***177***
friendly word • ***51***
from inflation to deflation • ***191***
from rapid growth to stable growth • ***193***
fucha-ryōri • *93*
fudoki • ***271***
Fujiko • *133*, ***161***
Fuji Santarō • *289*, ***310***
Fujiwara • *15*, ***66***
Fujiwara no Michitsuna's mother • *273*
funerals • *29*, ***97***, *297*
furi-sode • *87*, ***157***
fusuma • ***156***, *237*
Futabatei Shimei • *279*
Futabayama • *143*, ***162***
futon • *85*, *135*, ***156***

G, g

gagaku • *243*
gangster • *149*, ***162***
gardens • ***239***
Genji • *275*, ***309***
Genji Monogatari • *35*, *273*, *277*
Genji Monogatari Emaki • *259*
geki-ga • *289*
Genroku era • *19*
gestures • ***53***, ***55***
geta • *333*, ***340***
getting along with the Japanese • ***63***
ghosts • ***333***, ***339***
gift-giving • ***109***
Girl's Day • *101*
Gion Festival • ***105***, ***160***
giri and *ninjō* • ***41***
glutinous paste • *23*, ***69***
go • *151*, ***162***, *225*
golf • *33*, ***141***, ***225***
Gosen Wakashū • *285*
gosho dolls • *269*, ***308***
government • ***165***
government party • ***173***
Great Kanto Earthquake • *281*, ***309***
groundcloths • *137*, ***161***
group identification • ***213***
groupism • ***39***
growing cost of education • ***81***
growth of the SDF • ***187***
gyōsho • *257*, ***307***
gyūdon • *317*, ***338***

H, h

Hagakure • *37*, ***71***
Hagiwara Sakutaro • *281*
Hagoromo • ***303***
haikai • *287*
haiku • *27*, *35*, *279*, ***287***
hakama • *87*, *101*, ***157***
hakata dolls • *269*, ***308***
Hakata Dontaku • ***105***, ***160***
Hakuho culture • *15*, ***65***
hana-mi • ***137***, ***161***
hana-michi • *245*, *247*
Hanasaka Jijii • ***301***, *315*
haniwa • *269*, ***308***
hard-working Japanese • ***31***
Hasegawa Machiko • *289*
Hasegawa Tohaku • *259*
hashutsujo • ***121***
Hatsu Ebisu • *327*, ***339***
health spas • ***135***
Heian period • ***15***
Heiji rebellion • *275*, ***309***
Heike • *275*, ***309***
Heike Monogatari • *17*, *275*
Hieda no Are • *271*, ***309***
higan • *97*
(trips to Buddhist temples in the spring and fall) • *29*, ***70***
Higashiyama culture • *17*, ***67***, *253*
high saving rate • ***81***
high-technology products • ***207***
Higuchi Ichiyo • *279*
hikkoshi-soba • *109*
Himeji castle • *237*, ***304***
Hina Matsuri • ***101***, *269*
hina(-ningyō) dolls • *101*, ***159***, ***269***, ***308***, *331*
Hishida Shunso • *259*
Hishikawa Moronobu • *261*
hitotsume-kozō • *337*, ***340***
hōgaku • *241*, *243*
Hogen uprisings • *275*, ***309***
Hōjōki • *17*, *275*
Honen • *17*, *25*, ***66***
honne • *63*
honzen-ryōri • ***93***, ***158***
horses • ***317***
horse races • ***153***
Horyuji • *237*, *291*, ***304***
hot springs • ***135***, ***161***
household budget • ***81***, *221*
House of Councillors • *165*, *171*, *175*
House of Representatives • *165*, *171*, *175*
housing • ***83***

I, i

I am a Cat • *279, 315*
identity crisis • ***61***
Ihara Saikaku • *19,* ***277***
ikebana • ***253***
Ikenobo Senkei • *253*
iki • *35*
imperial anthologies • ***285***
imperial institution • ***169***
Important Intangible Cultural Asset *249,* ***305***
Inari • *29,* ***70***
inari-zushi • ***157,*** *319*
indicating the self • ***55***
indirect expressions • ***51***
industrial policy • ***199***
industrial relations • ***219***
industrial structure • ***197***
Ingen • *293*
Inoue Yasushi • *283*
insei • *15,* ***66***
Iseko • *133,* ***161***
Ise Shrine • *237,* ***304***
Ishihara Shintaro • *149, 283*
Ishikawa Takuboku • *279*
Issun-bōshi • *335,* ***340***
Izumo Shrine • *237, 247*

J, j

japan • *265*
Japanese aesthetics • ***35***
Japanese bath • *85*
Japanese brain • ***43***
Japanese business practices • ***231***
Japanese Constitution • *187*
Japanese consumer • ***107***
Japanese culture • ***23, 25***
Japanese day • ***77***
Japanese dolls • ***269, 308***
Japanese diet • ***89,*** *93*
Japanese food • ***91,*** *93*
Japanese language • ***43, 57***
Japanese literature • ***271, 273, 275, 277, 279, 281, 283***
Japanese National Railways • *119*
Japanese prototype • ***21***
Japanese-style furniture • ***85***
Japanese year • ***47***
Japanese sword • ***267, 308***
Japan's unbalanced trade structure • ***201***
Jippensha Ikku • *277*
Jodo Pure Land paradise • *37,* ***71***
Jodo sect • *15, 37,* ***66,*** *291*
Jodo Shinshu • *291,* ***310***
Jomon period • ***13, 64***
jōruri • *19, 37,* ***71,*** *335*
judicial system • ***181***
judo • *27,* ***145***
jūjutsu • *145*
juku • *49,* ***131***

K, k

kabuki • *19, 37, 143, 243, 245,* ***247,*** *249, 261, 269, 277,* ***305,*** *329, 333, 335*
Kabuki-za • *247,* ***305***
Kachikachi-yama • ***301, 311,*** *319*
kadō • *253*
kado-matsu • *99, 325, 327*
kagome-kagome • *155*
Kaifūsō • *15,* ***271***
Kairakuen • *239, 331*
kaiseki-ryōri • ***93,*** *158*
kaisho • *257, 307*
kakizome • *257*
Kamakura period • ***17***
kamigata dance • *249*
Kamo no Chomei • *275*
Kamo no Kurabeuma • *105,* **160,** *153*
kana • *15, 25, 57,* ***257,*** *271, 273, 327*
Kan'ami • *245*
kanji • *57, 271, 273*
Kano Eitoku • *259*
Kano Jigoro • *145*
Kano School • *259,* ***307***
kappa • ***337, 340***
karaoke • *33, 70, 241*
karate • ***27, 147***
karatedō • *145*
kashiwa-mochi • *101,* ***159***
Kato Kiyomasa • *105,* ***160***
Katsura Detached Palace • *237,* ***304***
Katsushika Hokusai • *137,* ***261,*** *307*
Kawabata Yasunari • ***281***
Kawatake Mokuami • *247, 277*
kayōkyoku • ***241***
kendō • *27, 145,* ***147***
Kenrokuen • *239*
keyhole-shaped tomb mounds • *13,* ***64***
kigo • *287*
kimekomi dolls • *269,* ***308***
kimono • ***87,*** *99, 101,* ***157,*** *249*
Kinkakuji • *17,* ***67,*** *239*
Kinkakuji garden • *239*
Ki no Tsurayuki • *273*
Kinrai Fūtei Shō • *287*
Kintarō • *303, 311*
kintarō-ame • *25,* ***69***
Kitagawa Utamaro • ***261,*** *307*

Kitahara Hakushu • *279*
Kitayama culture • *17*, ***67***
kitsune • ***319***
kōan • *293*
Kobayashi Issa • *287*
kōban • *121*, ***160***
Kōbō legends • ***303***
kōchi-kōmin • *15*, ***65***
kōdan • ***251***
Koda Rohan • *279*
Kodokan • *145*
Kofukuji • *265*, *291*
kofun • *13*
Kofun period • ***13***, *21*, ***64***
Kohaku Uta-gassen • *47*
koi-nobori • *101*, ***159***, *321*
Kojiki • ***15***, *249*, ***271***, *299*, ***331***
kokeshi dolls • *269*, ***308***
Kokin Wakashū • *15*, *285*, *329*
Kokugikan • *143*
Kokusenya Kassen • *249*, *277*
kondō • *239*, ***304***
Konjaku Monogatari • ***273***, *281*, *333*
konnyaku • *23*, ***69***
Korakuen • *239*
kōshaku • *251*
Koshien Stadium • 139
kotatsu • 47, 85, ***156***
koto • 243, ***305***
Kukai • *257*, *303*
Kumanoko • *133*, ***161***
Kurokawa Kisho • *237*
Kurosawa Akira • *149*
Kwaidan • *333*
kyōgen • *17*, *245*
kyūdō • *145*, ***147***

L, l

labor reform • *191*
lacquer ware • 23, *69*, ***265***, ***308***
Lafcadio Hearn • *333*, ***339***
land and people • ***11***
later hours • ***77***
legalized gambling • ***153***
legends • ***303***
life of a businessman • ***229***
life science • ***207***
life style • ***49***
lifetime employment security • ***215***
liquid glue • *259*, ***306***
living away from home • ***229***
Living Cultural Treasures • *249*, ***306***
longevity • ***45***
lotteries • ***153***
Love Suicides at Amijima • *249*, *277*
Love Suicides at Sonezaki • *249*, *277*

M, m

mahjong • *33*, ***151***, ***162***, ***225***
main industrial groups • ***197***
maku-no-uchi beauty • ***35***
Makura no Sōshi • *15*, *135*, *273*
mallets • *327*, ***339***
mana characters • *271*
maneki-neko • *315*, ***338***
manga • ***289***
manufacturing industries • ***205***
Man'yō-gana • *271*
Man'yōshū • ***15***, ***271***, ***285***, *303*, *325*, *331*
manzai • ***251***
maple-leaf viewing • ***137***
marriage and divorce • ***95***
Masaoka Shiki • *279*
matcha • *255*, ***306***
matsu-no-uchi • *325*
Matsuo Basho • *287*
mawashi • *143*, ***161***
meals • ***77***
medical insurance • ***125***
Meiji Constitution • *165*
Meiji period • ***19***, ***68***
Meiji Restoration • *59*, ***72***, *169*, *237*
memorial services • ***97***
menko • *155*, ***162***
miai • ***95***
microcomputers • *205*, ***233***
mikoshi • *105*, ***160***
millet dumplings • *301*, ***311***
Miminashi Hōichi • *333*
Minami-za • *247*
Minamoto no Yorimitsu • *303*, ***311***, *335*
Minamoto no Yoritomo • *17*, *59*, ***66***
Minamoto no Yoshitsune • ***59***, *303*
Minobuko • *133*, ***161***
min'yō • *241*, *243*, ***304***
miso • *91*
miso soup • *89*, ***157***
Mishima Yukio • *267*, *283*
Mito Komon • *59*
Mizoguchi Kenji • *149*
Miyagi Michio • *243*
Miyamoto Yuriko • *283*
Miyazawa Kenji • *281*
Miyazawa Kiichi • *177*
mochi • *99*
modern era • ***19***
modern games • ***155***
modern Japanese • ***21***
modern literature • ***279***
modern poets • ***281***

momiji-gari • ***137***
momo • *331*
Momo no Sekku • *101, 331*
Momotarō • ***301, 311,*** *315, 331, 335*
monsters • ***335, 337***
moribana • ***253, 306***
Mori Ogai • ***279***
morning commute • ***227***
Motoori Norinaga • *329*
motorboat racing • *153*
motorcycle racing• *153*
murahachibu • *39,* ***71***
Murasaki Shikibu • *273, 331*
Murata Juko • *255*
Muromachi period • ***17***
Mushanokoji Saneatsu • *281*
music • ***241***
mutual trust • ***231***
mythology • ***299***

N, n

Nagai Kafu • ***281***
Nagashima Shigeo • *139,* ***161***
nageire • ***253,*** *306*
Nakane Chie • *61*
Nakasone Yasuhiro • *177*
Nanakuri and Tamatsukuri (hot springs) *135,* ***161***
naniwa-bushi • *41,* ***251***
Naniwa Isuke • *251*
Nara period • ***15***
Naritako • *133,* ***161***
national conscience • *111,* ***160***
national holidays • ***232***
Natsume Soseki • ***279,*** *315,* ***338***
nattō • *23, 91*
natural gardens • ***239***
natural monuments • *325,* ***338***
naturalism • ***279***
Nawa Seizaemon • *251*
Nebuta Festival • ***105, 160***
nemawashi • *63*
nengajō • *99,* ***158***
new materials and life science • ***207***
newspapers • ***111***
newspaper strips • ***289***
New Year's holidays • *47, 295*
NHK • *47, 77, 113,* ***156***
Nichiren • *17,* ***67***
Nichiren sect • *291,* ***310***
nihon-ga • *259*
Nihon Ryōiki • *273, 333*
Nihon Shoki • *15,* ***271,*** *299*
Nijo Yoshimoto • *287*
nishiki-e • *261*
noh • *17,* ***245, 305,*** *325, 333*
nōh-gaku • *243*
non-glutinous rice • *91,* ***157***
nuclear family • *45, 79*
nuclear power industry • ***211***

O, o

obi • *87, 101,* ***156***
Oda Nobunaga • *19, 59,* ***68***
Ooka Shohei • *283*
Oe Kenzaburo • *283*
Ogata Korin • *259*
Ohira Masayoshi • *297*
Oh Sadaharu • *139,* ***161***
oil crisis • *167, 191, 207, 209, 217*
Okakura Tenshin • *255,* ***306***
Okamoto Ayako • *141*
ō-kubi-e • *261*
Okuni • *247,* ***305***
Oku no Hosomichi • *287*
old-fashioned games • ***155***
Omote Senke • *255*
oneness with nature • ***27***
oni • ***335, 340***
oni-gokko • *155*
onna-gata • *247*
Ono no Komachi • *303,* ***311***
Ono no Tofu • *257*
O no Yasumaro • *271,* ***309***
origami (paper) cranes • *103, 323,* ***338***
origins of the Japanese people • ***21***
Osaka • *19,* ***68***
Os and Xs • ***55***
osechi-ryōri • ***93,*** *99,* ***158***
o-tedama • *155,* ***162***
Otomo no Yakamochi • *271,* ***309***
o-toshidama • *99*
otogi-zōshi • *303,* ***311,*** *335*
overlapping religions • ***29***
overseas travel • ***133***
oyakata • *143,* ***162***
Ozu Yasujiro • *149*

P, p

pachinko • *33,* ***70, 153***
paid vacations • ***221***
painting • ***259***
parties • ***225***
pathos • ***35***
Peace Treaty • ***167***
peach • ***331***
Peach Festival • *101*
pensions • ***125***
people-oriented business • ***231***

perceptions of the group • ***39***
perilla • *23*, ***69***
Pillow Book • *15*, *135*, *273*
pine trees • ***325***
plum • ***331***
poetry (in Meiji period) • ***279***
political factions • ***177***
political parties • ***173***
pollution • ***123***
popular entertainment • ***251***
popular heroes • ***59***
porcelain • ***263***
portraits • *293*, ***310***
posthumous Buddhist name • *97*, ***158***
postwar economic recovery • ***191***
postwar literature • ***283***
postwar politics • ***167***
pottery • ***263***
prehistory and ancient history • ***13***
prices and distribution • ***209***
Prime Ministers • *171*, *177*, ***233***
Prince Shotoku • *13*, ***65***, *291*
Princess Nukada • *285*
principal manufacturing industries • ***205***
private lines • ***119***
professional baseball • ***139***
public order • ***121***
public outcry against pollution • ***123***
publishing • ***115***
puppet theater drama • *243*, ***305***

R, r

radio • ***113***
rail transport • ***119***
rakugo • ***251***, ***306***, *333*
rapid (economic) growth • *49*, *89*, *123*, *167*, *191*, ***193***, *203*
rapid graying • ***45***
Rashomon • *335*, ***340***
Rashōmon • *149*, *281*
recruitment and promotion • ***215***
regional dolls • ***269***
relations with the countries of Asia • ***185***
relations with the U.S.S.R. • ***185***
relaxing Japanese-style • ***33***
religion • ***29***
renga • *17*, ***287***
residences • ***237***
retirement • ***223***
rikka • ***253***, ***306***
ringi system • ***213***
Rinzai sect • *293*
Ri Sampei • *263*
ritsuryō • *13*, *15*, ***64***
rivers • *11*, ***64***
road construction • ***117***
roads • ***117***
rock garden • *239*
Rokumeikan • *237*, ***304***
role of language • ***43***
rōnin • *127*, ***161***
rural life • ***75***
rush hour • *77*
Russo-Japanese war • *19*, ***69***, *279*
Ryoanji • *239*, ***304***

S, s

sabi • *27*, ***35***, ***70***
sadō • *255*
saga dolls • *269*, ***308***
Saigyo • *285*, *287*, *329*
Sakaida Kakiemon • *263*
Sakamoto Ryoma • *59*, ***72***
Sakata no Kintoki • *303*, *335*
Sakata Tojuro • *247*
sake • *299*, *319*, *321*
sakura • *317*, ***329***
sakura-niku • *317*
samurai • *19*, *87*, *149*, *169*, *245*, *267*, *293*, *329*
samurai dolls • *101*, *159*
San Francisco Peace Treaty • *167*, *191*
Sanja Matsuri • ***105***, ***160***
Sanka-shū • *275*, *285*
Sanpitsu • *257*
Sanseki • *257*
sansui-ga • *27*, ***69***
Sanyutei Encho • *277*, ***309***, *333*
Saru Kani Gassen • ***301***
sashimi • ***91***, *321*
Sata Ineko • *283*
Sato Haruo • ***281***
Satomi Ton • *281*
Sato Sanpei • *289*
Sazae-san • *289*
SCAP • ***167***
school events • ***129***
science and technology cooperation • ***189***
Scrolls of Frolicking Animals and Humans • *259*
(early Kamakura) sculpture • *17*, ***67***
sea bream • ***321***
seasonal references • *27*, ***69***
seasonings • ***91***
Security Treaty • ***167***, ***187***
seibo • ***41***, ***109***
seika • ***253***, ***306***
Sei Shonagon • *135*, *273*, *331*,
sekku • *101*, ***159***
Self Defense Forces • *187*
Sengoku jidai • *17*

seniority-based promotions • ***217***
seniority-based rewards • ***217***, *219*
seniority-based wages • *217*, *223*, *229*
Sen no Rikyu • *35*, ***70***, *255*, *293*
senryū • *287*
seppuku • *37*, *267*
Sesshu • *259*, *293*
seto-mono • *263*
Seto no Toshiro • *263*
setsubun • *335*
Seven Samurai • *149*
shabu-shabu • *317*, ***338***
shakkei • *239*
shakuhachi (-gaku) • *243*
shamisen • *243*, *249*, *251*, ***305***
shamisen-ongaku • *243*
Shichi-go-san • *29*, *49*, *101*, *295*
Shiga Naoya • *281*
Shikitei Sanba • *277*
Shimazaki Toson • *279*
shinden-zukuri • *237*, *239*
shinjū • ***37***, ***71***
Shinjū Ten no Amijima • *249*, *277*
shinkansen • ***119***
Shin Kokin Wakashū • *17*
Shinran • *17*, *25*, ***67***
shinsho-ban books • *115*, ***160***
Shinto • ***29***, ***295***
Shinto architecture • ***237***
shiri'uchi • *251*
shiny-leaf culture • ***23***
Shirai Seiichi • *237*
Shirakaba • *281*
Shitakiri Suzume • ***301***
shite • *245*
shodō • *257*
shōen • *15*, ***65***
shōgatsu • ***99***
shōgi • ***151***, ***162***, *225*
shōhei-ga • ***259***
shoin-zukuri • *237*
shōjin-ryōri • *93*, ***158***
Shojoji no Tanuki Bayashi • *319*, ***338***
shōmyō • *243*
shopping • ***107***
Shosoin • *263*, ***307***
Showa period • ***19***, ***68***
shōyu • *91*
shūgaku-ryokō • *129*
Shūi Wakashū • *285*
shūji • *103*, ***159***
Shutendoji • *303*, ***311***, *335*
Sino-Japanese war • *19*, ***69***
sitting • ***53***
Six Ancient Kilns • *263*
69 Stations on the Kiso Kaido • *261*
sliding-door partitions • *83*, ***156***
soba • *89*, *99*, *109*, ***157***
socializing • ***225***
social welfare • ***125***
soft-core porn flicks • *149*, ***162***
Soka Gakkai • *173*, *291*
sōkyoku • *243*
some important *gengō* • ***232***
Sonezaki Shinjū • *249*, *277*
Sono Ayako • *297*
soroban • *131*
sōsho • *257*, *307*
sōshō • *287*
soul of the swordsman • ***267***
sources of Japanese culture • ***23***
soybean paste • *91*
soy sauce • *91*
spas • ***135***
standard of living • ***45***, ***75***
staples and side dishes • ***89***
steel industry • ***205***
stilts • *191*, ***233***
stopping off at the pub • ***225***
straw rice bundles • *327*, *339*
student life • ***129***
subways • ***119***
Sugawara no Michizane • *331*, ***339***
Sugawara no Takesue's daughter • ***273***
suiboku-ga • *259*
suicide • ***37***
sukiyaki • *93*, *317*
Sumiyoshi Shrine • *237*
sumo • ***143***, *161*, *337*
sumo ring • *143*, ***161***
sumo wrestlers • *87*, *143*, ***156***, *161*
Supreme Court • *165*, *181*
sushi • *89*, *93*, ***157***, *337*
Suzuki Daisetz • *293*, ***310***
Suzuki Harunobu • ***261***, *307*
Suzuki method • *241*, ***304***
sweet sake • *47*, ***71***, *101*

T, t

tai • *321*
Taiheiki • *251*, *275*
Taiho • *143*
Taika Reforms • *13*, ***65***
Taira • *333*, ***340***
Taisho democracy • *19*, ***69***
Taisho period • ***19***, ***68***
taiyō-zoku • *149*, ***283***
Taiyō no Kisetsu • *149*, *283*
Takamiyama • *143*
Takamura Kotaro • *279*, *281*

Takasago • *325*
Takeda Shingen • *59*, ***72***
Takeshita Noboru • *177*
Taketori Monogatari • *273*, *327*
Takizawa Bakin • *277*
Tale of Genji • *15*, *25*, ***273***
Tale of Genji Scrolls • *259*
Tale of the Heike • *17*, *275*
tales of battle • ***275***
tales of seclusion • ***275***
tales of the supernatural • ***277***
Tanabata • ***103***, *327*
Tange Kenzo • *237*
Tango *Fudoki* • *303*
Tango no Sekku • ***101***
Tanizaki Junichiro • ***281***
Taniguchi Yoshiro • *237*
tanka • *279*, ***285***
tanuki • *301*, ***319***, *338*
tatami • *53*, ***85***, *237*
tatemae • *63*
tattoo • *37*, ***71***
Tawaraya Sotatsu • *259*
Tayama Katai • *279*
taxes • ***183***
tea • *23*, ***69***
tea ceremony • *253*, ***255***, *263*, *293*
television • ***113***, *155*, *207*
temae • *255*, ***306***
tempura • *89*, *93*, ***157***
tengu • ***335***, ***340***
tennis • *33*, ***141***
Tenpyo culture • *15*, ***65***
terakoya • *19*, ***68***, *103*, *257*
36 Views of Mt. Fuji • *137*, *261*
Three Great Brushes • *257*
Three Nonnuclear Principles • *187*
Three Traces • *257*
tile roofs • *83*, ***156***
Tochinishiki • *143*
Tochuken Kumoemon • *251*
Todaiji • *291*
tōfu • *91*
Tojo Hideki • *167*, ***232***
Tōkaidō Yotsuya Kaidan • *277*, *333*
tokonoma • *237*, *253*, ***304***
Tokugawa Ieyasu • *19*, ***59***, ***68***
Tokugawa Mitsukuni • *59*, *303*
Tokugawa Tsunayoshi • *315*
Tokunaga Sunao • *283*
Tokutomi Roka • *279*
Tokyo Big Six League • *139*, ***161***
Tokyo Military Tribunal • *167*
Tokyo Story • *149*
Toneri Shinno • *271*, ***309***
"Tora-san" series • *149*
toshikoshi-soba • *47*, ***71***
Toshusai Sharaku • ***261***, *307*
Toshodaiji • *291*
tourism • ***133***
Toyotomi Hideyoshi • *19*, ***59***, ***68***, *137*, *245*, *255*, *263*, *297*, *323*
trade friction • *185*, ***201***, *205*
trade structure • ***201***
traditional Japanese dishes • ***93***
traditional Japanese music • *241*, ***243***
transfers • ***229***
Treasury of the True Dharma Eye • *37*
Tsubouchi Shoyo • *279*
Tsuchii Bansui • *279*
Tsukubashū • *287*
tsure • *245*
Tsurezuregusa • *17*, *275*
tsuri-gaki • *95*
Tsuruya Nanboku • *247*, *277*, *333*
two-day weekends • ***221***

U, u

Uchimura Kanzo • *207*
udon • *89*, ***157***
Ueda Akinari • *277*
Ueda Bin • *279*
Uemura Masahisa • *297*
Ugetsu Monogatari • *277*, *333*
ukiyo-e • *19*, ***261***, ***307***
ume • *327*, *329*, *331*
Umezaki Haruo • *283*
universities • *49*, ***127***
University of Tokyo • *127*, ***160***
Ura Senke • *255*
Urashima Tarō • ***303***
urban life • ***75***
urban housing • ***83***
us and them • ***63***
U.S.-Japan relations • ***185***
U.S.-Japan Security Treaty • ***167***
utai • *243*

V, v

vertical flute • *243*
vertical society • *197*, ***233***, *269*
verbal signals • ***51***
views of life and death • ***37***

W, w

wabi and *sabi* • *27*, ***35***, ***69***
wabicha • *255*
wages • ***217***, ***221***
waka • *15*, *27*, *257*, *273*, ***285***, *287*

Wakanohana • *143*
wakashū kabuki • *247*
waki • *245*
warrior dolls • *269*, ***308***
Watanabe no Tsuna • *335*
water trays • *253*, ***306***
wedding • *95*, ***158***
wedding industry • ***95***
Western clothing • ***87***
Western-style architecture • ***237***
Western-style painting • *259*
Western vs Japanese brain functions ***43***
Western vs traditional diet • ***91***
whisk • *255*, ***306***
wind instruments • *327*, ***339***
women's diary • ***273***
word processor • *205*, ***234***
work before pleasure • ***33***
worker participation in management ***219***
work ethic • ***31***
workweek and wages • ***221***

Y, y

yabu-hebi • *327*
yabu-isha • *327*
yagō • *247*, ***305***
Yakushiji • *237*, *291*
yamabushi • *335*, *340*
Yamada Yoji • *149*
Yamamoto Shichihei • *31*, ***70***
Yamato Court • *179*
yamato-e • *259*
yarō kabuki • *247*
Yayoi period • ***13***, ***64***
year-end bashes • *225*
year-end vacation • *47*
Yōjinbō • *149*
yōkai • *333*
Yokomitsu Riichi • ***281***
yokozuna • *143*, ***161***
Yosa Buson • *287*
Yosano Akiko • *279*
Yosano Tekkan • *279*
yose theater • *251*
Yoshida Cabinet • ***167***
Yoshida Kenko • *275*
Yoshida Shigeru • *167*, ***232***
Yoshizawa Ayame • *247*
Yotsuya Kaidan • *333*
yūgen • *27*, ***69***
yukata • *105*, ***160***
Yukawa Hideki • *43*, ***71***

Z, z

zaibatsu • *191*, *197*
zaibatsu dissolution • *191*
zazen • *293*, *310*
Zeami • *137*, *245*
Zen • *17*, *27*, *35*, *37*, *93*, *239*, *291*, ***293***
zenza • *251*
zōni • *99*, ***158***

R148907

140°
142°
144°
146°
オホーツク海
SEA OF OKHOTSK
44°
0
100km
北海道
Hokkaido
札幌
Sapporo
42°
中国地方
Chugoku District
34°
島根
Shimane
鳥取
Tottori
兵庫
Hyog
山口
Yamaguchi
広島
Hiroshima
岡山
Okayama
神戸
Kob
香川
Kagawa
大
Osa
佐賀
Saga
福岡
Fukuoka
愛媛
Ehime
長崎
Nagasaki
大分
Oita
徳島
Tokushima
32°
熊本
Kumamoto
高知
Kochi
和歌
Waka
四国地方
Shikoku District
宮崎
Miyazaki
鹿児島
Kagoshima
九州地方
Kyushu District
130°
0
100
200km
132°